Behavior Modification in Mental Retardation

WILLIAM I. GARDNER

Behavior Modification in Mental Retardation

*the education and rehabilitation
of the mentally retarded
adolescent and adult*

University of London Press Ltd

ISBN 0 340 05226 0

Copyright © 1971 by William I. Gardner

First published 1971 by Aldine-Atherton, Inc.
529 South Wabash Avenue, Chicago, Illinois 60605
Library of Congress Catalogue Number 79-149839

University of London Press Ltd
St Paul's House, Warwick Lane, London EC4P 4AH

Photo-litho reproduction by Clarke, Doble & Brendon Ltd, Plymouth

Preface

This book is addressed to all persons involved in the education and rehabilitation of those mentally retarded adolescents and adults who present
difficult problems of learning and behavior adjustment. It is written primarily for the rehabilitation personnel involved in the evaluation, training,
and vocational adjustment of retarded clients and for those special educators who are involved in the secondary level school program and the program of transition from the school to the work-rehabilitation setting; however, the psychologist, the psychiatrist, the social worker, the training and
sheltered workshop supervisor, and others who in one way or another contribute to the rehabilitation effort will find the book relevant to their own
specialty areas. These different groups have in common the single function
of providing expertise to the program which seeks to support the development of appropriate patterns of behavior in the mentally retarded client.
At the same time, these professional groups usually differ widely in the nature of the concepts which they hold concerning the development and modification of behavior patterns of the retarded. This conceptual potpourri
frequently results in poor communication, irrelevant activities, and a general lack of efficiency and effectiveness in the education and rehabilitation
of the mentally retarded adolescent and adult.

In recognition of these and other difficulties in present efforts with the
mentally retarded, this book presents a set of assumptions and related behavior principles concerned with the development and modification of behavioral characteristics. The objectivity of this position provides a basis for
evaluation of its therapeutic effectiveness. It focuses on the person as he
functions in an environment and emphasizes that the significant variables
which control his behavior are found in this environment. This provides a

basis for enthusiasm that something can be done in the natural surroundings to facilitate effective behavior change. In a sense, it provides an exciting viable position from which to view the possibilities of modifying the limited behavioral repertoire of the retarded. The positive approach engendered by the position that behavior is modifiable—even in the more severely limited retarded—is in marked contrast to the pessimism that is held by many other systems of therapy, education, and training.

No background knowledge of learning concepts nor experience in use of behavior modification techniques is assumed in this book. The behavior concepts are discussed in a nontechnical manner and in as much detail as is deemed necessary to provide the reader with clear understanding of the concepts presented. It is not intended as a comprehensive presentation or documentation of the conceptual model nor of the empirical basis for work with the retarded; however, the reader is introduced to the area of behavior modification and is provided with ample reference materials for more intensive study. To facilitate the acquisition of the concepts and related behavior modification techniques, a procedure of reinforcement through repetition is used by the writer. New concepts, once presented, are frequently rephrased immediately, re-presented in a new context, and later restated and integrated with additional concepts. An effort is made to build constantly on each new concept and to translate each into a workable and useful strategy or procedure of behavior modification. The university student or practicing clinician who is being introduced for the first time to the learning approach to behavior development and modification should find that this approach facilitates his task. The practicing clinician who is familiar with a learning approach can easily skip the repetition and quickly identify new information which may assist him in his contact with his clients.

In a further effort to make the learning concepts and related behavior modification procedures as meaningful and applicable as possible, numerous clinical illustrations, taken from experiences of the writer and his colleagues, are provided. The major focus of the book is on the practitioner who in his daily contact with the learning and behavior problems of the retarded is faced with the questions of "what to do" and "how best to do it." Relevant research results are also presented, where these are available, to emphasize the empirical data basis for many of the ideas represented. It is recognized that the clinical illustrations in many instances can provide only suggestive support for the treatment regimen described, and further that the legitimacy of the presumed relationship between behavior change and the treatment methods utilized must be evaluated with appropriate research. Many of the treatment ideas are just ideas. Most, however, have

been generated by an extension from basic behavior principles, or appear to be logical applications of available research data.

Special recognition is extended to those hundreds of retarded adolescents and adults who, even though seemingly in constant conflict with their social environment, have consistently demonstrated that they could learn if the environment would only provide appropriate support. Their failures and frustrations have provided the impetus for members of the rehabilitation team to examine their traditional concepts and methodologies and to explore new models of behavior development and modification.

Contents

PART ONE

Problems of Education and Rehabilitation of the Mentally Retarded Client

CHAPTER ONE

Introduction

With the intensive special education and rehabilitation programs provided in numerous communities, most mildly retarded adolescents and young adults are able to enter into a productive vocational life without undue difficulty. The percentage of such persons in any given community is more dependent upon social and economic conditions of the community than upon any pronounced personal deficiencies of the retarded. If sufficient work opportunities are available, most mildly retarded young adults have the basic occupational and personal-social characteristics to make them capable of at least a minimal degree of success in independent work and living without excessive assistance from community educational and rehabilitation resources. Additionally, many moderately and severely retarded persons are able to attain satisfactory adjustment in simple competitive and sheltered workshop environments. The number and quality of rehabilitation programs for this group are growing steadily.

There remain, however, a large number of retarded adolescents and adults with the general intellectual capabilities for educational, vocational, and social adjustment who do not gain satisfactory competitive or sheltered employment because they do not benefit sufficiently from educational and rehabilitation resources that are available. These individuals utilize an excessive amount of the efforts of educational and rehabilitation agencies and are typically viewed as "difficult rehabilitation" clients. These retardates are often viewed as having "limited feasibility" for vocational placement and are referred from one evaluation, counseling, social, or work adjustment or training program to another in the vague hope that someone or something will make a sufficiently suitable impression on the client to insure more satisfactory adjustment.

The factors identified as underlying the educational and rehabilitation failures of these retardates are viewed basically as personal in nature rather than being related primarily to negative social or economic conditions in the environment. Behavior problems, emotional disturbances, personality difficulties, poor social behaviors, poor motivation, erratic work behavior, and immaturity are all examples of the types of factors that are used to account for these failures. In numerous cases, the basic problems are viewed as emotional or personality ones and not as primary deficits in cognitive or learning factors.

Recent changes in legal, philosophic, and treatment concepts have included in this group of difficult rehabilitation clients a large number of moderately and severely retarded persons who previously had been viewed as possessing only limited and at best, unpredictable, vocational adjustment possibilities. Recent trends in rehabilitation programs present rehabilitation personnel with a multitude of new problems as efforts are being directed toward the more severely handicapped. Educational and rehabilitation personnel are confronted with numerous behavioral deficits in clients who respond only minimally to the typical treatment services provided. These services may include vocational and personal counseling, individual tutoring, social adjustment and vocational training programs, extended sheltered workshop placement, and the like. As a small percentage of the moderately and severely retarded does make a minimal adjustment in the simple competitive and/or sheltered employment and in general life adjustment, the rehabilitation agency is confronted with the problem of providing those effective and efficient programs which hold promise of contributing to the rehabilitation of much larger segments of these groups.

The efforts brought to bear on the problems of development, learning, and behavior adjustment which are presented by these retarded clients are varied and frequently ill-conceived and implemented. In too many instances the general conceptual and technological approaches used with the less difficult clients are categorically utilized with the more atypical difficult problems. The programs are aimed generally at creating a structured therapeutic work experience and are based on general psychodynamic and group dynamic conceptions of behavior development and change. Success is too infrequent and expenditures of personnel and program resources are typically excessive when viewed in terms of output.

Internal Causation Model

In dealing with the behavioral limitations of these clients, the total rehabilitation effort frequently assumes that the major deficits lie within the individual, with the result that the program focus is on modifying the in-

ternal causes. As suggested, such factors as emotional disturbance, mental retardation, minimal brain damage, personality problems, special learning disability, social immaturity, and poor motivation are viewed as the primary causes of the learning and work adjustment difficulty. Although it is recognized by educational and rehabilitation personnel that present environmental and social factors are of importance in behavior change, the major concepts providing direction to the rehabilitation effort are those denoting internal pathology. "He doesn't have a desire to work," "His attitude is generally poor," "He wants to remain dependent," "His passive-aggressive personality interferes with his handling stress satisfactorily," "His self-concept is too poor for satisfactory inter-personal contacts," are examples of these concepts. The program efforts are directed toward modifying these internal mental states or deficiencies—the "desire," "dependency," "personality," "self-concept,"—in order to render possible more satisfactory personality adjustment to the demands or requirements of the world of work and social living. In cases involving central nervous system impairment, it is usually routine to view much of the impulsive, erratic, distractible behavior seen in many problem retarded clients as being a direct result of the damage and to adapt the program requirements to these presumably "irreversible" behaviors. Little effort is directed toward changing these behaviors to any great extent, although there is some evidence that these behaviors are subject to modification by psychological means.

A frequent consequence of the assumption that the major causes of behavioral inadequacies reside within some internal pathology or deviation is the position that treatment should be undertaken only by highly trained mental health specialists. Further, this treatment usually takes place in a special location such as an office or hospital away from the environment in which the behavioral difficulties occur. Parents, teachers, and others in the natural environment of the client are typically warned not to attempt to "treat" the client as they may serve to intensify his condition due to a lack of understanding of or sensitivity to the complex and often subtle factors which are presumed to underlie the overt symptomatic behavioral difficulties. The client is referred from the natural environment of home and school to the artificial one of the expert's office or residential unit.

Six brief examples are presented to illustrate this general conceptual orientation. These examples will demonstrate how assumptions concerning behavior functioning influence program decisions by educational and rehabilitation personnel. Each of these cases subsequently was provided a program based on a behavior modification orientation. Aspects of these programs will be presented later in the chapter and at appropriate places throughout the book.

Case 1. John is an eighteen-year-old male attending a social adjustment-

work training program. He is functioning within a borderline range of intelligence, had been previously hospitalized as a simple schizophrenic, and had been dismissed from a work training program of a sheltered workshop because of disruptive outburst and generally poor progress. In the social adjustment program he is described as displaying little interest in the program, of engaging in frequent disruptive "silly" talk, and of leaving classes frequently without permission. In his workshop training, attention is poor, persistence minimal, and rate of task completion low. The staff views his poor behavior and minimal progress as being manifestations of his "schizophrenia" and are fearful that program demands which require consistent active participation would be too stressful and would involve the possibility of precipitating an additional hospitalization. In short, in view of the internal causation assumptions, the staff is somewhat helpless because the client is not responding to the free "therapeutic" environment nor to the group program provided all clients in the program.

Case 2. Barnard is a seventeen-year-old mildly retarded male who is presently attending a secondary special education program. He is highly disruptive in class, often refusing to comply with teacher requests. He cries when confronted with demands, falls out of his chair in "fainting like" spells without warning, is afraid of loud noises, and exhibits shouting episodes when frustrated. During these episodes he may throw chairs and desks or physically attack his peers or teacher. After these episodes, he verbalizes guilt and apologizes for his "bad behavior." He has been diagnosed as being emotionally disturbed and has been provided a series of psychotherapy sessions without noticeable effect. The teacher is fearful of requiring him to adhere to the program activities because "I might contribute to his emotional disturbance." Because she is not a "mental health expert" and thus does not feel that she can treat emotional disturbance and because the mental health experts were unable to modify the emotional disturbance, the teacher has no specific plan for dealing with the problems presented other than to send him to the principal's office or to send him home whenever he becomes unmanageable in the classroom.

Case 3. Sally is a moderately retarded twenty-year-old who has been placed in a sheltered workshop on a trial basis. She displays little interest in her work or social environment and is viewed as having limited motivation. She displays some seizure activity which medical authorities describe as being related to her diagnosed central nervous system damage. It is noted that when urged to conform to the workshop routine and to produce at a rate commensurate with that of her peers, she is prone to seizure activity. Observation by workshop personnel suggests that some of the seizures are fake but they do not know how to deal with the problems. The

low motivation and general low frustration tolerance are viewed as being related to her brain damage and emotional immaturity. The workshop "rehabilitation" program is designed to teach work behaviors, and because the client will not work, no specific plans are available to treat her work-related deficits.

Case 4. David, a twenty-two-year-old moderately retarded male, attends a social development and work adjustment program. He displays only minimal and erratic interest in aspects of the program. Program personnel report that they have "tried everything" to motivate him but with no effect. As a result, he is viewed as "not feasible due to his low motivation" and is being considered for termination. The motivational deficit or lethargy resides within him, it is assumed, and this internal deficit is viewed as the reason for his poor performance.

Case 5. Paul, a twenty-five-year-old adult who resides in a residential facility, spends most of his waking hours sitting or lying on the floor engaged in a complex variety of stereotyped behaviors. Efforts to get him involved in social and work behaviors have not produced results. He is viewed as a severely retarded, chronic stereotyper, with psychotic-like behavior patterns, and "not feasible for further rehabilitation efforts" due to these internal limitations.

Case 6. Bill, a nineteen-year-old and mildly retarded is an active client of a vocational rehabilitation program. He has attended a special education program for a number of years, has spent a few months in a residential setting for his delinquent behavior, and displays little interest in schoollike matters. He was described as being impulsive, socially difficult, and easily influenced by others in engaging in undesirable behavior. The vocational counselor reported that he displayed poor judgment in social situations, had difficulty maintaining acceptable work behavior, demonstrated only limited persistence at a task, and had limited work or achievement motivation. He frequently became aggressive and refused to cooperate in his training program. Because he was unable to read even simple instructions, he was referred for education and psychological evaluation as a basis for development of a remedial reading experience. The counselor viewed the illiteracy as a distinct vocational handicap. In view of the fact that he had been unable to develop reading skills during years of special education class attendance and considering his high anxiety response to educational testing, it was recommended that "a reading program be postponed until after psychotherapy has reduced the high anxiety and general emotional blocking" that is present. It was assumed that the illiteracy is caused by emotional factors and that these must be dealt with prior to the initiation of a reading program.

Behavior Modification Model

While such a psychodynamic or internal causation treatment or rehabilitation orientation may prove valuable in some cases, it may not be as effective and efficient as other educational and rehabilitation approaches in dealing with severe learning and behavioral difficulties presented by mentally retarded adolescents and adults. Alternatives to this internal causation approach should be developed and evaluated if education and rehabilitation programs are to meet the challenge of the difficult mentally retarded client. The orientation presented in this book represents one such alternative. This orientation has a primary *behavior* focus. It studies the person's behavior as it is observed to occur under defined environmental conditions. It is in agreement with the emphasis of Tharp and Wetzel (1969) that:

> . . . the most effective point of intervention with the individual displaying behavioral disturbances is most likely the disturbing environment rather than the disturbing set of internal conditions [p. 11].

The major conceptual system for behavior development and change is that of learning theory, although other principles of behavior development and change which have evolved out of the behavioral sciences are utilized. The major concepts are based on well established relationships which indicate that much behavior is influenced by the changes which the behavior produces in the environment. Behavior that produces positive consequences or removes or decreases the intensity of unpleasant ones is strengthened. It is more likely to occur under similar circumstances in the future. If the relationship between the behavior and the consequence is a reliable one, the consequence may be said to be contingent upon the behavior. The consequences come to control the occurrence or nonoccurrence of the related behavior in a given environment or situation on the basis of the likelihood that the behavior will produce the consequence. The retarded adolescent learns to complete his reading assignment as this results in his being permitted to participate in recreational activities in the gymnasium. An incompleted assignment results in his remaining in the classroom. Completion of assignment becomes a strong behavior as it produces a positive consequence. The positive consequence is not forthcoming if the assignment is not completed. Behavior that results in consequences that are unpleasant or aversive, under usual circumstances, is less likely to occur for a period of time in the future. A frown from the teacher, threats from the boss, or a ticket from a traffic monitor will typically render the behavior that preceded these unpleasant events less likely to occur under similar circumstances in the future. This relationship, as the examples suggest, includes

presentation of unpleasant events, a frown, as well as removal of desirable events, a fine of $10 for traffic violation. In general terms both are viewed as punishment and exert a similar effect—that of decreasing the likelihood of the behavior which produced these unpleasant consequences. These and many other specific relationships between behavior and environmental characteristics or events form the basis for a technology of behavior change. These principles tell us what we must do if we wish to influence behavior in a certain manner. These principles also provide some basis for estimating the amount of change that can be expected within a given period of time. A behavior pattern, for example, that has been followed by a desirable consequence on numerous occasions typically will be more difficult to eliminate than behavior that has just begun to produce a favorable consequence. At the same time, behavior that has resulted in a highly preferred consequence on only a few recent occasions may be stronger than behavior that has resulted in a low preference consequence on numerous previous occasions. These examples illustrate both the simplicity and the complexity of the concepts which are available.

The general application of these learning and related concepts to problems of human functioning is that of behavior therapy, or more general, *behavior modification*. Behavior, regardless of its kind or intensity, is viewed as being at least partially a result of learning processes. The role of abnormal physical, sensory and neurological factors in deviant or problem behavior is recognized. Whenever possible these factors should be corrected in order to insure a normal basis for behavior development. Little behavior, however, is directly related to and completely determined or controlled by physical factors. In the absence of suitable evidence to the contrary, most learning and behavior problems are assumed to be determined or at least influenced by learning variables. This orientation provides the rehabilitation personnel with a viable position which encourages an active treatment involvement. Again, behavior is viewed as the result of learning experiences. Principles of behavior development and function are used to account for behavioral inadequacies in the same manner as these principles are viewed as being involved in the development of appropriate socially desirable behaviors. Behavior is not viewed as being symptomatic of underlying psychic difficulties but as resulting from a history of an individual interacting with an environment. Thus the treatment of behavior patterns which have been termed neurotic, disruptive, behavior disorders, personality problems, emotional disturbances, and the like is viewed as involving the same general set of factors as would be involved in the task of increasing the work rate, reading skill, social graces, or achievement motivation of the same person. Therefore behavior development, maintenance, or modification, whether it be "neurotic" behavior or, for example,

reading behavior, is viewed as being related to a common set of variables. Various behavior patterns do indeed involve different combinations of these basic factors but it is assumed that the same general set of factors is involved in each.

One aspect of the behavior modification approach which recommends it to those interested in developing a positive rehabilitation environment is that specific procedures which can be followed to modify behavior can be derived from the behavior model. Although there is no magical assurance that the derived procedures will in fact have the desired effect, the rehabilitation specialist can draw on considerable experimental data and on the clinical experiences of others to provide some comfortable support for what he has devised. Additionally, he has a method for evaluating the effectiveness of his procedures and for changing to an alternative treatment strategy. These characteristics of the behavior modification model render it a great deal more valuable than does a similar adherence to other systems of behavior change such as those associated with, for example, psychoanalytic, client-centered, need-centered, or ego-centered models.

An example will illustrate the position that problem behaviors are not merely symptoms of some underlying pathology or deficit which must be dealt with in order to influence the problem behaviors. Also, the example demonstrates that the behavior approach provides direction as to what behavior change procedures might be utilized in given instances. In a recent project, the disruptive and bizarre behaviors of six young adult retardates were studied in an effort to identify factors which could exert control over the behaviors. Presently attending a basic social and work development program, all had been excluded from sheltered work programs because they failed to follow directions, worked very slowly if at all, attended little to the quality of their work, and engaged frequently in disruptive behaviors. In casual observation of these clients in different aspects of the social adjustment program, it appeared as if the problem behaviors were beyond control of aspects of the environment because these behaviors occurred across situations in a manner that appeared to be unrelated to what was occurring in the environment. It was easy to conclude that the behaviors were the result of some internal disturbances that were manifested in the disruptive behaviors—that is, some emotional disturbance, autism, psychotic process, personality disorder, or the like. All of these "diagnostic" labels had been used with these clients at some point in their recent history. The behavior modification program which was provided, however, ignored any assumption of internal causes of the behavioral inadequacies and dealt with the behaviors as if these could be modified directly by relatively simple environmental changes.

Observation of these clients in the social adjustment program revealed

that there were few consistent cues for organized and persistent work behavior. Further, there were no influential accelerating or decelerating
events provided consistently by those in charge of the program contingent
upon appropriate or inappropriate behaviors. The reinforcing components
provided by the program personnel were mainly social in nature and even
these were provided inadvertently, more for inappropriate than for appropriate behavior. It was also evident that much of the disruptive behavior
was being maintained by social feedback from peers.

Based on these observations, a work environment was designed to facilitate work behavior by positively reinforcing appropriate performance, by
providing mildly aversive consequences for behavior incompatible with
work performance, and by providing distinctive discriminative cues for
work behavior.

These six young adults were placed in a workshop and taught to engage
in simple assembly-type tasks. The daily work periods consisted of three
fifteen minute periods separated by ten minute rest periods. Records were
kept of the frequency of disruptive behaviors and of the total number of
items assembled within each work session. After learning the task, clients
were observed for 10 days under conditions of verbal instructions to perform the tasks. This was the same general procedure used in the social adjustment program to encourage performance.

During this baseline condition of ten days, the six clients exhibited an
average of 98 disruptive behaviors per daily 45 minute sessions. The average for each client is depicted in Figure 1.1. The treatment consisted of
three distinct procedures. First, the client was placed on a program in
which he was provided token reinforcement for assembly items comp'eted.
During the demonstration stage, the client was shown what the token could
purchase. These represented a range of items which had been selected on
the basis of the reinforcement value for these clients. Next, distinctive
prompting cues were provided for initiation and continuation of work and
as a reminder whenever inappropriate behaviors appeared. These prompting procedures, selected on the basis of their effectiveness with each client,
consisted either of verbal prompting presented through earphones which
the client wore or of a visual signal which was presented by means of a
small signal box placed on the person's work table.

The third procedure consisted of mild punishment following disruptive
behavior. Each client, when engaging in disruptive behavior, was warned
either verbally or by means of a flashing light from the signal box. If the
behavior did not stop immediately, the client was required to move from
the work table and sit in a "time-out" chair for 60 seconds. He was informed
that he would not earn tokens during the time-out period.

During the last week or so of the treatment period, the prompting condi-

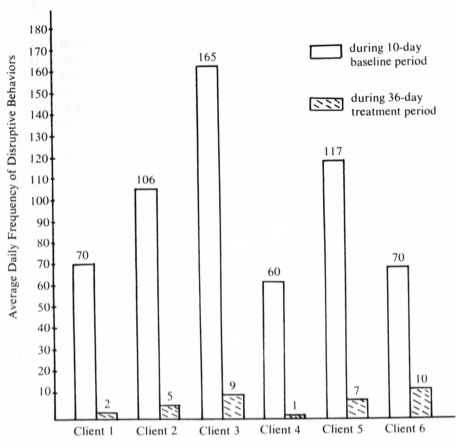

Figure 1.1. Number of Disruptive Behaviors During Baseline and
Treatment Periods

tion was removed as was the token reinforcement procedure. Instead, the
clients, at the end of the work session, counted their completed items and
marked them on record cards. These record cards became the mode of
exchange for reinforcers.

As shown in Figure 1.1, disruptive behaviors ouickly reduced in frequency, dropping from the average of 98 daily during the pretreatment
period to a rate of less than six daily during the treatment period. As noted
in Figure 1.2, production rate almost doubled in comparing the ten day
baseline period with the last ten days of the initial treatment period.

These data provide vivid illustration that at least some of the so-called
"symptomatic" behavior patterns of clients viewed as emotionally disturbed can be rather easily influenced by direct environmental treatment.

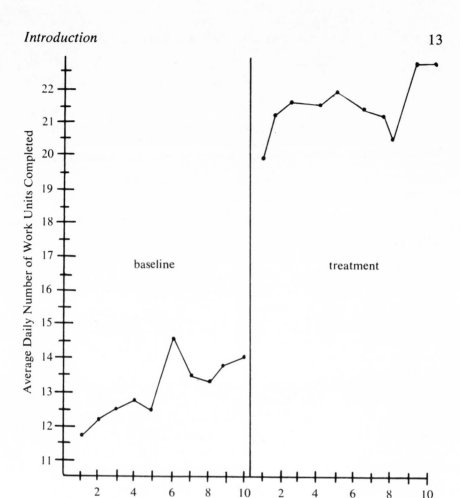

Figure 1.2. Average Daily Production During 10-Day Baseline Period and Last 10 Days of Treatment Period

The "pathological" disruptive behaviors were reduced dramatically as reinforcement was provided for appropriate behavior which successfully competed with the inappropriate mode of responding. The undesirable behaviors quickly came under the control of aspects of the new program environment and obviously were not merely manifestations of internal difficulties. In this environment the deviant behavior virtually disappeared and normal productive work behaviors appeared—behaviors which previous program personnel had not deemed possible.

To avoid any misinterpretation of this brief example, it should be noted that the clients behaved just as disruptively as they always had in other

settings. These environments had not changed. Their "emotionally disturbed" behaviors disappeared, however, whenever they entered the workshop environment which had been arranged to support positive behavior and these behaviors remained at a low level until they left the workshop. This illustrates even more emphatically that behavior, appropriate or inappropriate, is greatly influenced by specific environmental factors. As critical environmental variables are changed, behavior soon adapts to these changes.

Development of Effective Behavior

The basic position to be emphasized in this book is that major treatment efforts are directed toward the development of desirable effective behavior patterns. Once this occurs, and the retardate is better able to obtain more frequent and varied favorable consequences through his own efforts, inappropriate disruptive and bothersome behaviors characteristically disappear, or at least reduce in visibility. It is recognized that in some cases it may be necessary to decrease the strength of some high rate inappropriate behavior prior to being able to influence desirable means of responding. However, with an appropriate program, emphasis can be on developing desirable constructive behaviors which frequently will compete successfully with the inappropriate ones. Patterson, Jones, Whittier, and Wright (1965), in illustration, arranged an environment which systematically reinforced "attending" and "sitting at desk" behaviors in an aggressive, hyperactive retardate. These behaviors were incompatible with "constant looking around" and "out of seat" behaviors and these latter ones dropped in magnitude and frequency.

The focus of the behavior modification approach is on the behavior as it occurs in a specified environment. The primary treatment or behavior change focus is on *designing an environment* which will maximize the probability of the development and occurrence of appropriate behaviors, whether these behaviors be affective, cognitive, work, social, study, verbal or otherwise. As the orientation focuses on important environmental factors instead of on hypothetical, unobservable and unmeasurable internal factors, the rehabilitation and educational personnel are at a program advantage as the external environmental variables are potentially identifiable and manipulatable. To the extent that the critical environmental elements can be controlled and arranged, behavior can be influenced. A *behavior analysis* approach to evaluation and description of the problem areas (Kanfer and Saslow, 1965 and 1969; Lindsley, 1964) and the availability of a methodology of *applied analysis of behavior* (Baer, Wolf, and Risley, 1968) provide a means of developing hypotheses of effective behavior change

and of evaluating the value of these hypotheses as these are implemented in educational and rehabilitation programs.

The objectives of the behavior analysis are those of describing and pinpointing the problem behavior areas and of identifying factors which appear to be related to the behavior. Potential sources of reinforcement are sought. This analysis is conducted in the natural environment whenever possible and should involve those persons and events which are aspects of the natural environment.

Initial behavior analysis data are translated into programs in which functional relationships are identified by systematically modifying aspects of the environment and by noting resulting behavioral effects. If behavior changes as specified environmental events change, a functional relationship has been demonstrated; that is, the behavior is seen to be a function of the environmental events which are manipulated.

In a program of behavior modification, the basic questions raised are as follows: *How can new behavior patterns which the retarded has never exhibited be added to his repertoire?* Some behaviors are present, but these do not occur frequently enough or with sufficient reliance. *How can these behaviors be strengthened?* Other behaviors occur too frequently or else with excessive magnitude. *What can be done to weaken or eliminate these behaviors?* Still other behaviors are of suitable strength but do not always occur when desired. *How can the behaviors be brought under the control of appropriate aspects of the environment to insure that these will occur at the appropriate time or place?*

Although educational and rehabilitation personnel do not have precise control over the environment in which the retarded client presents learning and performance difficulties, nor do they have a detailed account of the history of the person which would permit them to identify the reinforcement variables which control the individual's behavior, there is research and demonstration evidence which suggests that sufficient control is possible to influence the behavior of the retarded in a significant manner. The reports of Ayllon and Azrin (1968) and Tharp and Wetzel (1969) and literally hundreds of other studies lend support to this position.

Studies by Wolf, Birnbrauer, Williams and Lawler (1965), Bijou, Birnbrauer, Kidder, and Tague (1966) and Zimmerman, Overpeck, Eisenberg, and Garlick (1969) illustrate the operational and analytic characteristics of the behavioral analysis approach to behavior change. These studies representing clinical, educational and vocational concerns also illustrate that there are no essential differences in the procedures and related learning concepts used in dealing with a wide range of problem areas. The Wolf et al. study provides one of the first examples of the successful use of a behavior modification procedure in work with a clinical problem of a men-

tally retarded client. The retarded, diagnosed as suffering from mental retardation, cerebral palsy, aphasia, hyperirritability, and brain damage, resided in an institution for the mentally retarded and was enrolled in a school program which met three hours daily. After a few weeks in class, the retarded girl began to vomit occasionally. This rate increased until within three months vomiting became practically a daily class occurrence. Drug therapy was of no value in reducing this rate. Noting that the girl frequently was returned to her dormitory following a vomiting episode, the behavior therapists hypothesized that such consequences were reinforcing and thus maintaining the vomiting behavior. The major modification procedure followed in eliminating this behavior was based on the learning principle of extinction. This principle suggests that behavior will decrease in strength upon the removal of those stimulus consequences which maintain it. The treatment consisted of keeping the girl in the classroom throughout the class period even though vomiting behavior occurred and of attempting to shape desirable behaviors by providing tangible and social reinforcers contingent upon the occurrence of such appropriate responses. Under such a program, vomiting behavior declined to a zero level over a period of thirty class days. Other behaviors that occurred with virtually every vomiting episode—screaming, clothes tearing, and destruction of property—also declined to a zero level along with the vomiting. It was noted that productive classroom behavior and responsiveness to the teacher's requests improved markedly.

In order to determine if the elimination of the vomiting and related tantrum behaviors was due to the extinction operations imposed, the original consequences were reinstated. Following the occurrence of the vomiting behavior in the classroom for the first time in a number of weeks, the child was immediately returned to the dormitory. Vomiting gradually increased until it occurred in over one-third of the class sessions over a three month period. The extinction procedure was reinstated with the result that the vomiting episodes were again virtually eliminated. This reversal or replication procedure demonstrated that the vomiting behavior was maintained by specific consequences and that it could be controlled (produced or eliminated) by providing or removing these reinforcing consequences.

This report also provides illustration of other characteristics of behavior modification programs. For example, the behavior was not assumed to be a symptom of some internal psychological disturbance. Further, it was not deemed necessary to delve into the history of this behavior to identify factors associated with its development even though the child had been vomiting in the dormitory since being admitted to the institution. This illustrates the position that the conditions which led to its initial development need not be the same as the current conditions which maintain the behavior. Nor

is it assumed that the reinforcement which maintains maladaptive behavior in one setting is necessarily the same reinforcement which maintains it in another. Additionally, behaviors other than those which are chosen as the focus of treatment may show change in a desirable manner. The temper tantrum behavior in this case reduced, although it was not provided specific and systematic attention. Numerous other studies in the behavior modification literature report these same results. Finally, a behavior therapy program not only seeks to eliminate maladaptive behavior, in this case vomiting episodes in the classroom, but attempts to provide more suitable behavior as a replacement. Had vomiting behavior been eliminated without replacing it with "increased productive classroom behavior", the treatment program would have been only partially fulfilled.

Bijou et al. (1966) describe the classroom program used to develop a motivational system for strengthening academic and appropriate social behaviors in a group of mildly retarded students. Initially, teacher approval provided for desirable classroom behaviors was ineffective in strengthening these classes of behaviors. Following the introduction of a token reinforcement system, higher rates of effective study and cooperation behaviors became evident. Various "study habits" including such behaviors as sitting quietly, paying attention to and complying with instructions, and working productively for sustained periods were strengthened and a range of disruptive behaviors was eliminated. Techniques involving frequent token and social reinforcement for appropriate social and study behaviors, and those utilizing extinction and punishment (time-out from positive reinforcement) operations, were used by the teacher personnel. The results of these behavior modification procedures along with the use of programmed materials can best be depicted by describing the study behaviors developed by one of the retarded students. It should be noted that initially the students were poorly motivated for academic achievement. That is, they engaged in "academic behaviors" for only short and inconsistent periods of time. The authors reported:

> Instead of being given his assignment by the teacher, he obtained his own "work folder," set his own watch, and entered the date and starting time on his daily record sheet. He chose his first task, completed it, and went on to the next. Starting and finishing times were entered for each item. When all the work was completed, he called a teacher and together they checked his work. Marks (token reinforcement) were given at this time [p. 512].

These authors provide an excellent discussion of the basic principles which guided the development of the procedures and materials used. Specific techniques for the development of the motivation system, prerequisite academic behaviors and programmed instructional materials are provided and

should be consulted by those interested in developing a behavior modification program for use with the mildly retarded in a classroom environment.

Zimmerman et al. (1969) illustrate the application of an applied analysis of behavior to the work production rates of mentally retarded adults who were participating in a prevocational training program and emphasize the crucial necessity of obtaining objective data as a basis for evaluating the effectiveness of any environmental changes which might be initiated. These writers suggested:

> We have found that objective measurement is essential because it alone provides a clear and certain description of a client's behavior and unambiguous feedback with respect to whether a client is being helped. Only by having a quantitative record of a client's behavior can his supervisor talk about this behavior in terms that communicate intelligibly to others. Only by examining the quantitative effects that a given treatment has on that target behavior can a supervisor immediately and clearly see whether that treatment is therapeutic, ineffective, or perhaps even noxious [p. 334].

Again, these three studies illustrate various characteristics of the behavior modification approach. In each, the major emphasis was on the development of effective behavior and on the objective evaluation of the effectiveness of the behavior modification program in meeting the treatment objectives. The focus was on specified behaviors as these occurred in the natural environment of classroom and work setting. In each instance the personnel in these natural settings functioned as the treatment agent. The teachers and work supervisors arranged the environment in terms of the designated program and, in the usual course of operation of the classroom and workshop, followed the treatment plan.

In most instances the natural environment offers the greatest resources for effective behavior change as the most powerful factors which influence the person's life are in the natural environment. The professional rehabilitation or mental health specialist who treats the person in a setting, away from the client's natural environment (for example, office, hospital) is at a distinct disadvantage in most instances as he frequently does not have control over the events in the natural environment which exert the most influence over the client's behavior. Whenever an individual is removed from his natural environment and is placed in another one for care and treatment purposes, it must be recognized that the new setting is an artificial one. If the client is to benefit from experiences in this artificial environment, there must be a high degree of similarity between critical components of this one and the natural environment in which the person is to reside. The types of social relations, the types of behaviors required, the schedules of behavioral requirements and reinforcements, and the like all

are quite critical in a consideration of adjustment to a future different environment. The artificial environment (therapeutic, supportive, rehabilitative, and the like) must teach and maintain those habits or modes of social and work behaviors which will be adaptive at a future time in a different environment. These behaviors are frequently not those that are adaptive in the artificial therapy environment. Habits of independence, self-sufficiency, individuality, freedom of choice, and the like are all needed for independence in a free enterprise system. These are hardly the behavior patterns which are fostered, for example, in many residential programs. In other programs which provide a therapeutic milieu, the client is provided new skills in arts and crafts, music, recreation and even "verbal insight." However, few of these skills will be maintained after return to the natural environment as there are few opportunities to utilize these new skills or else the social agents in the natural environment provide little reinforcement for these behaviors. Thus they disappear and the person is left without effective means of behaving.

Purpose of Rehabilitation Programs

The only justification for rehabilitation programs is that these hold promise of facilitating behavior change. Although the major focus may be on modifying school or work and work-related behaviors, rehabilitation efforts may be directed toward changing behaviors of numerous classes, for example, verbal, affective, cognitive, perceptual, social, or interpersonal. Once this behavior change focus is accepted, program personnel will find it necessary to identify and define the behaviors which require modification efforts. Such treatment statements as "develop a more positive attitude toward work," "create social sensitivity," or "decrease his dependency" are too general to provide specific treatment direction and are viewed as being inappropriate. These must be restated in more precise behavioral terms in relation to specific or general classes of environmental conditions.

An additional aspect of this treatment planning activity is that of describing the *direction* of change as well as the *extent* of change that is necessary in order to reach a given educational or vocational goal. It becomes apparent that this requirement is a difficult undertaking, but one that, if systematically pursued, will have a profoundly beneficial effect on program development and implementation. It is one thing to identify a goal as "to attain competence in self-help skills" or "social adequacy," but quite another to translate this general objective into specific behavior goals which lend direction to the day by day program efforts of the rehabilitation personnel. The behavior modification approach requires the program personnel to step out of the realm of general, and frequently vague, behavior

change methodology and into the arena of specificity. Thus, beyond specifying the behavior goals comes the problem of translating these into behavior modification procedures. What behavior modification procedures
will be used to bring about the desired behavior change? If verbal counseling, creation of a therapeutic milieu, information giving, classroom instruction, sheltered workshop exposure or relaxation training are to be used, for
example, the program personnel not only must describe the experiences but
also must justify in terms of behavior principle or hypothesis why these procedures of behavior change were selected for the particular problems presented by particular clients.

It is evident that all too frequently in rehabilitation practices involving
the mentally retarded, program placements are made (such as sheltered
workshop placement, social adjustment training) and specific treatment
procedures used (for example, verbal counseling, recreation therapy) without any clear conceptual or empirical indication of how such experiences
will result in better "adjustment" of the client. Some clients do, without
question, change during such experiences. The inefficiency and unpredict-
ability of such practices, however, become real issues in numerous difficult
problem cases. Zimmerman, Stuckey, Garlick, and Miller (1969), in support of this position, commented:

> We do not see how employability of any multiply handicapped clients can be-
> come a reality in the near future unless many sheltered workshops and other
> rehabilitation facilities focus more effort upon *both* the objective, *quantitative*
> assessment of their clients' target behaviors and the systematic application
> and objective assessment of training and therapeutic procedures employed by
> their supervisors, counselors, and other members of their rehabilitation staff
> [pp. 40–41].

The authors emphasized that rehabilitation workers should be trained in
the methodology of applied analysis of behavior and concluded:

> Workshops with supervisors and counselors so trained will be able to increase
> more effectively their armamentarium of therapeutic measures and *eliminate*
> from their repertoires the use of methods that may be at best ineffective, if
> not even noxious, from the point of view of improving their clients' behavior
> [p. 41].

Prescriptive Evaluation and Programming

The behavior modification approach requires *prescriptive programming*.
Every experience that is provided is viewed as one of a series of steps in the
direction of attaining a specified behavioral goal. The client is placed in a
program designed to develop functional academic skills, for example, only
if it is agreed that additional academic skills will increase his likelihood of

adapting to the requirements of given situations. He is placed in a work training program in order to develop designated work and work-related behavioral characteristics. These may range from learning to work under the pressure of an assembly line to the development of skills in changing quickly and easily from one assembly task to another. Again, the specific behavioral objectives are spelled out and the program experiences, whatever these may be, are selected as those which will best contribute to these behavioral objectives.

Evaluation is completed, not for the sake of categorization or diagnosis in the traditional sense, but for the purpose of giving precise direction to the program efforts. If evaluation provides no specific program direction, then it is a waste of effort for educational and rehabilitation endeavors. Such evaluation must provide the basis for differential programming. It is of little positive value, perhaps even of negative impact, for a teacher or a counselor to be informed that Client A is emotionally disturbed, brain damaged, culturally deprived or passive-aggressive unless these designations carry specific program predictions which are based on testable theoretical concepts or on established empirical relationships. Specific program predictions are too seldom provided by the evaluation procedures followed by the typical education and rehabilitation programs serving the retarded. As a result, program personnel are provided no differential program direction. They frequently are in no better position in terms of effective program development than they were prior to receiving the evaluation data.

Meyerson, Kerr, and Michael (1967) provide some pertinent comments about the usual evaluation data which are supplied by psychologists to rehabilitation personnel: "Most of the data obtained, however, seem strikingly unrelated to the behavior required in the rehabilitation center. They may lead the psychologist to believe that he 'understands' better why a client acts as he does, but the data lend little aid in changing unacceptable behavior to more acceptable behavior" [p. 215]. A further comment was made that reasons, usually stated in terms of some inaccessible trait of the client, are provided to account for the unacceptable behaviors. This was illustrated in a recent case with which the present writer had some contact. An adolescent mildly retarded girl was creating considerable distraction in the rehabilitation program, especially among the male students, by frequently exposing her legs while sitting at her desk or work area. A psychological evaluation, requested in order to assist the rehabilitation personnel in dealing with this problem, provided the following, "This problem is related to her great pregnancy longing due to her oral dependency." It would have been exceedingly difficult to provide more irrelevant information to rehabilitation personnel who were seeking some assistance in developing procedures for teaching more appropriate social behavior.

The question to be asked about all kinds of assessment information is a

simple practical one: What direction does the information provide about what to do with the specific student or client at a particular time in a particular place? Does it provide specific program direction or does it provide a basis for program decisions? If not, it must come under the heading of esoteric and irrelevant information.

Application to the Retarded

As the major task of educational and rehabilitation programs is that of creating an effective learning environment, the most defensible program approach appears to be one which makes use of established behavior principles. This program position will be followed in this book in an effort to understand the development of the educational and vocational difficulties presented by the mentally retarded and to provide effective means of modifying these bothersome characteristics. Although the practice of utilizing learning and other behavior principles as a basis for deriving behavior modification procedures is by no means new, the systematic application to a wide range of problem behaviors presented by the retarded is of recent origin. Nevertheless, some of the most exciting work in the application of behavior principles to treatment of developmental, behavioral, educational and rehabilitation problems has been that involving the mentally retarded.

Recent results of the application of behavior modification techniques provide illustration of behavior change of a range, degree, and rate that most psychiatric, psychological, rehabilitation, and educational personnel had not thought possible due to limitations assumed to be inherent in mental retardation. It has been demonstrated that at least a significant degree of the behavioral limitations of the retarded may well reside in an inappropriate or limited learning environment rather than being, as has been assumed too frequently, an unalterable manifestation of the individual's retardation. Severely and profoundly retarded persons who for years were beyond help or hope, have, as a result of treatment programs utilizing the systematic application of behavior modification procedures, developed language, motor, perceptual, cognitive, affective, social, and self-help skills which have rendered them more independent and more able to experience a meaningful personal and social existence. This application is illustrated, for example, by Gorton and Hollis (1965), Spradlin (1964), and Bensberg, Colwell, and Cassel (1965) in development of eating skills; by Roos (1965) and Minge and Ball (1967) in development of dressing skills; by Hundziak, Maurer, and Watson (1965), Giles and Wolf (1966), and Watson (1967) in development of toileting skills; by Gorton and Hollis (1965), Girardeau and Spradlin (1964), and Bensberg, Colwell, and Cassel (1965) in development of grooming skills; by Bensberg, Colwell, and Cassel (1965), Wiesen and Watson (1967), Gorton and Hollis (1965)

and Girardeau and Spradlin (1964) in development of socialization skills; by Meyerson, Kerr, and Michael (1967) in development of skills of locomotion; and by Hamilton and Stephens (1968), Sloane, Johnston, and Harris (1968), MacAulay (1968) and Kerr, Meyerson, and Michael (1965) in the development of language skills. Application has also been made to problem areas which are typically viewed as clinical in nature. The Tate and Baroff (1966) treatment of a self-destructive retarded child and the Wolf, Birnbrauer, Williams and Lawler (1965) treatment of an emotionally disturbed retarded with an inappropriate psychophysiological reaction illustrate this application.

Evaluation of these and similar reports emphasizes the particular applicability of these behavior change procedures even to the more severely retarded as no particular characteristics such as speech or a certain level of cognitive development are necessary for treatment effects. Additionally, there is ample illustration in published reports that various behavior modification procedures can be utilized by a wide range of personnel in the setting in which the retarded reside. This is of especial significance in view of the limited number of highly trained personnel who presently are available to provide general rehabilitation service to the mentally retarded. Some studies have even reported the use of retarded peers as major treatment agents in programs of behavior modification. Wiesen and Watson (1967) used peers to reinforce social interaction in a mentally retarded boy who typically almost totally ignored his peers. Social interaction with peers increased noticeably when made contingent upon tangible reinforcers which were provided by the peers. Peers were in turn reinforced by an adult counselor. Whalen and Henker (1969) demonstrated that moderately retarded adolescents could learn to use basic behavior modification techniques of social modeling and contingent reinforcement to modify the behavior of other younger more severely retarded children. These authors reported that the adolescent teachers became increasingly independent and were able to function with minimal supervision.

As will be discussed at some length in later chapters, the less disabled retarded exhibiting an array of deficit and nonadaptive behavior patterns have responded quite favorably to behavior modification efforts. The Birnbrauer, Bijou, Wolf, and Kidder (1965) report of remediation of academic difficulties and the Zimmerman, Stuckey, Garlick, and Miller (1969) effort to increase work productivity in a sheltered workshop illustrate this application.

Case Illustrations

The following chapter provides a scheme for describing problem behavior which is consistent with the behavior modification approach outlined in

this section. Following this and continuing the theme of environmental determination of behavioral inadequacies, Chapter 3 includes a description of a number of possible environmental deficits which contribute to poor behavior development. As a basis for these discussions and as a means of providing further illustration of the conceptual and procedural characteristics of the behavior model and how these differ from the more widely followed psychodynamic approach, brief descriptions will be provided of the behavior modification programs of two of the cases presented earlier in the chapter. While the more technical aspects of these and similar rehabilitation programs will be described in later chapters, these case descriptions will provide the reader with sufficient initial practical substance to reinforce his initial acceptance of the concepts presented up to this point.

David, described earlier as Case 4, presented a severe performance deficit. He just sat and did nothing for long periods of time. In viewing David's performance deficit in the work setting, it was determined initially that the tasks presented him were not too difficult; that is, it was noted that he could perform the task in a one to one situation in which considerable encouragement and praise were provided. Additionally, it was noted that in some tasks in other settings he was able at times to persist at the task over extended periods of time. Thus, it was discovered that David had in his repertoire the basic behavioral patterns for satisfactory work performance. His basic deficit was a "motivational" one. Motivation is viewed in the behavior model as residing in the reinforcing components of the environment; thus, an evaluation was made of the reinforcers which could be made available to David as a consequence of appropriate work. In interviewing the teacher and family, various items and activities were identified as possible reinforcers. Also, as noted earlier, praise, attention, and similar forms of social recognition were reinforcing to him. Initially, David was permitted to select items and activities (for example, pipe tobacco, bowling) which he chose to have or engage in. Following this, a token reinforcement system was initiated. David was shown that following work completion (for example, after 3 items completed or after 5 minutes of adequate work behavior) he would be provided tokens which were exchangeable for items or activities of his choice. Initially, David was reinforced frequently and provided opportunity for frequent exchange. After experience with the system, David was reinforced less frequently and could not spend his tokens earned until longer periods of time had elapsed.

After some success with this system, another procedure—that of charting—was used to maintain and to increase performance. After each work session, David and the supervisor would count the number of items completed and place the total on a bar graph. This bar graph was displayed over his work table. He was then encouraged to increase his performance

during the next work session, with the additional goal object of 10 bonus tokens for improvement. This charting procedure was quite valuable both in prompting higher and more consistent performance and also in increasing David's social interaction with peers and workshop personnel. The chart was a source of pride. David frequently would show his chart to others and explain what he did in order to make the lines go up or down.

David, although he was retarded and had previously demonstrated a general picture of apathy, laziness, and non-interest or involvement, was able to perform quite differently as the environment was constructed to be sensitive to his particular characteristics. In a sense, a prosthetic environment was created which supported the characteristics which were present. In the process, David's behavioral resources were rendered more functional. These prosthetic elements were gradually removed as David was able to function without them. The behavioral deficit was demonstrated not to be an unalterable aspect of his mental retardation or rigid personality structure. The behavior modification approach did not conceptually, or on any other a priori basis, accept the cause or reason for his general behavioral inadequacy to be internal. Rather, a search was made of the immediate environment for possible relationships between behavior and environmental determinants. In this instance, the prompting and reinforcing components of the environment were quite inadequate for David. As these were modified, David's behavior was modified. David is presently a valued worker in a sheltered workshop.

Bill, described earlier as Case 6, provides illustration of the close relationship between evaluation and treatment characteristics of the behavior modification approach. It will be recalled from the earlier description that Bill was referred for psychotherapy for treatment of his anxiety level and emotional blocking which apparently were interfering with his development of basic reading skills. When Bill refused to continue his "therapy" after the first session with the psychiatrist, he was accepted as an evaluation client in a clinic staffed by behavior modification personnel. The basic evaluation question presented by the counselor was "can he learn to read?" The behavior model assumes that the only legitimate strategy to follow in determining if a person can engage in or develop certain behaviors is one of placing him in an optimum program and of evaluating the question empirically. This practice deviates considerably from that followed by most evaluation approaches. Typically, following evaluation or diagnosis a set of recommendations is made for someone else to try out or implement. In the approach followed with Bill, evaluation data were used to design a treatment program which was implemented as a means of evaluating the validity of the program recommendations. The fact that Bill had failed to learn to read even though he had been in a special education program for

an extended period did not preclude the possibility that he would be able to develop reading skills if placed in an optimum program environment based on a careful appraisal of his learning and related behavior characteristics. In the absence of evidence to the contrary, the position is assumed that one should not declare that a person cannot learn or perform a given task or skill unless one also describes the training program that has been provided in arriving at this conclusion. Thus, behavioral predictions frequently are generated from a program designed to encourage the learning or performance of the behaviors under study. In Bill's case, the decision was made to provide him with a reading program based on learning principles and to evaluate his response to it. Thus, if he did not develop reading skills, the evaluation report could also describe the conditions under which this finding was obtained.

During the initial contact, it was established that Bill was functioning intellectually within the mildly retarded range. In addition, he demonstrated basic requisite skills for learning to read, that is auditory discrimination and memory, visual discrimination and memory, vocabulary, and comprehension of materials heard. It was observed that a number of overt anxiety responses were present during testing of his reading skills, stuttering, perspiration, facial grimaces, fidgeting, and the like. It was assumed that these behaviors could interfere with effective learning of new reading responses and should be dealt with in the program design.

A reading program based on a systematic application of learning principles was initiated. The objectives of the program were as follows: (1) to demonstrate that Bill could develop basic reading skills in a short period of time, (2) to demonstrate that attention to and persistence at the reading task could be established, (3) to establish a relationship between acceptable behavior and a positive consequence, that is, the basic elements of achievement motivation, and (4) to demonstrate that the anxiety responses could be eliminated by providing pleasant, relaxing and successful reading experiences. The basic technique used was that of immediate and frequent reinforcement of appropriate responses. Initially, reinforcers consisted of tokens which could be exchanged for a variety of items selected on the basis of Bill's preferences, such as cigarettes, pipe, pipe tobacco, cosmetic items, and movie tickets. After initial success, social reinforcement gradually replaced the tangible ones. The program was continued for some twenty sessions. Initially the sessions lasted for 10 to 15 minutes, the time determined by the client. After initial success, Bill requested that sessions be increased and soon worked for periods up to 75 minutes. At the termination of the evaluation-education program, all the objectives were attained. Bill had acquired some 400 new words and could read these in sentences and paragraphs with adequate comprehension. His overt anxiety responses

gradually disappeared, and he approached the reading sessions with enthusiasm. Achievement motivation was evident in that he, during the last few sessions, worked without tangible reinforcement, asked for homework assignments, and demonstrated considerable pride in his achievement.

In both of these cases, the focus of the behavior modification program was on designing that environment which would insure that the desired behavior would occur. Initially, it was necessary to provide rather intensive individual attention. However, as the behavior occurred, the program emphasis was shifted from concern for behavior development to concern for maintaining the behavior under more natural conditions. The procedures used and related principles which dictated these procedures will be described in later chapters.

CHAPTER TWO

Types of Problem Behaviors

The mentally retarded, influenced by the same set of learning variables that influence and control much of the behavior of all humans, can experience a wide range of learning difficulties and deficits. He may experience—just as every other human may—a wide range of adaptive behavior problems in a wide range of settings. Prior to a discussion of the types of learning and behavior problems which confront the mentally retarded, it should prove helpful to comment on a few general characteristics of the retarded.

Not only can the retarded learn, many retarded adults can learn well enough to become independent members of society. The retarded are no more or less prone to delinquency, psychoses, emotional difficulties, laziness, lethargy, happiness, enthusiasm, or sadness, nor to any other human characteristic than any other group. The retarded vary greatly along all known physical and psychological characteristics. Contrary to the misconceptions of many, the retarded do not behave and learn as they do because of their mental retardation.

There is no evidence that the variables operative in the learning and development of the mentally retarded are different in kind from those involved in the learning and development of any others. Thus it is assumed that the retarded can learn and further can learn most effectively and efficiently if the environment, both present and historical, is or has been designed and administered properly. In fact, it is even assumed that much of the learning and adaptive behavior difficulties are products not of mental retardation but rather of a faulty learning history.

The present chapter is concerned with the description and classification of types of adaptive behavior problems which confront the mentally retarded. The subsequent chapter focuses on the learning basis for these

28

problem behavior areas. In these chapters it is assumed that work behaviors, academic skills, social skills, verbal behaviors, and emotional behaviors are all acquired and maintained in terms of a common set of learning principles. Thus it is not assumed, as in other systems concerned with development and control of various classes of human behavior, that there is one set of learning variables involved in the development of academic skills, for example, and a different set involved in the development of interpersonal skills and social behavior. As a consequence, as will be emphasized throughout the book, there is no necessity for different systems of dealing with behavior characteristics that may be creating concern. There is no education theory and technology which is different in kind from a psychotherapy theory and technology which differs from a rehabilitation theory and technology. All problem areas are viewed, until demonstrated otherwise, as manifestations of inadequate educative procedures. The treatment or behavior change approach is an educational one. If a person is experiencing difficulty, he is presenting symptoms of a poor educational experience. He either has not been exposed to an environment appropriate to the behavior in question or else his exposure has been inappropriate. The program has not been designed to take advantage of what is known about behavior development and change.

Classes of Problem Behaviors

A simple but useful manner of classifying the educational and vocational problems of the mentally retarded is suggested by Eysenck (1960) in his statement:

> On the one hand we have *surplus conditioned reactions,* i.e., reactions acquired . . . where the reaction is unadaptive, even though originally it may have been well suited to circumstances. On the other hand we have *deficit conditioned reactions,* i.e., reactions normally acquired by most individuals in a society which are adaptive, but which . . . have not been acquired by a particular person [p. 7].

The retarded may exhibit too much behavior in terms of general environmental requirements. The behavior may be excessive regardless of where or when it occurs. In other instances, while not being inappropriate for some situations, the behavior may be under poor environmental control concerning the place or frequency of its occurrence. The behavior may be adaptive and even a common characteristic of many persons, but for a given individual it becomes inappropriate due to its excessive rate of occurrence. It is true also that in some cases behavior appears to be excessive merely because the retarded has so much general behavior deficit in rela-

tion to the requirements of specific situations. In these instances the gross limitations of appropriate behavior overemphasize the few behaviors that are present and render these excessive, bizarre and inappropriate. If the person had a wider range of appropriate behaviors, the "excessiveness" quality of certain behaviors would be diminished. In some cases the retarded may not know what to do; therefore, he engages excessively in what he does know.

Excessive behavior patterns are quite likely to be labeled as deviant or pathological by the social environment. Because of the apparent visibility of such behaviors, it is easy to notice conflict with or deviation from standards of conduct. Excessive behavior patterns also may create concern due to the fear that the retarded does not have control of his behavior and thus it might get out of hand. Such behaviors are most likely to be bothersome as these may interfere with the rights and privacy of others.

One other factor that renders excessive behavior patterns of particular concern to society is the apparent self-defeating character of such behaviors. It is difficult to understand what is accomplished by such behaviors. Thus there is a tendency to view such behaviors as a result of some pathology or sickness. In some instances the factors which maintain excessive behavior patterns are easily identified, even though casual observation may not provide such an impression. In illustration, in observing a group of "disturbed" retarded adolescents in a classroom, considerable disruptive behavior occurred even though this behavior was constantly rejected by the teacher. However, peer attention served to provoke and maintain the problem behavior. In other instances, excessive behavior patterns appear to persist in the absence of any discernable reinforcing conditions. These behavior patterns become even more puzzling when they persist in the face of obvious punishment, as is evident in some instances.

Under such conditions it may be that the retarded has no alternative behavior available. While the reinforcement associated with the excessive behavior patterns may be minimal, the retarded simply has no other suitable behavior to exhibit. In contrast, most persons will attempt various alternative behaviors when a particular behavior pattern does not result in desired consequences. The retarded, however, may have no alternative behaviors which can be utilized in an effort to be successful. He thus repeats the behavior that is available, even though it does not produce the consequences associated with more appropriate responses.

In summary, one major class of behaviors which interferes with the adaptation of the retarded to his social interpersonal and vocational environment includes those which occur excessively, either generally or in relation to specific situations. These behaviors in isolation may not be inappropriate. The major maladaptive component is the frequency or magnitude

of the behavior. The focus of the education and rehabilitation program objectives becomes that of eliminating or decreasing the frequency or magnitude of the problem behavior.

Behavior Deficits

The second class of problem behaviors stems from the fact that behaviors are absent in circumstances which require behaviors of a certain form. In illustration, the retarded may not be able to read well enough to follow written directions and as a result fails in his vocational tasks. At other times he may be unable to make the social responses required for adjustment to group living conditions. In these instances the person obviously will not be successful. In fact, in situations where deficit behaviors are common, active punishment in the form of rejection or isolation may be the result. The obvious program goal becomes one of developing new behaviors and of strengthening those that are present but which occur too infrequently or in an unreliable manner.

Deficit behaviors may represent a faulty learning environment as well as the absence of an appropriate learning environment. A person may be unable to make appropriate social responses due to his having been taught to make inappropriate responses. Another person may be unable to make appropriate social responses due to the absence of any opportunity for him to learn these behaviors. This is most obviously illustrated by the adolescent who has resided in an institution which has not permitted independent responses.

Relative Nature of Inadequacies

In viewing behavioral problems from the excessive-deficit viewpoint, it is important to recognize that behavior is not categorically or inherently inappropriate or inadequate. Behavioral characteristics, stated simply as what a retarded person does or does not do, must be viewed as inappropriate or being of an excessive or deficit nature only in relation to the requirements imposed by a given environment. To illustrate, John, a mildly retarded young adult, may read successfully at a fifth grade level. Job A may require only a minimum literacy level. John's reading skills would be appropriate for placement in this job. Job B on the other hand may require a higher level of reading skills than are presently characteristic of John. He would be viewed as exhibiting deficit behaviors in the reading area in relation to the requirements of this particular job.

Similarly, one behavior pattern may be viewed as excessive in one situation and acceptable in another. A person can be said to be "too aggressive"

only in relation to a given situation which does not accept behaviors which are viewed by those who control that environment as being too aggressive. In this environment the behaviors are likely to be responded to in a manner designed to eliminate or discourage the aggressive behavior. These same patterns which are viewed as aggressive in this situation may not be viewed as aggressive in others.

The consequences of these differences in behavioral requirements can be most significant in view of the problems presented by the retarded. That is, a person may adjust in one situation but not in another and never have to change one single behavior characteristic. This relatively simple concept becomes most important in planning a rehabilitation program for the retarded. Behavioral patterns which are present must be viewed in terms of environmental requirements prior to planning any program designed to change the behavior patterns.

It should be recognized also that some deficit or excessive behavior patterns are quite characteristic in a wide range of situations, for example: "He never has been able to do that." "He generally is too aggressive," "He always talks too loudly," "He most always disrupts any peer group," "He never has been able to get along with adults." On the other hand, other excessive or deficit behavior patterns are specific to situations or to types of situations. Additionally, appropriate behavior may be present in some situations and absent in others. It is not unusual to hear the statement, "He knows how to behave but he just doesn't." This statement suggests that desired behavior patterns are in the repertoire of the person but are not under appropriate discriminative control. That is, these behaviors do not always occur at the right time or place. This type of problem behavior is frequently different from that present when the behavior or any close approximation of that which is required has never occurred. In one instance the program task is that of teaching the desired behavior and then bringing it under appropriate environmental control. In the other, the task becomes one of strengthening the behavior that is already in the repertoire in relation to specific situations. The training program would differ in these two instances.

Behavior may be excessive in some situations, but of acceptable form or absent in others. It may be observed that the retarded is hyperactive in some situations but not in others, for example, very inattentive in classroom but "will sit motionless for an hour and watch television." A person learns to behave in certain ways in one situation and in other ways in different environments. It is essential to recognize all of these as important characteristics of the behavior of the retarded as education and rehabilitation programs are developed. All too frequently, behavior has been "rehabilitated" in the prosthetic environment of the rehabilitation agency, but to the

surprise of the program personnel, the desired behavior patterns do not occur or generalize to the environment of the real world. Also, it is not infrequent that the retarded client fails to present those problem behaviors in the rehabilitation environment which resulted in his being placed in this program initially. The behavior of the retarded client may change as significant components of the environment change. Again, "inappropriateness" or "excessiveness" or "deficitness" are not inherent or all-or-none characteristics of the retarded person's behavior. These gain essential meaning only in relation to the requirements or expectations of specific environments.

It is true that in a given broad environment certain behavior patterns are highly valued and will add to the adjustment potential of the person possessing these behaviors. This is true not only because these behaviors will be reinforced, but, in addition, the mere presence of these behaviors will result in greater tolerance for other behaviors which may be inappropriate. At the same time, certain behavior patterns, even when present at low frequency, will result in "out-of-proportion" nonacceptance of a range of borderline or tolerable behaviors. Inappropriate sexual behavior, in illustration, frequently results in the immediate rejection of the retarded and in the unrealistic negative evaluation of other behavior patterns which, under normal circumstances, would be viewed as acceptable.

Behavior Change Programs

The classification of problem areas as excessive or deficit in nature facilitates the development of specific rehabilitation goals and related behavior change programs. A group of behavior principles, which forms the basis for a set of behavior change techniques, is available for program planning and implementation. The principles and techniques are discussed in later chapters. Basically, the techniques focus on means of increasing desirable behavior and of decreasing undesirable behavior. These techniques are derived, as noted, from certain basic laws or principles of human behavior, notably those of operant reinforcement theory. The basic law of reinforcement, to be described in a later chapter, provides a procedure for the development of desirable behavior; the law of extinction provides a procedure for the elimination of an inappropriate behavior characteristic. It becomes important in some instances to identify correctly the types of behavioral processes underlying certain observable behaviors. In illustration, a "shy" client may be viewed as exhibiting behavior deficits in certain situations which require active participation. In analyzing the problem area from a behavior analysis viewpoint, it might be discovered that the shy behavior is not the result of aversive control and related avoidance learning

but rather has been shaped by positive reinforcement. The program technique would be clearly one of reinforcing more aggressive or assertive behaviors with no concern for extinguishing the situational aversiveness that typically is present when shyness represents avoidance learning. If, on the other hand, it was felt that the "shyness" did represent avoidance learning, a different treatment strategy involving the reduction of the aversive components of various situations might well be the treatment choice.

Program planning for education and rehabilitation activities must evidently begin with a description and reliable measure of the excessive and deficit behavior patterns which are creating difficulty. In many instances this requirement presents no problems; for example the retarded adult produces 30 work units per hour and must produce 42 in order to meet minimal production standards; he reads at the second grade level and must read at the fifth grade to be eligible for placement on Job B; he is unable to remember the numbers of the three different buses which he must take in order to travel from home to his job location. These are straightforward; these are easily definable, identifiable and measurable. Program goals can be stated in rather precise quantitative terms that are readily understandable.

In most instances, however, the requirements of definition and reliable measure of the problem behaviors are not so easily fulfilled. Behavioral problems are typically described in terms of typology, traits, dynamics, and the like. Even such general behavioral descriptions as "unable to assume responsibility," "socially insensitive," "can't get along with supervisor," "doesn't follow through," "blows up," "insufficient motivation," "gets angry too frequently" are quite inappropriate. These are very general, somewhat vague behavioral descriptions. It becomes necessary to reduce the general description to more precise behavior patterns that are definable in terms of what the person does or does not do. Additionally, the behavior patterns must be lodged in situations that require certain behaviors. The behavior description "can't get along with supervisors" is defined in terms of what the retarded does or does not do in relation to given environmental requirements. As "getting along with supervisors" may well entail a complex of behaviors, especially as supervisors vary greatly in terms of client behavior required, one is in a position to develop a meaningful behavior change program only after a detailed analysis of what the person does in relation to what is required.

It is often difficult to decide which of a range of possible behavior areas to select for education and rehabilitation efforts. Part of this difficulty is due to the fact that program personnel do not know what behaviors will be required in future settings. Programs, however, can become most effective

only after careful study of the behavioral characteristics needed for adjustment in the settings in which the client does or is likely to reside. With this information realistic and functionally meaningful program goals can provide direction to the experiences provided the client.

Categories of Problem Behaviors

In reviewing the rehabilitation and education agency records of ·a large number of difficult retarded clients, various categories of deficits and excessive behaviors have been identified. In most instances, any given individual presented a number of different types of problems. Although complex behaviors which occur in the natural environment of home, school, or rehabilitation center do not fit neatly into classes or categories, the following groups have been found useful as a basis for initial program development. The deficit and excessive behavior categories include:

1. *Specific task skill deficits.* These deficits refer to those that relate specifically to the educational task or job requirements such as not remembering the ingredients of a salad, forgetting to complete a record card on items sold, or not being able to complete in sequence the steps required for assembling a sheltered workshop task. While not identified as the major deficits resulting in rehabilitation failure for most mentally retarded clients, these specific skill deficits add significantly to the general personal and vocational inadequacy of the retarded. It is important to recognize that the same behavior change procedures would be used in dealing with these skill deficits as would be used in dealing with any of the other behavior deficits described below. That is, the same learning principles are involved in development of these skills as are involved in the development of any other behaviors.

2. *Task related deficits.* These behavior deficits include such behaviors as poor attention to a task, poor persistence at a task, poor quality output and inadequate quantity output. In many instances, difficulty is encountered by the retarded client, not because he does not have the specific task skills for satisfactory performance, but rather because he lacks the task-related skills needed for continuous performance. The terms "poor work attitude," "limited interest," and "poor work or achievement motivation" have been used by many education and rehabilitation personnel to describe or even to "explain" these behaviors. The behavior modification approach, on the other hand, rejects such explanations and focuses on designing a program environment which will facilitate the development of specific deficit behaviors such as attention, persistence, and quality output.

3. *Deficits in independent living skills.* Adequate adjustment to an independent social status is hampered in many adolescent and adult retarded

due to deficits in independent living skills. Poor grooming skills, poor travel skills, limited independence in handling money, limited functional academic skills, and the like all contribute to the adult adjustment problems of the retarded.

4. *Social behavior deficits*. This category of deficit behaviors includes a variety of classes of behavior involving interaction between the retarded and others, both in a close personal relationship and in a more general social context.

While there are a multitude of specific deficit behaviors and related factors involved in these behavior areas, in many instances the retardate just does not pay attention to the environmental cues that alter the behavior of others. He may be described as being socially insensitive or as being unable to behave in a discriminating fashion in his contact with other persons. He not infrequently is unable to discern and filter out from the multitude of social stimuli those that should have discriminative control over appropriate social behavior. Either these cues have lost their meaning or control function or else many typically controlling stimuli (for example, verbal requests, tone of voice, facial expressions, or affective reactions) have not acquired discriminative properties for the person.

5. *Affective behavior deficits*. This class of deficits includes both a limitation in the range of affective behaviors available to the person as well as a limitation in the intensity or degree of affective behavior expression. In illustration, this category would include such deficits as being unable to anticipate danger or aversive situations. As a result, adaptive defensive behavior is frequently absent. Stated in more popular language, with such deficits, the retarded person would not experience sufficient emotional reactions such as fear, apprehension, or "social anxiety" to avoid situations having aversive or punishing consequences.

6. *Deficits in self-direction and self-control behaviors*. Many retarded adolescents and adults experience considerable adaptive behavior difficulties due to their excessive dependency on direction from the external social and physical environment. Stated differently, there is a limitation in self-direction or self-control. The person may perform quite satisfactorily in a highly structured environment which provides reliable and distinct directions concerning time and place for behaviors of certain forms to occur. However, when placed in a less structured environment, behavior becomes less predictable and even disorganized. There appear to be deficiencies in verbal mediational processes to such an extent that the intervening behaviors fail to lend adequate direction to overt behavior in the absence of distinct external control stimuli. The retardate does not appear to verbalize or cue himself sufficiently in "decision" or in conflict situations or else, if he does engage in such behaviors, there appears to be a deficit con-

trol relationship between such processes and resulting behavior. That is, the intervening verbal or other mediational behaviors do not provide direction to what the person does in the situation. The person may be described as too situationally bound or outer-directed. He demonstrates deficits in internal cueing, controlling, or mediational processes.

7. *Excessive disruptive behaviors.* This class of behaviors includes a variety of motor, affective, social, and verbal behaviors which disrupt the education and rehabilitation program environment in which the retardate is placed. In illustration, Steve is a 20-year-old mildly retarded male attending a work adjustment program. In different classes over a four hour period, he was observed to make 54 disruptive comments, exhibit excessive inappropriate laughter three times, initiate conversation with peers at inappropriate times on 18 occasions, and engage in disruptive motor behavior (tapping on desk, knocking, gesturing a mustache, and the like) 14 times. Such excessive behaviors not only were disruptive to the teachers and peers but obviously rendered it impossible for Steve to participate in the program provided him.

8. *Excessive social reactions.* Some problems are created by the relatively excessive amount of social behavior in comparison with other types of behavior engaged in by the retarded. Too much of the person's time is spent in interacting with or seeking the company or attention of others, with the result that other responsibilities or types of involvements are neglected.

9. *Excessive motor reactions.* This class of excessive behaviors includes reactions that are described as hyperactivity, distractability, stereotyped movements, aimless activity, and the like. The person apparently is under stimulation to respond motorically, but the behavior is either disruptive to other social or physical components of the environment or else interferes with more integrated, purposeful activity.

10. *Excessive affective reactions.* Such reactions as excessive fearfulness, crying, display of affection, laughing, becoming angry, aggressiveness, and the like create considerable adaptive behavior difficulties for the mentally retarded. These behaviors may serve to disrupt more adaptive behavior patterns. Additionally, emotional reactions which appear to be unrelated to, or else an overresponsiveness to, identifiable external environmental events are disconcerting to many educational and rehabilitation personnel as they are unable to understand why the person is behaving as he is. This may result in overconcern by the program personnel with the result that the emotional behavior is further facilitated.

In viewing these behavioral deficits and excesses, it is important to recognize that these are not of an all-or-none fashion. For example, in analyzing one client's failure to adjust to a work task, it was found that he had 90 percent of the required behavior in his repertoire. The work deficit was

eliminated following his acquiring the additional 10 percent of the task behavior. Frequently, problems created by the presence of excessive behaviors may be solved by a rather minor reduction in the frequency or intensity of the excessive behavior. A retardate may be viewed as unsuitable for employment in a competitive setting due to an excessive amount of talking behavior which interferes with the attention required of co-workers. A reduction of 20 percent in frequency of talking behavior may result in behavior which, while still undesirable, is within the tolerance range for being maintained on the job.

CHAPTER THREE

Characteristics and Bases
of Problem Behaviors

As noted in the initial section, it is rather popular to account for the behavioral inadequacies of the mentally retarded in terms of general factors such as the "mental retardation," "emotional disturbance," "poor environmental background," or by invoking concepts which imply more circumscribed and dynamic internal difficulties such as "inadequate ego controls," "excessive hostility," or "poor self-concept." From this orientation involving internal causes of behavior problems, the inadequacies are viewed as symptomatic of the underlying hypothetical factors. Since some of these are viewed as essentially unchangeable (such as mental retardation) and others of a serious or extreme pathological nature (for example, depressive reaction, character disorder, psychotic state), it is not surprising that educational and rehabilitation personnel typically assume a rather pessimistic orientation that little can be done to modify those behavior patterns that are creating adjustment difficulties. An example of this attitude is provided by the following report of a special education teacher concerning one of her sixteen-year-old mildly retarded male students. The teacher, with the assistance of a psychological report, views the adolescent as emotionally disturbed. The teacher wrote:

> Robert sits day after day and plays with his physical education padlock which is on a basket that he keeps his books in. He never can get an assignment done during the period that it is due, but sneaks it home and then it comes back with only about 50 percent or less done correctly. When he isn't playing with the lock, he's up and down disturbing others. Some days he sits and rubs his

39

legs and rocks. He always says, "I don't know the answer" and stops trying when helped individually. Outside of my room he is a constant problem also. I feel he will waste *four* years of his life here as we are not equipped to handle this type of student.

The teacher presents an attitude of helplessness. She does not believe that her teaching approach, although a special education one, is appropriate for the problems presented by the retarded adolescent. This "type of student" needs some program other than her special education one.

Treatment from this viewpoint focuses on the hypothetical internal factors which are assumed to be causing the problems. This orientation creates considerable difficulties for most educational and rehabilitation personnel since they are not specially trained to deal with these presumed internal factors. The preceding case as well as those discussed in the initial chapter illustrate the possible negative consequences of such an approach. The major concern becomes one of treating the pathology that is presumed. This focus detracts considerably from efforts to build positive behavior patterns by means of more direct procedures of behavior development and modification. This is illustrated by the following experience with Dena, a nineteen-year-old mildly retarded female residing in a private boarding facility. Dena, upon arriving at the residential facility, was placed in the school rehabilitation program. An individual program was designed for development of a wide range of educational, work, social, and independent living skills. In the school unit as well as on the living unit, Dena displayed low frustration tolerance and frequently engaged in emotional outbursts. Following these outbursts, she was more hesitant about becoming involved and demonstrated other "depressive" behaviors such as loss of interest, minor crying episodes, and preference for remaining in her room alone. The educational staff devised a plan for Dena with the objectives of increasing her frustration tolerance, of developing self-control over emotional outburst, of teaching her to react appropriately to failure, of providing considerable success experiences, of reinforcing problem solving behaviors generally and especially those that demonstrated personal competency, and the like. In short, the educational program was designed to provide her with a range of new positive behaviors. Early in the program Dena became quite upset at one of the nursing staff and engaged in a rather violent temper tantrum. As was the routine practice following such confrontation with the medical staff of the facility, Dena was referred for psychiatric evaluation and possible treatment. She was declared to have a "hysterical reaction with depressive tendencies." Further, the nursing staff was instructed to watch Dena carefully and at the initial sign of losing emotional control she was to be removed from the situation. She was placed on drug therapy and a once weekly psychotherapy contact with the psychiatrist.

This diagnosis of her being hysterical and depressive created considerable anxiety within the teaching staff. How could they deal with these conditions? What caused these conditions? Were they contributing to these disorders? What program should be provided her in the school and living units? As the "internal pathology" concepts did not provide answers to the questions, the teacher-counselors were at a loss as to how to handle this client. They were afraid to require much of her as they did not wish to provoke a depressive episode. Their educational plans for teaching a range of positive behaviors suffered greatly.

In contrast to this internal disorder concept, the learning position views the behavioral inadequacies from an educational viewpoint and utilizes a small number of behavioral variables and related principles in an effort to understand and plan for the modification of these inadequacies. Explanation is in terms of the learning process and how the person's learning history has resulted in a repertoire of behaviors which characterizes the person at the present. Biological, physical, and sensory factors are considered in terms of their influence on what a person is physically able to do and in terms of the effect these characteristics have on the reactions of others to him as a social being. Although causation of inappropriate behavior in the traditional etiological sense is of little concern, consideration is given to a small number of possible contributing factors. These become important to the rehabilitation personnel as general treatment directions evolve from consideration of these factors.

Characteristics of Inappropriate Behaviors

Prior to a consideration of these possible contributing factors, it should be valuable to comment briefly on the nature of the behavioral inadequacies which characterize the problem retarded. It is not infrequently assumed that the retarded fails because he has a general paucity of behavior. The concepts of mental *deficiency* and *subnormality* imply that there is a deficiency or limitation in the sheer quantity of behaviors which the retarded can produce. There are no data, however, which would substantiate this as a general characteristic of the retarded. It is true in a relative sense for the more severely retarded. However, even at this level, the person has many behaviors which potentially could be used to produce positive consequences if the environmental contingency system were appropriately arranged.

Generally, the retarded adolescent or adult, with behavioral inadequacies of such severity that he is unable to adapt satisfactorily to various aspects of the environments, does not have the particular behaviors which result in the positive consequences that are frequently present and avail-

able all around him. He does not have, or does not utilize appropriately, certain social, verbal, affective, work, self-help, and other behaviors which are required by a given environment as a condition for obtaining positive feedback from that environment. The reinforcing events are available but not for the behaviors that are engaged in by the retarded. Frequently, the retardate has the kind or class of behavior that is required, but the behavior is not of the specific topology or quality required. Further, to add to his difficulties, the retarded frequently has acquired various behavior patterns which provoke a negative reaction from important segments of his environment. In illustration, a sixteen-year-old mildly retarded boy, attending a special class located in a middle class neighborhood, talked to himself in a voice loud enough for all to hear. Additionally, he frequently brought a pocket full of coins to class and constantly jingled them to the distraction of the teacher and classmates. He also dressed in a gaudy manner that made him a target of numerous derogatory comments from his peers. Although these behaviors obviously evoked attention from his social environment, this social reaction was of a negative reprimand or derisive nature. In spite of this, the attention apparently was sufficiently reinforcing to maintain the inappropriate behaviors. He evidently did not have the appropriate behaviors which would produce more appropriate social attention.

As suggested, most of the retarded who create unusual educational and rehabilitation problems do not as a rule suffer from a general paucity of behavior reactions. Neither the retardate's behavioral frequency nor his range of different behavioral reactions is low. He engages in many behaviors, but not those that are appropriate in relation to the behavioral requirements of various situations. In observing a group of retardates in a secondary level special class, record was obtained on four students who were viewed as well adjusted and four others identified by teacher and work adjustment counselor as presenting severe patterns of unadaptive behavior. Behavior was observed over a three week period and evaluated as to its appropriateness in relation to a structured group participation activity, an independent study activity, and an unstructured social recreation activity. In terms of the number of different behaviors and in terms of the amount of time engaged in active (observable) behaviors, the behavior problem students exceeded the nonproblem ones by five percent. The major difference between the groups resided in the inappropriateness of the behaviors which were exhibited by the problem group. Again, the problem of the retardate is not merely a function of a behavior repertoire that is too restricted in sheer frequency or to a repertoire that represents a gross limitation in the range of different behaviors. Rather, the difficulties usually stem from the fact that the wrong behaviors occur too frequently and that other appropriate behaviors, which may be in the repertoire, do not occur at appropriate times in the frequency or intensity that is required.

As will be discussed in more detail later in the chapter, this observation implies that much of the failure of the retarded could be avoided if there was a more satisfactory arrangement between what the retarded could do and the behavioral requirements of the social environment for reinforcement attainment. The retarded fails frequently not because he is not "capable" of more adequate performance or because of an absolute limitation in the range of behaviors at his disposal but because the environment is insensitive to the behavioral characteristics of the retarded. This environment imposes standards which are too stringent in order for the retarded to attain reinforcement. As a result, not only is there a failure for simpler forms of the appropriate behavior to be shaped gradually into more complex patterns, but in addition the retarded is forced to engage in "neurotic" or maladaptive forms of behavior which bring only less preferred reinforcement consequences.

It is also evident that many behavior patterns which are present but which are nonfunctional in terms of environmental requirements are as complex as those that are required. Thus it is frequently no more difficult to engage in the desired behavior than to engage in the usually inappropriate behavior. The general difficulty in adjustment appears to reside, then, not in a neurophysiological limitation in what can be acquired or in a limitation in a hypothetical intelligence, but rather in a learning history that renders more likely inappropriate instead of appropriate behavior. It is no more difficult, in terms of the amount of "ability," "intelligence," or "self-concept" required, to learn to sit at a work table for an hour and engage in high rate and quality assembly type work than to learn to play cards, shoot billiards, and to make numerous disruptive comments during a personal adjustment class. It is evident that a *different* set of skills or groups of behaviors are required in the former situation, but it would be a mistake to blame the failure on limited intelligence or to other internal hypothetical factors.

It should be emphasized that it is not being suggested that those adolescents and adults who are viewed as mentally retarded have unlimited behavioral potential. There is obviously a limit to the range and complexity of behaviors which can be acquired. Whether a retardate can or cannot acquire a given type, range, or level of behavior, however, is an empirical question which can be answered only by providing a maximal learning environment.

The case of Paul, mentioned in the first chapter provides dramatic illustration of this concept. Paul had been viewed for a number of years as an individual who was too retarded and unresponsive to benefit from training efforts, although on occasion he was included in new training or recreation groups. However, he was soon dismissed from such programs as he would not become involved in them. He had been provided physical care but

otherwise left to engage in his stereotyped behavior. Observation of Paul revealed a level of physical agility and dexterity considerably higher than that required by simple workshop tasks. Additionally, eye-hand coordination was excellent as demonstrated in his self-feeding skills and in his habit of picking up small pieces of food and other objects and putting them in his mouth. Based on these and similar observations, it was assumed that he could engage in more complex and socially desirable behavior than that presently characteristic of him. A behavior modification program was devised to test this assumption. Initially, the program objective was to gain some specific external stimulus control over some specific motor response that would compete directly with classes of his stereotype behavior. From this beginning, Paul progressed through successive programs aimed at building positive work, verbal, cognitive, social, and self-help skills. Today, Paul seldom engages in stereotyped behavior. He is an active productive worker in a sheltered workshop. He engages in rather complex social behavior, is developing some speech, and has acquired primary level skills of color, form, size, and quantity discrimination. Paul has acquired a level of functioning that for a number of years was not deemed possible due to his mental retardation and related self-stimulatory behaviors. The empirical attitude of a behavior therapist challenged the edict that Paul could not learn and demonstrated that if the environment were right, even the Pauls could learn.

Factors Contributing to Inappropriate Behaviors

If behavior is the product of learning, it becomes meaningful to identify the kinds of learning deficits or distortions which have contributed to the behavioral deficits and excesses which characterize the retarded. That is, what types of learning and related factors may account for the poor work skills, excessive disruptive behaviors, poor manners, excessive quarrelsome behavior, limited work motivation, poor compliance to instructions, inadequate social behaviors, and the like which are reported to characterize those retardates who present serious adaptive behavior problems?

As noted earlier, the assumption that appropriate behaviors are absent due to some distortion or deficiency in the learning environment implies that something can be done if the learning environment could be modified. Such an optimistic position offsets the pessimism that is generated among educational and rehabilitation personnel by the viewpoint that places causation within some internal limitation or pathology.

The following groups of factors, most of which have been discussed by Bijou (1966a), are suggested as having significance in accounting for the excessive and deficit behavior patterns which the retarded present. The

inadequate behavioral repertoire of a particular individual may be related in part to any one or to a combination of these factors. Additionally, these groups of factors are not mutually exclusive. A behavioral analysis will be helpful in suggesting the specific factors operative in a specific case. In many cases, the absolute and relative significance of certain factors may be estimated only after a maximum program experience has been provided the person.

Deficiencies in Reinforcement Components

Many of the behavioral inadequacies involving both excessive and deficit behavior patterns may be viewed as resulting from various deficiencies in the reinforcement characteristics of the environment. There may be deficiencies in the *kind, amount,* and/or *frequency* of reinforcing events available in the past and present environment of the retarded. Poor discrimination training, limited tolerance for delayed reinforcement, excessive aversive experiences, and deficits in self-reinforcement skills are among other reinforcement-related variables which may underlie the difficulties presented by the retarded. Although these will be discussed separately, it is evident that there is considerable interdependence among all these reinforcement and reinforcement-related factors.

Inadequate Contingent Reinforcing Events. The behavioral inadequacies of the retarded may result from an improper reinforcement history and from a present environment that is deficient in the available reinforcing events that are presented contingent upon desired behavior. The individual does not develop behavior which education and rehabilitation programs attempt to teach because the consequences of the desired behavior are too *small, infrequent,* or *inappropriate.* The school and work activities required, instead of being intrinsically interesting to the retarded, are frequently difficult and unpleasant. This is true even though in some instances the behavior required may appear to be quite simple. It is not unusual to find that the person experiencing difficulty with acquiring or performing seemingly simple school or work required behavior may have competing responses of high strength which interfere with or disrupt the occurrence of these new behaviors. This was illustrated in the case of Peter who failed in three consecutive job placements due to his "being unable to persist at his work task for periods in excess of 30–40 minutes at a time." At the end of this time period, he would leave the job and wander around, talking with others, going to the toilet, smoking a cigarette, drinking a coke, or just sitting in the lounge. An examination of the history of this client revealed that this pattern of behavior had been reinforced for the previous three years during his residence in a program that permitted him

to work whenever he felt like it. In this ultra-therapeutic environment, Peter had developed strong behavior patterns that rendered prolonged work behaviors quite unlikely. Persisting at a task was a difficult undertaking. Learning this behavior pattern required a highly structured program that involved appropriate reinforcing events.

Programs all too frequently assume that the retarded client should be influenced by consequences or reward factors that are quite abstract (such as reinforcement by being involved in the group activity or by the feeling of achievement which task completion brings) or which are too far removed from the behaviors being taught (such as grades or pay check provided at end of week or month). One result of an environment with too small, infrequent, or inappropriate reinforcing components frequently is that of disruptive behavior. The disruptive behavior is strengthened as such behavior results in the client being removed from the activity requirements imposed by the program. Such activities acquire aversive components and any behavior that removes these stimulus events is strengthened. This was evident in the case of Peter. Whenever he was prodded to persist in his work behavior, he characteristically would become negativistic and at times would engage in rather noisy emotional outbursts. Whenever these occurred, job requirements were terminated and he was removed from the work environment. This consequence of removal from an aversive environment requirement served to make more likely the occurrence of this disruptive behavior when he was again placed in similar circumstances. This pattern of behavior did not occur because he willfully enjoyed upsetting his supervisors and counselor. It occurred because those responsible for the program inadvertently permitted the wrong aspects of the work environment to gain powerful control over this behavior pattern.

Another consequence of an inadequate reinforcement history is the development of a generally disinterested or lethargic involvement. Behavior patterns in relation to environmental requirements are not developed, with the result that the person is described as being unmotivated. A more meaningful description would focus on the deficits in the reinforcing components of the environment and the resulting limitation of behaviors supported. As noted previously, program personnel should discriminate between what the retardate is able to do but does not and those behavior patterns required by the rehabilitation program which he does not have in his present behavior repertoire. In the former case, rapid improvement in behavior adjustment may be realized once a more appropriate reinforcing environment is provided. For example, a person may have all the skills necessary for acceptable performance in a sheltered workshop. He may, however, present a general pattern of high absenteeism and low quality and quantity production when he does go to work due to the limited rein-

forcing consequences associated with workshop attendance and performance. A dramatic change in performance may be noted merely by changes
in the kind, magnitude, and schedule of reinforcement provided for more
appropriate behavior. In the latter case, a longer period of behavior development may be required to offset the behavior deficits which are present.

Some education and rehabilitation programs impose behavioral requirements which the person is unable to fulfill at the moment. The required
behavior represents too large an increment from what he is presently able
to accomplish. The person may not know what to do or how to do it. The
symbolic verbal models (instructions) which are frequently used by
teacher and supervisor may not provide the direction which is intended. As
a result, reinforcement, even if available, is not obtained as the retarded does
not perform appropriately. This excessive failure may result, as noted, in a
limited interaction with various elements of the environment—a passive, low
motivated, noninvolvement. As suggested, the situation may even become
aversive due to excessive failure and thus actively avoided.

Inadequate Discrimination Training. It is not sufficient that the retarded
is able to perform. In fact, it is not unusual to observe that the difficulties
caused by the person's apparent deficit behaviors are related, not to the
fact that behavior patterns are absent from his repertoire, but rather to the
low or erratic probability that the behavior will occur at the appropriate
time and with sufficient frequency. Those situations which designate the
time and place in which specific behaviors will result in reinforcement do
not have sufficient control over the behaviors to insure their occurrence.
The retarded adolescent may know how to be polite, for example, since he
has engaged in such behavior in the past. He may even presently act in a
polite manner from time to time or under certain restricted situations. Such
behaviors may, however, be of low strength relative to other behaviors that
compete successfully with and may even be physically incompatible to
such "politeness" behaviors. Politeness behavior is not reinforced sufficiently in specified situations or else the reinforcement is of low magnitude
in relation to that provided other competing behaviors. The politeness behavior has not been reinforced differentially in those situations that require
such behavior.

Much inappropriate behavior, therefore, is due to a lack of adequate discrimination training. The environment has not provided differential reinforcement for certain desired behaviors in the presence of distinctive cues.
Thus, behavior does not appear at the proper time or place with the desired
frequency or magnitude as it has not been brought under control of specific
stimulus events. The procedures of discrimination training will be discussed in a later chapter.

Limited Range of Reinforcing Events. The limited behavioral repertoire

of the retarded may be due both to the infrequency and inconsistency with which reinforcers are available. It may also be due to the limited range of stimulus events which have reinforcing properties for specific individuals. As will be described in a later chapter, there are a few primary stimulus events which have a reinforcing function for most everyone, for example, food, water, warmth, and the like. Most stimuli, however, gain their reinforcement function through consistent association with other reinforcing events. The retarded may fail to acquire appropriate behavior patterns due to a paucity of reinforcing events available in his environment. Many events which are available to most people in our culture just do not exert a reinforcing effect on the retarded. This is due partly to the fact that these events have not been available to the retarded in the past and partly to the fact that these events have not been associated sufficiently with other reinforcing events in order to acquire secondary reinforcing properties. Many events such as listening to music, carrying on a conversation, playing cards, attending a concert, going to a movie, bowling, swimming, or watching sports events may hold neutral or even aversive reinforcing value for the retarded as he has never had the opportunity to participate successfully in these, or has done so too infrequently. Such social events as teacher praise or work supervisor approval may have little reinforcement value since such events have not been associated consistently with other events which are reinforcing to the individual.

Educational and rehabilitation personnel typically represent a subcultural status different from that enjoyed by the retarded student and client. One of the outstanding differences between groups representing different subcultures lies in the differences in events which are reinforcing and in the pattern by which these events are provided. The special education teacher, in using praise, approval, and grades in an effort to reward desired behaviors, frequently finds these events to be totally ineffective with many of her retarded students. She, in a sense, is imposing her subcultural reinforcement system onto her retarded students and is expecting them to be influenced in the manner that she would be by these events. Likewise, the rehabilitation counselor, by urging the retarded client to adhere to the requirements of the work setting and by praising him for desired behavior, is depending upon these abstract social reinforcers to be effective events. As educational and rehabilitation personnel well know in their work with those retarded who present adaptive behavior problems, such events are most likely to exert little systematic influence over the behavior of the retarded. Such practices of depending upon a limited range of inappropriate stimulus consequences add considerably to the behavioral limitations of the retarded.

One additional result of a limitation in the amount and range of effective

reinforcing events available is the possibility that the retarded will become excessively dependent upon and thereby overly controlled by the social reinforcement provided by his retarded peers. This is especially devastating in the not uncommon practice of isolating a group of highly disturbed retardates into a special program. In such a group the retarded person who is disruptive is most likely to receive social feedback from his disruptive peers. If he behaves in a manner which is consistent with the program goals, little peer attention is forthcoming. Standards of behavior which the retarded as a social reinforcing agent holds (that is, those behaviors which he will socially reinforce in his retarded peers) are typically different from those deemed desirable by the education program. Thus, the retardate will get attention from his peers if he behaves inappropriately. This excessive peer control of disruptive behavior was forcefully illustrated by a group of retarded young adults attending a personal and work development rehabilitation program. The instructor spent most of his time attempting to control a wide range of disruptive behaviors presented by various members of the group. He had little success in doing so as the disruptive behavior was quickly reinforced by peer attention. A silly comment resulted in laughter from the peers which served not only to maintain the strength of this type of disruptive behavior but also served as a stimulus for other silly behavior from some other class members. Teacher attention for appropriate behavior was of insignificant strength in relation to the influence of the social feedback provided by peers.

Excessive Dependency on Immediate Reinforcement. Closely related to the limited range of events which are reinforcing is the observation that the retarded with excessive adaptive behavior difficulties may be overly dependent upon immediate reinforcement. If newly emerging behaviors are not reinforced frequently and immediately, these behaviors do not gain strength. Additionally, tangible events are frequently more reinforcing than abstract ones. Delayed reinforcement serves as no reinforcement for the previous behavior for which it was intended. Behavior extinguishes under such circumstances and other behaviors which produce immediate reinforcement are strengthened. In a rehabilitation program these other behaviors frequently are inconsistent with the objectives of the program designed for the client.

A related dimension is the poorly developed skill of self-reinforcement. The person has not learned to "pat-himself-on-the-back" for appropriate behavior and thereby unable to maintain the behavior until other external sources of reinforcement are provided. He has limited self-imposed standards which are then self-reinforced when the imposed goal is attained. All of these are reinforcement deficits which render the person more under the control of immediate sources of reinforcement. Under those circum-

stances in which immediate tangible reinforcing events are not provided in a systematic manner following desired behavior, a range of problem behaviors may result.

Noncontingent Reinforcement. In some environments, reinforcement is provided in an indiscriminate or unsystematic fashion. That behavior which by chance is reinforced most frequently becomes the dominant response. In other environments a whole range of behaviors is provided reinforcement. These are sometimes an aspect of a "therapeutic" program which is based on the belief that the person should behave as he feels like behaving. It also may be the result of an environment which views the retarded as being sick, being unable to learn, and thus not responsible for his behavior. In such a welfare-type environment, a variety of behaviors—adequate and inadequate—are strenghtened by this free distribution of desirable consequences. This was seen recently in a workshop in which a client exhibited unpredictable emotional outburst. For fear that the person might create unusual management difficulty, the workshop supervisor permitted the person to do whatever she wished. She was free to work or not work without any requirement that she produce on the same schedule as her peers. In spite of the fact that she spent considerable time in a variety of nonwork activities, she still received the same monetary and privilege consequences as did the others. The program, by this noncontingent reinforcement procedure (reinforcement not systematically provided following specific target behaviors), was strengthening a range of behaviors which was incompatible with appropriate work skill development.

Excessive Extinction Conditions. Behavior that has gained some strength must be reinforced occasionally in order to be maintained. In the absence of such occasional reinforcement, the behavior is weakened and eventually eliminated. Such conditions are not infrequently present as the retarded is removed from a highly specialized and well staffed program in which reinforcement had been provided on a frequent and systematic manner. As he is placed in a less structured environment which cannot follow the reinforcement regimen that was routine in the treatment program, much of the retarded client's behavior disappears to the surprise and dismay of the program staff. Likewise, the special education teacher may find that as she moves from one lesson to another, her retarded student has forgotten what he learned last week. Frequently, this is a result of assuming too early in the learning process that the behavior is well developed and thereby maintained by intrinsic or irregular extrinsic reinforcing events.

Limitations of the Stimulus Environment

Behavioral deficits and excesses frequently may be correlated with a restricted or inappropriate stimulus environment. Either the range and type

of stimulation or the lack of consistency or distinctiveness of the stimulus components may have resulted in limited behavior development. The retarded, by definition, has difficulty in acquiring the complex range of adaptive behaviors which are required for general social and vocational independence. Adequate behavior development requires prolonged exposure to a systematic set of conditions designed both to initiate and to reinforce desired responses and to discourage and eliminate undesired behaviors. It becomes readily apparent to even the casual observer of the American education scene that too few retarded persons have such an environment available throughout their developmental years. Secondary-level special education and rehabilitation programs are confronted with the task of offsetting the effects of the highly inappropriate conditions which most retarded adolescents and adults have experienced throughout earlier critical years.

As suggested earlier, inappropriate stimulus conditions are created by the prevalent practice of placing those persons with the most difficult school and work adjustment problems together in the same program. Such a practice insures that the social models for behavior will be provided by those who are least discriminating concerning those behaviors which would be socially appropriate. In the example provided previously, inappropriate behavior in a group of highly disruptive young adults was almost constantly facilitated by social stimulation and reinforcement of other equally disruptive retarded peers. The teacher, who was the only person in the environment who could represent appropriate social and cognitive models of behavior, was of little influence as she spent most of her efforts in attempting to manage the disruptive environment. These high rate disruptive behaviors were being maintained by sources of reinforcement that were beyond the control of those responsible for the program.

As noted initially, the stimulus environment may result in poor behavior development due to a restriction in the amount of stimulation or to the inappropriateness of the environment. The environment may be quite rich in type, range, and frequency of stimulation. However, many such education and rehabilitation programs may represent a limited stimulus environment for the retarded who exhibits excessive behavioral inadequacies. The program may simply be geared to a level of behavior development which is too complex for the clients involved. The retarded person is unable to behave successfully in the environment. Many clients require rather basic behavior development programs prior to being able to profit from a work development program, for example. That is, experiences of developing basic skills of attention, persistence, and basic discriminations should be provided prior to attempts to teach more complex school or work skills. In a recent experience with an eighteen-year-old mildly retarded male who was unable to read, it was discovered that the reading program provided

in a secondary special education class was geared at too high a level. In a sense, the program environment was restricted in terms of the type of instruction which was needed for this student for appropriate development of basic reading skills.

Excessive Contingent Aversive Experience

Contributing to the inadequate behavioral repertoire of the retarded are those contingent consequences which are aversive in nature. Cultural, physical and cognitive factors associated with mental retardation all render aversive consequences more likely to occur than is true of a nonretarded group. Presentation of aversive stimulation following behavior results in the suppression of this behavior. The more intense the aversive consequences the greater the suppressive effects, not only on the specific behavior punished but also across a broad range of behaviors. In addition, excessive aversive stimulation may result in inappropriate affective or emotional behaviors which frequently serve to compete with those more desirable behaviors which are within the retardate's repertoire. There is frequently seen a broad generalization of suppressive effects. Not only do those behaviors which are punished decrease in frequency of occurrence, but also there is frequently a reduction or temporary elimination of other behavior patterns which are quite unrelated to the punished behavior. A generalized pattern of stubbornness or withdrawal represents an example of this effect.

When the retardate is unable to perform due to his behavioral deficits, he becomes a target of a wide range of aversive stimulation. He is not reinforced in situations that require the behavior deficit. In addition, he is apt to receive considerable general social punishment. His more able peers and adults criticize him, make fun of him, require him to become involved in situations in which he cannot perform, increase their demands upon him, reject him, and the like. Thus, an excessive amount of his behavior produces negative social reinforcement from the normal social environment. Except in a highly controlled therapeutic, and, therefore, somewhat unnatural or artificial environment, the retardate's behavior or his general social stimulus features obtain few consistent positive social reinforcements. He has low social prestige; his behavior has few reinforcing properties for general social relationships and interactions. Few aspects of his social environment will find his behavior reinforcing and consequently will not attend to or seek his company or services.

In most cases, the social environment will not even encourage his physical presence. Only limited social reinforcement is forthcoming to support appropriate behaviors which could serve to facilitate the development of

more social prestige. Consequently, much of his general social experience merely serves to extinguish attempts at appropriate social behaviors, or, through suppression and aversive control, to limit the total behaviors which are expressed. As he has no adequate group or gang with which to interact, appropriate social reinforcement is greatly reduced. As Ferster (1958) has suggested, under these circumstances the probability is greatly decreased that the individual is able to make a successful social adjustment in view of the fact that a major most readily available source of reinforcement—social in nature—is not provided.

This excessive aversive stimulation also results in extensive escape and avoidance behavior. The retardate learns to stay away from those situations that have resulted in punishment as well as those persons who are associated in time and place with these aversive conditions. This type of avoidance behavior pattern develops because these behaviors initially lead the person to escape from the aversive conditions—such behaviors removed the painful or unpleasant conditions and were thus strengthened, a process called negative reinforcement. If excessive aversive stimulation is provided in a school or work setting, the retardate may learn to avoid teachers, adults, task involvement, and the like. In those situations where the adolescent is forced by parent or "truant officer" types to be physically present in a situation that has greater aversive than positive features, a pattern of passive disinterested behavior may occur. The person just does not become involved. He may sulk or pout; he may spend excessive periods of time in preparation for initiating a task or may even sit idly for extended periods. It is quite logical that much of the low motivation or lack of interest which characterize many difficult rehabilitation clients is a manifestation of excessive aversive stimulation. The negative components for "not doing" are less intense than those associated with attempts at becoming involved.

Observation of the retarded in many situations reveals that many are excessively hesitant about entering into various activities, especially those that involve competition against people or a standard performance requiring cognitive skills. This hesitancy may be a reflection of a previous history of insufficient positive reinforcement, of excessive aversive stimulation, or, as is more likely, of a combination of the two factors. Such "becoming involved" behavior is of low magnitude because it has been associated with a low probability of positive reinforcement. Additionally, as has been suggested, the hesitancy may represent active avoidance behavior which indicates that previous attempts at participation have resulted in aversive consequences. Nonparticipation in such activities avoids the possibility of repetition of these aversive events.

In recent experiences with a group of learning problem adolescent and

adult retardates, the following types of comments were heard frequently whenever they were provided an opportunity to earn reinforcers in an unfamiliar situation: "Oh, no. I can't do that," "I'd never earn that even if I did good," "Oh, you're kidding me—I couldn't do good enough to get that." Such terms as "low generalized expectancy of success" (Gardner, 1966a), "failure avoiders" (Cromwell, 1963) and "negative reaction tendency" (Zigler, 1966) have been used by various writers to describe such behavioral characteristics. These writers generally agree that the behavior tendency has resulted from a history of excessive failure or nonreinforcement in a wide range of settings. By avoiding situations and by demonstrating "low effort behavior" when confronted with situations which present the possibility of obtaining positive reinforcement for appropriate responses, reinforcement is highly improbable. Consequently, the probability of developing new appropriate behaviors is quite low.

Excessive Reinforcement of Aversive Behavior

A segment of inappropriate behaviors is reinforced positively by the environment either because such reinforcement temporarily removes or stops the inappropriate behavior (for example, the teacher or parent giving in to the person's demands in order to terminate crying, temper tantrum, or hyperactivity) or because the environment is unaware of the reinforcements that are contingently available to the behavior. An example will illustrate each of these. Jack, a seventeen-year-old moderately retarded adolescent, tends to "lose control" whenever he is confronted with tasks that require concentrated activity. The teacher, fearful that this emotionally disturbed boy will become too upset, gives in to his demands and tries to comfort him. Joyce, a nineteen-year-old, has dizzy spells while working. The supervisor and the co-workers are very sympathetic toward Joyce whenever she complains of the dizzy spells and provide her with considerable concern. In both instances the inappropriate behaviors are reinforced by the consequences provided by the peers and staff members.

Behaviors that are aversive to others may be rather weak, but these may be the dominant behaviors engaged in by a person because other appropriate behaviors are less frequently reinforced by the environment. It is not unusual for the environment to ignore appropriate behavior whenever it occurs because this behavior is expected to be present in everyone. On the other hand, inappropriate behaviors bring all kinds of reactions or results from the environment ranging from attention to removal of those task requirements which may be aversive to the retarded. Such contingent consequences frequently strengthen this inappropriate behavior.

It is also essential to recognize that inappropriate behavior may be quite

strong or resistent to elimination as a result of a peculiar history of partial or intermittent reinforcement. An individual presently may be reinforced only infrequently for inadequate behavior but the behavior may still remain at relatively high strength due to the previous history of reinforcement. The manner in which negative behaviors can become highly resistant to extinction will be described in later chapters.

In some cases inadequate behavior which results in punishment is maintained due to positive reinforcement that follows. In illustration, a client may behave disruptively in the workshop even though he is reprimanded by the supervisor and has a reduction in pay consistent with the piece rate pay schedule. However, these aversive consequences may be followed frequently by the client's being sent to the counselor's office for a "therapy session," an activity which is highly reinforcing to the client. He thus is reinforced inadvertently for behaving inappropriately.

It is evident that the absence of available or attainable positive reinforcers renders numerous situations rather aversive. Environments acquire aversive components in which failure has been the routine rather than the exception or in which the retarded has been required to expend more effort than is reasonable for the amount of reinforcement payoff available. In these environments inappropriate behaviors develop which are reinforced because these either remove the retarded from the aversive environment, or, at a minimum, reduce the time required to spend in the work behavior. this negative reinforcement strengthens the inappropriate behavior and becomes the predominant controlling factor.

As noted earlier, limitations of appropriate behaviors in a situation may overemphasize the few behaviors that are present and render these excessive, bizarre, and inappropriate. These may result in the person being removed from the situation. Consequently, the negative reinforcement effect may result in the nonadaptive behavior to be increased in strength as a result. These same behaviors, it should be noted, if occurring as one of an array of appropriate behaviors, may be viewed as mildly odd or inappropriate but not nearly as bizarre or maladaptive as when they occur within a limited behavior repertoire.

Behavioral Potential

If the behavioral problems presented by the mentally retarded client are viewed in terms of these and related classes of factors, it becomes apparent that his behavior potential is quite closely related to the *type of environment* that is provided him. In many instances, behavior potential in education and rehabilitation settings is significantly restricted by *environmental limitations*. Maximum benefit from an education or vocational program in

many instances is less related to limitations in the cognitive, physical, personality or emotional structure of the client than it is to the type of program that is provided, the program viewed both in terms of content as well as in terms of behavior change methodology. This position is supported by research, for example, with schizophrenic adults (Poindexter, 1962; Blachely, Stephenson,and Levy, 1963; Saslow, 1965). The development of a variety of behaviors including new occupational skills was found by these studies to be unrelated to the severity of the psychiatric disability as clinically defined, to the diagnostic label, or to the current level of disorganization. Saslow concluded from these results that "present behavioral capability has to be conceived of as frequently, if not generally, independent of much past historical information and present personality diagnostic formulations" [p. 288]. Experience with a wide range of difficult mentally retarded clients, including the institutionalized severely retarded, provides ample support for this position.

In the chapters to follow, it is assumed that the education and vocational potential of the mentally retarded can be assessed adequately only by observing his responsiveness to a maximally designed program based on a careful appraisal of his learning characteristics. The position is taken that a statement which declares that an individual cannot perform a certain task, learn a certain skill or adjust to a certain environment must also describe the program that has been provided the person in arriving at these conclusions. It is evident that most present educational, psychological, and vocational evaluation procedures provide little reliable information concerning what a person can or cannot do in relation to a given environment. The evaluation techniques are frequently quite unrelated to factors of a learning nature.

Numerous recent studies have suggested that the severely involved client, including the mentally retarded who had been viewed as having limited learning potential, can develop a variety of skills which greatly facilitate their independence level (for example, Ayllon and Azrin, 1968; Gardner, 1970). The retarded who for a number of years had been fed, dressed and toileted have, after appropriate learning experiences, become independent in these areas (for example, Gardner and Watson, 1969: Watson, 1967). Others who have been rejected from rehabilitation programs as having limited potential for development of work skills have shown promise of becoming suitable workshop clients (Zimmerman, Stuckey, Garlick, and Miller, 1969). Allyon and Azrin (1968) have provided ample evidence that chronic psychotic adults, including those who are mentally retarded, can develop a wide range of more appropriate behaviors. It should be emphasized that in none of these cases did the "potential" of the person change. The clients did not gain insight, develop a better attitude

or regain interest in their environment prior to these changes. The change was obtained in a designed environment which influenced individual behavior development. Additionally, the environmental changes were initiated without any extensive investigation of the possible origin of the behavioral difficulties treated. It was assumed that a significant amount of the previous limitation resided in the environment and not within the "lack of potential" of the client.

PART TWO

Behavior Modification: Concepts and Principles

CHAPTER FOUR

The Nature of
Behavior Modification

Behavior modification is a term that applies both to an orientation to clinical problems that is conceptually consistent with experimental psychology and to a number of different behavior change techniques that have the goal of changing human behavior in a beneficial manner. Techniques are available for the task of influencing change in deficit behavior areas as well as for dealing with excessive behavior patterns. That is, behavior modification procedures may be used both for the task of development of behaviors which are absent in the form desired as well as in a program designed to strengthen behaviors which are present but of low strength. Other procedures are appropriate for the elimination or reduction in strength of behavior patterns which occur excessively, either in sheer frequency or in magnitude. These techniques are based on concepts of various learning theories and on behavior principles and experimental data concerning stimulus-response relationships.

The learning concepts that provide the basis for most of the behavior modification work with the mentally retarded are those derived from the operant conditioning model of Skinner and colleagues (for example, Ferster and Skinner, 1957; Skinner, 1961). In addition, some behavior change procedures available to education and rehabilitation personnel are based on other concepts that are closely associated with experimental psychology, notably those of classical conditioning and imitation or social learning. In short, "The basis of behavior modification is a body of experimental work dealing with the relationship between changes in the environ-

ment and changes in the subject's responses" [Ullman and Krasner, 1965, p. 1]. Further, in a treatment program based on learning concepts "the subject is exposed to an environment which is manipulated by the therapist to provide meaningful contingencies for the subject's differential responses to stimuli" [Ullman and Krasner, 1965, p. 50]. These learning concepts form the basis for the behavior modification techniques to be discussed throughout the book.

It should be emphasized that even though most behavior change techniques used by contemporary behavior therapists are based on learning concepts, the general behavior modification approach is open to any concepts based on reliable data which support a functional relationship between an environmental event and a behavior event. From a pragmatic viewpoint, any "therapy" that reliably and efficiently results in behavior change or which supports the occurrence of behavior which can be strengthened may be accepted in terms of its operations. That class of behavior which is controlled by its consequences must occur before it can be reinforced. In view of this, any environmental design that produces the desired behavior may become part of the technology of behavior modification. If, for example, verbal and insight therapy, group relationship, and the like produce measurable behavior changes, they may be viewed as behavior modification techniques. The basic criterion, however, is that a functional relationship is demonstrated between observable behavioral changes and measurable environmental events; for example, the client produces more positive verbal statements after social reinforcement by the therapist. As noted earlier, a functional relationship is a statement which denotes the nature of the reliable influence which an environmental event has on behavior. An assumed or hypothesized behavioral influence resulting from internal processes that are beyond observation, measurement or manipulation is not acceptable. While the basic assumptions and concepts of behavior modification will be presented in this chapter, reference should be made to Bandura (1969), Eysenck (1960, 1965), Kalish (1965), Ullman and Krasner (1965), Wolpe (1958), and Yates (1970) for more extensive and varied descriptions of the nature of this approach to behavior change, and to recent works of Bijou and Sloane (1966), Bucher and Lovaas (1968), Gardner (1969, 1970), Gelfand and Hartman (1968), Leff (1968) and Watson (1967) for selective comprehensive reviews of its use with a range of childhood and adult problem areas.

Learning Basis for Behavior

One of the basic concepts of the behavior modification model is that most behaviors, whether these are labeled as inadequate, inappropriate, maladaptive, pathological, or as adequate, appropriate, adaptive, or acceptable,

are viewed simply as learned behaviors. Ullman and Krasner (1965) summarize this position very adequately in stating that "the development and maintenance of maladaptive behavior is not different from the development and maintenance of any other behavior. There is no discontinuity between desirable and undesirable modes of adjustment or between 'healthy' and 'sick' behavior" [p. 20]. The implication of this position is that the education and rehabilitation personnel will look toward learning concepts to provide a basis for understanding problem behaviors as well as to provide direction to a program designed to change these behaviors. As suggested earlier, the behavior therapist depends mainly on learning concepts to assist him with the questions: "How can inappropriate behavior be weakened or eliminated?" "How can new forms of behavior be developed?" "How can behavior be brought under the control of appropriate aspects of the person's environment?"

The focus of the educational or rehabilitation program is on the overt behavior which is causing difficulty or concern to the environment in which the retarded reside. Major consideration is provided the development of constructive means of behaving—those that result in maximum independence in the vocational, social, and economic spheres—and not, as is characteristic of many other therapy systems, on dealing with internal pathology. In illustration, if a person is avoided by his peers because of his excessive complaining, no attempt is made to "understand" the presumed internal dynamics of the complaining. Rather, the major strategy becomes one of teaching alternative ways of behaving which will result in positive social feedback from peers.

An example of this approach is provided by a recent report by Wiesen and Watson (1967) of the behavior treatment of a retarded boy who exhibited excessive attention getting behavior. This behavior, directed toward adults, was described as "almost unbearable" and consisted of constant grabbing, pulling, hitting, untying shoelaces and the like. Unlike a psychodynamic model that would view the behaviors, for example, as symptoms of emotional disturbance or of an excessive need for attention and affection, the behaviors were hypothesized as being maintained by the adult attention that such behaviors brought. It was hypothesized that the excessively high rate (over six responses per minute during the baseline or pretreatment observations) was being maintained by "an inadvertently established partial reinforcement schedule carried out unwittingly by harried attendant counselors who periodically reinforced Paul with prolonged attention" [p. 50]. This hypothesis was translated into a treatment program designed both for the elimination of the bothersome behaviors and for the development of more appropriate means of interacting socially with adults and peers alike.

No attempt is made within the behavior modification model to "cure" the

person of all his quirks and idiosyncratic behaviors. Only those that functionally interfere with the attainment of those educational and vocational goals which are deemed desirable and feasible for a given individual are identified as requiring change. Such an approach is both efficient and meaningful since various "quirk" behavior patterns frequently lose their visibility or negative social stimulus value as other behavior patterns are developed that render the retarded more generally successful in a variety of settings.

Problem behavior is not viewed as symptomatic of some more basic internal hypothetical events such as hostility, conflicts, repressed wishes, minimal brain damage, learning disabilities, or poor self-concept. Behavior is not assumed to have such inferred causes. The concept of low intelligence is frequently used as an explanation for much of the behavioral inadequacies of the retarded. For example, it is reported that the retarded adolescent is "socially inadequate due to his low intelligence." Limited intelligence is thus viewed as the active causative agent involved in the socially inadequate behavior pattern. That is, low intelligence is veiwed as the independent variable that greatly influences the behavior under study. No one, in fact, however, has been able to spell out the manner in which "low intelligence" does influence behavior. It is evident that persons who are designated as scoring low on intelligence tests do experience difficulty in learning new responses and in maintaining newly acquired ones. However, nothing is gained by proclaiming that the cause of this learning difficulty resides in the limited intelligence.

A related concept is contained in the frequently heard statement, "He is unable to learn because he is retarded or has low mental abilities." Mental retardation and low mental abilities are viewed as causing poor learning. In this type of conceptualization, the only observations or direct measurements that are made are those of the behaviors under question. As the behavior is inadequate, an inference is made that something inside the person, "low mental abilities," "mental retardation," or the like, does actively account for his inadequate behavior. Such concepts, in addition to being scientifically unsound, create the impression that little can be done to influence the behavior as it is merely a reflection of the internal unmodifiable cause, "low mental abilities."

Education and rehabilitation personnel, however, have the alternative of viewing behavior in terms of environmental requirements and of attempting to provide those programs that will in fact influence the behavior. There is ample evidence that even the more severely involved can learn. The rehabilitation worker has the task of creating that environment which will best promote learning and performance within the retarded. Present behavior, in a sense, may be the end result of literally thousands of pre-

vious experiences. That is, there are numerous historical events that add up to the person who, under certain present stimulus conditions, behaves as he does, whether appropriate or inappropriate. In illustration, a mildly retarded workshop trainee interrupts her task assignment by frequent trips to the work supervisor's office to seek assurance that her completed assembly items are satisfactory. Whenever the supervisor attempts to ignore or to reprimand her quest for assurance, Mary becomes sullen and will not return to her work station for a period of time. It could be said that Mary is emotionally disturbed, overdependent, negativistic, has a high need for attention or has poor achievement motivation, and further, that the excessive assurance seeking behavior is merely a surface sympton of any one or a combination of these hypothetical conditions.

The learning approach, in contrast, would view the excessive trips to the supervisor as the end result of a complex set of previous experiences which provide various present environmental events with given stimulus control functions, that is, with certain influence over the trainee's behavior. An examination of the environment in which this behavior occurs may reveal that the work environment is aversive and the work stoppages are strengthened as this behavior removes her temporarily from the aversiveness of the work environment. A complete understanding of the behavior could require such data as (1) a designation of the manner in which the work environment acquired aversive properties, (2) a description of the manner in which the person developed the behavior pattern of leaving the work bench to obtain supervisor approval, (3) the types of response which the supervisor makes to the client, and the like.

The Cause of Behavior

From a functional viewpoint, behavior is viewed as being controlled by present stimulus conditions. The causes of the behavior are viewed as those environmental events which are effective in influencing the occurrence or nonoccurrence of the behavior patterns. The manner in which these environmental events acquired their respective influences is another matter. An elaboration of this process may be of general interest but in a specific case may be quite unnecessary for an effective program of change to be devised. Appropriate explanation, therefore, is viewed as demonstration of a functional relationship between behavior and present controlling events.

In explaining behavior, the behavior therapist does not resort to such explanations as, "He does it because he needs to," or "He fights because he is angry." Such explanations are viewed as inadequate because they do not provide information about the conditions that will reliably produce or control the behavior. A person may be angry and fight under certain conditions

and angry but not fight under other conditions. If one is interested in the fighting behavior, it would be sufficient to identify those conditions under which fighting occurred, including the contingent consequences of such behavior. Being angry may be one of the conditions which increases the likelihood that fighting will occur, but anger is not viewed as a meaningful explanation for the fighting behavior. As another example, instead of stating that a person goes to the restaurant and orders hamburger and coffee because he is hungry or because he needs food, an attempt is made to state the conditions under which he is likely to engage in this behavior pattern. A statement similar to the following would be more acceptable, "At about 12:00 each day, when he has enough money, John will go to the restaurant and order food." It may be necessary to add other qualifying conditions such as deprivation of food for four hours and the company of peers in order to increase the reliability of the predictions. Explanation of present behavior is in terms of a specification of the conditions under which certain behavior patterns are likely to occur. The focus, as is evident, is on the person in an environment. Our knowledge of the "person-conditions-behavior" relationship is gained from observation of the person under similar conditions—that is, through a knowledge of the history of the person and of the conditions which, when present, will result in given behavior.

Although behavior is controlled by present events acting upon the person, it is evident that these present events have gained certain stimulus functions or behavior control features through previous exposure. A retarded adolescent does not scream because he is angry. He screams, as previously suggested, because screaming has produced certain changes in the environment, for example, attention from adults, removal of punishment, receiving permission to engage in desired behavior, and the like. Knowledge of these historical experiences is needed in order to describe how present stimulus conditions exert influence over the screaming behavior. That is, in response to the question, "How did the child learn to scream when frustrated?", it may be necessary to look into the history to identify the previous consequences which have strengthened the response of screaming under certain environmental conditions. A person reads his lesson not because he likes it but because such behavior previously has produced certain consequences and has promise of doing so presently. The retarded adolescent makes disruptive comments in social adjustment class, not because he is delinquent or naughty, but rather as a result of certain consequences which this behavior has produced under similar circumstances in the past. The behavior will continue to occur if these consequences continue to be produced by the endeavor.

Knowledge of these historical events which result in present determinants of behavior becomes valuable in attempts to control or modify the behav-

ior. Knowing that these behaviors are controlled by certain effects which are produced, it may be possible to eliminate or otherwise alter these effects with the result that the behavior pattern will change along with the environmental events which cue, prompt or mark the time or place for the behavior to occur.

Skinner (1953) summarizes this position quite succinctly in his statement:

> The external variables of which behavior is a function provide for what may be called a causal or functional analysis. We undertake to predict and control the behavior of the individual organism. This is our "dependent variable"— the effect for which we are to find the cause. Our "independent variables"— the causes of behavior—are the external conditions of which behavior is a function [p. 35].

The external conditions include those stimulus events which are external to the person as well as those stimulus events which are created by the person's own behavior. These behavior-produced stimulus events provide the basis for further behavior. The particular form or strength of any behavior pattern which may occur at a given time is related to a number of factors including (1) the environmental events which precede and are present as the behavior occurs, (2) consequences (events) which are produced by the behavior and, (3) the person's previous experience with these events which precede, accompany, and follow the behavior. The effective preceding or following stimulus conditions for a given person may represent a wide range of events, social or physical, which may or may not have any obvious "face validity" as influential events.

Very little behavior has a 100 percent occurrence rate. That is, not many behaviors invariably occur as designated conditions are presented. Rather, behavior has a higher or lower likelihood of occurrence under varying environmental conditions. With knowledge of a person's history, one can predict with a certain likelihood of being correct that under given environmental conditions a specific pattern of behavior will occur. The behavior modification model merely attempts to influence the likelihood or strength of those behavior patterns which are nonadaptive when viewed in relation to situational requirements.

Learned Behavior or Symptoms?

Symptom substitution, as the concept is used in the psychodynamic approach to psychological functioning, is not a consideration in a program of behavior modification because problem behaviors are not viewed as being symptomatic of some more basic or central underlying difficulty. As sug-

gested, the behavior modification position is quite a departure from that of the general psychodynamic model which focuses treatment on what is assumed to be the internal causes of the symptomatic problem behavior. By treating the internal or central causes, it is assumed by the psychodynamic position that the danger of "symptom substitution"—one inappropriate behavior symptom substituting for or appearing after treatment of another one—is averted. Commenting on this difference, Skinner (1953) noted: "Where, in the Freudian scheme, behavior is merely the symptom of a neurosis, in the present formulation it is the direct object of inquiry" [p. 373]. Eysenck (1960), another behavior therapy proponent, reports: "Learning theory does not postulate any such unconscious causes, but regards neurotic symptoms as simple learned habits; there is no neurosis underlying the symptom, but merely the symptom itself. Get rid of the symptom and you have eliminated the neurosis" [p. 3].

It should be noted that no psychological treatment procedure actually removes or eliminates behavior. Behavior modification, or any other form of psychological treatment, can only change the functions of the environmental conditions which control the behavior. Thus, even though behavior patterns may be reduced to zero frequency of occurrence in one or a dozen situations, it cannot be said that the behavior has been eliminated completely. It can only be said that the behavior is no longer under the control of present environmental conditions, or conversely, that other behaviors have a higher likelihood of occurrence in these situations. This same behavior may well appear in other situations at high strength.

Following the reduction in strength of a specified behavior pattern, it is quite possible that the behavior pattern may reappear if the initial or similar environmental conditions reappear. Additionally, new patterns of unadaptive behavior may be developed or other patterns which had not been highly functional may gain prominence.

Bandura (1969) has suggested that:

> According to the social-learning point of view, in the course of social development a person acquires different modes of coping with environmental stresses and demands. These various response strategies form a hierarchy ordered by their probability of effecting favorable outcomes in certain situations. A particular mode of responding may occupy a dominant position in various hierarchies; subordinate strategies may differ from one situation to another and may vary widely in their frequency of occurrence relative both to the dominant response tendencies and among themselves. Consequently the effects of removing a dominant response pattern will depend upon the number of different areas of functioning in which it is characteristically activated, and the nature and relative strength of the initially weaker response dispositions [p. 50].

The weaker response dispositions may well be behavior patterns that are viewed as maladaptive by the dominant social environment. In this case, what appears to be symptom substitution may be explained easily by rather simple principles of learning.

As will be emphasized in later chapters, behavior modification programs designed only to eliminate behavior are quite apt to result in the display of other unadaptive behaviors. Such a strategy which focuses on the elimination of behavior provides no guarantee that appropriate ways of performing will occur. A maladaptive behavior may produce a reinforcer appropriate to a state of deprivation. This behavior may not occur except under extreme states of deprivation. A program which eliminates this symptom without providing for other means of producing stimulus events which will reduce the deprivation state may well result in the development of other maladaptive behaviors. Reynolds (1968) has suggested that, depending upon previous learning conditions, attempts to eliminate behavior under one set of conditions through suppression (punishment) may actually facilitate that behavior under other conditions. Controlling a person's aggressive behavior by means of threat of punishment may be effective as long as the person who can provide the aversive consequences is present. However, in the absence of the controlling person, the aggressive behavior may actually become more frequent than before the punishment procedure was initiated.

Likewise, programs that result in only minor changes in stimulus conditions can produce only temporary changes in behavior. An individual usually has a number of alternative patterns of behavior which will produce reinforcing or controlling consequences. Failure of one mode of problem solving will frequently result in other patterns being attempted. These alternative means of behaving are often as unacceptable as the initial unadaptive behavior pattern.

Role of Emotional Behavior

Some systems of behavior functioning view "emotional" variables as being of primary significance in unadaptive behavior patterns. The behavior modification system views moods, complaints, feelings and other subjective components of a person as behavioral events which may, or may not, be functionally related to other behavioral events. A retardate may report, "I feel depressed today and can't work" or "I don't feel good. I need to rest." This verbal report is viewed merely as verbal behavior and is not categorically viewed as being related in a reliable fashion to other classes of stimulus or response events. Whether verbal reports are related to other events is an empirical question that cannot be determined on an a priori

basis. In illustration, a twenty-two-year-old mildly retarded adult attending a work training program frequently complained of not feeling well and of not being able to work. The supervisor assumed that the verbal report did in fact represent some internal feeling state that did render it difficult or impossible for the client to engage in work behavior. This verbal behavior routinely resulted in his being able to take a break, or to go to the office and "lie down for a while." Later, when placed in a workshop, this verbal behavior was not attended to by the supervisor and work behavior was reinforced systematically, with the result that such verbal complaints were eliminated within a short period of time. Even though the client reported initially "I can't work," work behavior was reinforced and it did continue to occur. In this instance the verbal report, "I can't work," was not a reliable predictor of the subsequent work behavior. It should be noted that the retarded client quickly formed a discriminated response. While extinguished in the workshop, the complaining behavior continued in the social adjustment period of the work training program. However, after extinction operations were instigated, the behavior reduced in frequency in this class. This complaining behavior apparently was being maintained and encouraged by an environment which negatively reinforced the behavior—that is, such behavior removed the retardate from an environment which apparently was not only nonrewarding but also was aversive to him. It was interesting to note that after being reinforced for work behavior for a few sessions, this young man not only refrained from complaining but instead reported that he liked to work. It appears that the positive or negative content of such verbal statements are quite related to, or even controlled by, the reinforcement which is associated with the activity. Initially, the work behavior had not been reinforced sufficiently and the verbal content was negative. After positive reinforcement became associated with the work behavior, not only did the strength of this behavior increase but further, accompanying verbal statements were of a positive nature. It seems safe to conclude that both content of verbal behavior as well as the work behavior were controlled by the nature and magnitude of the subsequent reinforcing events. Ayllon and Azrin (1965; 1968), in work with hospitalized psychotic adults, report similar observations.

These examples emphasize the position that the major responsibility for the inadequate behavior resides in the environment rather than within the retarded person's "apathy," "emotional disturbance," "lack of motivation," or other "mental" states. This position also rejects such pseudoexplanations as, "He works well when he *wants* to," or "He can get along fine if he is in the *mood* for it." These and similar statements imply that the retarded behaves inappropriately as he wishes or wants to and controls such behaviors at will. As a result, it is easy to assume that it is the retarded person's

fault that more appropriate behavior does not occur. The responsibility for inappropriate or inconsistent behavior is placed within the individual and removed from the environment. Meyerson, Kerr, and Michael (1967) in rejecting such constructs, suggested that such "not only places an overwhelming, needless, and often unfulfillable responsibility for the client to be the architect of his own rehabilitation, but also neglects two other basic variables that can be manipulated for the client's benefit: his environment and, as a result of the manipulation of his environment, his behavior" [p. 215]. The behavior approach, again, places the blame for "poor motivation" or "lack of interest," for example, in the hands of the treatment program. The cause of the lack of behavior implied by the term "poor motivation" resides in the lack of success of the program to provide an environment which utilizes appropriate consequences or which requires performances which presently are in the person's repertoire. The problem becomes one of, "How can a program be designed to increase the frequency and durability of certain patterns of behaviors?" Satisfactory solution of this problem also solves the problem of getting the client to "want to" or to "be motivated."

Diagnostic Activities

Although diagnostic activity in the traditional sense is not pursued in the development of a program of behavior change, the behavior therapist does engage in what has been termed a behavioral analysis. The goal of this behavior evaluation process is the development of a set of speculations, stated in terms that are testable, concerning the conditions under which certain behaviors can be obtained. As the treatment focus is on observable behavior, the initial step in developing a treatment strategy is on a specification of the problem behavior. What behavioral deficits or excesses are creating difficulty or concern in what environmental situations? Emphasis is on rendering this description as precise and quantitative as possible. It is not sufficient to indicate that the retarded is schizophrenic, delinquent, emotionally disturbed or passive-aggressive. Lovaas (1967), in his behavior modification approach to schizophrenia, for example, raises the possibility that schizophrenia does not constitute a psychological variable in a functional sense and suggests that "instead of addressing treatment to the hypothetical condition, 'schizophrenia,' one could concentrate treatment on some of the behavioral deviations covered by that term. . . . This kind of approach leads to the attempted modification of functionally identifiable behaviors in such areas as verbal, intellectual, and interpersonal behaviors" [p. 110].

It even becomes necessary to translate more circumscribed behavior descriptions such as "aggressiveness," "cries easily," "hyperactive," "socially isolated," "poor worker," "does not persist" into terms of specific behavioral reactions and to describe the frequency of occurence under specific environmental conditions. Burchard (1967), for example, defined "antisocial retardates" in terms of frequency of occurrence of such behaviors as fighting, lying, stealing, cheating, physical and verbal assault, and temper tantrums. These specific behaviors were selected as the target of treatment, with the goal being that of reducing the frequency of these behaviors below that observed during the initial behavior analysis.

In addition, information is gathered only in relation to those behaviors which are relevant to the treatment goals. In a rehabilitation program the basic pertinent question is, "What specific behavioral characteristics must this person have if he is to function satisfactorily in a given work, social, or other specified setting?" Such an individual may have all kinds of "unhealthy behavior," quirks, limitations, or deviations, but these may have little if any relevance to job adjustment, for example. Reporting that a retarded adolescent engages in homosexual practices may be irrelevant as it may be totally unrelated to job adjustment. If unrelated, such information should be ignored. It is even possible in a sheltered environment that a client may be permitted to hallucinate, for example, as long as this does not interfere greatly with his work behavior or does not significantly disturb his co-workers. If the hallucinatory behavior does interfere with his own work production or with his co-workers, then reduction or elimination of this behavior pattern in the work setting may become an object of treatment.

Only after the problem behaviors have been pinpointed is the behavior therapist in a suitable position to begin to formulate specific program goals. In delineating these goals, emphasis is on precise quantitative specification whenever possible. The delineation of specific observable behaviors that can be readily identified will remove the mystery from whether a given treatment procedure does or does not exert a desirable influence on the goal behavior. Goals such as "motivate him more," "decrease his disturbance," "improve his work attitude," "strengthen his self-concept," and "increase his social skills" are much too general as stated. As statements of final program objectives, these general concepts must be translated into specific frequency behavior in specific situations. "Improve his work attitude," for example, is stated in terms of a series of specific behavioral goals such as (a) beginning work on time, (b) decrease in number of arguments which he has with his supervisor, (c) increase in positive work-related verbal statements, (d) completing tasks without prodding or complaint. "Motivate him more" may become, for example, "Increase by 25 percent

the frequency of his initiating classroom work behavior without teacher prompting." These behavioral goals are described for a given individual in terms of frequency counts so as to provide a baseline against which future behavioral change can be evaluated. These goals are then translated into specific treatment plans.

In summary, the program personnel must identify the behaviors to be developed, strengthened, eliminated, or otherwise altered and then delineate the treatment concerns in behavioral terms: What can be done in order to strengthen present behaviors, to insure the continuation of present behaviors under new environmental conditions, or to decrease or eliminate the occurrence of behaviors under certain circumstances (such as horseplay while working) or under all conditions (for example, apathy)? Following the specification of the problem behaviors and the related treatment goals, specific treatment strategies are decided upon. While the specific techniques used are not categorically dictated by the nature of the problem, it is true that a given behavioral pattern may be treated differently depending upon the nature of the learning variables involved in the development and maintenance of the observed behavior. As noted earlier, an adolescent may present a group of behaviors in relation to a given situation which results in his being described as disinterested or unmotivated. This lack of participation or involvement may be due to the fact that such participation has not been reinforced sufficiently, either in terms of kind or amount of reinforcement, to gain any strength. It has a low likelihood of occurrence. The treatment approach in this case would be one of designing the environment so that participation by the person would result consistently in meaningful consequences. On the other hand, this same behavior may represent avoidance learning wherein nonparticipation serves to remove the person from the presence of aversive consequences. In this case, previous attempts at participation had resulted in aversive consequences such as reprimand, ridicule, or criticism from, for example, the teacher or work supervisor. Nonparticipation removes these aversive conditions and is therefore reinforced or increased in strength. Participation behavior may have high strength but incompatible avoidance behavior which is under stronger aversive control successfully competes with such involvement. Requiring or attempting to force or cajole the retardate to participate carries the danger of eliciting disruptive emotional states which would only further confound the "disinterested orientation." The treatment strategy followed in this instance may consist of a procedure of counterconditioning which would serve to eliminate the emotional components associated with the previous aversive experience and at the same time reinforce participation behavior. The learning principles which form the basis for these different treatment procedures are presented in the following chapters.

In some cases, even an unsuccessful treatment program may produce fruitful results in that study of the program could reveal the conditions under which a behavior or group of behaviors cannot be obtained. Further, the deficits in the program which may account for this may become apparent. As there are no projective, psychometric, or interview procedures available which have suitable powers for reliable prediction of these conditions, it frequently becomes necessary to "try out" the initial stages of a program of behavior change prior to reaching a decision concerning the acceptability or rejection of a client for rehabilitation services or for reaching other major decisions concerning the conditions needed for suitable behavior change.

Kerr, Meyerson, and Michael (1965) provided an example of the use of a limited behavior modification program to demonstrate that a severely retarded girl could profit from further rehabilitation efforts and to establish the conditions under which the desired behaviors could develop. In a matter of a few hours of contact with a mute, cerebral palsied, epileptic, emotionally distrubed, severely retarded child, the therapists followed a program based on the principles of reinforcement and "altered her mute, antisocial behavior in the direction of spontaneous vocalizations under the control of adult vocal stimuli and a first approximation to true echoic behavior" [p. 369].

In a related study (Baer, Peterson, and Sherman, 1967), three severely retarded persons who lacked both imitative and verbal behaviors responded favorably to a behavior modification program. These children developed both reinforced and generalized imitative behaviors. The results provided important information to the treatment personnel as the conditions under which learning could take place were empirically identified.

Motivational Components

Consistent with the objective environmental focus of the behavior modification model, inferred internal states such as needs, attitudes, motives, interests, drives, and similar motivational constructs are not utilized as explanations of behavior. Such statements as, "He constantly makes disruptive comments because he has such a strong need for attention," are rejected because the construct "strong need," is not measurable independent of the behavior it is presented to explain. It is not infrequent for the retarded to be dismissed from an educational or rehabilitation program for the reasons that "he is not sufficiently motivated" or "he exhibits no interest in the training program." Lack of motivation and poor interest, both internal deficiencies, are used to explain his poor adjustment to the program.

When we speak descriptively of someone as indifferent, unmotivated,

interested, with high needs, timid or minimally involved, we have reference to the general probability of occurrence of a class of behavior. The factors involved in the development of the probability of occurrence of a particular behavior reside in the history of the individual. The behavioral probabilities may vary widely from one setting or situation to another or these may be quite similar across a number of different settings. When we speak of the person as being highly motivated at work, for example, we have reference to a high probability that various work and work-related behaviors will occur in certain settings. This same person may be viewed as "lazy" or as highly unlikely to assist with household chores. As another example, if a retardate is described as being disinterested in social interaction, we have reference to a low probability that such social behaviors will occur.

The behavior modification model approaches the topic of motivation from this descriptive empirical viewpoint. Environmental events are identified which have the effects of increasing or decreasing the occurrence of behavior when presented contingent upon that behavior. These reinforcing events will vary considerably from person to person and even from time to time, for any given person. Certain classes of environmental events, such as social attention or praise, may be quite effective in influencing the probability of a wide range of behaviors. Social attention is thus identified as a reinforcing stimulus of high value to this individual. It also may be true that such a reinforcing event shows little satiation effect under normal use. That is, it may be found that social attention can be used effectively as a reinforcing event on a number of different occasions without temporary or permanent loss of its reinforcing properties. In short, instead of inferring an internal state as implied in the statement, "He has a high need for attention," attention from peers is viewed as an effective reinforcer if it can be determined empirically that it strengthens those behaviors which precede its presentation or suppresses behaviors which result in its removal. Knowledge of such a relationship between attention and its influence on behavior is quite helpful in planning and implementing a program of behavior modification.

The empirical observation that the reinforcing effectiveness of certain stimulus events (such as smiles, money, cigarettes, food) can be influenced by operations of deprivation and satiation is an important motivational variable. Behavior that produces a cigarette for a chain smoker can become more probable by depriving the person of cigarettes, or new behaviors can be generated more quickly by providing cigarettes contingent on this behavior. Satiation effects, or decrease in effectiveness of a controlling consequence or reinforcer following frequent presentation of the consequence, influence both the probability of occurrence of learned behaviors as well

as the probability that new behaviors will be generated due to the reduced reinforcing effect of this stimulus event.

In the behavioral analysis which precedes the development of a rehabilitation program, an attempt is made to identify those effective stimulus events which have the effects of increasing or decreasing the occurrence of behavior when presented in a contingent fashion. A search is made for a variety of stimulus events which can be used to strengthen (praise, grades, approval, money, privileges, and the like) or to weaken (such as frown, fine reprimand, loss of privileges) behavior. These events will vary considerably in their effect from person to person and even from time to time for any given person. Identifying potential reinforcing events for many problem mentally retarded clients presents a challenge. Although social reinforcement in the form of praise, approval, or attention is effective with some, these events show quick satiation effects or are rather unreliable with others, especially with those displaying antisocial behavior as suggested by studies of Johns and Quay (1962) and Quay and Hunt (1965). Studies have found tangible reinforcers such as food, toys, trinkets, money and other generalized token reinforcers, and access to preferred activities to be more effective than social events with some retardates (for example, Bijou, Birnbrauer, Kidder, and Tague, 1966; Burchard, 1967). In addition, the behavioral effects of mild aversive or punishment consequences vary considerably as suggested by Striefel's (1967) work with a removal-from-positive-reinforcement procedure. In this study with retarded adolescents, isolation or removal of the person from a source of social reinforcement decreased contingent behavior in some, had a neutral effect in others, and even increased it in others. In contrast, and emphasizing the relative effectiveness of tangible reinforcers, Culkin's (1968) work illustrated that high level disruptive behavior of behaviorally disturbed retarded adults could be significantly influenced by following such behavior with a timeout period during which the retarded adult was unable to work and, thus, unable to earn tokens or generalized reinforcers.

As was suggested earlier, and as has been emphasized by Bijou (1966a), much of the behavior limitations present in the retarded appear to be due to the inconsistent, inappropriate, and infrequent nature of the reinforcing events provided by the environment. Many retardates are unable to exhibit certain behaviors required in various situations because these behaviors have not been followed by appropriate, frequent and consistent consequences. These observations emphasize the necessity of identifying a wide range of stimulus events which can be used as potential reinforcers when providing a behavior treatment program for the retarded.

In some retarded clients who manifest striking deviations in behavior development, the range of reinforcing events may be too limited to expect

suitable progress in the development of new behaviors. One basic abnormality may be viewed as a distortion in stimulus functions. That is, certain social events such as a smile, adult attention, closeness, approval, affection and the like may have no reinforcing effect. In such cases, the range of reinforcing events available in the natural or even in a carefully designed treatment program may be designed to alter stimulus functions so that previously neutral stimuli acquire reinforcing or aversive properties. These new reinforcing events become quite valuable in the subsequent program of remediation of the deficit behaviors. Lovaas (1967) in his work with schizophrenic children not only has demonstrated the value of altering stimulus functions, but also has emphasized the differences in treatment operations between this procedure and those concerned with the remediation of deficit behaviors such as speech or social interaction. In other cases, it may be necessary to attach aversive components to certain stimuli in order to provide for environmental control of certain inappropriate behaviors. Tate and Baroff (1966) and Watson (1967) illustrate this strategy in their reports of procedures used in attaching a behavior control function to certain verbal and other auditory stimuli.

Additional Features of Behavior Modification

As the focus is on modifying behavior which will be more suitable in the natural environment of the retarded client, treatment frequently is conducted in the setting in which the problem occurs. If the client is being disruptive in the classroom or in the workshop, for example, efforts are made to change this behavior in the natural setting of the classroom or workshop. Providing treatment in another setting such as a therapy room or counselor office creates the problem of generalization of treatment effects. Treating the behavior in the natural environment as it occurs insures greater generalization of treatment effects. The natural environment also provides a wide range of possible reinforcing conditions and a supply of caretaker personnel which can become involved in the treatment plan.

The behavior modification approach uses a general functional analysis of behavior methodology which provides the rehabilitation personnel with a specific means of evaluating the effectiveness of the treatment program. As noted earlier, Baer, Wolf, and Risley (1968) present an excellent discussion of the components of such an approach. In the initial behavioral analysis, treatment personnel obtain a reliable record of the frequency of occurrence of the target behavior. These baseline data serve as a reference point against which behavior change, if any, which accompanies treatment can be evaluated. After a reasonable period of time, the treatment strategy can be modified and further systematic observations can be obtained in

reference to the new treatment regimen. Under such a procedure the rehabilitation personnel do not have to guess about behavior change or do not
have to wait for an extended period of time before deciding whether treatment has its effects, as in the case in many other rehabilitation or treatment
practices.

It should be quite evident that a behavior modification approach is applicable to complex as well as simple patterns of behaviors. A treatment
program can be as specific as teaching a series of word recognitions or as
complex as teaching appropriate peer interaction in a work setting. Limitations of application reside more in the procedural limitations imposed by
most treatment environments than, at least theoretically, in the behavior
therapy principles and practices. Most environments, even those viewed as
structured rehabilitation programs, are not designed in such a manner to
facilitate optimum development in the retarded adolescent and adult who
present special learning and behavior problems. Suitable illustration of
this is provided in the final section of the book.

Summary

The focus of behavior modification is on the relationship between the person's behavior and environmental consequences. The goal is to change aspects of the current life situation which control the occurrence of inappropriate behaviors or which impede the development and maintenance
of more appropriate ways of responding. The emphasis is not on the person's deficiencies, but rather on the development of behaviors which are
more suitable to the behavioral requirement of the environment in which
the person resides. In practice the treatment techniques seek to modify the
relationship between the behavior and those stimulus events which control
the behavior, either those discriminative stimuli which mark the time or
place in which the behavior will result in suitable reinforcers or those reinforcing stimulus events which maintain or otherwise control the rate of occurrence of the behavior. By altering the stimulus events, the behavior is
altered in its rate or frequency of occurrence or in the conditions necessary
for its occurrence or continuation. In short, "all behavior modification boils
down to procedures utilizing systematic environmental contingencies to
alter the subject's response to stimuli" [Ullman and Krasner, 1965, p. 29].

CHAPTER FIVE

Concepts of Respondent Learning

Consistent with the previously stated environmental bias of the behavior modification approach, this discussion of learning concepts focuses primarily on an examination of stimulus functions and the manner in which certain functions may be developed, modified, or eliminated. The environment contains various classes of stimulus events. Some events precede behavior and serve an eliciting function. That is, when these stimuli are presented, the related behavior occurs. A person who behaves in a fearful manner during thunderstorms represents an example of this relationship. The fear response pattern occurs consistently whenever the thunderstorm begins.

Other stimulus events serve to influence those responses which precede these stimulus consequences. These serve to strengthen the preceding behavior and are called reinforcing stimuli or reinforcers. A third class of stimuli has a discriminative function and signals the time and place at which a behavior will produce a reinforcing event. The stimulus event "Now you may come to the dinner table" acquires discriminative control over the behavior of sitting at the table if this behavior pattern has been reinforced on previous occasions by the availability of food.

A final class, neutral stimulus events, has no systematic effect on behavior. The function of any stimulus event can be determined by observing its effect on behavior. Is behavior more likely to occur in the presence of certain stimulus conditions? If so, these stimuli have a discriminative control function. Does an event which follows a behavior pattern strengthen that behavior? If not, it does not fill a reinforcing function for that particular behavior or person. It may do so at another time or for other behaviors or persons. The numerous factors which may influence the functions of stimulus events will be described in the sections to follow.

Stimulus events are potentially manipulatable events. To the extent that we can identify the functional relationships between certain stimulus events and behaviors, we have the means of influencing these behaviors. As Bijou and Baer (1961) have emphasized, a study of "stimulus functions concentrate simply and objectively upon the ways in which stimuli control behavior: produce it, strengthen or weaken it, signal occasions for its occurrence or nonoccurrence, generalize it to new situations and problems, etc." [p. 19].

As learning principles are statements of relationships between classes of stimulus events and various response characteristics and as the major concern is with procedures of behavior change, the following discussion of learning focuses on a description of the *operations* which, when followed, demonstrate the learning relationships. With this orientation, it is recognized that some of the finer technical aspects of the learning concepts discussed have been treated lightly and, at times, perhaps even oversimplified. The interested reader should refer to Keller and Schoenfeld (1950), Skinner (1938, 1953, 1961), Ferster and Perrot (1968), and Bandura (1969), for a more detailed and technical presentation of these principles.

To increase the meaningfulness of these learning principles for those readers with an applied or treatment orientation, examples are provided for translating these learning operations into procedures for influencing the behavior of the mentally retarded. The major questions which the materials presented attempt to answer are: What can be done to facilitate the development of new behaviors by the retarded? How can behavior which the retarded has in his repertoire be strengthened, weakened or eliminated? How can the behaviors of the retarded be brought under the control of appropriate aspects of the environment?

There are two different ways in which behaviors are related to environmental (stimulus) events. First are those behaviors called *operants* that are influenced by stimulus *consequences*. Such behaviors alter or "operate upon" the environment, thus producing a following consequence which comes to control the frequency of occurrence or strength of that behavior. *Respondent* behavior, in contrast, is that behavior which is controlled by *preceding* stimulus events. This chapter is concerned with the development, control and elimination of this latter class of behaviors. Operant behavior will be discussed in the following chapter. While major attention in a rehabilitation program may be concerned with the modification of various features of operant behaviors, rehabilitation personnel must be sensitive to the procedures of respondent learning as most components of emotional behaviors are of a respondent sort and come under the control of numerous environmental aspects through the process of conditioning.

Conditioning of Respondent Behavior

Some behavior exhibited by humans can be viewed as unlearned or reflexive; that is, it will appear under specified stimulus conditions without benefit of previous experience. When certain eliciting stimulus events, called *unconditioned stimuli,* are presented, the unlearned or unconditioned responses invariably follow, assuming that the person's nervous system is mature or not unduly injured. In view of the natural, "built-into-the-organism," automatic nature of the relationship between these preceding stimuli and responses, such respondents are viewed as involuntary behavior. This unlearned behavior, basically physiological in nature, includes such responses as coughing, sneezing, pupilary reflex, salivation, perspiration, changes in heart rate, blood pressure, adrenal secretion, and stomach, bowel, and bladder activity. These behaviors are elicited whenever related unconditioned stimuli are presented. It should be noted that many of these unconditioned physiological responses are aspects of "emotional" reactions. An angry or fearful person, for example, is one who displays many of these smooth muscle and glandular responses—increased heart rate, heightened blood pressure, increased adrenal secretion, decrease in digestive activities, involuntary bowel and bladder activities and the like. These reflexive glandular and other smooth muscle reactions frequently are viewed as "emotional" responses and occur concomitantly with learned verbal reports of unpleasantness. Stimulus conditions are created by these reflexes which are correlated with a variety of reactions which have the function of disrupting much ongoing motor or operant behavior. This relationship will be discussed in the following chapter as it has numerous implications for the understanding and treatment of problem behaviors.

Respondent behavior becomes important in a consideration of complex human behavior as many of these responses can come under the control of previously neutral stimulus events through a procedure of *respondent conditioning.* The range of autonomic physiological responses which can be brought under control of conditioned stimuli is great. In fact, although differing in degree of difficulty of conditioning, almost every variation of somatic response can be conditioned to previously neutral stimuli. Although no new response is created in the conditioning process, components of the unlearned reaction can be attached to new stimuli by a procedure of association. A neutral stimulus can acquire the eliciting properties of an unconditioned stimulus through its repeated and consistent pairing with that unconditioned stimulus and the resulting response pattern. The eliciting function of the conditioned stimulus is strengthened by this association. Again, frequent temporal pairing of an initially neutral stimulus with one

that does elicit respondent reactions will result in respondent conditioning. The new stimulus will gradually come to elicit highly similar reactions which initially were controlled only by the unconditioned stimulus.

This type of learning is seen in the example of the retarded adolescent who was provided frequent physical punishment by a remedial reading teacher who, quite thoughtfully, always wore a white laboratory jacket while she administered the spanking. These painful unconditioned physical stimuli elicited a variety of "emotional responses," or unconditioned reflexes. The teacher and white robe, previously neutral, were repeatedly paired or associated with the aversive unconditioned stimuli and the resulting emotional reactions and soon acquired the eliciting properties of the unconditioned stimuli. Learning had occurred. The adolescent gradually became upset or "emotional" whenever he saw the remedial teacher. Later, other aspects of the environment such as the white jacket became effective conditioned stimuli and elicited the emotional reactions whenever presented. These substitute stimuli came to elicit the respondent behaviors independently, that is, in the absence of the initial aversive stimuli. The respondent behaviors, which previously had been elicited by the aversive stimulus components of the physical punishment, are elicited whenever the conditioned stimulus, the white jacket, is present.

Once a conditioned stimulus gains well-established control of respondent reactions, this stimulus may serve the function of an unconditioned stimulus in a *higher order conditioning* process. Other neutral stimuli, when paired with the well-established conditioned stimulus, will acquire independent power to elicit the respondent behavior. In this manner stimulus aspects of the environment which are quite removed from the initial conditioning may come to contol the respondent behaviors. The aversive components of the white jacket may be transferred to, or acquired by, other stimulus events even though these new events have never been present when the physical punishment was administered.

These new conditioned stimuli which elicit the aversive response components associated with the spanking can interfere significantly with a whole range of behaviors with which the teacher and white robe are associated. Various operant behaviors become involved. For example the adolescent may "play hookey" or "feign sickness" in order to escape from and later to avoid the teacher and the conditioned aversive stimuli associated with her. These escape and avoidance behaviors can be reinforced by the consequences of removal of the aversive stimuli. This illustrates the intimate and continuous relationship between respondent and operant behavior and learning. An elaboration of this relationship will be presented in the next chapter following a discussion of operant learning principles.

Many emotional response patterns exhibited by the mentally retarded

are not the result of direct association with the unconditioned stimulus objects or events, but rather result from higher-order conditioning. Many situations, objects or events are avoided, not because the person has had direct aversive contact with these stimuli, but because these have acquired aversive characteristics through higher-order association with other stimulus events which do elicit the respondent reactions. Additionally, there is evidence that respondent emotional behavior may be acquired through a process of vicarious conditioning (Bandura, 1965; Berger, 1962). That is, the person may observe others undergoing a conditioning experience and display respondent conditioning himself although he was not directly exposed to the aversive and neutral stimulus pairing.

Due to the general behavioral and physical limitations of many mentally retarded clients, relatively few positive stimulus events are made available to the retarded by aspects of his social and work environment. The rehabilitation environment will find it relatively easy to criticize, shout at, reprimand, ignore, isolate, reject and otherwise provide aversive events to such an individual. In so doing, the rehabilitation worker is acquiring, through respondent conditioning, some of the aversive stimulus properties associated with these negative stimulus events. Such learning merely serves to compound further the behavioral difficulties of the retarded client. Although such aversive procedures may be justified in some instances of a systematic treatment program, the negative aspects of such procedures should be weighed carefully against the possible positive behavior control effects.

Just as disruptive emotional reactions can become attached to those stimuli which systematically precede the elicitation of these, a variety of other more favorable reactions which some have called relaxation, "comfortable" or "pleasurable" responses, can be so conditioned. Neutral cues repeatedly associated with stimulus conditions which elicit the relaxation responses will become conditioned stimuli for these responses. On future occasions, these favorable respondent reactions can be elicited by presenting the new conditioned stimuli. Some behavior therapy techniques attempt to attach respondent relaxation responses to a variety of stimuli in an effort to compete with, and extinguish, disruptive emotional states associated with anxiety or fear (Wolpe and Lazarus, 1966; Wolpe, 1958).

Setting Events

Certain patterns of respondents which we have called "emotional states" of the person including "disruptive" as well as "relaxation" reactions, may be viewed as *setting events* (Bijou and Baer, 1961; Kantor, 1958). These represent stimulus-response interactions which influence other behavior

patterns which follow. These setting events render more likely the occurrence of certain subsequent behaviors. A person who is "angry" is less likely to engage in cooperative, productive behaviors than one who is not so aroused. These respondent behaviors thus change other subsequent stimulus functions. On the other hand, a person who is smiling, relaxed or otherwise in a "positive emotional state" is more likely to engage in behaviors of cooperation, concentration, and persistence in the face of difficulty. Although these behaviors are operant in nature and are controlled in strength by their consequences, it is important to recognize that such stimulus-response relationships can be influenced by respondent behaviors or other setting events. These stimulus-response interactions are potentially controllable as the respondent behaviors can be conditioned to stimulus events which can be presented by those attempting to modify the behavior of the retarded. The counselor or teacher who "charms her clients" or "has a good personality" is one who creates positive setting events, that is, who through her own behavior and the environment which she controls, elicits positive respondent behaviors. As a result, task-oriented, cooperative, participation behavior is more likely to occur.

As another example, typical comments about the difficult mentally retarded client are "He's in a bad mood today." "He just won't do anything right." "He worked hard and was cooperative yesterday, but he won't do anything today." These comments imply that his emotional state influences his responsiveness to a variety of aspects of his environment. Again, the rehabilitation personnel should either (a) attempt to identify and control the stimulus conditions which create such setting events or (b) attempt to counterbalance such by presenting conditioned stimuli which will elicit a more appropriate emotional state. Verbal instructions, encouragement, and statements of future consequences are significant setting events. "Let's settle down now and finish our work so that we can go to the basketball game" serves to evoke a range of respondent and operant behaviors which contribute to the final goal attainment. Again, subsequent stimulus-response relationships will be facilitated, for example, when provided work assignment, the client will produce at a constant high rate.

Elimination of Respondent Behavior

Repeated presentations of the conditioned stimulus without pairing it with the initial eliciting stimulus will result in the gradual weakening and eventual elimination of its effectiveness in eliciting the respondent behavior. The conditioned stimulus thus loses its function of controlling the respondents. The conditioned stimulus regains its neutral status in relation to control of the conditioned response. The control relationship between the

conditioned stimulus and the conditioned response is terminated. This procedure is known as *extinction*. The response is not extinguished or eliminated. It still remains as a reflex but it no longer is elicited or controlled by the conditioned stimulus. The stimulus can regain control over the respondent behavior only through additional pairing with the unconditioned stimulus or one which serves as one in higher order conditioning.

The rate of extinction of conditioned respondents generally depends on the level of previous conditioning. A relationship between a conditioned stimulus and respondents, which developed gradually over a large number of pairings with the unconditioned stimulus, will be slow in extinguishing. The response must occur in the presence of the conditioned stimulus, but without the unconditioned stimulus, many times prior to extinction.

During extinction, a condition called *spontaneous recovery* typically is present. Following the apparent elimination of the conditioned response to the conditioned stimulus, the response usually reappears. It is necessary to re-present the conditioned stimulus in order to completely eliminate the respondent reaction to it.

As suggested earlier, a procedure of *counterconditioning* can be used to accelerate the extinction of conditioned stimulus control of undesirable respondent reactions. This involves both the presentation of the conditioned stimulus in the absence of the unconditioned stimulus (extinction) and the added feature of presenting other stimuli which simultaneously elicit more favorable reactions which are incompatible with the undesirable respondents. The "fearful reaction" exhibited toward a new work supervisor by a young retarded adult whose previous supervisor had been quite punitive could be eliminated in the work setting itself by this counterconditioning procedure. The new supervisor initially presents himself under pleasurable circumstances, such as when the retarded adult is having lunch, during rest time, during "cigarette break" time, and during the recreation period. At these times, more favorable emotional reactions which are incompatible, and which could successfully compete with the disruptive emotional reactions, are likely to be present. Assuming that the "fearful reaction" is never reinforced by some new aversive event in the presence of the new supervisor, an extinction procedure is in operation. Additionally, the supervisor, through association with those stimulus events which elicited the more favorable emotional reactions, gradually acquires the stimulus function of eliciting these respondent behaviors. Counterconditioning is in evidence.

It should be noted that extinction is not always a smooth process when working with the retarded in a complex social environment. Aversive experiences, for example, other than those controlled by the rehabilitation personnel can intervene between the contacts which he has with the client.

These can serve to increase the strength of the conditioned stimulus worked with in treatment. Such a process involves the phenomenon of stimulus generalization which is discussed in the following section. Additionally, conditioned stimuli that have acquired considerable strength through association with intense aversive stimulation such as severe physical punishment and other traumatic experiences producing intense fear reactions are quite difficult to eliminate. Literally hundreds of nonreinforced experiences, that is, presentation of the conditioned stimulus without the unconditioned stimulus, may be required before reduction in strength of the conditioned respondent is evident.

In many cases involving intense emotional reactions, extinction is a most difficult undertaking because the presentation of the conditioned stimulus or fear object produces highly painful reactions. It is not unusual to find that the retarded person avoids those situations completely in which conditioned aversive stimuli is, or is even likely to be, present. Thus, extinction of the conditioned respondents becomes highly unlikely. In this situation, desensitization or extinction of the emotional reaction can be undertaken by presenting approximations of the conditioned stimulus. Initially, stimuli that are only vaguely similar to the conditioned stimuli are presented. Gradually, through a series of graded presentations, the stimulus events closer approximate the conditioned stimulus. In this manner, there is a gradual extinction of the respondent reaction until a point is reached at which the conditioned stimulus loses its control function over the behavior.

Generalization and Specification of Stimulus Control

Stimuli other than those involved in conditioning may elicit the respondent behavior. This *respondent stimulus generalization* occurs along dimensions of quantitative and qualitative similarity to the conditioned stimulus. That is, after conditioning to some stimulus, a variety of other stimuli which resemble it will elicit the respondent behavior. Generally, the greater the similarity between the conditioned stimulus and other stimuli not present during conditioning, the greater the generalization. In the previous example involving the remedial reading teacher who wore a white robe while she administered physical punishment, the adolescent was noted to respond in a fearful manner toward the art teacher and the janitor who also wore light grey laboratory coats during school hours. These people acquired some of the eliciting stimulus function initially associated with the reading teacher due to the stimulus similarity of their coats.

The eliciting power of the conditioned stimulus can generalize to stimuli which differ along dimensions other than a physical similarity one. There is some evidence that generalization occurs along semantic and cognitive

associative networks (Diven, 1937). As a result, respondent emotional be-haviors may occur which appear to be totally unrelated to any experience which the person may be able to describe.

Respondent discriminations may be acquired through the process of dif-ferential reinforcement. In the previous example of generalization of a fear reaction to the art teacher on the basis of the physical similarity of some of her dress apparel, a discrimination was formed after some exposure. The conditioned stimulus provided by the art teacher's coat gradually lost its control over the respondent behavior as reinforcement was never provided. Effective stimuli that would elicit the respondent reaction were soon *re-stricted* to those which were reinforced, that is, to those specifically in-volved in the conditioning.

Concepts of Operant Learning

It will be recalled that operant behavior is that class of behavior which is controlled by stimulus consequences. Such behavior is viewed by some as voluntary behavior in the sense that it does not have an invariant relation to preceding stimulus events as is true of respondent behavior. The greatest proportion of the behavior of the mentally retarded which comes under the scrutiny of education and rehabilitation personnel is of this operant class. *Operant conditioning* refers to the procedure of changing the strength of a behavior by following it with a class of stimulus events called *reinforcers* or *reinforcing stimuli*. As noted, the result of such conditioning is operant behavior, or behavior controlled by consequences. The strength of behavior at any given time is dependent upon the number and type of previous consequences with which it has been associated.

This reinforcement procedure by which the strength of behavior is influenced represents the fundamental principle of operant learning. As such it provides educational and rehabilitation personnel with a most powerful technique for use in their contact with retarded clients as the major objective of education and rehabilitation programs is that of changing the strength of a wide range of problem behaviors. The major techniques of behavior modification which have been used with the retarded (for example, Burchard, 1967; Bijou, Birnbrauer, Kidder & Tague, 1966; Lindsley, 1964) are based primarily on this fundamental reinforcement concept. Burchard (1967) used positive reinforcement in influencing mildly retarded adolescent boys who frequently engaged in antisocial behavior. When provided positive reinforcers contingent upon appropriate school and workshop behaviors, the strength of these behaviors increased significantly. Lindsley (1964) describes a range of applications of operant learn-

ing principles and methods to the behavior development of the retarded. Bijou, Birnbrauer, Kidder and Tague (1966) provide a detailed analysis of their pioneering work in developing a total education program for the mentally retarded on a behavior modification model. Table 6.1 presents an

Table 6.1. *Procedures of Influencing Strength of Behavior*

	Operation	Behavioral Effects	Examples of Events	Learning Principle
I	Behavior produces positive event	Increase in strength of behavior which produces the event	Smile, money, food, approval, special privilege, affection, passing grade, promotion, pay raise, participation in game	Positive reinforcement
II	Behavior produces removal of aversive event	Increase in strength of behavior which removes the event	Frown, poor grade, electric shock, threat of removal of play period, criticism, rejection, nonattention, penalty	Negative reinforcement
III	Behavior does not produce the positive event associated with previous positive reinforcement	Decrease in strength of behavior which was reinforced previously by the presentation of the positive event	Same as events in Row I	Extinction
IV	Behavior does not produce the removal of the aversive event associated with previous negative reinforcement	Decrease in strength of behavior which was reinforced previously by the removal of the aversive event	Same as events in Row II	Extinction
V	Behavior produces aversive events	Decrease of strength of behavior which produces the aversive event	Same as events in Row II	Punishment
VI	Behavior produces temporary or permanent loss of positive events	Decrease of strength of behavior which produces the loss of positive events	Same as events in Row I	Punishment: Time out, response cost

overview of the procedures, behavioral effects, and related learning principles involved in influencing operant behavior.

Concepts of Reinforcement

Positive Reinforcement. The principle of reinforcement states that a behavior, for example, beginning to work when requested to do so, being polite to peers, will be strengthened or maintained by the presentation of certain stimulus consequences called *positive* reinforcers, for example, a smile, money, praise, or approval. Any stimulus event is by definition a positive reinforcer if, when presented following a response, it strengthens that response. The reinforcer is defined in terms of its effects upon behavior. Such reinforcing events thus are empirically determined. If an event does influence the strength of the behavior, it is a reinforcer. If it does not, it is a neutral event. Reinforcing events increase the rate of responding during the initial learning period. Following reinforcement there is an increase in the likelihood that the behavior will appear again under similar circumstances. After a stable rate of performance is obtained, reinforcing events are needed to maintain the behavior pattern that has developed. It can be said that the behavior produces the consequence. Good teachers and counselors will be sensitive to such behavioral contingencies, or relationships between behaviors and the consequences which the behaviors produce.

This procedure of influencing behavior through presentation of reinforcing events is a simple one. If the counselor or teacher wishes to strengthen some operant behavior, he must arrange for some desirable consequences to follow that behavior. If the behavior is not followed by favorable consequences, the behavior will simply not reappear with any reliable frequency. It is important to note that *any* operant behavior, desirable or undesirable, appropriate or inappropriate, will appear more frequently if followed by favorable consequences. These consequences may not appear to be reinforcing to a casual observer. For example, some behaviors may be reinforced by the scolding or threatening behavior of a teacher. Thus, a reinforcer cannot necessarily be identified by its surface features of pleasantness.

Observation of rehabilitation personnel interacting with the retarded client reveals that much inappropriate behavior is inadvertently reinforced by the staff member who is attempting to establish and maintain a positive emotional relationship with the client. In a recent observation of a class of retarded adolescents, it became evident that the social attention provided by the teacher was reinforcing nonattentive, disruptive, out-of-seat behavior in one of the students. During a 20-minute observation period an adoles-

cent student walked away from his work table on 12 different occasions during a time when everyone in the group had been provided tablework and requested to "remain in your seat until your work is finished." On every instance of out-of-seat behavior, the teacher directed him, through casual verbal request, gesture or physical guidance, to return to his work. This teacher, in her effort to be therapeutic and controlled in her contact with this boy, was strengthening inappropriate behavior by the attention or social reinforcement which she provided.

Stimulus events which are reinforcing for one person may not be reinforcing for another. This principle of reinforcer effectiveness cannot be emphasized too strongly since one of the most apparent deficits in many educational and training programs for the retarded is that the same reinforcers (for example, grades, teacher approval, pay check at end of week) are provided for all. Little consideration is given to the possibility of individual differences. The types of consequences which are of primary importance for one person may be insignificant for another. This observation is of especial significance when working with the behaviorally disturbed mentally retarded client. There does not appear to be any highly effective common reinforcing event that can be used with most efficiency with these clients. Social reinforcement in such forms as attention, praise or approval, for example, may be neutral or even negative or aversive to some. The range of positive reinforcing events is greatly limited for many retarded adolescents and adults and at times can be quite idiosyncratic. It is also characteristic of many retarded individuals who present unusual learning and social adjustment difficulties that satiation occurs rapidly, that is, the effectiveness of a given reinforcement class, such as attention or opportunity for peer interaction, diminishes rapidly on any given occasion. Additionally, the reinforcing properties of a given stimulus event may be high on one occasion and low or absent on another. In illustration, counselor approval or opportunity to participate in recreation activities may be most effective in influencing contingent behavior one day but have little if any effect on the following day or week. As another example, teacher approval may be valuable at one time in maintaining study behavior and quite ineffective on another occasion.

In view of these observations, it becomes crucial that education and rehabilitation personnel have available a range of stimulus events which can be made contingent upon appropriate behavior. If given events are not effective, or if these lose effectiveness, others can be substituted quickly and evaluated as to their effectiveness. As a general rule, best learning will occur with the difficult retarded client when a wide variety of reinforcing events are provided. In such an environment satiation and adaptation are less likely to occur. Additionally, behavior patterns of enthusiasm, coopera-

tion, and persistence are frequently engendered by an environment which provides the novelty of a variety of available reinforcers. The counselor who depends primarily upon social reinforcement such as counselor approval or praise or upon the usual reinforcers provided in a training workshop, such as end-of-week paycheck, noncontingent rest periods and the like, will have little success in substantially influencing the behavior of many clients. The counselor must search for those events which do in fact strengthen the behavior of the retarded client and make these available following appropriate behaviors. This is accompanied by empirical investigation and not by a priori notions of what *should* be effective.

The opportunity to engage in certain activities (for example, playing pool, shooting basketball) or the possibility of gaining access to certain events or stimulus environments (such as resting, attending a movie, watching a ball game) are readily available sources of reinforcement which are frequently at the disposal of the rehabilitation environment. It has been noted that behaviors which systematically precede the occurrence of high probability behaviors are increased in strength. This general principle has been described by Premack (1959) and has sufficient experimental and clinical support to recommend its use. Everyone has some preferred activities which can be used to reinforce less preferred or probable behavior. These high probable behaviors can be identified easily merely by observation of what the person does when provided an opportunity. Sitting idly, smoking, being included in a certain group, looking at comic books, listening to jazz records, drawing, eating, and talking with the counselor are all possible reinforcing events. Rest periods immediately following completion of a production goal and being permitted to play table games following completion of a low preference academic task are examples of this reinforcement procedure.

The utilization of this relationship greatly enhances the effective environmental design capabilities of the rehabilitation personnel. One of the most frequent and immediate objections that the teacher, counselor, or work supervisor has against the application of the principle of reinforcement is that adequate reinforcers are not available for use. Creative application of this high preference behavior relationship vitiates this objection.

Negative Reinforcement. In addition to this positive reinforcement procedure, another procedure called *negative reinforcement* may be utilized in a program designed to increase the frequency of behavior. This procedure of strengthening behavior consists of removing an aversive stimulus condition following that behavior. Those aversive stimuli which serve this function are called *negative reinforcers.* Aversive stimuli are those stimulus events which strengthen behaviors when they are terminated, removed, or avoided. Behavior which results in escape from these events is strength-

ened. Both positive and negative reinforcement result in an *increase* in the strength of behavior, positive reinforcement through presentation of a stimulus and negative reinforcement through removal of a stimulus. This procedure should not be confused with *punishment* procedures which refer to the *presentation* of aversive stimuli following behavior or to the removal of positive reinforcers following behavior. The operations of presenting aversive events and removal of positive events contingent upon certain behaviors are followed with the objective of weakening the behavior. The same aversive stimulus can be a reinforcing one to that behavior which terminates it or a punishing one to that behavior which produces it. This punishment procedure and its relationship to the aversive control of behavior is discussed in a following section.

The most prevalent aversive events in human behavior gain their aversive properties through contingent association with the termination or withdrawal of positive reinforcing events. The person acquires a range of behavior which avoids the withdrawal or discontinuation of these positive events. For example, the admonition "stop being so noisy" results in less noisy behaviors as these behaviors remove the threat of withdrawal of an enjoyable social experience with playmates. The person avoids the possibility of loss of positive reinforcers (for example, playmates, play activities, etc.) by engaging in a set of behaviors which removes the possibility that the game will be ended. The "less noisy" behaviors are thereby strengthened through negative reinforcement. Driving behavior in city traffic is regulated chiefly by negative reinforcement. Driving faster than 25 miles per hour in a 25 m.p.h. zone produces the threat of loss of certain positive events (for example, loss of money through payment of traffic fine, loss of driving privileges through suspension of driver license, loss of time through appearing in traffic court, loss of approval of family members, etc.).

It should be remembered that the conditioned aversive cues (for example, threats, frowns, signs) which come to control avoidance behavior acquire discriminative and secondary negative reinforcing properties through prior association with other aversive consequences. The more intensive the aversive event, the more frequently the aversive event is associated with the conditioned cues, and the closer the proximity of the aversive event to the conditioned cues, the greater the strength of the conditioned aversive event. A threat of removal of positive events in the face of inappropriate behavior which only infrequently results in removal of these positive events will develop little control over appropriate behaviors. The threat acquires little conditioned aversive components and thus has little reinforcing effect on behavior which results in the removal of the threat.

Much behavior which escapes or avoids aversive events and thus is

strengthened by negative reinforcement is viewed as "good adjustment" or adaptive behavior. A significant amount of that behavior which conforms to society rules and regulations is present as it avoids the negative consequences associated with violation of these rules. With the difficult mentally retarded client, however, it is not unusual to find that considerable inappropriate behavior has been developed under negative reinforcement and is under the control of aversive stimulus events. In a recently observed client, high strength disruptive behaviors (such as talking out of turn, laughing, poking peers, getting out of chair) were reinforced by the person being sent out of the classroom on occasion. The class, concerned with teaching quantitative concepts, was rather aversive to the retarded adolescent. His being dismissed from class removed him from the unpleasant task of working arithmetic problems, being criticized by teacher for poor performance, and the like. Thus that behavior of being disruptive which terminated or removed these unpleasant consequences was strengthened. On future occasions of these unpleasant events, the disruptive behavior is more likely to occur. The consequences—removal or termination of aversive events—come to control the disruptive behavior. He is not disruptive because he is naughty, delinquent or emotionally disturbed. He is disruptive due to the previous consequences of such behavior.

As with positive reinforcers, there is considerable variation in the types of stimulus events which have an aversive function for groups of problem mentally retarded clients. Being isolated may be aversive to one and neutral or positive to another. Being given attention in a group may be quite positive to one and negative to another. In the former case that behavior which resulted in the attention will be strengthened. In the latter case, that behavior which will terminate the attention will be strengthened. The student, for example may bury his head in his arms, run out of the room, shout or attack the person providing the attention. Any of these which terminate the aversive stimuli will be strengthened and be more likely to occur under similar circumstances in the future. The only test of the particular function of a given stimulus event is to observe the behavioral effects upon its presentation or removal. If the behavior increases in strength upon stimulus presentation, the stimulus event has a positive reinforcer function. If its removal increases the behavior which preceded it, the stimulus has a negative reinforcer function. If no effect, the stimulus has a neutral function.

Although there is a class of aversive stimuli that is *primary* in the sense that these have biological significance, such as extreme states of deprivation of food, water, air or sexual contact, "painful" stimulation such as shock, loud noises, extremes in temperature, those aversive events of most significance in human behavior are *secondary, derived,* or *acquired.* As suggested by Ferster and Perrot (1968), such stimuli become aversive because

they signal reduction in frequency or amount of positive reinforcement or because they precede or mark the time or place for other aversive stimuli. Scolding, yelling, criticizing or reprimanding behavior by the workshop supervisor may function as aversive stimuli as they mark the occasion for a reduction in positive reinforcement. Under these conditions, the supervisor is much less likely to provide positive social comments or to grant a cigarette break or the like. Additionally, such may also set the occasion for other aversive consequences, for example, reduction in pay, removal of privileges and the like. These events can serve as negative reinforcers which can function to strengthen the behavior which precedes their removal or termination.

Events may be aversive at one time or in one situation and not in another. A person's social conversation may be quite enjoyable most of the time. However, it could become an aversive event in a situation in which the listener was required to concentrate on a cognitively complex task under time pressure. Under these conditions, those behavioral strategies used to terminate the conversation could be strengthened as these remove the aversive distractive conversation.

An interesting aspect of negative reinforcement should be mentioned as it has possible widespread implications. The behavior of the rehabilitation personnel which produces aversive stimuli, for example, frowns, scolding, nagging to control the behavior of the client, may, in turn, be controlled by the effects it has on the client's behavior. In illustration, the client's disruptive behavior during workshop activities, an aversive event to the supervisor, may be terminated by yelling loudly at the client. Yelling loudly is thus negatively reinforced—increased in strength—through its effect of termination of the disruptive behavior. Yelling behavior can thus become a high strength behavior without the supervisor "realizing" or "planning" it.

Evaluating Effectiveness of Reinforcing Events

In observing the mentally retarded in his natural environment, for example, classroom, workshop setting, social group and the like, it becomes rather difficult to isolate the relative reinforcing effects of the numerous consequences which follow various behavior patterns. Although difficult to ascertain, it nevertheless becomes essential from a practical viewpoint to determine those aspects of a program which are in fact exerting beneficial effects. As noted earlier, the methodology of the experimental analysis of behavior is available to education and rehabilitation personnel and can be used with precision with only minor investment of time or effort.

The relatively simple *replication procedure* is useful in the determina-

tion of the reinforcing effects on a designated target behavior of a given stimulus event presented in a contingent manner. Initially, a frequency count of the behavior (or some other measure of behavior strength such as magnitude or latency) is obtained prior to the presentation of the "treatment" condition. After a stable measure of the behavior is obtained during this baseline or pretreatment period, treatment operations are initiated. This may involve such procedures as providing social approval or a token following the desired behavior. If the target behavior changes after initiation of treatment, this effect is studied for a few days. Although there is great temptation to conclude that the behavior change which coincided with the initiation and continuation of the treatment procedure was controlled by the treatment, there is no basis for arriving at this conclusion. In order to gather more data concerning this possible relationship, it is desirable to remove the treatment condition and return to the environmental status present during the baseline period. If the treatment effects disappear or, at minimal, if there is a definite trend in the direction of baseline data, it can be concluded with some reasonable reliability that the specific stimulus events used during the treatment condition did in fact control the behavior change that was noted. The treatment condition would again be instated with the expectation that the behavior effects would once again become evident. The reappearance of treatment effects would further demonstrate the control which the treatment conditions exert over the target behavior.

This replication evaluation procedure, also called a same-subject or ABAB design is outlined in Figure 6.1. A successful treatment effect using token reinforcers to strengthen work behaviors is illustrated. It is noted that behavior changes in a reliable manner as reinforcement—no reinforcement conditions change.

A second procedure for evaluating the reinforcing influence of designated stimulus events or of determining the precise event which is maintaining a target behavior involves the initiation of a DRO (differential reinforcement of other behaviors) schedule of reinforcement. Such a procedure also is useful in answering the question of whether behavior is maintained by general reinforcing components provided on a noncontingent basis or if it is maintained by specific contingent reinforcing events. In this procedure, following baseline data, the stimulus event under study is used to differentially reinforce behaviors other than the behavior previously reinforced. If the baseline behavior decreases in strength as the newly reinforced behaviors increase in strength, it can be concluded that the baseline behavior had been maintained by the stimulus event in question.

This general procedure becomes an effective treatment strategy in those instances in which it is desirable to eliminate a behavior pattern. For ex-

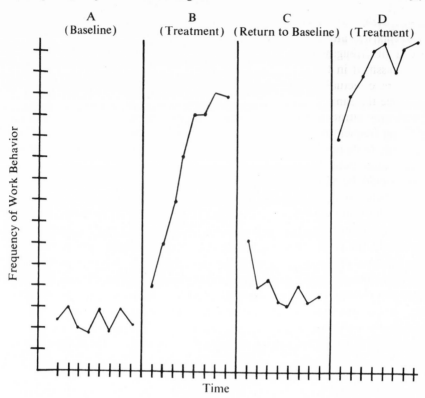

Figure 6.1. Change in Work Behavior as a Function of Reinforcement
Conditions

ample, if it is discovered that disruptive comments in a classroom are being
maintained by teacher and peer attention, a DRO procedure would be
initiated. No attention would be provided the disruptive comments by
either teacher or peers. Additionally, no behavior would be reinforced for
a short period of time following disruptive comments. This second step is
followed to insure that there is no generalization of reinforcement effect
back to the disruptive behavior. Finally, after lapse of the designated time
delay following disruptive behavior, any appropriate behavior would be
provided social attention from teacher and peers. This strategy should result in elimination of the disruptive comments through nonreinforcement
and at the same time should result in the strengthening of a range of appropriate behavior which produces the reinforcing consequences.

Functional Equivalence of Behaviors

As noted earlier, stimulus events are placed in classes on the basis of their
functional similarity. Stimuli, regardless of their quantitative or qualitative

dissimilarity, are viewed as similar reinforcing events if these have the effect of strengthening preceding behavior patterns. Similarly, responses are classified in terms of their functional equivalency. However dissimilar in terms of actual physical form, behaviors are viewed as equivalent if they produce the same reinforcing event. An adolescent in a work training program may attract peer attention by achieving a high production record, by making frequent disruptive comments, or by creating a loud noise by dropping his tools on the floor. All of these may be grouped together as attention-getting behaviors. Although the former attention-getting behavior pattern would be viewed as most desirable by the rehabilitation supervisor, these behaviors are all similar and functionally equivalent as each produces the same consequence. In general, one behavior will become more dominant than the others in the triad to the extent that it more frequently results in the reinforcing consequences. If, on occasion, the dominant behavior does not produce the reinforcer, other behaviors which are functionally equivalent will appear. This may well account for the observation that the elimination of one inappropriate behavior through one means or another results in the appearance of another bothersome behavior pattern, a process identified by some as symptom substitution. Decreasing the frequency of a response high in the functionally equivalent response hierarchy may serve to raise the strength of the next response in the hierarchy. A hierarchy may include a number of inappropriate behavior patterns. It may be necessary to eliminate each prior to declaring the person "symptom" free. Ullman and Krasner (1965) provided illustration of this phenomenon. In their program to promote appropriate social behavior in a disruptive youngster, it was necessary to eliminate self-punishing behavior, tantrums, public nudity, stealing, smearing feces, and piling the shoes of other children in the group living unit in a single pile. It was necessary to extinguish each as these occurred.

This does not imply that in every case of elimination of inappropriate behavior that other inappropriate behaviors will appear. It may well be that the next behavior in the hierarchy is an acceptable one. At other times, the inappropriate behavior that is eliminated may be functionally unrelated to other responses. In this event of independence in origin and consequences, elimination of the inappropriate behavior should have no systematic influence on other behaviors, appropriate or inappropriate.

It is possible that a group of behaviors may also be related in terms of similarity of discriminative stimulus control. Rachman (1967) has suggested this possibility in asserting that behavior symptoms are functionally interdependent and that extinction of one should weaken all other behaviors which are controlled by similar discriminative stimulus events.

A significant characteristic of functionally equivalent behaviors is that

reinforcement of one response may also increase the strength of other behaviors belonging to this class. Keeping in mind that a group of behaviors
can be functionally equivalent, it becomes evident that certain of these
behaviors may appear at high strength in a specific situation without a history of reinforcement in that situation. This may well provide another manner in which inappropriate behavior may appear to "substitute" for one
which has been discouraged or eliminated.

Components of Behavior Strength

The strength of behavior is usually measured in terms of the *rate* or *frequency* of occurrence in a specified set of conditions within a given period
of time. The number of work units completed within a given period, the
number of words recognized, the number of appropriate social contacts
made, the number of minutes spent in productive study are all examples of
this aspect of behavior strength. Reinforcement operations are designed to
increase the percentage of times appropriate behavior occurs or the rate or
speed of this behavior. In addition, reinforcement is designed to increase
the resistance to extinction or its persistence over time on those occasions
where reinforcement is not provided for every response. This consideration
involves the manner in which previous reinforcement has been provided
or scheduled. This topic of *schedule of reinforcement* will be discussed in
a later section.

Another component of response strength and thus a measure of reinforcement effectiveness, is that of the *magnitude* of the response. Although more
difficult to measure quantitatively in complex human behavior, the "vigor"
or "enthusiasm" components of behavior are sometimes important and may
be viewed as goals of program effort. A third component of response
strength that is of importance in some instances is that of response *latency,*
that is, the promptness of response following the presentation of a stimulus
or occasion for its occurrence. In illustration, a withdrawn "schizophrenic-
like" retarded adult in a sheltered workshop may be quite slow in responding to a signal to begin work. One program goal may be that of increasing
his promptness in initiating task performance.

Factors Determining the Effectiveness of Reinforcing Stimuli

The degree of influence of any stimulus event on the behavior which preceded its presentation or removal depends upon a number of factors. A
most important variable, and one that is frequently overlooked by education and rehabilitation workers in providing programs for the retarded, is
that of the temporal interval between response and reinforcer. The more

immediately the response is followed by a reinforcer the more it is strengthened by that reinforcer. The behavior that immediately precedes the occurrence of the reinforcing stimulus will be strengthened the most. Other behaviors which are more temporally separated will also be strengthened but not to the extent as the immediately preceding behavior. That last behavior which produces the reinforcer will gain most strength. This was most interestingly illustrated in a recent experience with a severely retarded adult who was in a work development program. According to workshop procedures the adult brought her completed task, consisting of a number of long nails which had been sorted into a box, from her work table to the supervisor's desk. Upon approaching the desk with this box of nails, the client accidentally turned the box over and spilled some of the contents on the desk. The supervisor, gratified at the fact that Jane had completed a box and had brought it to her, smiled broadly, patted her on the shoulder, praised and immediately presented her with a token reinforcer. Within a few trials it occurred to the supervisor that she inadvertently had reinforced a "spill the nails" response as Jane, upon approaching the desk, would spill them out and reach for her token. The spilling behavior had been the last response prior to the presentation of the social and tangible reinforcers. The supervisor promptly modified her reinforcement procedure and made presentation of token contingent upon placing a full box on the desk.

This requirement of immediate reinforcement following the behavior to be strengthened imposes considerable difficulty in the typical educational and rehabilitation setting. The teacher, counselor or supervisor is not immediately available to provide social or tangible consequences following the occurrence of every desirable response. In addition, even if it were feasible, such frequent presentation would lead to distracting bothersome interruptions of the person's school or work behaviors. A solution to this problem involves the use of similar stimulus events which are called *secondary reinforcers*. These are stimulus events which have previously been associated with the later delivery of reinforcement. Visual and auditory signals, tokens, attention, approval, money, grades, points, stamps, and similar events are all effective secondary reinforcers as these have been associated previously, after varying time delays, with other reinforcers. In work with the retarded the more tangible and physically durable these events are which bridge the time gap between behavior and the subsequent final reinforcing event, the more effective these are. The development and use of this class of stimulus events are described later in the chapter.

Another factor influencing the strengthening value of a stimulus event is the *magnitude* of the reinforcer. A response which removes a mild aversive electric shock is strengthened less than one which removes a more in-

tense shock. Presenting a dollar bill following completion of a task would add more strength to the response than would be the case had a nickel been presented. A smile from a stranger may not be nearly as reinforcing as a smile from a highly admired individual. Reinforcers of high value can result in rapid learning. Also as long as the high magnitude event is present, the frequency of this behavior is high. Work behavior which results in praise from an attractive teacher may remain at high strength, that is, may occur on every occasion when requested. This same behavior may reduce suddenly and drastically when a low magnitude reinforcer, for example, that of approval by the male supervisor, is provided.

A related variable is that of the *kind* of reinforcer. Approval, praise and other social stimulus events may be quite powerful for some but relatively uninfluential for others. As suggested earlier, the rehabilitation worker must utilize those consequences which are in fact reinforcing and not assume that certain classes of stimulus events do have reinforcing properties for specific problem mentally retarded clients. The client "could care less" about some of the consequences which are provided by the rehabilitation program. Thus it should not be surprising that systematic behavior change does not result.

It is also important that the client have some familiarity with the reinforcer which is being provided. Many retardates are not influenced by, and may even at times actively avoid, participation in or consumption of certain events because they have had no previous experience with these. Thus many events can become reinforcing if the retardate is given an opportunity to experience or sample these events. Shooting pool, making a voice recording, taking snapshots with a Polaroid camera, and spending time in a library initially may all be low preference activities with limited or neutral reinforcing properties. All may become high preference, highly reinforcing events for a group of retarded adolescents after exposure to these activities. In a recent study with a group of young adults in a rehabilitation program, these and similar events, initially presented noncontingently or in a free manner in this environment, were later provided as rewarding events following behavior which was being developed. In this manner a variety of academic, work, and social behaviors was strengthened.

The value of a given reinforcing event can be enhanced in some instances by providing a limited sample of the reinforcing event or by permitting the client to observe others consuming or participating in the event. This experience is terminated prior to satiation and the client is provided an opportunity at a later time to gain the event. In popular language, this procedure creates a "need" for the event. Stated in functional analysis terms, this procedure of *reinforcer sampling* increases the likelihood that behavior will occur which will result in this event.

The state of *deprivation* or *satiation* of the person in relation to the specific reinforcer used at the time reinforcement is provided is of considerable importance in influencing the effectiveness of that event. Conditions of deprivation or satiation are examples of the previously discussed setting events. These conditions influence the general level of responsiveness to those classes of cuing and reinforcing stimuli related to the setting events. The deprivation state of a person who has not eaten for some hours will increase the strengthening value of food as a reinforcer and increase the cuing or discriminative value of those stimuli which in the past have marked the time and place for "food seeking behavior." Satiation results whenever a reinforcer is presented too frequently or in excessive amounts. Many potentially influential reinforcers are not fully effective in educational and rehabilitation programs as these reinforcers are freely available to the mentally retarded outside the rehabilitation setting. In fact, in some instances the excessive presentation of reinforcing stimuli may serve to neutralize the positive reinforcing properties of given stimulus events. Only under the conditions of controlling these events and increasing the deprivation state can these become valuable events. As suggested earlier, one charactertistic of many difficult mentally retarded clients is that they become satiated easily in relation to a variety of reinforcers, especially those of a social nature. Related to this satiation-deprivation relationship to reinforcer effectiveness is a more general observation. For many mentally retarded, especially the more severely limited, satiation of one class of reinforcers generalizes to other classes of reinforcing events.

The *type of response* is involved in the effectiveness of a given reinforcer. Simple responses are more quickly strengthened than more complex responses. This would suggest that, in order to dispel discouragement on the part of the treatment staff and in order to more quickly obtain an indication of the effectiveness of a given reinforcing consequence, complex behavioral goals should be arranged in smaller, more manageable segments. Progress will be more observable. This will decrease the likelihood that treatment will be terminated prematurely by the staff due to lack of progress. Additionally, a response or response pattern that had previously been strengthened in some other situation, is more likely to develop at high strength in a new situation than a response pattern that has had limited or no previous reinforcement history.

The final consideration of those variables which influence the reinforcing properties of stimulus events in relation to a specific response pattern is that of the *number* of reinforcements. Generally, the greater the number of times the response has resulted in the reinforcing consequence, the stronger the response. Of course there is a practical limit beyond which response strength would not be increased. It should be recognized that this relationship between number of reinforced responses and strength of the

response is influenced by the interacting effects of all previously mentioned factors: temporal relationship between response and reinforcer, magnitude and kind of reinforcer, state of deprivation, and the type of response being considered. A reinforcer of high magnitude may be of limited value if delivered a number of times when the individual is satiated in reference to that stimulus event. Or a response may be noticeably strengthened when followed a number of times by a generally uninfluential reinforcer if the individual is in a high state of deprivation in relation to that reinforcer. The practical implication of these multifactor interrelationships is apparent. Optimal learning will occur generally in those situations where all of the factors are maximized, that is, short time delay, high preference reinforcer, high magnitude reinforcer, high state of deprivation. At the same time, it should be recognized that these same factors which maximize learning can interfere with continued or persistent high rate performance of these same response patterns. These factors may become highly specific discriminative cues for subsequent responding and if these change significantly, performance may weaken quickly. In illustration, during training behavior may be reinforced immediately with a high preference and high magnitude reinforcer under conditions of deprivation. The behavior continues to occur at a high rate of correctness as long as these setting and reinforcing stimulus components are present. A significant change in any of these, for example, delay in reinforcement following performance or decrease in the magnitude of reinforcer, may result in a rapid decline and perhaps even the cessation of the behavior. Thus, although certain stimulus events and relationships between environment and response may maximize performance, a rehabilitation program must plan also for the essential requirements needed for the continuation of this behavior under different conditions. Many programs fail because inadequate attention is provided this problem. Factors relating to schedules of reinforcement, secondary reinforcement, and discriminative control, all to be discussed in later sections of the present chapter, must be considered.

The reinforcement properties discussed in this section are characteristic of both positive and negative reinforcers. Those behaviors which remove mild aversive stimuli are strengthened less than those which remove more intense aversive events. Avoidance responses of high strength can develop rapidly under instances of response contingent removal of intense aversive conditions, for example, a highly threatening supervisor, being accused of illegal behavior, and the like.

The Weakening and Elimination of Operant Behavior

Extinction. Just as there are two basic procedures for the strengthening of behaviors, those of presenting positive events and removing aversive

events, there are also two major sets of operations for decreasing the strength or frequency of occurrence of behavior. One major set of operations involves the removal of stimulus events. The set of operations may involve the removal of contingent stimulus conditions which maintain the behavior, a procedure called *extinction*. Or the operations may involve the loss of certain positively reinforcing events following inappropriate behavior. Unlike extinction, however, those events which are removed are not those which had served to reinforce or strengthen the behavior which is being eliminated. This distinction will be described in some detail following an examination of the extinction operation.

The second major set of operations for the weakening of behavior involves the presentation of certain stimulus events following a response to be eliminated. This would include primary and secondary aversive consequences. Such a procedure is called *punishment*. Aversive stimulus consequences are viewed empirically as those response contingent consequences which do in fact result in a reduction in the frequency of occurrence of a particular behavior. It is evident in working with the difficult mentally retarded client that many stimulus consequences which are aversive to most do not exert a behavior deceleration or aversive effect on the retarded. Verbal threats, frowns, gestures of disappointment and other signals for additional future aversive events do not influence many retardates. This punishment procedure will be discussed in a later section. Reference should be made again to Table 6.1 for a summary of these procedures for eliminating operant behavior.

If those reinforcing conditions which previously were produced by a learned behavior pattern are discontinued, the behavior decreases in strength and eventually disappears. Thus, if a performance had occurred at high frequency because it produced praise from a teacher or parent, the strength could be reduced if the praise were no longer provided. As noted, this is called an extinction or nonreinforcement operation. It is easily demonstrated in a laboratory setting in which the reinforcing events controlling the behavior can be removed. This operation is most valuable in a functional analysis of behavior as it serves to identify the events controlling the behavior. That is, it serves to identify those stimulus events (consequences) without which the behavior would decrease in strength. If, in this example, the performance reduced in rate and eventually ceased to occur following the removal of contingent praise, it could be said that praise was a reinforcing event which caused or controlled the behavior. If the performance did not decrease, praise as a consequence evidently did not hold a functional relationship.

The rate of extinction is dependent upon a number of factors. Further, extinction effects following removal of the reinforcing conditions typically are not immediately evident. Some of the factors which influence the rate

with which extinction does take place include: (a) the frequency and magnitude of previous reinforcement, (b) the schedule by which previous reinforcement had been obtained, (c) the amount of effort involved in the performance of the behavior which is to be eliminated, (d) the state of deprivation or satiation in relation to the maintaining reinforcer during extinction, (e) the availability of other ways of behaving which will produce the same or equally valuable reinforcing events, and (f) the level of assurance held by the person that reinforcement is no longer forthcoming following the behavior to be eliminated. If the person is informed that reinforcement will no longer follow the behavior in question and further if he has a history which renders this information highly reliable, the behavior may be eliminated quickly as other modes of behavior which will produce the reinforcer are sought. This emphasizes the value of informing the person of the changes in contingencies which have been imposed in the intervention program. Thus the rate at which extinction occurs in a given case is dependent upon a large number of interacting factors.

It should be noted that the behavior is not literally eliminated, or removed as such, through extinction. An extinction procedure merely modifies the behavior pattern by changing the environmental events that influence its rate of occurrence. Thus a behavior pattern, virtually eliminated under specific stimulus conditions involving extinction operations, may reappear as these conditions change. In illustration, behavior eliminated through nonreinforcement under a relative low state of deprivation for the reinforcer, may reappear under conditions of a high level of deprivation for that reinforcer. Further, behavior may be eliminated through nonreinforcement in one situation but not in others in which extinction conditions are not in effect. This observation further emphasizes the notion that behavior is not removed from the repertoire. Rather the stimulus events which control various behaviors are changed.

After the behavior ceases to occur following a period of nonreinforcement, it is not unusual for the behavior to reappear after an interval of time has elapsed. The behavior typically will not be at the same rate or precise form as initially, but must be placed under extinction conditions in order to once again eliminate that behavior. Most every teacher or counselor has had this experience and has frequently commented, "I thought we got rid of that behavior last week." As this is a predictable type of occurrence (a temporary reappearance of behavior previously extinguished), the educational and rehabilitation program must be prepared for its appearance so as to ensure that reinforcement is not produced. Inadvertent reinforcement could well result in an immediate reappearance of the behavior at a rather high strength requiring a much longer period of elimination, although not as long as required for initial extinction.

It is known that after continuous reinforcement the response ceases

rather quickly upon initiation of a nonreinforcement procedure. Of course the extinction rate is dependent upon a number of factors even here, such as the number and magnitude of previous reinforcers. In illustration, it is highly unlikely that a quarter placed in a cigarette machine which did not produce cigarettes would receive too many additional quarters in an effort to obtain the cigarettes even though the machine had produced cigarettes on numerous previous occasions following the response of placing a quarter in the slot.

Of considerable interest is the manner in which a person can develop a resistance to deterioration or cessation of behavior in the absence of reinforcement. One of the essential behavioral characteristics which the retarded must acquire if he is to be successful in general life adjustment is that of perseverance or persistence of behavior under conditions in which external reinforcement becomes scarce or infrequent or in which behavioral requirements become difficult. Many retarded adolescents and adults requiring special education and rehabilitation services have a low resistance to extinction; that is, they stop performance in the face of difficulty (which may produce conditions of infrequent reinforcement) or may avoid situations entirely which require some competitiveness on their part. Gardner (1966a, 1966b) and others (for example, Cromwell, 1963) have suggested that problem solving behavior extinguishes quickly under these conditions of infrequent reinforcement. On the other hand, some writers (for example, Zigler, 1966) report an extreme resistance to extinction for some retarded persons. The individual is reported to persist in the same behavior for excessive periods of time following the initiation of nonreinforcement. Both extremes obviously are maladaptive and should be eliminated as a predominate mode of reaction to extinction conditions.

The retarded may stop performance readily when faced with difficulty because he has experienced numerous successive conditioning and extinction sequences. His behavior in the face of difficulty closely approximates what is called *one-trial extinction*. He has learned that any single response or at least a small number of responses are discriminative cues that further responses will not be reinforced. Thus, behavior stops suddenly upon occurrence of unreinforced responses. Such is highly adaptive in numerous situations but when it occurs as the general mode of responding it becomes increasingly maladaptive. "If you don't succeed, try and try again" is a bit of advice that pays handsome dividends at times. The education and rehabilitation program will find it valuable to teach the retarded to discriminate between situations in which one-trial extinction is most adaptive and those in which persistence or increased efforts in the face of nonreinforcement will eventually result in reward attainment.

Laboratory research indicates that behavior is sustained for longer pe-

riods of time and with greater frequency following a history of intermittent reinforcement than following continuous reinforcement. The adolescent whose somatic complaints have resulted on an irregular but somewhat frequent basis in his being able to be excused from participating in an activity which is unpleasant to him will persist for a long period of time following nonreinforcement of the complaining behavior. If the complaining behavior had been reinforced on a continuous schedule prior to the initiation of nonreinforcement, the behavior would have been eliminated in a shorter period of time. This relative effect is illustrated in Figure 6.2. Other relationships between rate of extinction and patterns of previous reinforcement will be discussed in a later section.

The rate at which the behavior under extinction decreases in strength is somewhat irregular. If the behavior had not undergone extinction previously, it would not be unusual to observe at the initial removal of reinforcement an actual increase in strength as reflected in rate, magnitude or la-

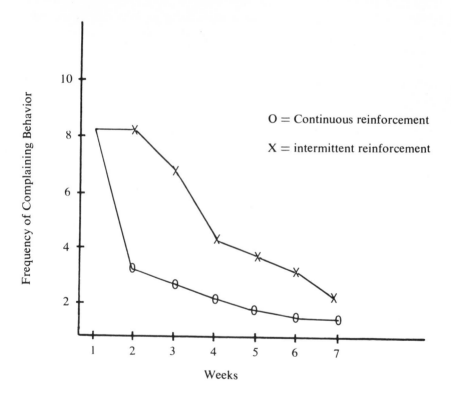

Figure 6.2. Relative Extinction Rates for Behavior with Histories of Continuous and Intermittent Reinforcement

tency. That is, the behaviors may occur at a higher frequency initially than when they were being reinforced. There is an immediate increase in rate. This increased strength is usually accompanied by other behaviors which are emotional in nature as seen, for example, in the aggressive or temper tantrum outburst of a child after failing to receive a usual reinforcer following certain behaviors. A retarded adolescent was observed recently as he placed a coin in a candy vending machine. He had used the vending machine on a number of previous occasions. After he pulled the lever which previously had resulted in delivery of the candy, and no candy appeared, he suddenly began pulling the lever vigorously. As this did not produce the candy bar, he began yelling at the machine and soon was pounding on it with his fists. Next his feet entered the controversy and began kicking vigorously at the machine. After no success, the adolescent burst into a string of expletives and walked down the hall muttering to himself. The lever pulling response which on numerous previous occasions had produced the candy reinforcer had been extinguished on this occasion. Other behaviors quickly appeared and intensified for a short period of time. These gradually reduced as no reinforcer was produced. This frustration or temper-tantrum behavior is seen frequently as a reaction to sudden discontinuance of previously available reinforcers. Response rate is highest just after reinforcement becomes unavailable and gradually decreases in an irregular form over time.

The actual appearance and intensity of these frustration behaviors are related to the schedule of previous reinforcement as well as to other characteristics of the person. If the behavior has been reinforced on a high schedule, the person is more likely to become upset when reinforcement is not provided. Thus frustration behavior is apt to occur early in the extinction process. In contrast, the more intermittent the previous reinforcement, the greater the number of nonreinforcement behaviors which will occur without the appearance of the frustration behavior. In some cases no observable frustration effects may accompany extinction as a person has been reinforced for "self control" of such reactions. In the individual case, it is not possible to predict what the nature or intensity of the side effects will be without an intimate knowledge of the person's history of reinforcement and related reactions to frustration or removal of scheduled reinforcement.

During the course of extinction, both the frequency as well as the form of the behavior changes. In a highly developed response pattern, there is noted an increase in variability of form and intensity of the behavior. That is, during extinction there is a decrease in the quality of the behavior.

In working with the mentally retarded, however, it is not unusual to find some intensive emotional reaction to the extinction operation. A program utilizing an extinction procedure should anticipate a possible temporary

increase in frequency of the behavior as well as other frustration reactions. In the Wolf et al. (1965) study described earlier, the writers reported a significant increase in the inappropriate vomiting behavior following initiation of extinction. In addition, related temper tantrum behavior increased in intensity.

It is not unusual for disruptive, frustration behavior to be strengthened and maintained by the frequent return of the reinforcer following the behaviors. As an example, the special education teacher who upon being provided with new time-consuming tasks in the classroom suddenly no longer provided Tom with immediate attention whenever he raised his hand. Tom's handraising behavior increased in rate. As this behavior did not result in teacher attention, he next threw a mild temper tantrum involving both operant and respondent reactions. This behavior pattern finally attracted the teacher's attention and was immediately reinforced by her responses to him. The repetition of this sequence a few times would result in a strengthening of vigorous handwaving, temper-tantrum behavior. In cases when the behavior continued to go unreinforced, this behavior gradually reduces in strength and eventually will drop out completely.

An important adjunct to the extinction operation is that of teaching some more appropriate behavior. In fact, extinction is seldom used alone in an education or rehabilitation program. Extinction merely removes the behavior from the person's repertoire. The program must teach the person what to do under those conditions in which the extinguished behavior previously occurred. Ideally, the new behavior should be shaped by using the reinforcing events which were maintaining the behavior being extinguished. This combination of extinction and teaching new incompatible behaviors not only facilitates the elimination of inappropriate behavior patterns, but it also decreases the probability that such inappropriate behaviors will reappear in the same situation in the future as some new competing behaviors which produce the reinforcer are present.

The extinction procedure, that of weakening behavior through removal of its reinforcer consequences, provides an important treatment procedure for the rehabilitation personnel when used in combination with techniques of creating and strengthening positive behaviors. Considerable inappropriate behavior presented by the difficult mentally retarded can be reduced in strength by a systematic utilization of this extinction procedure. The extinction procedure is most useful when the behavior being considered for elimination or reduction is being maintained by reinforcers that are readily controlled by the treatment personnel. Additionally, simple behavior patterns are eliminated easier than more complex behavior patterns. The more complex the behavior and the longer the period of time these have been in the repertoire of the individual, the greater the likelihood of multiple rein-

forcing events controlling the behavior; thus, the less likely that an extinction operation in isolation will result in suitable reduction of the behavior.

Complaining behavior involving various referents, such as "I can't do," "This is too hard," "I'm sick or tired," "I need to rest," will frequently reduce in strength, for example, if not provided attention. "Behave as if these complaints were not heard" is a strategy that frequently pays dividends. Such a procedure may not be effective when the undesirable behavior occurs in a group setting as reinforcements may be provided by various members of the group. In observnig the disruptive behavior of talking in a loud voice, talking out of turn, repeating nonsense statements, and the like of a young retarded adult in a social adjustment program, it became evident that the reactions that these behaviors evoked from his peers and teacher were maintaining the behavior. In order to evaluate the relative reinforcement effect of her attention, the teacher systematically ignored the behaviors for a two-week period. During this time there were no noticeable extinction effects. Following this, peers were reinforced by the teacher if they did not respond to the disruptive comment of this student; that is, teacher and peers behaved as if these disruptive behaviors were not occurring. Following an initial increment, the behaviors reduced in strength and eventually dropped to a level of infrequent occurrence. It is evident that in many group settings where reinforcement for inappropriate behaviors is provided by various persons it is difficult to control these reinforcing events and thus not possible to utilize an extinction procedure as the only behavior change strategy. Some other techniques of weakening behavior must be used.

Although extinction has its place in a behavior modification program, there are certain practical problems involved when working with the retarded. As suggested by Hamilton and Stephens (1968), analyzing and controlling the reinforcing contingencies especially of complex behavior and behavior of long standing may be a most difficult undertaking. It is difficult to identify the reinforcing events and to control them once identified. Some behaviors are maintained by several reinforcing events. Additionally, powerful primary and secondary reinforcers are attached to or are aspects of the problem behavior itself. Thus, the behavior is not one event and the reinforcer a distinctly different and separate event.

As noted previously, in the early stages of extinction there may be an actual increase in the rate of behavior. This characteristic renders an extinction procedure quite undesirable in those instances in which the behavior is either highly disruptive or of potential danger to the client or others. Also, as noted, as most behaviors have developed under and are maintained by a partial reinforcement schedule, a strategy of behavior elimination based solely on extinction operations promises to be a slow undertak-

ing. This was noted by Birnbrauer, Bijou, Wolf, and Kidder (1965) in attempting to eliminate behavior problems of groups of retarded boys in a classroom setting by an extinction procedure, that is, by ignoring instances of inappropriate behavior. After some experience, additional behavior change procedures were added to supplement the extinction procedure "since extinction is often difficult to implement effectively in a classroom . . ." (p. 360).

Bucher and Lovaas (1968) used an extinction procedure with a retarded boy who, due to high rate self-injurious behaviors, was kept in restraints on a 24 hour a day basis. After eight days of being released from restraints for one and one half hours daily, the behavior was gradually reduced to near extinction level by removing a presumed source of contingent reinforcement. However, during this extinction process the boy hit himself more than 10,000 times. In another case of severe self-destructive behavior in a sixteen year old retarded female, these writers reported that "because of the extreme severity of her self-injurious behavior . . . it is impossible to place such a person on extinction. Marilyn could have inflicted serious self injury or even killed herself during an extinction run" [p. 91].

Watson's observation (1967) is also quite pertinent:

> When a child is engaged in acts that are physically damaging such as breaking windows with his head, arms or hand, beating his head against the walls, stabbing himself or others with a safety pin, or throwing another child down with great force the cottage staff cannot wait for the effect of extinction to gradually end or eliminate the behavior. Someone might be injured severely before the effects of extinction could eliminate the behavior in question [p. 13].

In light of these and related considerations, it must be concluded that, even though from a theoretical viewpoint removal of reinforcement may be a most reliable and effective manner of eliminating some behaviors whose controlling reinforcing events are known and manipulatable, considerable difficulty may be encountered in its application in a field situation, especially with cases of complex or extreme behavior deviation. In these instances such a procedure at times is a highly inefficient and impractical procedure.

Time-Out and Response Cost. A second procedure for decreasing the strength of behavior also involves the removal of reinforcing events but not those which in the past had systematically followed the response. In this second procedure the person has to relinquish other positive reinforcers which he has or which are forthcoming. One variation of this procedure is called *time out from positive reinforcement.* Following inappropriate behavior, the person is removed from that environment in which he has previously received positive reinforcement or in which is available a range of

reinforcers. Engaging in disruptive behavior in a group is followed by the removal of the adolescent from the classroom. He is deprived of the presence of other people and of that environment in which are available other social, tangible or token reinforcers. He is removed from the positive reinforcers. An additional variation of this procedure involves what has been called a *response cost* procedure. Following inappropriate behavior, the person must pay a *fine;* he loses privileges, freedom, money, opportunity to go to the gym and the like. These procedures again involve the *removal* or *loss* of reinforcing events and have the effect of decreasing the frequency of occurrence of the preceding behavior which resulted in this consequence.

Time-out procedures used with the retarded usually include any of three elements, each of which could contribute to the deceleration effects frequently obtained. The typical operation involves the removal of some aspect of the present stimulus environment which is identified either as a reinforcing stimulus or as a discriminative stimulus for the occurrence of reinforcing events. In some studies with the retarded, (a) a positive reinforcer has been removed for a designated period of time following negative behavior, for example, consumption of food has been interrupted for 30 seconds for inappropriate response or food is lost as a response cost, or (b) the retarded either has been removed from the general stimulus environment in which he typically receives reinforcers or from a present source of reinforcing stimuli, for example, subject is removed from peers who provide social reinforcement and placed in an isolation area following disruptive behavior, thus reducing the possibility of further social reinforcement. In addition, in instances of withdrawal of social reinforcement or when the person is placed in isolation, conditions are created which may contain conditioned aversive properties, such as removing a child to an isolation room when the child is fearful of being left along, Further, merely turning your back on someone or not responding for a designated period of time may be a discriminative stimulus for "rejection," or other unpleasant affective responses as suggested in a review by Hill (1968). Thus, a time-out may be effective either due (a) to the *removal* of the possibility of positive reinforcement for the negative behavior or of the person receiving *any* positive reinforcers for any behavior for a period of time or (b) to the suppressing effects of the *presentation* of conditioned aversive stimuli. It is also possible that factors relating to the reinforcing properties associated with the termination of time-out may be operating. The separate contributions of these have not been evaluated in studies involving the mentally retarded.

Studies with the retarded have demonstrated that both isolation from social reinforcement and interruption of consummatory behavior involving

primary positive reinforcement have influenced the rate of the behavior which preceded these events. It should be noted, on the other hand, that isolation or the removal of social reinforcers for a period of time does not prove to be aversive universally. Isolation may be neutral or even positively reinforcing for some. Striefel (1967), after studying the effects of isolation as a behavior management procedure with a group of retarded children residing in an institution concluded that:

> The data support the contention that isolation is not very effective as a means of behavioral management when used indiscriminately. Rather the effects of isolation vary from child to child and in many cases with an individual child, from one time to the next. In many cases isolation actually reinforces the very behavior one is trying to eliminate, since some children find stimuli associated with isolation reinforcing [p. 8].

These results emphasize that treatment strategies used in specific cases must be an aspect of a carefully planned program which evolves from a systematic behavioral analysis of the individual being treated.

Environmental Control of Operant Behavior

Observation of the behavior of the mentally retarded reveals certain consistency in his activity. Most behaviors occur only under certain conditions. He routinely makes appropriate social responses when he meets his teacher. He routinely enters the classroom when the 8:15 bell rings. He only infrequently enters the classroom prior to this time. He promptly discontinues his disruptive behavior upon seeing the principal enter the classroom. He opens his lunch box only during the noon recess period. In each of these examples, the behavior described has a high probability of occurrence in the presence of certain environmental conditions. When the conditions are not present, the behavior is unlikely to occur. These are illustrations of a most significant aspect of learning, that of discrimination and the resulting control which environmental events gain over behavior. In each of these instances that behavior occurred which was likely to result either in positive reinforcement or in the avoidance of aversive consequences. Cues or stimulus events were present that marked the occasion for a given behavior or a range of functionally equivalent behaviors to result in reinforcement. Any other behaviors in these situations would likely have resulted in neutral or negative reactions from the environment. These appropriate behaviors come under the control of specific stimulus events or *discriminative stimuli* due to the reinforcement which has reliably followed their occurrence. The development of the stimulus control which is appropriate to certain environments is dependent upon such factors as contin-

gent reinforcement, magnitude of reinforcement, and the consistency of reinforcement in the presence of given stimulus cues. Those cues that are present when a behavior pattern is reinforced, acquire some control over the occurrence of the behavior. If the behavior is reinforced a number of times in the presence of the cue and not reinforced when the cue is absent, the cue comes to control the occurrence of the behavior. Its presence denotes that a given behavior pattern will result in specific reinforcing consequences. To continue the preceding example, as the bell rang, Jim entered the classroom, sat in his chair at the work table and opened his book. This response sequence following the 8:15 bell previously had been reinforced by a variety of events, including those of greetings from teachers and peers, the attention provided as he answered the roll call, and the like. Additionally, such behavior may have gained strength as it resulted in the removal of certain aversive conditions including such events as criticism and threats from the teacher and principal. To repeat, a particular cue, signal, or stimulus gains discriminative control over the behavior as a result of its consistent association with the subsequent positive or negative reinforcement. When the relationship between a behavior and the related reinforcing conditions is disrupted, the discriminative stimuli will lose the control function. The behavior will no longer occur at a high or consistent rate whenever the discriminative stimulus is presented. Other behaviors that are reinforced more reliably in the presence of these stimulus conditions will come under the control of these stimuli.

The act of opening the lunch box at times other than during the noon lunch period, as another example, had not been followed in the past with the student being able to eat his sandwich or other delectables contained in the box. He had developed a discrimination. *Preparatory* behaviors result in his eating his lunch only during the lunch period. Such preparatory behaviors thus are controlled by those cues that mark the time and place for these behaviors to result in reinforcement.

As noted earlier, one of the prominent deficits characteristic of the problem mentally retarded client is his lack of fine discriminations. Much behavior that results in difficulty is not unusual or bizarre in any absolute sense. It is nonadaptive as it occurs under inappropriate stimulus conditions. The complaint is frequently made that the retarded does not know when to make responses that he is perfectly capable of making. Or even more aggravating or damaging from a point of view of developing appropriate peer relations, many retarded do not know when to stop responding. The behavior itself may be appropriate. The frequency or magnitude of the behavior, however, may be most inappropriate. This was illustrated to the writer recently by a seventeen-year-old adolescent who was referred by a

school-work counselor. The chief complaint, "she is unable to make new friends because she does not know when to stop talking," was viewed as a problem of poor discrimination training. This mildly retarded girl was not controlled by certain cues provided by her unappreciative audience such as changes in facial expression, negative verbal comments, and attempts to ignore her lengthy verbal episodes. Inquiry into the reinforcing history of this client revealed a mother and an aunt who would patiently listen to her for extended periods of time, reinforcing her for her nondiscriminating verbal behavior as a result of their pleasure that their "dull" child was so verbal. Behavior that resulted in reinforcement under one set of cues was not appropriate in another. Generalization of behavior across similar stimulus situations occurred. The behavior had not acquired the *specificity* needed to meet the requirements of adequate social interaction. In popular terms, the girl had no tact or had poor social sensitivity. This failure to discriminate resulted in behavior which was aversive to peers and which decreased the possibility that appropriate social relationships could develop.

Another discrimination deficit characteristic of many mentally retarded persons who exhibit problems of social and vocational adjustment is that the behavior of peers is imitated without discretion. The person is easily influenced. He attends to too few stimulus components of a complex environmental situation and thus engages in behavior that results in neutral or negative consequences. Certain subtle discriminative cues do not control his behavior as these either have not marked the occasion for sufficient reinforcement in the past or else the reinforcing consequences of inappropriate behavior are more powerful than those associated with socially defined "discriminated" behaviors. In illustration, the retarded adolescent may follow the "gang" into socially deviant behavior in order to receive the attention and possible acceptance provided by the members of the gang. Socially sanctioned behavior does not produce adequate reinforcers and thus is not under the control of relevant environmental cues.

Other persons are controlled by an overly restricted range of cues. Too much of their behavior is controlled by the social cues provided by certain people in their environment. These overly dependent persons will respond in socially significant situations only upon excessive prompting, urging, and prodding by others. Decisions cannot be made, behavior cannot be initiated except in imitation of similar actions by others. Social approval or acceptance is a powerful reinforcer to them. The behavior of others becomes the discriminative stimulus controlling their own behavior. Other discriminative stimuli which also mark reinforcement occasions are relatively uninfluential due to a differential reinforcement effect. Behaving in many situations without the guidance of another person may be an occa-

sion for highly probable failure or other aversive events. Such a restricted range of controlling stimulus events, however, creates a type of dependency behavior which impedes adult adjustment.

As implied, behavior is not controlled categorically by a specific discriminative stimulus. Other similar stimuli acquire the same control properties or functions without ever having been associated with the response-reinforcement sequence. Generally, the more similar the stimulus events the greater the *generalization* of stimulus functions. In many instances this generalization of stimulus control function is quite adaptive. Behaviors learned under one set of stimulus conditions may be quite appropriate under a variety of similar environment conditions. In other instances, such generalization can result in neutral or even aversive consequences. Differential stimulus control must be developed for appropriate adjustment. These finer discriminations are formed through the process of *differential reinforcement* or *discrimination training*. Behavior occurring in the presence of certain specific cues or stimuli is provided reinforcement. That same behavior occurring in the presence of similar events is not reinforced. In this manner, highly similar situations, as a result of discrimination training in the presence of subtle stimuli differences, can come to mark the occasion for highly different behaviors resulting in quite contrasting reinforcing consequences.

The transference of stimulus control from one component of the environment to another can be facilitated by the simultaneous presentation of both stimulus components and the additional procedure of gradually removing the original discriminative stimulus. In illustration, a teacher of a class of highly disruptive mentally retarded adolescents has acquired excellent control of the disruptive behavior of the adolescents. If the teacher is abruptly replaced by a new teacher, control of the disruptive behavior may be lost. However, following a period during which both teachers are present in the classroom, gradual removal of the initial teacher as the new teacher spends an increasing amount of time alone in the class should facilitate the transference of class control to the new teacher.

One aspect of the "limited intellectual capacity" which by definition characterizes the retarded is a reduced facility to form fine discriminations. The retarded is frequently confronted with situations that require him to respond differentially to stimulus conditions which differ in a most subtle or complex manner. The discrimination requirements are too difficult for many to handle. In numerous instances the discrimination difficulty is due to poor or inadequate discrimination training and not to an inherent limitation in discrimination skills. Even so, being forced to respond in a nondiscriminating manner and receiving unpredictable positive and negative consequences produces a variety of "neurotic" behaviors such as hyper-

activity, distractability, and a loss of previous discriminations. In other individuals, such patterns as behavioral rigidity or perseveration may result.

Acquired Reinforcement

It will be recalled that a wide range of stimulus events may serve a reinforcement function. Only a few of these, called *primary reinforcers,* have this function as a result of a basic relationship with certain physiological characteristics of the human organism. Food and water, for example, have primary reinforcing properties without the influence of learning. However, the most important reinforcing events for people in our culture are *acquired, learned,* or *secondary.* Any neutral stimulus event potentially can acquire reinforcement properties through being associated with other reinforcing stimuli. As noted earlier, many reinforcers are available to the rehabilitation personnel including such social and tangible events as praise, approval, visual and auditory signals, tokens, grades, points, stamps, privilege cards and the like. These events gain reinforcement properties as they mark the time and place for other reinforcing events; that is, they are associated with the reinforcement which follows certain operant behavior. Thus, a stimulus event that acquires secondary reinforcing properties does so as it functions initially as a discriminative stimulus. On a number of occasions it has preceded a response which was reinforced and thus gained discriminative stimulus properties. As a result of the temporal association with reinforcement, it gradually acquired reinforcing properties as well. Smiles, winks, gestures, headnods, praise, and other social stimuli known as *social reinforcers* all become reinforcing as these on numerous occasions have signalled the occurrence of behaviors which resulted in other reinforcing events. Social events do not acquire all-or-nothing reinforcing characteristics. Wide individual differences among the retarded, for example, are evident in responsiveness to social agents as reinforcing events. A person may be influenced by one class of social agents, for example, peers and not by other classes, for example, police authorities. He may be quite influenced by male supervisors but not nearly to such an extent by older female counselors. This was illustrated by Tony who was not influenced in any positive manner by social events provided by his fifty year old female teacher. However, a young graduate student who wore a full-face beard was quite influential in strengthening behavior by means of social praise and attention. In fact, Tony would even work at workshop tasks for three or four hours in order to receive a 15 minute conversation period with the student. Each person has a different history of experience with social reinforcement and will thus respond differently to different types of social reinforcement.

The acquired reinforcer can be of either a *positive* or *negative* nature. An event which marks the occasion for the presentation of positive consequences following behavior acquires a *positive reinforcing function*. Such a stimulus event can now in its own right strengthen that behavior which precedes it. A smile can come to reinforce or strengthen behavior which precedes or produces it. It should be noted that once acquired, such events can strengthen a whole range of behaviors even though these had not been strengthened by the primary reinforcer during the conditioning process. A smile, in illustration, may initially have acquired reinforcing properties as it was associated with a primary reinforcer such as food or removal of painful or aversive stimuli. Once the smile acquires reinforcing properties, however, a whole new range of other behaviors can be strengthened by this new reinforcer. This principle of generality of function is of prime importance in the development of a significant array of human behavior. Of importance is the fact that such acquired reinforcers must once again be associated with other reinforcing events on occasion or the reinforcing properties will diminish in strength and finally extinguish entirely. This relationship to some continuous back-up reinforcing stimulus is of especial significance in work with the difficult retarded client due to the rather tenuous nature or strength of numerous acquired reinforcers.

Many events acquire *secondary negative reinforcement* properties. Those behaviors which result in their removal will increase in strength. A frown or verbal threat, in illustration, will serve to reinforce that behavior which results in its removal. Returning to the work table, replying "I apologize," or initiation of a reading task, may all be strengthened if followed by removal of the frown or threat. As noted earlier, the frown or threat acquires negative reinforcing properties through association with other aversive stimuli. Additionally, as with the acquired positive reinforcer, the secondary negative reinforcer will lose its function unless associated with other aversive stimuli on occasion. A verbal threat, "I'll remove your privileges," will continue with repeated use to strengthen behavior that removes the threat only if such is followed by the threatened negative consequences on occasion. Otherwise these become empty threats and lose their stimulus control function.

In summary, stimulus events which become discriminative stimuli for specific behaviors begin to reinforce or strengthen other behaviors which precede them. The same stimulus events can thus serve both functions of strengthening preceding behavior and also of controlling the occurrence of behavior through its signaling properties.

The strength of the acquired reinforcer at any given time is a function, not only of the recency of its association with the conditioning reinforcer, but also of the (1) number of times it has been paired in the conditioning

process, and (2) the amount or magnitude of reinforcement paired with the acquired reinforcer. In establishing a token economy in a class or workshop for the retarded, in illustration, the strength or value of the acquired reinforcers or tokens (for example, points, marks, checks, stars, metal tokens, poker chips, foreign or American coins) will be dependent upon both the number of times these tokens have served as discriminative stimuli for other established reinforcing events as well as upon the amount, kind, or magnitude of these reinforcing events.

There are many significant classes of *generalized reinforcers* in addition to tokens that are of crucial significance to the development, maintenance, and control of appropriate social behavior. Skinner (1953) and Lundin (1969) have identified the most important of these as attention, approval, affection, and submission of others. Attention, for example, becomes a generalized reinforcer as it frequently has been merely a condition preceding other reinforcements. Attending to a person is the first step in providing him with a wide range of positively reinforcing events. Attending may acquire secondary negative reinforcement properties in the same manner. Attention from others has been the initial discriminative stimulus for numerous aversive consequences. Thus, the initiation of attention from a stranger may serve as a discriminative stimulus which results in avoidance behavior. The avoidance behavior is thereby strengthened by the termination of the attention.

Approval in the form of verbal responses and various gestures may acquire powerful reinforcement properties. Being recognized as "right," or "good," and being praised or provided some other social honor come to be reinforcing as they have served to signal the subsequent appearance of other reinforcing events. In the same general manner, other classes of events come to acquire effective secondary reinforcing properties.

As suggested previously, many adolescent and young adult retardates presenting exaggerated difficulties of personal, social, and vocational adjustment show idiosyncracies, not only in the types of stimulus events which are reinforcing but additionally in their reaction to the manner and frequency with which these events are available. It is not unusual to find retarded adolescents and adults who are influenced only minimally by the usual events of attention or approval. The teacher and counselor can spend an excessive amount of time praising and generally approving certain types of behavior but with little effect. As suggested, such attention may even be aversive to some. On the other hand, the behavior of other retarded individuals may be excessively dependent upon frequent and intense approval and affection for behavior development and maintenance. Other types of generalized social reinforcers such as affection may have minimal effect.

It is also observed in this group that many respond with excessive de-

pression or dejection whenever reinforcement is terminated or temporarily removed. Morale drops suddenly; behavior rate and intensity reduce abruptly. Such change in reinforcement schedule apparently is a powerful secondary aversive stimuli developed through its association with frequent unpredictable or prolonged withdrawal of reinforcement.

As a final comment, it cannot be emphasized too strongly that inappropriate as well as appropriate behaviors can be reinforced by a wide range of secondary reinforcers. Much disruptive and socially self-defeating behavior is the result of inadvertently provided social reinforcers. As has been illustrated previously, other behaviors of nonparticipation have been strengthened because these have resulted in the removal of the person from certain conditioned aversive stimuli such as disapproval or failure.

Developing New Response Combinations

The basic principle of reinforcement states that behavior must occur prior to being reinforced. How then is behavior which is not in the repertoire of an individual ever strengthened? This is accomplished through a process of behavior differentiation. After specification of the target behavior, or response which is desired, behavioral characteristics which are similar to or which approximate the goal behavior are strengthened; those aspects which are most similar to the target behavior are next selected for differential reinforcement and other aspects are ignored. Thus, through a series of *successive approximations* a new response pattern is shaped or developed. It is significant to note that differential reinforcement means that one aspect of behavior is reinforced and others are not. Unless followed consistently, behavior differentiation is an unpredictable result. This *behavior shaping* procedure has been utilized with considerable success in teaching basic self-care skills to the severely and profoundly retarded, as described by Watson (1967) and Meyerson, Kerr, and Michael (1967), and in teaching a wide range of social and work behaviors as reported by Lent (1968). In each of these reports, the education and rehabilitation personnel (1) initially identified a final desired goal behavior pattern, and (2) evaluated the present level of functioning along this and similar behavior dimensions. With the present behavior patterns which did occur, the treatment programs provided differential reinforcement for those behaviors that were in the direction of, or which approximated, the desired goal.

The approximation sequence which is reinforced is not a random matter. In most cases, the program provides various prods, physical guidance, prompts, prosthetic devices and redundant stimulus cues in an effort to insure continuous movement toward the goal behavior. As the behavior begins to closely approximate the final goal, the stimulus environment is

changed to coincide with that environment which will eventually acquire discriminative stimulus control over the target behaviors.

Highly inappropriate behavior patterns such as aggression may be shaped inadvertently by the procedure of reinforcement of successive approximations. Gradually, through a complex series of steps extending over a long period of time, such behavior is shaped by reinforcement perhaps in the form of social attention or removal from aversive conditions.

It is most important that there is a gradual shift in the performance that is reinforced and that reinforcement is provided just at the right time if effective learning is to result. "Just at the right time," must be translated rigidly into the concept of immediately following the desired response. Most educational and training environments are highly inefficient in promoting behavioral development in the retarded because reinforcement is so far removed from the response to be developed. Either the wrong response is reinforced or the desired one is reinforced so infrequently that it never gains much strength or else disappears through extinction as a result of inconsistency of reinforcement. Practice does not make perfect in the development of new responses. Behavior increases in strength only if it results in reinforcement. Additionally, as the reinforcement shift is made from one approximation to another which is more similar to the goal or target behavior, care must be exercised that the shift is not too great or that the behavior to be reinforced is not too difficult.

This requirement of immediate reinforcement translated into operational procedures to be followed in an educational or training environment requires the use of secondary reinforcement in most instances. That is, tokens in the form of visual or auditory cues, marks, coins and the like can be provided successive approximations without unduly disrupting the natural flow of behavior. This would not be possible if it were necessary to deliver reinforcers such as food after each approximation of the target behavior.

Aversive Control of Behavior

Mention has been made previously of the control of behavior by a class of aversive stimulus events. These are stimuli that strengthen that behavior which precedes their removal or termination. These same events can also weaken or suppress that behavior which produces them. The former is called *escape learning* by negative reinforcement. In escape the behavior terminates an aversive event after that aversive condition has begun. That behavior increases in strength and is more likely to occur on the next presentation of the aversive conditions. The person learns to take his coat off to escape the discomfort of being in a room that is too hot. He learns to get out of the crowd into a quiet restaurant when the noise becomes too great

in the street. He learns to adhere to authority demands in order to remove the threat of loss of positive reinforcers. A second means of controlling behavior by aversive stimuli is through a *punishment* procedure of following a behavior with an aversive event. Such a procedure results in the suppression of the preceding behavior. The adolescent stops his disruptive comments after being reprimanded by the teacher. In addition to these two basic procedures for influencing behavior by means of aversive stimulation, the related topics of *avoidance* and *anxiety* are of significance in human behavior. In *avoidance learning,* a behavior avoids or postpones the presentation of certain aversive stimuli or prevents the postponement or loss of positive ones. In other situations in which a neutral stimulus is followed reliably by one that is aversive, a condition of *anxiety* is developed. In such a situation, the person is unable either to avoid or escape the aversive event. He merely has a cue that signals the future appearance of the aversive event. The behavior which appears in the interim is known as anxiety. This condition usually serves to disrupt ongoing behavior and to render the individual less able to engage in adaptive behaviors.

In summary, the precise stimulus function served by an aversive event depends upon its relation to the person's behavior. If the behavior terminates the aversive stimulus, the strength of this behavior is increased. Behavior that is followed by aversive stimuli may decrease in frequency of occurrence. Additionally, as noted in the earlier chapter on respondent learning, aversive stimuli may produce a range of unconditioned "emotional" reactions. These respondent behaviors can come under the control of new stimuli through respondent conditioning. Thus, aversive stimuli can have a variety of effects on both operant and respondent components of human behavior.

Escape and Avoidance Behavior. Behavior that terminates a present aversive event is strengthened through the process of negative reinforcement. A wide range of behaviors may belong to the same class as each serves the same function of terminating the aversive condition.

As an individual is confronted with aversive events and terminates them through engaging in various behaviors, he soon begins to do those things that result in his avoiding altogether the presentation of the aversive stimuli. That is, he learns those behaviors which prevent the initiation of the original noxious condition. Some cue or preaversive stimulus becomes discriminative for avoidance behavior. This stimulus condition which in the past had preceded the aversive condition acquires the function of a discriminative stimulus. Such a stimulus also, through its initial frequent association with the aversive consequences, acquires aversive stimulus properties. These neutral stimuli become aversive as they precede or set the occasion for subsequent aversive events. Thus, the stimulus acquires the

function of a discriminative stimulus for avoidance behavior. Additionally, the avoidance behavior is strengthened as it removes or terminates the cue which also has acquired aversive properties. In this manner both escape and avoidance behavior are strengthened through the process of negative reinforcement or the removal of aversive conditions.

As noted earlier, many other conditioned aversive stimuli involved in strengthening avoidance and escape behavior acquire aversive properties as these events signal a lowered frequency, a delay in receiving, or even a possible loss of positive reinforcement. A teacher's frown is aversive as it signals a reduction in the possibility that positive reinforcement will be forthcoming. The teacher who is angry or who is frowning is not likely to provide positive reinforcement. Behavior that terminates the frown is thus strengthened. In numerous instances, appropriate behavior is evident as it avoids the loss or reduction of reinforcers in the possession of or at least available to the person. This type of aversive control is of particular importance in governing social behavior. Much of our social behavior is controlled by the threat that reinforcement will not be provided unless our behavior is "up to par" or "fits the mold." Academic and work behaviors are maintained at high quality levels due to the aversiveness associated with being deprived of a passing grade or of failure to graduate from a work training program. Traffic regulations and many other legal and social rules or conventions are followed as a result of the threat of loss of positive events such as money, acceptance by group, privileges, freedom, job, reputation, and the like. Such negative consequences are avoided by a range of behaviors which result in acceptable performance. The adolescent retarded in the work study program, as an example, does return to his classroom promptly from the training center in order to avoid the loss of his privilege card. The privilege card permits him considerable freedom of movement during recess, lunch, and recreation periods. This "returning to school promptly" behavior is thus under aversive or threat of punishment control and is being negatively reinforced as it removes the threat of loss of positive reinforcers. Such control is easily upset, however, under the conditions that the privilege card would lose its positive reinforcement value. This emphasizes the value of using a variety of positive events to strengthen those appropriate behavior patterns which may initially be controlled by aversive means.

In observing many problem mentally retarded clients, it becomes evident that the attainment of high quality performance or even task completion are not reinforcing events nor are these reliably associated with suitable reinforcing consequences. Making a mistake or producing an inferior paper or object is not an aversive event as it does not postpone or result in the loss of a positive reinforcer. Under such conditions the client could care

less about the quality of his output as high quality output is not a highly reinforcing event. The treatment procedure in such a case would call for rendering task completion with a quality product a highly reinforcing event through associating it with suitable consequences. Under these new conditions the retarded client will find aversive the production of unacceptable (nonreinforceable) items as these serve to postpone the receipt of the positive reinforcer, an aversive event. A higher performance level should become evident.

It should be noted that a teacher's frown or threat may also be aversive as such events set the occasion for the presentation of other aversive events, such as being sent to the principal's office or of being spanked. That behavior pattern which terminates the frown and thus avoids these additional aversive events is strengthened. The preaversive signal (frown) functions as a discriminative stimulus which controls avoidance behavior which in turn is reinforced by the termination of the frown or the conditioned negative reinforcer.

In an earlier example it was noted that such behaviors as scolding or yelling by teacher or work supervisor may be negatively reinforced as it terminates those disruptive behaviors of the retarded clients which are aversive to these adults. Such aversive control, however, is a self-defeating type of procedure as (1) the aversiveness associated with criticism may generalize and the supervisor may lose whatever conditioned positive reinforcement properties he may have, with the result that the client may avoid not only the criticism but the supervisor as well, (2) no new appropriate behaviors are being generated, just temporary control of inappropriate behaviors, (3) the discriminative and reinforcing control of the strength of the teacher's scolding behavior resides in the client's behavior, and (4) the effectiveness of the scolding as a conditioned aversive stimulus depends upon its intermittent association with the primary aversive stimulus involved in conditioning. Thus, the scolding would gradually lose its aversiveness unless associated with some other aversive event on occasion. In view of these factors, such aversive control procedures have little to offer and should be provided low priority as treatment strategies are being devised.

It is not unusual for some behaviors to be strengthened as these are incompatible with some highly aversive stimuli, that is, these behaviors avoid the appearance of events which are aversive. As an example, a retarded adolescent may engage in high rate disruptive behavior in the classroom as such behaviors are incompatible with attempting to read in front of the class. As reading aloud in front of the class results in being laughed at by peers for his poor reading skills, he is able to avoid such aversive events by being disruptive. As long as he is disruptive, the teacher will not

require him to read. In another case monotonous incessant talking by a mildly retarded adult may avoid verbal comments from others that may be of a critical nature. Thus, some inappropriate behavior may reflect avoidance learning resulting from negative reinforcement involving secondary or acquired aversive stimuli. Similar types of behavior, of course, could also be shaped by positive reinforcement, for example, attention or approval. In planning a program to change such behavior patterns, it becomes valuable to identify the factors controlling the behavior. The procedures used to eliminate or modify behavior patterns which were maintained by positive reinforcement would differ somewhat from those used in modifying behavior maintained by aversive stimuli.

The reduction or extinction of avoidance behaviors becomes a most critical aspect of a program designed to promote positive behavior development. Many retarded adolescents and adults have acquired through negative reinforcement a wide array of avoidance behavior. Work situations, situations involving competition, new situations, social interaction with strangers, situations that require a change in routine, contact with authority figures, to identify a few, become aversive situations and are avoided frequently. As a consequence the person selectively and effectively removes himself from a wide range of situations which hold promise of considerable positive reinforcement. Such avoidance behaviors may be maintained for long periods of time due to the difficulty involved in the extinction of avoidance behaviors. If the behavior is quite successful in avoiding the appearance of the aversive events, the person may not be confronted with the originally aversive conditions. He thus is unable to discover any reduction in the aversiveness previously associated with certain events or situations. In such situations, the program personnel must insure that the person does approach the originally aversive situation so that he may discover the change in reinforcing characteristics of the environment. In illustration, the aversiveness of a classroom or work situation may be reduced drastically by reducing the requirements needed for goal attainment. Requirements of completion of 30 minutes of reading, 25 correct spelling words, or 40 items produced in 15 minutes may be quite difficult and thus aversive. The retarded adolescent may engage in a range of disruptive and/or competing emotional behaviors and thus successfully avoid the requirements altogether. Reduction of the requirements by 20 percent, for example, may reduce the aversiveness of the tasks to the point that successful completion and thus reinforcer attainment would be possible. In this case a combination of describing the changed contingencies to the retarded adolescent and appropriate positive reinforcement of approximations of the desired behavior may prove successful in extinguishing the avoidance behavior.

Punishment. The operation of punishment involves the presentation of

aversive stimuli following a given performance. The effects of punishment are complex and depend on such factors as the strength of the behavior being punished, the intensity of the punishing stimuli and on whether the behavior being punished is still being positively reinforced. Typically, the more severe the punishment, the greater the suppressive effect. At the same time, the stronger the reinforcer maintaining the behavior, the more intense and frequent the punishment must be to suppress the behavior. Additionally, other neutral stimuli associated with the punishing stimulus will acquire aversive properties and may thus come to serve the same suppressing and reinforcing functions of other aversive events. Finally, aversive stimuli are typically conditioned stimuli for respondents which comprise an emotional state. This state in turn frequently disrupts a range of behaviors other than the ones being punished. In spite of these varied components of punishment, this behavior control procedure is quite popular in education and training programs mainly because of its immediate, albeit, temporary effect. The presentation of aversive stimuli following disruptive behavior may stop the disruptive behavior. The teacher's behavior of delivering punishment is thus negatively reinforced and thus strengthened as it resulted in the removal of the aversive disruptive behavior.

Punishment is not the opposite of positive reinforcement. Characteristically, it reduces the strength of behavior only temporarily. After the punishment and the threat of punishment is removed, the behavior returned to original strength, assuming that the performance still results in positive reinforcers. In many instances of intense punishment, behaviors that are incompatible with the punished performance are negatively reinforced by escape from the aversive stimuli. These behaviors that avoid the possibility of receiving further punishment make it appear in some cases that punishment resulted in permanent elimination of behavior when in reality it only removed the person from the situation in which the behaviors could occur.

Mild criticism, rejection, threats, fines, and other secondary aversive stimuli presented following behavior are effective in controlling future occurrence of the punished behavior as long as some agent or signal is constantly present to function as a discriminative stimulus for avoidance behavior. Even with these present, these cues lose their aversive properties unless associated intermittently with the aversive stimuli from which they initially acquired the aversive components.

Just as with positive reinforcement, punishment must be delivered immediately following the behavior to be most effective. Consistent punishment results in greater aversive control than does intermittent punishment. However, as noted above, once punishment is removed the behavior may return in full strength unless incompatible behaviors have been brought under the control of positive reinforcement.

It is not unusual to note a widespread behavior depression effect following punishment, especially following the presentation of more intense aversive stimuli. The shy retarded adult who is criticized severely by his supervisor for making derogatory remarks to a fellow worker may not talk to anyone for a few days, especially when the supervisor is present.

Anxiety. As noted in the preceding chapter, a class of behavior, typically referred to as emotional, assumes a central role in many systems and theories of human behavior. In the usual theoretical system, anxiety assumes a central role in the development of numerous patterns of maladaptive behavior.

In the present consideration of behavior functioning from a learning viewpoint, anxiety is treated in a manner that is consistent with the empirical orientation which characterizes this position. Anxiety is defined in terms of the behavior effects of certain stimulus conditions. As noted earlier, whenever a neutral stimulus event is followed by an aversive event on a number of occasions, the neutral stimulus takes on some of these aversive properties. It becomes a conditioned aversive stimulus. Under these conditions a disruption of behavior is noted that occurs at the time the conditioned aversive stimulus is presented. This suppression or behavior disruption effect may be viewed as *anxiety*. It is noted whenever a stimulus event through previous pairings has come to signal the later occurrence of some aversive event under conditions which do not permit the person to terminate or avoid the aversive event. If the person is able to avoid the later delivery of the aversive condition, avoidance behavior and not anxiety behavior is the result. Again, anxiety refers to the behavior suppression effects which arise from the situation in which a preaversive stimulus signals the later occurrence of an aversive experience. Further, the person is unable to avoid the aversive event. It is inevitable. The behavior which results from the presentation of the preaversive or conditioned aversive events and which occurs prior to the appearance of the primary aversive event is anxiety. This behavior will have both respondent and operant components. The range of respondent behaviors which can be acquired were identified in the preceding chapter. These respondent behaviors have stimulus components which may serve as a cue for verbal reports of such feelings as "fear without knowing why," "vague apprehension," and the like. There frequently is an increase in activity level, usually described as general restlessness and heightened muscular rigidity.

The anxiety reaction may be seen in the adolescent retarded who is required to attend an academic program that has become quite aversive to him. When he approaches the school he may exhibit a range of respondent and operant behaviors that serve to interfere with such classroom behaviors as attention, concentration, cognitive problem solving, and the like. Such

anxiety behaviors merely serve to increase the aversiveness of the school program.

The mentally retarded with a range of learning and behavior difficulties is in an ideal position to develop a large number of anxiety reactions. As he has little positive behavior that produces appropriate reinforcement, he is highly susceptible to numerous aversive consequences. He frequently is threatened with punishment and is placed in situations where aversive consequences are inevitable. As a result, his behavior becomes disorganized and inflexible. Attempts to reprimand him for not attending or to prod him into more persistent organized behavior merely serve to provoke more intense anxiety behaviors.

In view of this presumed proneness to anxiety reactions, it becomes essential that education and rehabilitation personnel become aware of the operations which produce such behavior effects. Effective learning and performance can occur only when anxiety reactions are absent or of low magnitude.

Effect of Pattern of Reinforcement on Behavior Development and Elimination

Reference has been made to various procedures for effective and rapid strengthening of behavior as well as to techniques not only for developing high rate behaviors but also of insuring persistence of these over periods of time when reinforcement is infrequent. These are areas of concern which involve a consideration of the pattern or schedule by which reinforcement is provided.

It has been noted that it is critical for most effective learning that reinforcement be provided immediately following behavior. Additionally, although behavior will develop under less optimal circumstances, behavior will be most rapidly strengthened when reinforcement is provided on every occasion. A regular or relatively even pattern of responding is produced under this condition. Reinforcement continues to be essential after behavior has been acquired. Although continued reinforcement may not add to the strength or to an improvement in skill level of behavior, it is necessary in order to maintain the behavior. A great deal of the behavior required for adjustment is in the repertoire of the mentally retarded person. An important question becomes one of insuring that the behavior will be maintained under future conditions in which reinforcement may be infrequent and variable.

A schedule or pattern of continuous or 100 percent reinforcement has some critical negative features. First, from a practical management point of view, it is difficult to provide reinforcement on every occasion of the be-

havior. Reinforcement in the natural environment obviously is not continuous. Some of our activities are reinforced on one occasion but not on another. Social responses which the retarded make are not always given suitable reciprocal social courtesy. Verbal requests are refused at times. The work behavior does not always bring about desirable consequences. Attending to teacher request is sometimes ignored. Typically, the more complex and social the behavior, the less likely it is to be reinforced on every occasion. The reinforcing agent, for example, the teacher or supervisor, may not be attentive to the behavior occurrence. The teacher may be preoccupied. The supervisor may be planning new activities for the group. These and numerous similar factors render continuous reinforcement of most behaviors virtually impossible. Further, the natural environment is so structured that a certain amount of behavior or number of responses has to be made before reinforcement is available. In other instances, reinforcement is available only after certain intervals of time have elapsed.

While it is true that behavior is strengthened most effectively by continuous reinforcement, it also is found that behavior extinguishes most rapidly following a history of continuous reinforcement whenever reinforcement is discontinued or significantly reduced. Schedules or patterns of intermittent or partial reinforcement which are more practical to implement also result in a behavior that is more durable, resistant to extinction, or which is maintained in strength over periods of time in which there is a reduction or elimination of reinforcement. More behavior will occur over longer periods of time. Intermittent reinforcement is a procedure by which behavior can be rendered resistant to extinction. In a real sense, it is a procedure which has a much greater payoff than continuous reinforcement. Given the same number of reinforcements, more behavior is maintained over periods of nonreinforcement after a history of intermittent reinforcement than following a history of continuous reinforcement. This would suggest that some therapeutic educational and rehabilitation programs in which the client is showered with attention and other forms of reinforcement may be contributing to the client's range of nonadaptive behavior patterns. A more appropriate procedure would involve intermittent reinforcement following appropriate behaviors.

Illustration of the durability of intermittently reinforced behavior after reinforcement has been discontinued was provided by the behavior of Mary K., an "emotionally disturbed" client in a work adjustment program. . After observation of highly disruptive behavior episodes involving yelling, throwing objects, crying, swearing, and general negativism, it was evident that this pattern had been provided reinforcement by the attention it attracted and the privileges it gained. Mary K. was viewed as emotionally disturbed and was not required to participate in work activities following

such episodes because it "might upset her too much." However, some of the work supervisors followed these instructions; others did not. The behavior had been reinforced on an intermittent schedule. Following the intitiation of a program of treatment involving ignoring the outburst, requiring her to continue work, and a continuation of a procedure of reinforcing appropriate work behavior, the behavior remained at high strength over an extended period. Only after persistence on the part of the environment for a four week period did the behavior noticeably reduce in strength. The history of intermittent reinforcement had rendered these behaviors quite resistant to decrease in strength during periods of nonreinforcement. She had been taught that in spite of long periods of nonreinforcement, if she persisted long enough, occasional reinforcement would be provided.

These relationships between pattern of reinforcement and response characteristics would be translated in a classroom or work training setting into the following procedures. Initially, in developing a new behavior (simple or complex), reinforcement should be provided as frequently as possible; after the behavior is occurring with some strength, the reinforcement should be provided less and less frequently. This procedure of periodic reinforcement increases the durability and persistence of the behavior. This procedure of changing the schedule of reinforcement in relation to the strength of behavior would result both in the effective development as well as the effective maintenance of this behavior.

The particular nature and pattern of intermittent reinforcement also exerts an influence on certain characteristics of the behavior being reinforced, such as the frequency or rate as well as the pattern of behaving within a designated period of time. The teacher and workshop supervisor are faced with two basic concerns in relation to the school and work behavior of their trainees. First is the question of the dependability with which a certain behavior will occur, that is, will the client follow the correct sequence in assembling a particular work item? Secondly, the supervisor is concerned with the question, "How many items will be completed within an hour, day, or within any other designated period of time?" A related question concerns the pattern of performance. Will the rate be relatively stable or will there be erratic interspersed spurts and work stoppages? The same basic questions are pertinent to the classroom teacher in the form of, "Will the retarded make the desired reading or arithmetic responses, that is, will he pronounce the words, will he solve the computational problems, and will be read or solve arithmetic problems at a high steady rate for a designated time period? The pattern or schedule of reinforcement has considerable bearing on the solution of these problems.

As suggested earlier, reinforcement on occasion is provided in the natural environment only after a certain performance level or number of

responses have been made. This pattern of reinforcement is known as a *ratio reinforcement schedule*. There is a ratio of a given number of responses to one reinforcement. On other occasions behavior is reinforced after a certain passage of time. This procedure defines an *interval schedule*. Reinforcement is provided the first response occurring after the interval elapses. Reinforcement under each of these may be either fixed or variable in nature. Under a *fixed schedule* the behaviors are reinforced only after these have occurred a specific number of times. Reinforcement requires the same number of responses over periods of time. Payment of the retarded client on a piece rate basis illustrates a *fixed ratio schedule*. Payment of the worker on an hourly basis illustrates the *fixed interval schedule*. In the variable reinforcement arrangement, the behavior is reinforced randomly around a given time or ratio value. Reinforcement depends upon elapsed interval or number but the specific values vary from time to time. Under these conditions there are no particular cues which forecast that reinforcement is imminent. Under a *variable ratio schedule* a response is reinforced on the average, for example, one time for every twenty-five responses, while the actual number of responses separating reinforcement may range from three to seventy.

Under a fixed interval reinforcement schedule, it is typical to observe behavior to increase in rate prior to reinforcement and suddenly to drop for a time after reinforcement is received. The number of responses vary widely from reinforcement to reinforcement. Thus, rather variable behavior is present. As the number of responses is irrelevant to reinforcement, the person learns to "tell time." Responding just after reinforcement delivery has never been reinforced. This is seen in "Blue Monday," a day in which work output is greatly reduced over Friday. Friday, as it just precedes the reinforcement associated with weekends, produces relatively high performance. If the interval between reinforcement is too long, behavior is difficult to maintain. Paychecks for the retarded on a biweekly basis frequently are quite inadequate to maintain high rate behavior. It is not surprising under such conditions that work behavior is erratic and of low rate and that absenteeism is frequent. Thus, a fixed-interval schedule fails to maintain a consistent level of behavior over a period of time and is a relatively poor schedule to follow.

A variable interval schedule of providing reinforcement reduces the pause following reinforcement. A stable and uniform overall response rate results. Further, it is difficult to extinguish behavior after development under this schedule. Much social behavior is under this type of control.

The ratio schedule represents the patterns of reinforcement which control most of human behavior. There is some evidence to suggest that the mentally retarded will function best under a ratio schedule that provides

frequent reinforcers. Under high fixed ratio schedules, for example, the rate of behaving is relatively low after reinforcement as a large number of behaviors must be produced before the next reinforcer is provided. Thus, it would be best to reinforce the retarded with low magnitude reinforcers on five occasions following a small number of behaviors than to reinforce him one time after a longer number of required behaviors even though the total amount of reinforcement may be the same. This is especially true in cases where adequate secondary reinforcers have not been established to span the time lag between the performances and later delivery of reinforcement.

Another means of dealing with the inefficiency involved in a high fixed ratio schedule is that of shifting from a fixed to a variable schedule. As reinforcement is provided in a variable manner, a smooth high rate of behavior can be generated as long as the reinforcers are of sufficient magnitude and do not occur too infrequently.

As suggested, behavior under intermittent reinforcement is more resistant to extinction than under the conditions in which continuous reinforcement has been provided. It should also be noted that resistance to extinction is a function of the number as well as the size or amount of previous reinforcements. Additionally, extinction is a smoother process following a pattern of intermittent reinforcement than is observed following continuous reinforcement. It can be said that the person has more frustration or stress tolerance after a history of intermittent reinforcement. He is less prone to exhibit aggressive or emotional outbursts as is observed in extinction following continuous reinforcement. Such relationships between certain classes of behavior and schedules of reinforcement would suggest that the low frustration tolerance and low disposition to perform in the face of failure characteristic of many problem mentally retarded clients could be viewed as a result both of insufficient reinforcement and of insufficient training on intermittent schedules of reinforcement.

Typically, intermittent reinforcement regardless of the nature of the schedule or pattern followed produces a greater rate of behavior than does continuous reinforcement. Although rate of performance does fall as the frequency of reinforcement is reduced, optimum rates are found under conditions where reinforcement is provided intermittently. Also, in general, decreasing the probability of reinforcement serves to increase the resistance to extinction. Such a schedule teaches a person perseverance. The person learns that following a period of nonreinforcement, reinforcement will occur once again if performance is maintained.

Of course, there is a limit to the infrequency with which reinforcement can be provided and behavior maintained. Increasing the number of performances results in longer and longer pauses after reinforcements. As the ratio increases the pause increases up to a point until behavior is lost. Re-

quiring the retarded to complete twenty-five problems or work units prior to reinforcement, for example, may well result in a complete loss of the desired behavior. Too much is required for each reinforcer. In general, it may be said that a low disposition to perform is a result of limited (infrequent) reinforcement.

Respondent and Operant Relationships

It is apparent from the previous descriptions of the principles of respondent and operant behaviors that both response systems typically are involved in the daily activity of an individual. A given stimulus event can result in both operants and respondents. In illustration, a workshop supervisor may admonish a retarded trainee who is being disruptive during work hours. An emotional reaction (a respondent) may occur as a result of previous aversive experiences with the supervisor. Concomitantly, the trainee may engage immediately in appropriate work behavior (an operant) and discontinue the disruption. As the supervisor (a conditioned aversive stimulus that exerts aversive control over the appropriate behavior) leaves the room and as the aversive stimulus components of the emotional behavior dissipate, the disruptive operant behavior may reappear.

It is possible, on the other hand, that the initiation of disruptive behavior, or even the initiation of verbal behavior related to the possible occurrence of disruptive behavior, may serve to elicit respondent behaviors. The stimulus components of the emotional reactions may in turn exert aversive control over the disruptive behavior. Appropriate behavior will be reinforced negatively by removing the aversive stimuli. These complex and frequently subtle respondent-operant interactions characterize much of human behavior.

CHAPTER SEVEN

Concepts of
Observational Learning

There is a growing body of data which suggests that the mere observation of the behavior of other people under certain prompting and reinforcing conditions produces predictable effects on the behavior of the observer. Bandura (1969) has suggested that:

> one can acquire intricate response patterns merely by observing the performances of appropriate models; emotional responses can be conditioned observationally by witnessing the affective reactions of others undergoing painful or pleasurable experiences; fearful and avoidant behavior can be extinguished vicariously through observation of modeled approach behavior toward feared objects without any adverse consequences accruing to the performer; inhibitions can be induced by witnessing the behavior of others being punished; and finally, the expression of well-learned responses can be enhanced and socially regulated through the actions of influential models [p. 118].

A variety of terms are used by different writers to refer to this class of learning, including those of "imitation," "modeling," "learning through observation," "vicarious learning," "social learning," and "role-playing." The term which appears to be most appropriate is that of observational learning. This term best describes what the learner does. He observes the behavior of another person or "model" and gains information about certain behaviors and related consequences under specific environmental conditions. This chapter will consider the various types of behavioral effects

134

which such observation has on respondent and operant behaviors of the observer. The major concern is with the operations which must be followed in order to produce a specified effect on the potential learner. What characteristics should the model have in order to insure maximum behavior effect? How should the situation be arranged and what classes of behaviors can be influenced? The reader who is interested in a detailed technical discussion of the factors involved in observational learning or in a discussion of the theoretical positions and issues involved in observational learning should refer to Bandura (1969), Bandura and Walters (1963), Kanfer and Phillips (1970), and Miller and Dollard (1941).

As noted, exposure to the behavior of others has three types of effects. First, the observer may acquire new response patterns that were not in his repertoire prior to exposure to the model. Second, exposure to the behavior of a model and the resulting environmental consequences may exert either an inhibitory or disinhibitory effect on the behavior of the observer. The nature of the effect is dependent upon the positive or aversive consequences which are produced by the model's behavior. The third type of effect which exposure to a model may exert on the observer is that of response facilitation. The behavior of the person observed serves as a discriminative stimulus for similar behavior on the part of the observer. Each of these behavioral effects will be evaluated.

Acquisition of New Responses

New responses, or new combinations of responses which are in the person's repertoire, may be acquired through observation of these behaviors in others. Mere exposure, however, is no guarantee that the behavior of the model will be imitated. Obviously, the observer must first possess the sensory capacities for appropriate perception of the multiple cues provided by the model. In addition, he must, as noted by Bandura (1969), have the capacity for representational mediation and covert rehearsal which appear to be necessary for acquisition and retention of more complex chains of behavior. The observer must attend to the critical discriminative and reinforcing cues in order to imitate successfully the appropriate response sequences. Thus, a person with a limited behavioral repertoire, as is true with many mentally retarded clients, may display only fragmentary imitation of behavior of a desired model.

To be usefull with the mentally retarded, a modeling procedure designed to promote the development of new behavior patterns must utilize a procedure of successive approximation. Complex patterns of behavior must be reduced to smaller subunits which are later integrated into more complex chains. Ullman (1969) has emphasized that one frequently does

not begin by modeling the final and perfect performance. Such may be too difficult for the observer to perform, or in instances involving conditioned emotionality, may be too aversive and thus may produce unwanted intense emotionality and resulting avoidance behavior.

In modeling new behaviors for the retarded, it is essential that the critical discriminative cues be distinct and that the characteristics of the appropriate behavior be emphasized in the model. Further, maximum effects of exposure to a model will be realized if the model is reinforced by those events which are reinforcing to the observer. Previous discussions have emphasized that the mentally retarded client presenting difficult problems of adaptation are idiosyncratic in the events which are reinforcing. It is also critical that the models used be of some significance to the retarded observer. Models that have little or no reinforcement value to the observer are not likely to attract the attention of the observer and thus not likely to be imitated. Models should be selected to match the characteristics of the observer. Appropriate behaviors modeled by a teacher or work supervisor who has neutral or perhaps even aversive stimulus value will exert no positive effects. The same behaviors modeled by a high prestige (high reinforcement value) peer are much more likely to influence the observer. He is more likely to attend to the critical discriminative cues and the precise forms of the behavior. Additionally, he is more likely to gain information about the contingency in effect between the correct form of the behavior and the subsequent consequences.

To the extent that modeling is a form of prompting, it is essential that the model or prompt be faded out in order that more natural components of the situation will serve the discriminative function of controlling the time and place of the behavior. Thus, as the observer engages in the behavior, he must be reinforced for that behavior in the presence of naturally occurring prompting or discriminative cues.

The modeling of new behaviors for the retarded learner often assumes an additional function. Such a demonstration removes some of the uncertainty over outcome. This is somewhat critical for many retarded adolescents and adults as new situations and new behaviors produce unpleasant emotionality due to a history of unpredictable aversive consequences. New situations have been unsuccessful. New behaviors have not met reinforcement criteria with the result that such behaviors have been punished or quickly extinguished through nonreinforcement. Modeling a new behavior by a prestigious model, including the contingent positive consequences, will provide valuable information to the observer.

There is evidence to support the position that emotional or respondent behaviors can be acquired through observation just as operant behaviors

are acquired. Bandura and Menlore (1968), in illustration, report that many phobic behaviors are displayed by persons who have no actual injurious experiences with the feared objects. Rather, the phobic behaviors result from observation of others being hurt by or responding fearfully toward the feared objects. Additionally, there is evidence that emotional response patterns can be eliminated vicariously. This is accomplished by having persons observe models engaging in feared behaviors without experiencing aversive consequences. This vicarious extinction of emotionality may be enhanced by evoking an antagonistic positive affective response. Bandura, Grusec, and Menlore (1967) provided some evidence of this in their demonstration of vicarious extinction of avoidance behavior in persons demonstrating strong fear of dogs. Repeated exposure to a model who displayed fearless interactions with a dog in a party setting and similar exposure to a model displaying the same interaction, but in a neutral context, resulted in greater extinction of avoidance behavior in comparison to control groups. An important feature of this and related studies concerned with vicarious extinction of conditioned emotionality and related avoidance behavior is the manner in which the model interacted with the feared object. The modeled approach behavior and the interactions with the feared object were presented gradually over a series of exposures and became more intimate and direct toward the end of the sessions. Thus, a gradual and systematic desensitization or extinction of the conditioned emotionality was realized.

Inhibitory and Disinhibitory Effects

A second effect of exposure to the behavior of a model relates to the strengthening or weakening of the observer's inhibitions of established response patterns. The observer may observe that certain behaviors of a model result in punishment. As a result there is a reduced likelihood that similar behaviors will be exhibited under similar circumstances. In some instances, especially if the observed consequences are quite aversive, there may be a general reduction of responsiveness on the part of the observer.

The observer may also experience a disinhibitory effect following exposure to a model who is either rewarded or who experiences no adverse consequences for engaging in behaviors that are typically prohibited. The degree of influence which a model may exert is dependent upon a complex array of factors. Although there is no pertinent research which has specifically identified the critical variables controlling the behavior of the mentally retarded, a range of model characteristics have been identified in research with other subject groups. Such factors as the age, sex, socioeco-

nomic status, ethnic background, social presitge, intellectual and vocational status, and the like have been demonstrated to influence the degree of disinhibitory effect which a model may exert.

Response Facilitation Effect

In addition to influencing the acquisition of new response patterns and to decreasing or increasing the inhibitions of established behaviors, the behavior of models may function as discriminative cues for behaviors of the observer which are not under aversive control. Observer behaviors that are neutral or socially acceptable have an increased likelihood of occurrence following exposure to a model who engages in these behaviors. A wide range of behaviors have been demonstrated to be responsive to such influence; assisting persons in distress (Bryan and Test, 1967), seeking information (Krumboltz and Thoresen, 1964) and volunteering one's service (Rosenbaum, 1956) represent examples of this influence. The degree to which an individual's behavior is facilitated by observation of others is related not only to observer characteristics but also both to the reinforcement contingencies associated with matching the behavior of others in a specific situation and to the characteristics of the model (Flanders, 1968).

Summary

It is evident from this brief presentation that the behavior of the mentally retarded may be influenced by exposure to the behavior of a model. In teaching new responses, the behavior should be demonstrated by a person who holds some positive reinforcement value to the observer. This exposure will increase the likelihood that the critical discriminative and reinforcing components of the situation will be attended to. It is also desirable to utilize effective reinforcing events following the modeled behavior. Such a procedure should increase the likelihood that the observer will recognize the contingency between the behavior and outcome.

In representing a desired performance through a model, the discriminative and related behavioral components should be emphasized. This may be done through verbalizing the essential stimulus components of the environment and the appropriate related behaviors and by increasing the physical characteristics of the critical discriminative stimuli.

The behavior that is modeled should be within the realm of replication by the observer. If the modeled behavior is too difficult for the observer to imitate, the situation may become aversive and thus result in avoidance behavior. The observer will stop his observation of the behavior and the modeled behavior loses its potential influence. As noted earlier, it is neces-

sary to model successive approximations of the final behavior. As each sub-unit of behavior is imitated and strengthened through reinforcement, additional segments are modeled. A final performance will result if the procedure is followed systematically.

Prompted rehearsal of the observed behavior adds to the effectiveness of exposure to the model. Following behavior rehearsal, the model can demonstrate the behavior again, with emphasis on those components which the observer is missing.

The concepts of response facilitation and inhibitory and disinhibitory effects may be used to good advantage by the education and rehabilitation program. These concepts would suggest that it is essential that appropriate models be available in a rehabilitation program. Desired behavior exhibited by an influential model is likely to produce desired behavior on the part of the observer. This behavior can be increased in strength through appropriate reinforcement procedures and thus rendered more likely to occur independently of the model as the discriminative cue. The practice of placing a group of highly inadequate retarded clients together in a program could not be recommended as there would be no suitable behavior models. As noted in previous illustrations, such a procedure merely produces the strengthening through various modeling effects of the very ineffective behaviors which are in need of change.

Finally, since avoidance behavior and related conditioned emotionality represent major problems in the rehabilitation of the mentally retarded, the use of modeling procedures should supplement more direct approaches to elimination of such inappropriate behavior patterns.

PART THREE

Psychological Evaluation of the Mentally Retarded Client

CHAPTER EIGHT

Behavioral Evaluation:
A Basis for Rehabilitation

Introduction

It is evident that many mentally retarded adolescents and adults require special educational and rehabilitation services due to various problems of learning and performance. An essential aspect of these services is that of the assessment of various educational, social, work, and psychological characteristics of these retarded clients. In this initial section, after a brief elaboration of the purposes or objectives of the assessment process, the relationship between the types of decisions regarding the retarded client which are made by educational and rehabilitation personnel and the requirements placed on the assessment procedures will be explored. Also, some of the problems involved in obtaining appropriate assessment data will be discussed. The following section will present the conceptual and methodological characteristics of evaulation procedures based on various typological, trait, and psychodynamic systems of behavior.

From the rehabilitation viewpoint, the basic purpose of any assessment activity is one of providing information about the client which will assist in making those decisions that are most beneficial to the client. All assessment activity, regardless of the discipline of the person or the methods involved in the assessment, must be evaluated from the pragmatic position: Do the data evolved from the assessment procedure contribute positively to the decision-making function of the rehabilitation personnel? Do the evaluation data provide differential direction in the development of general and specific programs for the client?

The initial question which precedes any assessment activity is a general one of "assessment for what?" What decisions must be made about the education and rehabilitation programs for the client and how might assessment

data assist in making these decisions? What types of information would increase the possibility that the decisions which are made will be most beneficial to the client? It is evident that numerous decisions concerning clients are made by educational and rehabilitation personnel and further that the types of decisions made as well as the types of assessment data needed differ at different stages of the rehabilitation process. The decisions may be of a *program* nature (for example, Is he mentally retarded and thereby eligible for placement in a residential program?) or of a *treatment* nature (for example, Should he be provided client-centered therapy, a remedial reading program, or a highly structured sheltered work placement?). Obviously the types of assessment data required to assist in these various types of decisions differ.

In illustration, following the general decision that the retarded client has the "vocational adjustment potential," that is, is eligible and feasible and thereby acceptable for further rehabilitation efforts, the next decisions revolve around such questions as, "given the present behavioral and physical characteristics, in what type of rehabilitation environment should this person be placed in order to insure maximum behavior development or to best insure broad vocational adjustment?". Stated differently, "What behavioral (that is, job, social, verbal, emotional, and the like) changes must be made in order to maximize the possibilities of vocational adjustment?". Related questions concerned with "how can these goals best be accomplished" are then posed for the assessment process to answer. Later, after exposure to rehabilitation experiences, decisions concerning placement or termination of the rehabilitation plan must be made.

In the special educational setting, the teacher and schoolwork counselor will be confronted with such questions as: "Will this adolescent benefit from an intensive remedial program?" "John has lost interest in the school program. What can I do about it?" "Sue has become a real discipline problem. Should I punish her or should I send her to a counselor for therapy?" Obviously various types of assessment data are needed for the program and treatment decisions which will be made in each of these cases.

Nature of Assessment Data

The specific information gathered during the assessment process and the levels and nature of recommendation which assessment personnel render are functions of numerous factors. Of significance is the nature of the conceptual or theoretical model of personality or behavioral functioning which various rehabilitation and evaluation personnel follow. For example, if the evaluation personnel view the social environment as being of prime sig-

nificance in the functioning and modification of behavior, it is evident that study will be made of the social environment in which the person is residing or in which he is to be placed for treatment services. The evaluation techniques used and the data gathered are quite influenced by these basic concepts of behavior functioning. Evaluation personnel with a psychodynamic orientation concerning behavior functioning, when assessing certain personality problem areas, would use certain data gathering procedures such as the interview. This information then would be interpreted in terms of the evaluator's constructs in the process of generating hypotheses concerning underlying factors which might account for the difficult behavior. He is interested in the *why* or *cause* of the behavior. More specifically, a psychologist with a psychoanalytical orientation of one sort or another would routinely use projective techniques as a means of gathering data. A psychologist functioning from a learning theory orientation would seldom if ever use such data gathering procedures. Similarly, a person with a general client-centered or self-concept orientation typically would use procedures providing information concerning the person's self concept and its respective components. The use of psychometric and other objective tests would be emphasized by trait theorists.

In turn, the types of data gathered greatly influence and in a sense even limit or restrict the types of recommendations or conclusions which can be derived. The data obtained, whether it is gathered in an interview, from the Rorschach, or in a learning task, will be interpreted by the person conducting the assessment (for example, psychologist, social worker, work evaluator, diagnostic teacher, psychiatrist, and the like) in a certain fashion by using constructs of his theoretical views of human functioning. Depending upon his orientation, he may render a diagnosis, a description of the personality organization and dynamics of the individual, and may speculate about the why or etiology of the problem behaviors. Even the work evaluator may render a "dynamic" diagnosis in his statement that the client has a "poor work attitude" and "minimal motivation" for sustained work. The cause of the work adjustment difficulties is viewed as being determined in part by the internal factors of "attitude" and "motivation." These differ little from such concepts as "fragmented self-concept" or "intense feelings of insecurity." Both imply internal sources of pathological influence which determine the overt work or work-related patterns of behaviors. A person with a social learning orientation may ignore altogether etiological or diagnostic considerations of the general psychodynamic sort and concentrate on describing the learning environment, along with the client's assets and deficits which he brings into this environment, which should be provided in order to promote adequate behavior development or functioning.

Role of Counselor in Assessment

Within the secondary level special education program and in the vocational rehabilitation agency, the school-work or rehabilitation counselor assumes a most critical and difficult role in the assessment process. Although he may not be involved in the assessment through any formal procedure involving direct contact with the client, he is a central figure in identifying the decisions that must be made and in gathering data from various sources pertinent to these decisions. In this decision-making process, it is not unusual to find that most of the information upon which the decisions are based is provided by personnel outside the vocational rehabilitation agency. The counselor must gather and synthesize information from a variety of sources. The psychologist, the educator, psychiatrist, social worker, work evaluator, and the like who are involved in various stages of the assessment process may be staff members of various private and public organizations. The counselor must select from among all the assessment resources available to him those components which not only are most pertinent to the problems presented by a specific client but which also hold promise of providing those data that will be most beneficial to him in evolving the best rehabilitation plan for a client.

As suggested earlier, the types of decisions which the counselor will make may be of a general or specific program nature or of a general or specific treatment nature. There co-exists with each decision the tacit prediction that the retarded person will adapt to or profit from the resulting program or treatment environment which is to be provided. Enumeration of these classes of decisions and examples of each are as follows:

1. *General program decisions:* acceptance of retarded individuals as rehabilitation clients; placement in a residential facility which provides a wide range of specific program and treatment possibilities.

2. *Specific program decisions:* placement in a sheltered workshop; termination of a social adjustment experience; providing on-the-job training; psychotherapy.

3. *General treatment decisions:* provide a well-structured environment; encourage social interaction with peers; do not use punishment or criticism; emphasize social reinforcement in the form of praise or other supportive comments; provide directive therapy.

4. *Specific treatment decisions:* whenever the client engages in disruptive comments during production hours, fine him 25 cents; following an appropriate social response, attend to him by smiling; whenever he makes comments denoting positive self-regard, reflect his feelings and provide warmth and acceptance.

Although the role of the rehabilitation counselor in the assessment process is examined in this section, many of these same factors would characterize the role of the special education teacher in an educational setting. Chapter 12 provides more specific consideration of the special education teacher and her role in evaluation.

Relationship Between Decisions and Assessment Data

It is evident, as suggested, that the types of assessment data needed may differ substantially depending upon the types of decisions which are being made. The assessment data needed for a specific treatment decision is most frequently quite different from that needed for most general program decisions. In illustration, quantitative test data concerning intellectual, verbal, and educational skills of a young retarded adult may be of significant value in the general program decision to accept the person as a rehabilitation client; however, it may be of absolutely no value in the specific treatment decision to use or not to use a variable reinforcement schedule of contingent social reinforcement.

After the general program decision has been made to accept the person as a rehabilitation client, the counselor is faced with the task of evolving the best match between the specific client's characteristics and the requirements of certain "environments." Should he be placed in a job environment in which he can be successful and at the same time gain experience and new skills which will render him eligible for other more remunerative positions in the future? If so, which one? Should he be placed in an on-the-job training environment? If so, which one? Should he be placed in a social adjustment and prevocational training environment? If so, which one? Should he be placed in a vocational training program? If so, which one? Should he be placed in a sheltered work environment? If so, which one? Each environment has many components which require adaptive behavior skills and all must be considered in making a decision concerning placement in each. This requires, obviously, that the counselor have an adequate knowledge of the behavioral requirements of these various environments. For example, the counselor must know what the various behavioral requirements are for successful adaptation to a given job as a busboy in a busy downtown drugstore before placing a client in such an environment and thereby making a prediction that the client does in fact have the necessary characteristics for adequate adjustment in that job environment.

With this information about environmental requirements, the counselor is in a position to request an assessment designed to determine what behavioral characteristics the client does have. In this behavioral evaluation, the emphasis should be on what the person does do in response to different

types of situations. The client may be able to follow verbal instructions but only in a slow deliberate manner. Under rush hour conditions in a busy downtown drugstore, to continue the previous example of the busboy position, the client may become confused, forgetful, and prone to cumbersome and disorganized behaviors.

In obtaining data to be used in predicting the manner in which a client will adapt to the behavioral requirements of given environments, observation should be made under those conditions, or under highly similar conditions, in which the behavior is expected to occur or is to be required in the future. Every psychologist is familiar with the case who has been described by the teacher or counselor as being highly disruptive in school or work setting but who is most cooperative during the evaluation conducted in the privacy of the psychologist's office. While the evaluation in the office provides valuable data (for example, that the person is not disruptive under all conditions), these data reveal little about the factors which relate to the disruptive behavior pattern observed in other settings. It may be valuable to know how the person will behave in work activities across a variety of work settings. It should be evident, contrary to usual practice, that highly reliable information concerning how a person will respond in a variety of settings or situations cannot be obtained by observing the person only in one setting.

A person may behave in one manner under one set of conditions and in another manner under a changed set, even though great similarity exists between the two situations. Behavior may be observed to occur under conditions in which frequent supportive social reinforcement occurs but may not occur under conditions where this social reinforcement is absent. Thus, to be most valuable, an evaluation report must describe the conditions under which behavior evaluation data were obtained. Such concerns for the stimulus conditions in which evaluation data are obtained limit the value of many objective and projective procedures which are used frequently in the behavioral evaluation of the mentally retarded. Such procedures as personality inventories, check lists, projective procedures, and the like are based on trait, type, and dynamic theories of behavior functioning. The use of these procedures is predicated on the assumption that data obtained under one set of conditions (for example, responses provided to test stimuli under standardized procedures of administration) are quite representative of response data obtained under a broader range of contemporary and future conditions. Such assumptions are generally faulty and result in data with poor predictive value.

After obtaining information about the behavioral characteristics of a client, the counselor is in a position to decide upon the relationships between the client's behaviors and the requirements of certain environments.

If there is a discrepancy between what a person does do and the requirements of given situations, the conclusion is drawn that a behavior deficit is
present. However, this deficit is not an inherent or absolute characteristic
of the person's behavior but rather a characteristic of situations which require more than the individual does in fact perform. The deficit may represent a performance problem or a more basic acquisition one. That is, under
other conditions the behavior may occur. Or under appropriate learning
conditions the performance required in a given environment, but which the
client does not have, may be acquired. In other instances, performance
deficits may in fact represent acquisition limitations. The retarded client,
even under optimal learning conditions, may be unable to acquire the kind
of level of performance required for adaptation to components of a given
environment or environments.

As a further example, in concluding that an adolescent has a reading
deficit, an observation may be made that he does read with appropriate
speed and comprehension at a fourth grade level on test materials X and
Y. The requirements of job B may be for sixth-grade reading skills. Thus,
there is a two grade level discrepancy between what the person does do
and what the environment does require. Assuming reliable measurement,
the class of behavior required is more than is in the client's repertoire. This
focus on what a person does do generally and/or in relation to specific environments is essential for appropriate placement in a work or social environment and as a basis for developing a meaningful program of behavior
change.

Predictions About Training Potential

The discussion up to this point has focused on a consideration of the match
between the present behavioral characteristics of the retarded client (or
more precisely on what the client exhibits under the conditions of our
observations) and the behavioral requirements of various environments.
The counselor, in making the decision to place the client in a certain work
and social living environment, is predicting that the client can in fact
adapt to these settings either with the behavioral patterns that are present
or with those which are reasonably expected to be acquired as a routine
function of the experiences provided in these settings. The counselor also
assumes that the environment will support the adaptive behavior patterns
which presently characterize the retarded client.

If the counselor, on the basis of assessment data concerning the client's
behavior patterns, makes the decision that there is no appropriate match
between the client's present behavior and the requirements of various work
and social living environments available in the client's community, the

counselor is faced with deciding (1) about the possibility that the client could acquire more adaptive behavior and (2) about the conditions under which the new behaviors would most likely be acquired. If the decision is made that the client would not profit from a training environment, the counselor may next consider the possibility of placement in a prosthetic or a sheltered environment which is designed to adapt to and utilize the behavior patterns which the client has. If the program decision is made that the client would not adapt to the minimum task performance requirements of a competitive employment setting, for example, the client may be placed in an environment which will adopt the performance requirements which the client is able to meet.

In making decisions concerning placement in various training and sheltered work programs, concepts of rehabilitation potential or behavior capacity are frequently utilized. Many evaluation reports conclude with statements about the potential or capacity of the client and related predictions about the limitations which the presumed potential or capacity imposes on the client. The reader will recall the previous discussion of behavior potential in Chapter 3. The retarded client fails to benefit from many training programs, not because of inherent limitations in his psychological structures, but rather because of limitations in the training programs that are provided. As there are no general means of assessing a person's "capacity" or "potential" for all classes of behavior, it is assumed that one can determine what a person can do only by observing his responsiveness to a maximally designed environment organized to teach or support that behavior. A statement which indicates that a retarded client has no potential to profit from a training program or which states that he cannot perform a certain task, learn a designated skill, or adapt to a given environment must be held suspect unless the conditions in which these observations were made are also provided. As suggested earlier, most present educational, psychiatric, psychological, and vocational evaluation procedures provide little reliable information concerning what a retarded client can or cannot do in relation to designated environments except in broad general terms. The person is described in typological, statistical, and hypothetical dynamic terms and not in observable behavioral terms.

Again, the counselor must make decisions relative to the types of learning or work adjustment experiences which would result in positive behavior development. Will an intensive personal counseling program produce those behavior patterns needed for adjustment to the work and social environment? Would an individualized work training program produce better results? What is his predicted maximal level of functioning in a specific behavioral area or in a number of identified behavioral areas? These are representative of the types of questions posed by the counselor. These

obviously are difficult questions to answer but the counselor must become involved in such questions as program and treatment decisions are made.

As suggested, many decisions about the behavior functioning of the retarded under future conditions (for example, what will he do? what can be acquired?) are made on the basis of questionable data. Some of these data represent standardized test results. Other data used as a basis for predicting what the retarded will acquire or how he will perform under future conditions represent little more than misconceptions about the predictive significance of various historical, etiological, and psychological variables. Data showing that an adult retarded has a history of complex and frequent stereotyped behavior and of limited language usage and has present IQ and SQ scores in the severely retarded range are not sufficient to decide that the person cannot develop useful patterns of social and work behaviors. Such historical, psychometric, and observational data are not sufficient to predict what a person could do under different conditions unless the person has been provided experience under these conditions. This position was illustrated, the reader will recall, in the cases presented in Chapter One.

In summary, the counselor is faced with the task of making a variety of decisions about the client. In making these decisions, predictions are being made about the person's adaptations to a range of work, social living, training, and sheltered environments. It is critical that highly appropriate assessment data are available to the counselor in order to insure appropriate decisions, even though such data are difficult to obtain.

Difficulties In Obtaining Adequate Assessment Data

Obtaining the best assessment data in relation to the types of decisions which the counselor must make is a most difficult undertaking for a variety of reasons. One set of factors relates to counselor inadequacies. Another set relates to inadequacies in those who conduct the assessment. The counselor may not ask the right questions of the assessment personnel. In other instances the counselor may be unable to pull out and organize the pertinent data having relevance to specific problems from more voluminous irrelevant and misleading information available to him.

Some of the reasons involving the counselor and the evaluation resources which account for the limitations or lack of usefulness of assessment data include the following:

Counselor Limitation. (1) *The counselor may be unaware of the types of data which will in fact be helpful in making the most beneficial decisions.* He may not know the absolute or relative predictability or lack of predictive validity of various types of data. Thus, he is unable to give sufficient direction to the assessment process. In other instances, the counselor

attempts to make predictions about what a person will do in a broad range of settings over extended periods of time and as a result seeks to obtain such "general factor" data from assessment personnel. The assumption in such predictions is that there is a broad trait of adequacy or inadequacy. For example, the counselor is faced with the question "Should this client be accepted for rehabilitation services?" He is asking "Will this client benefit from such services?" There are no assessment techniques which can provide answers to such questions unless these are stated in much more specific and detailed terms. What services are available? How much specific behavior change must occur in order for the client to be considered as having benefited from the service? What behavioral dimensions must be changed? These and numerous other similar questions must be posed. These questions should be in the form "Will the client make at least a minimal adaptation to situation A which requires behavior patterns S, T, V, and Z?"

(2) *The counselor may ask for assessment data prior to delineation of appropriate questions.* This may be done in the vague hopes that the data will provide something which turns out to be helpful. It does not require much clinical acumen to request, "This young adult has graduated from special education and is being considered for rehabilitation services. Please conduct a psychological examination." Nor does much useful information result from such requests. To continue, it does not require much to refer the client for a "psychiatric evaluation" or to an "educational diagnostician for evaluation of educational skills." With this general request, a psychological evaluation, for example, may test certain functions such as the client's intellectual, perceptual, memory, or verbal skills, or may study "personality characteristics" through such means as interviews or projective procedures. A composite report may be written which presents the psychologist's view of the client. Such a report may be interesting reading, and even in some aspects, a valid characterization of the person's behavior patterns, but may be of only limited relevance to the decisions which the counselor must make. Some of the data obtained from such evaluation procedures are more likely to be helpful generally than others. Data relative to cognitive skills, educational skills, perceptual or motor disabilities, and the like are more likely to be useful than many statements about broader "personality" characteristics. In any event, without specific requests for data which are empirically related to the decisions which are to be made, such shotgun evaluations are not apt to be too useful.

(3) *In other instances the assessment questions raised by the counselor may not be pertinent to the resources which are available to the client.* As an example, it may be helpful to learn that the client is reading at a beginning second grade level as such would influence the types of job or training

program placements which would be recommended. However, it would be of no value to request a psychoeducational evaluation for the purpose of identifying the specific factors underlying reading limitations unless the possibility of a remediation program existed.

Limitations in Evaluation Resources. A second major source of difficulty in obtaining pertinent assessment data resides in the resources for psychological, educational, vocational, social, and psychiatric assessment which are available to the counselor. These resources may be unable to provide the types of data necessary for most appropriate decision making. As noted earlier, data provided by different sources frequently represent different theoretical or conceptual systems. The language used, the assumptions made, and the inferences drawn from the data frequently are at best confusing and at worst create a false impression of erudite insight into the real characteristics of the retarded client. Too few personnel providing assessment data to the counselor are sensitive to the types of data which would be most helpful in the decision-making activities of the counselor. In other instances, the evaluation procedures used in gathering data or the inferential systems used in interpreting the data do not produce information which has a high degree of relevance to the decisions which the counselor must make.

Many of the objective and subjective evaluation procedures used in assessment just do not have sufficient predictive validity when used with the retarded. Many techniques and procedures designed to provide personality and personal-social adjustment status data are, for example, of questionable value when used with the mentally retarded due to such subject characteristics as limited language skills (that is, reading, verbal, and conceptual-cognitive deficits), limitations in self-perception and those of time-boundedness and stimulus-boundedness. Gallagher (1959) suggested that the feeling tones verbalized by the retarded are more likely a reflection of immediate experience rather than being representative of "a deeper core of personality." Similarly, Guthrie, Butler, Gorlow, and White (1964), in recognition of the limited ability of the retarded to verbally report feelings and thoughts, suggested that "their reports do not give us sufficient material to identify the patterns of attitude which they have developed toward themselves and toward others" [p. 42]. Burg and Barrett (1965) concluded that "assessing the interest patterns of the mentally retarded is complicated by their inability to read, questionable comprehension, poor attention span, and lack of abstractive power " [p. 552].

Other similar results suggest that the general language deficits characteristic of the mentally retarded would render many techniques of personality measurement of questionable value. Sternlicht and Silverg (1965), for example, obtained an average of 28 words per story on the Thematic

Apperception Test from a group of retardates in the IQ range of 52–69. Stories frequently were simply enumerative of what was on the card. In an effort to evaluate differences in fantasy aggression between a group of acting out, hostile, and destructive adolescents in an institutional setting and a group of peers who were docile and of conforming behavioral reactions, these writers (Sternlicht and Silverg, 1965; Sternlicht, 1966a) administered a battery of objective tests, including drawing and thematic procedures. About the only difference reported was that the females tended to draw more cats and the males more dogs—a result hardly startling or revealing. These results were similar to those obtained by Lipman (1959). The Rosenzweig Picture Frustration Study and the Children's Manifest Anxiety Scale were administered to groups of retardates identified as behavior problems or as behavior models. No differences between groups were found on any of these measures.

As a more specific illustration of the types of problems which are encountered when the usual test procedures are used with the retarded, evaluation of a self-report personality test, the California Test of Personality, which is used with some frequency with the retarded will be presented (Gardner, 1967a). In using the California Test of Personality with the mentally retarded, a number of questions arise. Initially, which level of the test should be used? Due to the lower mental age, reading, and general language skills, problems arise when a level appropriate to the person's chronological age is administered. When a level appropriate to the mental age of the person is used, some obvious difficulties are created by the nature of the items and their meaningfulness or appropriateness to such a chronological age level. A level appropriate to the mental age of a person which is administered to a seventeen-year-old retarded adolescent with an IQ of 65 would include such items as: Do you feel like crying when you are hurt a little? Is it alright to cry when you cannot have your own way? Does someone usually help you dress? These items may be appropriate for the typical youngster in the five- to nine-year-old range for which this level is recommended, but is of questionable appropriateness when used with the seventeen-year-old adolescent with a mental age of ten. In contrast, if the level of the test which is appropriate to the individual's chronological age is used, the following items would be provided: Do your friends seem to think that your folks are as successful as theirs? Would you rather stay away from parties and social affairs? Do you like to go to school affairs with members of the opposite sex? These items appear to be rather inappropriate for the retarded whose intellectual and social age levels are quite below the level for which the test was designed.

Finally, certain characteristics of the test items would suggest the hypothesis that the test is not an appropriate instrument for use with the re-

tarded. First, the test items reflect a middle class set of values (for example, Would you rather stay away from most parties? Is it necessary to thank those who have helped you? Should people be nice to people they don't like? Do others decide to which parties you may go? Do you usually act friendly to people you do not like? Do you visit many of the interesting places near where you live? Is it alright to do as you please if the police are not around?). As a great majority of the retarded are from low income and culturally disadvantaged families, questions concerning parties, social graces, and respect of middle class authority are of questionable value in evaluating general personal-social adjustment. Should the retarded be viewed as maladjusted if he does not respond in terms of the values reflected by the item content? There is obviously no easy or categorical answer to this question but at least those who have used this test with the retarded should examine their concepts of normality and personal-social adjustment prior to interpreting California Test of Personality scores.

In addition, other items if answered realistically in terms of the typical experience of the retardate, especially those who attend regular classes in the public school system, would be scored as deviant responses (for example, Do your classmates think you cannot do well in school? Is your work often too hard that you stop trying? Is schoolwork so hard that you are afraid you will fail? Do your classmates and friends usually feel that they do know more than you do? Do people often think that you cannot do things very well? Do you feel that most of your classmates are glad that you are a member of the class? Do most of your friends and classmates think you are bright?). Again, realistic answers to these questions would lower the personality adjustment score of the retarded. Thus, the retarded is viewed as having adjustment problems if he does not deny reality. If on the other hand he denies what is present his adjustment score is enhanced. This type of procedure is an inappropriate approach to defining and evaluating adjustment-maladjustment with the mentally retarded.

It is evident from this and numerous related illustrations that many procedures used in the assessment process do not provide data which are reliable or pertinent to the decisions made by the counselor. Presence or absence of color responses on the Rorschach are not related to whether the person will or will not be a reliable worker or an intelligent voter. Whether or not the adult has a higher performance score than a verbal score on the Wechsler Adult Intelligence Scale is not predictive of job success, social skills, or anything else that relates to the decisions the counselor must make about the client.

Use of diagnostic labels frequently contributes to the limitations in utility of much assessment data, and may in fact even hamper beneficial program and treatment decisions. This was illustrated earlier in the case of

Dena in Chapter 3. Psychiatric diagnosis of depressive reaction and hysterical neuroses resulted in a series of program and treatment decisions that removed the client from potentially beneficial experiences. The treatment focus shifted from an environmental educational one to an internal illness one. A conceptualization of her behavior as "being extra sensitive to criticism and thus requiring a treatment environment which would encourage and reinforce positive behaviors and which provided her with warm responsive support when she made a mistake or lost control" would have resulted in decisions which would have differed noticeably from those made. Under this latter orientation, the rehabilitation staff could do something. From the "disease" system, the staff merely watched for outbursts and sent her for psychiatric consultation when these occurred.

Additional Limitations of Assessment Data. The characteristics and limitations of such psychodynamic, trait, or "internal pathology" systems are discussed in some detail in the next section; however, three other sources of difficulty with assessment data are:

(1) *Faulty assumptions concerning generality of test findings.* The assumption underlying many tests based on trait or dimensional areas is that if the person demonstrates the trait in the test or in specific observational settings, he is highly likely to demonstrate the behavior pattern in all other environments. This is a most faulty assumption. Some behavior is highly specific. Other behavior does occur across numerous situations. This was illustrated in the data presented in Chapter 1 concerning the group of highly disruptive adolescent retardates. It will be recalled that inappropriate behavior patterns were eliminated in the treatment environment but remained at high strength in other settings.

(2) *Inappropriate interpretation of statistical data.* Statistical or probability statements are sometimes included in evaluation reports. As an example, the assessment report may state "Approximately 66 percent of people who present this test profile do not make satisfactory adjustment in program A." It should be recognized that this is a group prediction. It does not indicate that a given client has a 66 percent chance of being successful. Client A either will be or he will not be successful in program A. Certain probability statements have reference to groups but are not predictive of what an individual will do. Other types of behavioral data are needed as a basis for making the most appropriate decisions concerning the type of program or treatment environment which is best for the client.

(3) *Low relationship between specific decision and type of assessment data.* Data provided may have utility in making some decisions but may be of no value in making other ones that the counselor must make about Client A at time B. For example, information concerning the general intellectual skills or general educational skills may be of value in making a

general program decision but be of limited or no value in making specific treatment decisions. Thus, as has been emphasized, the gathering of data should be guided by specific questions provided by the counselor. In the absence of these questions the relevance of much assessment data is questionable.

A Psychodynamic Approach to Evaluation

Much assessment activity is based on various psychodynamic and typological systems of behavior functioning. In such diagnostic evaluation, attempts are made to understand the deficit and excessive behavior patterns of the retarded in terms of constructs of personality organization and dynamics. A search is made for underlying causes of the behavior which result in rehabilitation difficulties. Typically, the client is assigned to a category or categories within a diagnostic classification scheme, or at least speculations are evolved concerning various diagnostic possibilities. Examples of some of the questions that might be asked are as follows: Is this person brain injured or emotionally disturbed? Is this a mentally retarded adolescent with an emotional overlay or is he emotionally disturbed and functioning as a retardate? Is his excessive shyness due to unconscious concern about his masculinity? Is anxiety an aspect of a deep-seated neurotic disturbance or is the anxiety caused by some realistic factors in the home environment of this individual? Is this adolescent retardate's suspiciousness situationally induced or is this an aspect of a schizophrenic process with paranoid elements? Is the reading difficulty related to an emotional block? Such questions are raised, it is assumed, in order to generate information which will provide meaningful differential rehabilitation efforts. An example of the end result of such a typological disease-oriented approach is presented to illustrate the nature of the information provided. This report represents an extensive psychological and psychiatric evaluation of an adult retarded female. The report concluded:

> The final impression is of a primary mental retardation of a mild degree, very likely related to genetic and organic etiology. Chronic depressive reaction, related to passive-aggressive personality adaptation, passive type, and immature ego structure which is subjected to easy fragmentation under stress, is present. It is felt that even though an organic factor is definitely related to the retarded functioning in the intellectual, social, and emotional areas, this is further aggravated by the lack of a consistent parental figure, both maternal and paternal, related to real experiences of deprivation and rejection which has led to her poor, unstable, self-concept. The fixation of her psychosexual development on about a puberty level is related to the outlined emotional problems.

What decisions can the rehabilitation counselor make with this information? Should this client be provided further rehabilitation services? What types of treatment services should be provided? Is there an established relationship between "passive aggressive personality adaptation" and level of responsiveness to a rehabilitation program designed specifically to promote vocational skills? In view of the diagnosed "immature ego structure," how should the rehabilitation personnel respond to this client? Should the "ego" or "poor unstable self-concept" be treated, and by whom, or should the client be provided job training and these personality constructs ignored? These and a multitude of similar questions evolve from such an evaluation report. It would appear that the information provided is of minimal usefulness in decision making, especially in relation to those of general or specific treatment natures. Most of the constructs are quite unrelated to the specific client behaviors dealt with in a rehabilitation program.

In addition, in a traditional psychological/psychiatric evaluation, concern for the so-called dynamics of the behavior in question is routinely expressed. What is causing the behavior? What are the personality dynamics or conflicts of a young adult retardate which might be resulting in her inability to function in a social setting? As suggested, speculation about these questions is presented in terms of constructs of various personality theories. And *various* should be emphasized as most evaluation personnel are quite eclectic in their use of personality constructs.

Diagnostic activity is pursued, (for example, assigning to diagnostic categories and/or rendering psychodynamic speculations) under the assumption that such will give direction to treatment and provide some encouragement to the diagnostician in his predictive statements about the efficacy or relative efficacy of alternative treatment strategies. However, the lack of reliable relationships between test data, demographic variables, diagnostic categories, or other measures taken on the client *and* duration of illness or disturbance, response to specific treatment, degree of recovery, and the like preclude the possibility that one should be entirely comfortable engaging in such activity. This is especially true when the difficult rehabilitation client is involved. As one illustration, a number of studies (see Saslow, 1965) of hospitalized schizophrenics who had been provided training programs aimed at developing new occupational skills reported no relationship between learning and sustaining occupational skills *and* such variables as severity of psychiatric disability, psychiatric diagnostic label, or current degree of disorganization.

In light of these and similar data, the following conclusion by Saslow (1965) appears to be most realistic: "Present behavior capability has to be conceived of as frequently, if not generally, independent of much past

historical information and present personality diagnostic formulation"
[p. 288]. If the major function of the diagnostic task is to give direction to
rehabilitation efforts which hold promise of producing more appropriate
adaptive behavior, one should look for other types of data more empirically
related to the task at hand.

From a psychodynamic viewpoint, and this obviously reflects the orientation of the vast majority of people who conduct psychiatric or psychological evaluations, the inappropriate behaviors, whatever they might be (for
example, aggressiveness, suspiciousness, reading difficulty, hyperactivity,
inability to relate to others) are viewed as *symptomatic* in nature and as
reflecting some underlying deficiencies, defects, psychic illness, or pathology. Usually, recommendations concerning treatment strategies, especially in the case of the more deviant individual, are directed toward treatment of the underlying pathology under the assumption that once this is
removed, or at least reduced in influence, the symptomatic behavior will
disappear or improve. In other cases, considerable time is spent in specu-
lating about the why or underlying cause of behavior, but no differential
or specific treatment strategy is suggested.

An example mentioned earlier provides an illustration of this observation. A mildly retarded adolescent female was referred for psychological
evaluation due to a persistent habit of exposing her legs to the male members of her special education class whenever she sat at her desk or work
table. As noted earlier, the report provided an explanation for the behavior
in the statement "This problem is related to her great pregnancy longing
due to her oral dependency." In reviewing the case record for the basis for
this statement, it was noted that projective techniques were used. The response data from the projective test had been translated into the constructs
of the psychologist's personality theory. The disturbing element of such a
report is that it provided nothing of value to the rehabilitation personnel.
The major emphasis was on providing a theoretical explanation for the
behavior and not on providing meaningful suggestions about what could
be done to alleviate the problem.

Psychodynamic Model of Questionable Utility

Rehabilitation personnel should question whether the agency can afford
the luxury of such a time consuming, inefficient, and mostly ineffective
evaluation orientation which attempts to place the etiology or why of behavior in historical or internal pathology constructs. The statement of Kanfer and Saslow (1965) is most pertinent: "Among the current areas of ig-
norance in the field of psychology and psychiatry, the etiology of most
common disturbances probably takes first place" [p. 531]. In addition, as

suggested, there appears to be at best a tenuous relationship between psychodynamic constructs and level of response to specific environmental treatment. These observations force the conclusion that if an orientation, with related behavior constructs, does not provide direction in rendering reliable and specific treatment recommendations, such should be discarded and a search made for other alternatives with more functional and less esoteric value.

One additional problem posed by the psychodynamic orientation is that related to the concept of symptomatic behavior. Much of the problem behavior exhibited by the difficult mentally retarded client is viewed as symptomatic of some more basic or fundamental internal factors. The diagnostic and therapeutic efforts are directed toward identifying and changing the more remote but "basic" cause of symptomatic behavior. But how can the counselor decide if behavior is symptomatic or not? If behavior is labeled as symptomatic, the task becomes one of looking for underlying pathology to account for the behavior. If not symptomatic, no assumptions are made concerning *underlying* causative factors.

This exercise of labeling some behaviors as symptomatic and others as not symptomatic is further confusing because it appears that this is done so very infrequently on the basis of knowledge of etiology and rather frequently or almost always in the manner that Kanfer and Saslow (1965) implied that "symptoms as a class of responses are defined after all only by their nuisance value to the patient's social environment or to himself as a social being" [p. 529]. These symptoms, they conclude "are also notoriously unreliable in predicting the patient's etiological history or his response to treatment" [p. 529]. Restated, it appears that the assumption is made that there are two processes of behavior development in operation: (1) If behavior is a nuisance, it is labeled symptomatic and as resulting from some intrapsychic factors. (2) However, if behavior is not a nuisance, it is accepted as being the result of experience, learning, and the like, and if one wishes to modify this behavior, it could be worked with directly by manipulating learning variables.

Such an orientation is difficult to follow. A possible solution to the problem is contained in a simple but inclusive statement presented by Ullman and Krasner (1965):

> Maladaptive behaviors are learned behaviors, and the development and maintenance of a maladaptive behavior is not different from the development and maintenance of any other behavior. There is no discontinuity between desirable and undesirable modes of adjustment or between "healthy" or "sick" behavior. . . . because there are no disease entities involved in the majority of subjects displaying maladaptive behavior, the designation of a behavior as

pathological or not is dependent upon the individual's society. . . . Maladaptive behavior is behavior that is considered inappropriate by those key people in a person's life who control reinforcers [p. 20].

An Alternative Approach to Evaluation

In summary, the basic purpose of an evaluation from a rehabilitation counselor viewpoint is to provide support for program and treatment decisions and not to identify cause of behavior in terms of underlying intrapsychic difficulties unless these causes are reliably related to treatment decisions. Kanfer and Saslow (1965) have suggested that there is little relationship between methods of modification of a patient's behavior, attitudes, response patterns, and interpersonal actions and various dimensions of diagnostic systems.

It is evident that an alternative approach to evaluation must be sought— one that differs not only in terms of technology but in concept as well. Peterson (1968), in discussion of this topic, has suggested that as there are serious flaws in the traditional approach to psychodiagnosis, the methods of evaluation should be complemented and perhaps even replaced by more useful methods. He further suggested:

Not only have we been using faulty methods, we have been trying to get the wrong kinds of data, in the framework of misleading conceptions of disordered behavior.

The main difficulty with the topological disease-oriented approach to the study of human problems is simply that we are not dealing with disease types in the assessment and modification of disordered behavior. A child who strangles kittens or spits at his mother does not have a disease. He *does* something somebody defines as a problem, and this is so even when the behavior is covert and the judgment of the problem is subjective. The therapeutic need is to get the client to change his behavior, not to cure his illness, and the vital diagnostic need is for information contributory to the behavior changing enterprise [pp. 4–5].

An alternative orientation to the psychodynamic one which supports this basic purpose of behavior modification is one which focuses on the identification of those variables which have a functional relationship to the client's behavior. With such a focus, behavior is viewed as resulting from present life and environmental conditions, including interpersonal experiences. This represents a clear conceptual change from a traditional "internal pathology" one. It is of little value to report merely that the retarded adult has a "weak ego structure," "poor self-concept" or "passive-aggressive

personality" as these do not provide answers to such questions as: How can new forms of behavior be developed? How can behavior be strengthened or weakened? What are relevant functional relationships between the behavior and present environmental conditions? This orientation which emphasizes a behavioral analysis as a basis for specific program development will be described in the following chapter.

CHAPTER NINE

A Functional Analysis
Approach to Evaluation

Introduction

Rehabilitation personnel require assessment information that provides program direction. Decisions must be made about program and treatment activities. The assessment must provide those data that will result in the most useful program and treatment decisions. Explanation of academic, work, social, interpersonal, and other classes of behavior problems, to be functional, must be not only in terms of present factors, but additionally, in terms of factors which can be manipulated or controlled by rehabilitation personnel. An evaluation procedure, to be viable, must reflect a direct relationship between treatment[1] procedures and assessment data. An interview procedure designed to identify the effective reinforcing events in a person's life would meet this requirement as this type of information would be most helpful in a program designed to modify certain behavior patterns. An interview procedure designed to uncover presumed unconscious conflicts would not meet this requirement unless data so generated would provide

1. Treatment is used throughout to refer to various educational, rehabilitation, behavior therapy and other such programs. Regardless of the label attached to a program designed to influence the strength of designated behaviors, the basic principles and procedures remain the same. Although the equipment, materials, physical setting, and the like may differ depending upon who is administering the program and on the classes of behavior being modified, the program consists of strategies of environmental changes designed to influence the behavior.

assistance to the rehabilitation personnel in developing an effective treatment program. Additionally, if the general assumption is made that behavior, deficit or excessive, normal or adaptive, is significantly related to the social environment, the assessment process must involve the person as he interacts with and is influenced by components of this environment. What events, social and physical, prompting and rewarding, positive and aversive, are available in what manner to the person as he functions in various situations? This assumption has implications not only for concern for "explanation" but also for treatment considerations. Treatment becomes a psychoeducational task which utilizes the functional relationships discovered through direct evaluation or those based on hypotheses generated from assessment data.

As suggested earlier, one of the major deficits of many systems of assessment is found in the observation that little or no specific treatment direction evolves systematically from the data. As illustrated, what can be done if it is concluded that the client exhibits schizoid tendencies or is disruptive because he is emotionally disturbed? Does this render him unable to learn or develop new skills? Does this provide differential direction to treatment? The hodgepodge of terms used in evaluation reports and related conclusions are frequently a result of the fact that the evaluation procedure and related concepts are not related to any theory or integrated set of constructs or behavior principles. For effective treatment, one initially must have concepts of behavior development, functioning, and change which provide direction to the assessment process. With such a system, the assessment task becomes one of precise measurement and a resulting description of the behavior, and one of searching for the operations of the critical variables which hold functional relationships to this behavior. In this manner both behavioral deficits and assets are identified and these can be translated into program components. As has been noted, a learning approach offers this close relationship between evaluation and treatment. Evaluation seeks to identify present controlling variables which can be modified by treatment personnel.

Identification of functional relationships impose certain requirements on the assessment process. It is not possible to study the person in response to an artificial situation similar to that imposed by most psychological test procedures. Behavior is not viewed as being a function of some small number of stable internal factors which control behavior rather independently of the environment. As Peterson (1968) has suggested, "the object of clinical study is not the individual alone nor his environment alone, but the individual in his environment, as both aspects may be viewed in the context of general behavior science and as both may be changed for the benefit of man and society alike" [p. 11].

The primary task becomes one of describing an individual as he functions in various environments and of identifying those environmental factors which influence his behavior. Which factors may be manipulated? What environmental changes correlate with what behavior changes? How reliable or stable are these behavioral changes? In this endeavor, disease designations, types, traits, internal dynamics, and the like are all discarded in favor of a series of statements concerning functional relationships pertinent to the behaviors under consideration.

Such a functional approach explains the behavior by providing a precise description of the problematic behaviors and the factors that are known to control this behavior. Such an approach also suggests means of changing the behavior. Ferster (1965) has indicated:

> . . . a functional analysis of behavior has the advantage that it specifies the cause of behavior in the form of explicit environmental events which can be objectively identified and which are potentially manipulable. . . . Given an individual for whom money, social approval, control of other individuals, and various forms of social contact are reinforcing events, the environment available to the individual has a vast potential for selectively reinforcing those performances that would be effective in producing the reinforcing consequences [p. 11].

The behavioral analysis is an ongoing endeavor, ending only after the behavioral goals have been accomplished. Kanfer and Saslow (1965) have suggested that "in a functional approach it is necessary to continue evaluation of the patient's life pattern and its controlling factors, concurrent with attempted manipulation of these variables by reinforcement, direct intervention, or other means, until the resultant change in the patient's behavior permits restoration of more efficient life experiences" [p. 533]. As implied, the functional analysis also provides a systematic means of determining the effectiveness of the rehabilitation program in reaching the program goals. Continuous evaluation requires continuous attention to the elements of the program. If program components are ineffective, changes can be made and their effectiveness evaluated. In this manner, there is a continuous interplay between assessment and treatment strategies, with the result that maximum behavior change is likely.

In summary, a functional analysis of behavior is characterized by the following:

1. The focus is on the client's present observable behavior. The concern with a given behavior is with *what* he does, *how* he does it, *where* he does it, and *when* he does it. The behavior may be simple or complex, may be of various classes (for example, motor, social, work, academic, verbal, interpersonal, or affective), and may occur in a single setting or in numerous

settings. The focus may be on behavior patterns which are excessive in nature or on those which are deficit in nature. Such a behavior focus results in data which will lend direction to treatment strategies aimed at influencing observable behavior patterns. This behavior approach precludes concern with such internal constructs as self-concept, attitude, ego, wishes, and the like unless these are defined in terms of observable and therefore measureable behaviors. Such an approach does not deny categorically the operation of numerous internal factors. It merely assumes the position that an approach which focuses on that which is observable and potentially manipulatable is more likely to be effective in influencing behavior than any approach which deals with unmeasurable hypothetical events that provide little direction to the details of a treatment program.

2. The assessment activity is organized to identify those environmental variables of which the client's behavior is a function. These variables, instead of presumed underlying etiological constructs, are viewed as the most relevant causes of behavior. Those variables are sought which are potentially manipulatable by the treatment agents. Most personality constructs are ruled out in this assessment endeavor as being redundant as these are beyond observation, measurement, or control. An example will illustrate this position. A psychological evaluation of a retarded client included the statement, "John loses his temper and refuses to work when reprimanded by his supervisor because he has considerable poorly controlled hostility." The construct "hostility" is presented as being the cause of John's refusal to work. As "hostility" is not observable independently of John's temper tantrum and refusal to work behavior, such a factor cannot be viewed as having any utility. It would be most meaningful to report that certain actions of the supervisor result in John's refusal to work. That is, John's inappropriate behavior is a function of the supervisor's behavior and of other identifiable events in the present environment.

As has been emphasized previously, knowledge of the person's biological (sensory, physical, neurological) status is needed as the behavior analysis is conducted. It is evident that various sensory, physical mobility, and neurological limitations do influence not only what a person can learn to do but also influence the manner in which the social environment responds to the person. Caution should be exercised, however, in imposing preconceived functional relationships. Neurological defects may or may not determine, influence, or limit various behavior patterns. Until demonstrated otherwise, behavior patterns should be viewed as determined by, or at least partially influenced by, learning variables.

Explanation of behavior is in terms of present factors. Explanation in terms of presumed internal constructs has no place in this endeavor unless these can be measured and related to specific behavior measurements.

Even though historical events do not directly control present behavior, knowledge of historical events can prove valuable. Major group memberships in the past (for example, ghetto poverty subculture) and major sets of experiences (for example, spent five years in institution for the delinquent mentally retarded) may have distinct influences on the manner in which a person responds to various environmental conditions. Historical data can be valuable in that these may elucidate the conditions under which present events gained or acquired certain stimulus functions. The person's behavior, nonetheless, is controlled by present events. Factors which were involved in the initial development of a behavior pattern may have little or no relevance to present factors which control that behavior. Present events are manipulated in a treatment program, not historical ones.

3. Data are gathered to describe the person using behavioral and environmental dimensions that have relevance to procedures of behavior change. The basic *unit of analysis* is the relationship between behavior and an environment which maintains that behavior.

The study is made of an individual as he functions under environmental conditions. The emphasis is on *individual* assessment as the client's behavior is a function of a unique set of factors. The same general set of factors may influence different persons, but never to the same extent and in the same precise manner.

4. The evaluation is not completed until the desired repertoire is established. The initial evaluation data lend direction to development of a tentative treatment program. This program is evaluated, and modified if needed, to insure that it is most relevant to the program objectives. As the person is exposed to the treatment program, his reactions to it provide additional information about the factors which influence him. Again, initial formulations result in an initial program. The effectiveness of this program is evaluated from the moment it is instituted and is reformulated if needed. This interaction between program evaluation and program changes continues until the objectives are attained.

5. As it is not feasible to evaluate everything that a person does in all situations nor to identify the total range of variables which may exert some influence over these behaviors, the focus of the behavior analysis must be predetermined. If the adolescent is presenting problems in the social adjustment class, the focus may well be restricted to the problem behavior in this setting. In other instances, the concern may well be with much broader classes of behavior which occur across numerous settings. It should be recognized that most traditional evaluations are too broadly based and result only in generalities about behavior and controlling variables. Such information provides little treatment direction.

It may be beneficial to identify the total number of problems which a

person presents so that a priority listing may be established. In most cases, certain problem areas will be evaluated and treated initially. As changes occur in certain areas, treatment focus may shift to other areas.

6. The behavioral analysis produces a set of behavior change recommendations. These may be of a specific treatment nature concerning a specific education or rehabilitation program, for example, placement in a work training program in which frequent verbal direction and social reinforcement in the form of praise and the like is provided or in the form of more general recommendations, for example, the majority of client's disruptive behavior in the classroom setting is under aversive control. The environment should be restructured to provide more effective and consistent positive consequences. In other cases, general environmental changes may be recommended. For example, the present sheltered environment holds limited possibility of changing to the extent needed to insure John's development of more appropriate social and affective behavior patterns. The foster parents rely too heavily on punishment and negative reinforcement procedures and are not willing to provide the tangible and social reinforcement needed for positive behavior development. It is recommended that John be placed in a residential setting other than his present one.

In the following section of the chapter, attention is focused on the questions: (1) What types of data should be sought in the initial clinical functional evaluation? (2) What procedures are used in obtaining these data? In the final section, a detailed description will be provided of evaluation procedures for analyzing the effectiveness of various components of a program designed to change behavior. Baer, Wolf, and Risley (1968), Birnbrauer, Burchard, and Burchard (1970), Ferster (1965), Kanfer and Saslow (1965), Lindsley (1964), and Peterson (1968) have presented excellent descriptions of various aspects of the functional analysis approach to evaluations and should be consulted for more detailed expositions.

Types of Data in Behavior Analysis

The behavior analysis would provide quantitative and qualitative information about (a) the problem behaviors and the factors which appear to be related to these patterns of responding, (b) the interrelationship of problem behaviors, (c) the reinforcement hierarchy of the client, (d) the behavioral resources of the person which may be used in a treatment program, including a description of major positive behavior patterns and self-control characteristics, (e) the broader environmental settings in which the client resides, (f) the treatment resources in the client's natural environment of work, home, school, etc., and (g) the aversive control components

of the client's environment. A series of program and treatment recommendations would result from this assessment activity. Each of these areas will be discussed.

ANALYSIS OF THE PROBLEM BEHAVIOR

As noted earlier, the unit of analysis is a designated behavior pattern as it occurs in a specific environmental setting. Beginning with this behavioral unit, the analysis focuses on a number of related variables which hold promise of providing better understanding of the unit and the factors which influence it. The major activity of this analysis involves: (1) a quantitative-descriptive specification of the focal behavior, (2) a description of the antecedent stimulus events, and (3) a description of the consequences of the behavior. Following is an elaboration of the procedure of analysis.

Behavior. What behavior or behaviors are creating difficulty? The behavior should be described in terms of what the person does, including some indication of the strength of the behavior in terms of frequency, intensity, or duration. Additionally, it is valuable to know the history of the behavior. How long has the pattern been present? Under what conditions did it develop? In what other settings does the behavior occur? All of these questions provide information about the strength of the behavior. If the client is reported to be unable to hold a job because he does not get along with supervisors, is unable to budget money sufficiently well for independent living, and experiences difficulty in using leisure time, these specific behavioral areas will be studied. In each case, the general problem statement should be translated into the behavioral unit of what the person *does* do in a designated environmental setting. What behaviors are involved, for example, in his not getting along with supervisors? Such a description of the problem behavior should include an enumeration of other behaviors which accompany and appear to be an aspect of the problem. Description of a problem area such as "poor reading skills" may be accompanied by such reactions as "when he begins to read he begins to perspire, fidget, frown, stutter, and make derogatory comments about himself."

Another client may be reported to have limited reading skills and thus precluded from various jobs. In this instance, an analysis would be made of the client's reading and related skills as these occur in the presence of specific types of stimulus materials under specific conditions. This analysis would serve as the basis for determination of the feasibility of providing a reading program. For some clients, the problem areas will be few in number and well delineated in nature. Other clients will present a long list of problems which are present in many situations. In either event, it is desirable whenever possible, to analyze the problem behaviors as these occur

in a natural setting. The complaint, "he can't get along with people" cannot be analyzed except in relation to what is done with specific people under specific conditions.

Following an elaboration of what the person does, a description is obtained of what the person *should do*. This delineation of what the client should do is accompanied by an identification of aspects of the environment which set the behavior requirements or standards. The question is asked: Who is dissatisfied, irritated, displeased, or concerned over what the client is doing? This is of significance, for example, as those who are judging the client's behavior may be unreasonable in their requirements.

An examination of the discrepancy between what the client *should do* (for example, what behavior must be present prior to reinforcement delivery) and what he *does do* provides an impression of the nature of the problem behavior.

Nature of Behavior Problem. As indicated in previous chapters, behavior is typically inappropriate in relation to the specific requirements of a designated environment. Some behaviors are viewed as excessive in terms of *frequency* of occurrence (for example, disrupts co-workers too frequently with his conversation), *magnitude* or intensity (for example, he laughs too loud and distracts everyone in the room), or *duration* (for example, he stays angry for days at the time following some minor disagreement). Other response classes may be viewed as representing a behavior deficit due to a low frequency, magnitude, or duration in situations that require more than is present. The behavior in the form required may not be in the repertoire or it may be there but be of insufficient frequency. Thus, the problem behavior should be described in terms of the degree or amount of excessive or deficit behavior present in relation to the situation or situations in which the behavior is viewed as a problem. How much of the class of behavior is excessive or deficit? How much change must occur for the problem to be eliminated? If an individual is making an average of ten disruptive comments during a work session, he may be tolerated if he would make only five. Thus, the initial program goal may be that of "reduction of 50 percent of the disruptive comments made in the work session."

In viewing inappropriate behavior (deficit or excessive), it is important to determine if the appropriate form of the behavior is in the repertoire of the person. Has he or does he engage in the desired behavior (what he *should do*) in other settings or at other times? If so, the treatment plan becomes one of developing discriminative control over the behavior in the specific situation in which it is creating difficulty. If there is no evidence that the desired behavior has ever occurred, the treatment strategy becomes a different one of behavior shaping.

Environmental Setting. A general description should be provided of the

environmental settings in which the behavior occurs as well as an enumeration of the specific antecedent stimulus events which cue or appear to cue the behavior. Although neither the specific discriminative events nor the relative strength of various events can be determined in every case, it should be possible to develop some meaningful hypotheses about these events. Is the behavior more likely to occur at certain times, preceding certain scheduled events, in the presence of certain persons, at the presentation of specific types of tasks, etc.? An identification of these antecedent events is critical in some cases as simple modification of these events can produce important behavior change.

Consequences of Behavior. The most important type of data has reference to the question of what happens following the behavior. Does there appear to be any consistent type of consequences? On what schedule are these consequences provided? Do the behaviors result in the presentation of events or the removal of events? What are these events and do these events appear to be positive or aversive? Data about the schedule of reinforcement which controls the behavior can be of considerable value in some cases. The behavior may be undergoing extinction when observed. The maintaining conditions may no longer be present but, due to the reinforcement history, the behavior may still be occurring at a high rate.

From these data will come a series of functional hypotheses concerning those factors which are strengthening and maintaining excessive modes of responding or which are related to deficit behavior areas. For example, it may be hypothesized: The poor production rate is the result of the use of low preference reinforcers and a schedule of reinforcement that presents reinforcers too infrequently. As another example the excessive talking and disruptive activities are reinforced negatively.

Severity of Behavior. Some impression should be gained of the severity of the behavior under consideration. What are the short and long term consequences of the behavior if it were to remain at present strength? Will the client lose his job, be dismissed from the training program, be rejected by his peer group, continue to avoid those situations that openly reinforce those behaviors in others which are deficit in him, receive a salary cut?

Impressions about the severity of the behavior, if continued in its present form or in a less desired form, provide the basis for deciding upon the priority of treatment. As it is not possible in most instances to deal with all deficit and excessive behavior patterns, which ones should be given initial consideration? The top behavior item on the treatment priority list may appear to be unrelated to later job adjustment, for example, but may be of critical significance presently as the continuation of the problem behavior may result in the client's dismissal as a workshop trainee.

An impression should be gained as to the aspects of the environment

which view the behavior as being of a severe nature. The behavior problem may appear to be of a minor nature in one environmental setting but may be of considerable severity in numerous other settings. Is the behavior pattern alienating critical sources of positive reinforcement? The problem behavior may be of critical severity due to a limited range of positive reinforcers which may be available to the person. If the person has only a limited number of friends, a behavior pattern which threatened to alienate all of them would be viewed as more severe than a similar behavior pattern of one who had numerous friends and stood to lose only a few of these with continuation of the behavior pattern.

Effects of Behavior Change. Impressions about the effects that changes in behavior would have on other behavior patterns become important both in lending direction to the treatment program as well as in establishing treatment priorities. In illustration, assume that a bothersome behavior pattern is being maintained by social attention which the behavior receives from peers. Prior to a decision to eliminate the behavior by means of an extinction procedure (this is, through removal of the peer attention following the behavior), it would be necessary to determine if the client had other means of obtaining social attention. If not, or if these were limited, it would be desirable to insure that social attention from peers was forthcoming contingent upon other behaviors available to the person. As another example, a punishment procedure used to eliminate excessive talking may be quite aversive to the client and result in suppression of all speech or in suppression of spontaneous speech in social groups for a period of time. In other instances, the elimination of one bothersome behavior may result in the appearance of an equally bothersome pattern.

The possible positive effects of behavior change should also be estimated. For example, a socially isolated client who lacks certain recreation or social skills may, following development of these skills, be included in various peer groups where he may be able to receive a wide array of new reinforcing events.

In summary, impressions about the possible effects of remediation of deficit and excessive behavior patterns will be most valuable in deciding upon treatment procedures and in assigning treatment priority. This consideration emphasizes the critical and frequently complex interrelationships among the multiple variables involved in the development of treatment programs.

Related Behavior Patterns. A behavior problem, defined in terms of the discrepancy between what a person does do and what he should do as determined by environmental requirements, is only one of many behaviors in the person's repertoire. In an analysis of the problem behaviors, it is valuable to identify other behavior patterns which appear to be related to the problem behavior. Is the problem created by the absence of required

behaviors in the person's repertoire? If so, it would be desirable to identify the presence and strength of related skills. Does the person have the basic components of the required behavior or will it be necessary to strengthen these components prior to teaching the final behavior pattern required? Such data provide some basis for predicting what a person may do under various training programs. In illustration, a person with minimal reading skills is placed in a setting which requires functional reading skills. A deficit behavior problem is present. In this case, it would be valuable to obtain information about related skill areas such as vocabulary level, visual and auditory discrimination skills, comprehension and memory skills, and the like. These related data would be helpful in decisions about the type of program which should be provided. Such an evaluation of related skills, combined with impressions about other factors which have impeded the acquisition of learning the desired behavior in previous teaching situations, may result in the development of a successful treatment program similar to that provided Bill as described in Chapter 1. In other instances, related skill behaviors may be minimal or absent as was present in the case of Paul described in Chapter 1. In this case, it was necessary to build basic behavior components prior to shaping more complex work skills in a workshop setting.

Source of Information. Finally, the source of the information used in the behavior analysis should be identified. The most ideal source consists of direct observation of the person as he behaves under conditions of that natural environment in which the behavior is viewed as a problem. If this is not possible, a number of other means of data gathering is possible. First, those persons controlling various aspects of the person's life can be interviewed. The interview is conducted so that data can be obtained about each of the previously described categories. The informant may be the teacher, parent, sibling, peer, counselor, neighbor, workshop supervisor, or anyone else who has knowledge of the client's behavior.

Previous reports and records concerning the client will provide some useful data. Data obtained through observation under standardized test conditions can be most helpful in some instances. However, test data should be used with caution due to the factors enumerated in the previous chapter.

The client himself may provide valuable information about his behavior and those environmental events which appear to influence him. Information so obtained may or may not be reliable. For example, the verbal report of intentions, likes, etc., may or may not be related to what this same client will do under future conditions. The client, nonetheless, should be utilized in the analysis of his problem behaviors.

In summary, an analysis of the problem behavior involves an examination of a range of factors. The Specific Behavior Analysis Report has been developed as a means of reporting the results of the analysis. A brief ex-

ample of the use of the Specific Behavior Analysis Report is provided in Table 9.1.

Table 9.1. Specific Behavior Analysis Report

Name of Client: John K. Jackson   *Name of Evaluator:* Janelle K. Huitt
Date of Analysis: June 12–19, 1970

---

1. *Behavior*
   A. While sitting at his work table during work hours, John spends excessive time staring blankly into space.
   B. At other times, John spends excessive time making comments to his co-workers. These comments are unrelated to the work tasks and serve to distract the co-workers to the extent that their work rate suffers.
   Both these behaviors have developed during the last three months. There is no history of previous occurrence.
2. *Nature of Behavior Problem*
   A. The staring behavior occupies about 5 percent of the working day. The supervisor is requiring that such behavior be eliminated totally during working hours.
   B. John averages about 15 disruptive comments during the course of a work day. The supervisor would not be concerned if these comments occurred only three or four times a day.
3. *Environmental Setting*
   A. The staring behavior occurs most frequently during rush periods, especially when co-workers will not respond to his verbal comments.
   B. John initiates the verbal interaction. Such behavior occurs most frequently when work is routine.
4. *Consequences of Behavior*
   A. The supervisor frequently instructs John to return to work when he sees him staring. On occasion, his co-workers will remind him to return to work.
   B. The supervisor frequently reminds him to refrain from talking. His co-workers frequently make comments in return.
5. *Severity of Behavior*
   The supervisor has informed John that he will be returned to a sheltered workshop if he does not cease staring and talking during workshop hours. He has given John one week to make these changes. John is a capable worker and will be generally underemployed if returned to the workshop.
6. *Effects of Behavior Change*
   The anticipated effects of elimination of these bothersome behavior patterns are quite positive. His co-workers would view him as a more desirable peer. He would receive more positive comments from his supervisor. His production rate and his salary would be higher. The added social reinforcement that would result from elimination of the staring and talking behaviors would more than offset that which is obtained by these behaviors.
7. *Related Behavior Patterns*
   John has the skills to persist at the work task without disruptive staring and talking behaviors. John is aware of the problem behaviors and feels that he can learn to control them.
8. *Source of Information*
   Information was obtained by direct observation of the client in the work setting, by interview with the supervisor, and by interview with the client.

ANALYSIS OF INTERRELATIONSHIP OF PROBLEM BEHAVIORS

Following the behavior analysis of the specific problem behaviors that are present, it is necessary to speculate about the interrelationships of these various behavior patterns. In some instances, the various problem behaviors may be unrelated and treatment of one would have little effect on the strength of others. In other instances the problem areas may be functionally related or even equivalent. As a result, treatment of one would influence the strength of others. In illustration, a client may be excessively disruptive in a situation which requires behavior which is somewhat deficit in his repertoire. A program designed to decrease the deficit behavior and thus render the situation less aversive and more reinforcing may result in the decline and elimination of a number of different types of disruptive behavior. As an example of one functionally equivalent behavior pattern, an adolescent in a personal adjustment class may have various means of attracting attention from his female friend. He may attract her by (a) receiving praise from the teacher for his completion of classwork assignments, (b) helping his friend with her work assignment, (c) being critical of other females, or, (d) giving his friend presents that he has to steal due to his limited financial resources. He uses the first two methods of obtaining attention most frequently. As class assignments get too difficult, his behavior is deficit in relation to the requirements of obtaining teacher praise or of being able to assist his girl friend with her work assignments. These two behavior patterns become nonfunctional due to his behavior deficit. The remaining two behaviors become stronger in the hierarchy as these are the only means left of obtaining attention from the female. As a result of areas of deficit which make the attainment of desired reinforcement (female attention) impossible, other functionally equivalent behaviors appear more frequently. Changes in the difficulty level of class assignments which could render functional the first two behaviors could result in the disappearance of some highly inappropriate behavior patterns.

ANALYSIS OF REINFORCEMENT HIERARCHY

In addition to the reinforcers identified during the analysis of specific behavior problems, it is desirable to identify other reinforcing events which could be used in a treatment program. The success of a behavior modification program depends upon the degree of control which the program has over the reinforcing events which are of high value to the client. Relatively weak reinforcers may be maintaining rather disruptive or bothersome behavior patterns due to the fact that there are no more powerful positive events available for appropriate behavior. The availability of more powerful reinforcers may result in dramatic changes in a person's behavior when

these are used to strengthen and maintain behavior which competes with the problem behaviors.

The types of reinforcing events which influence behavior have been discussed in previous chapters and will be elaborated upon in the following chapter. It should be remembered that the types of events as well as the relative strength of events will vary considerably from person to person and even from time to time for the same person. Tharp and Wetzel (1969) have suggested that potential reinforcers can be grouped into activity reinforcers, material reinforcers, and people reinforcers. Other writers have suggested additional classification systems such as those which can be consumed, those which can be manipulated, and those which can be exchanged for a range of back-up reinforcers. The important factor to remember, however, is that most every setting includes potential reinforcing events. An analysis of an individual and his environment will produce both a range of events and a tentative hierarchy of these events on the basis of relative strength. It is desirable to be highly specific in this enumeration. In illustration, it is usually not sufficient just to indicate that a person is influenced by social reinforcement. It would be necessary to identify the types of social reinforcement (attention, praise, approval, affection, control of others, etc.) and the classes of influential social agents (peers, male authority figures, older females, athletes, etc.). A person may be influenced by social reinforcement of attention and affection, but only if provided by peers. The same consequences may have neutral or even negative effect if provided by adult authority figures.

There should be some data concerning the schedule of reinforcement under which the person may function. Some persons require frequent reinforcement in order to maintain behaviors. Others can function for extended periods of time prior to presentation by others of a reinforcing event.

It is also important in this analysis to obtain some information about (a) the availability of various events which hold a reinforcing function for the client and (b) the possibility of providing various events in the setting in which the problem behavior occurs. Who controls the important reinforcers and how willing are these individuals to make the reinforcers available contingent upon desired behavior? Some people are unable to provide reinforcers on a contingency basis. Institutional regulations and philosophies preclude the administration of a contingency management system in some settings regardless of the abundant availability of reinforcers.

A final consideration in identifying and ranking reinforcing events is that of the satiation level of each event. Some events are highly reinforcing but lose their value quickly after being used a few times. Others maintain high value over long periods of use, however. These satiation aspects should be noted.

In summary, the development of a reinforcer hierarchy should include the following information: (a) specific description of reinforcer, including the agent dispensing it, (b) the availability of the reinforcer in various settings, (c) the magnitude of the reinforcer required for effectiveness, (d) the general schedule of reinforcement required for strengthening and maintaining behavior, and (e) the satiation characteristics of various reinforcers.

ANALYSIS OF SUPPORTIVE BEHAVIOR RESOURCES

In evaluating problem behavior patterns, it is valuable to identify behavior assets which may be used in a program of treatment. The behavioral assets identified are in addition to those more directly related behavior patterns discussed earlier. What does the person do well in the setting in which the problems occur? What other positive behavior patterns are present which may be used as a starting point for developing more appropriate behavior in the problem areas?

The analysis should also include a study of the self-control components of the person's repertoire. Does he have any patterns of self-control? Is he able to control his behavior in problem situations or is his behavior mostly under the control of events in the external environment? Answers to these and related questions provide valuable direction to the development of a treatment program.

ANALYSIS OF AVERSIVE ASPECTS OF THE ENVIRONMENT

We have seen that much of the problem behavior of the retarded client is related to aversive components of the environment. It is not unusual to find that an excessive amount of the person's behavior is controlled by aversive events, either through punishment or negative reinforcement. It becomes important to determine the proportions of a person's repertoire which are controlled by positive and by aversive events. Severe deviant modes of behavior functioning may result when too much of the person's repertoire consists of escape and avoidance patterns. A person may become excessively nonresponsive to components of his environment under this condition. The specific aversive components of the person's environment, along with the magnitude and manner of control by the aversive components should be identified. Such information is necessary in order to design a program which is most relevant to a specific client. A program objective, for example, of shifting behavior control from aversive control may result in highly disruptive behavior patterns, as an attempt is made to shape desired behviors through positive reinforcement. Such reactions can be most disconcerting to the treatment personnel as well as to the client. A knowl-

edge of the aversive components in the person's environment and the degree of control which these components hold over various behavior patterns could be used in designing a program which would avoid such consequences.

ANALYSIS OF BROADER ENVIRONMENTAL SETTING

The client functions in a variety of settings—home, neighborhood, peer group, work, school, and the like. An analysis should be made of the major components of these settings in order to gain an impression of those factors which influence the client's behavior. A treatment program may be successful in strengthening various behavior patterns. A critical consideration, however, becomes one of how the behaviors will be maintained in the natural environment outside the treatment setting. What behaviors will be reinforced and therefore maintained? What behaviors will be ignored or even actively punished through ridicule, rejection, or even direct physical assault? All of these factors must be given consideration in development of a treatment program.

AVAILABILITY OF TREATMENT RESOURCES IN THE NATURAL SETTING

A closely related consideration concerns the identification of persons in the natural settings who can be used in a program designed to modify the client's behavior. The most desirable place for instigating behavior modification programs is the client's classroom, living unit, work setting, recreation setting, home, and the like. Whenever the client is removed from the natural surroundings, the environment becomes an artificial one. Such a practice creates problems of generalization of treatment effects. How available and how adequate are these agents in the natural environment for initiating and maintaining a treatment program? Can the workshop supervisor, teacher, attendant, nurse, counselor, parent, sibling, peer, etc., be used?

An equally important question is that of "to what extent can the person be used in his own program of behavior change?" Will knowledge of the treatment objectives and the reinforcement contingencies influence his self-cuing and self-reinforcing behaviors? How much verbal control does he have over other classes of his behavior? Is there a suitable relationship between what the person commits himself to accomplish and what he will in fact accomplish under appropriate reinforcing conditions? These are questions of the degree of self-control which he will be able to utilize.

Treatment Program Recommendations

The end result of the analysis of these numerous components of the person's behavior and his environment will be a series of recommendations. These may, using the classification mentioned in the previous chapter, consist of general and specific program recommendations as well as general and specific treatment recommendations. As emphasized earlier, the treatment recommendations are stated in terms of functional hypotheses and are tentative in nature. As the recommendations are implemented, these functional hypotheses are modified to reflect the empirical findings.

Analysis of Program Effectiveness

FUNCTIONAL ANALYSIS OF BEHAVIOR

In the preceding clinical behavior analysis, hypotheses were generated concerning those environmental conditions, both discriminative and reinforcing, which exert control over specified behaviors. These hypotheses concerning functional relationships between stimulus events and behavioral events, must be accepted as mere hypotheses initially and not viewed as relationships which do in fact exist. Both antecedent and subsequent events which do control behavior are frequently subtle and complex, and are quite difficult to discern through limited observation. As discussed briefly in an earlier chapter, there are procedures which the behavior therapist can use in the natural work, school, or training setting either to determine more precisely the nature of factors which do control behavior in an environment or to evaluate the effectiveness of various components of a treatment or intervention program. In evaluating treatment effects, the analytic procedures not only must reveal that some behavior change has in fact taken place but additionally must identify the events that are influencing this change. Or in determining the behavior control function of any event in the person's environment, there must be demonstration of a reliable relationship between changes in the stimulus event and changes in the behavior under study.

The analytic procedures are basically the same in both instances. In attempting to identify the factors that control behavior as it presently occurs in a given natural environmental setting, observation is made of the behavior and functional hypotheses are developed about maintaining events which are occurring naturally in this environment. These suspected controlling events are modified in some systematic manner and the effects on behavior of these changes are studied. In evaluating a treatment program, various procedures are instituted, either in the natural environment of the person or in a "treatment" environment (for example, specially de-

signed work training program, behavior-oriented counseling, etc.) and behavioral effects are determined. The functional analysis procedure is comprised of the closely related operations of: (a) specification of behavior, (b) description of environment in which behavior occurs, (c) measurement of strength of behavior under specified conditions of the environment, (d) initiation of treatment, and (e) continued measurement of behavior strength. Each of these operations will be described. Following this, a description will be presented of additional means of establishing the reliability of the relationship between specific treatment procedures and changes in behavior strength.

Specification of Behavior. This initial step in a functional analysis of specification of the behavior under study can present considerable difficulty. The behavior must be *observable*. It also must be defined in such a manner that reliable observations can be obtained. This implies that independent observers can with regularity agree on the presence or absence of the behavior. Unless persons involved in the treatment program can agree on the definition and on the occurrence or nonoccurrence of the behavior, this initial criterion of specification of behavior has not been met. Under these conditions, the effects of treatment cannot be evaluated. The value of most education and rehabilitation programs are difficult to determine because the program objectives are stated in such general and frequently vague terms. Unless the objectives of a program are stated in terms of behaviors that can be observed reliably, the influence of components of the program cannot be evaluated. Program objectives stated in such general terms as development of emotional maturity, skill in getting along with peers, good work attitude, ego strength, positive self-concept, vocational adjustment, and the like do not meet the initial criterion of specification of behavior. It becomes necessary to translate general program objectives into specific observable behaviors. Similarly, it becomes necessary to translate general behavior descriptions of problem areas into specific observable behaviors. Description of problem areas in such terms as poor social skills, poor work attitude, emotional immaturity, low motivation, and the like are much too general. As an example "poor work attitude" is a class name for a wide variety of behavior. The specification of behavior requirement states that the general term "poor work attitude" be translated into specific behaviors which a person exhibits in the work or work-related setting. Poor work attitude, in illustration, may be defined in terms of (a) being late for work frequently, (b) initiating arguments with supervisor, (c) open criticism of work setting and co-workers, (d) low rate of work output, (e) frequent absenteeism, and (f) refusal to work overtime. If delineated in operational terms, these behaviors can be observed by anyone and described in terms of frequency of occurrence.

It should be valuable to digress briefly to recognize that "attitude" is viewed in some psychodynamic systems of behavior as an internal factor which causes the specific behaviors enumerated. These behaviors are viewed as symptom manifestations of this internal factor. In this model, the attitude becomes the focus of treatment under the assumption that changes in attitude will result in changes in the symptomatic behaviors. Such conceptualization, however, is rejected by the behavior modification approach as such a concept of attitude does not meet the specification of behavior criterion. In the behavior system, attitude is merely a descriptive label that is applied after observations are made of the manner in which a person responds to various environmental settings. Attitude is not observable or measurable independently of the group of behaviors enumerated. Behaviors which are observable are potentially modifiable. If reliable observations of a behavior cannot be completed, the behavior, for treatment purposes, does not exist.

Description of Environment. As noted in an earlier section, behavior is described as it occurs in an environment. The environment contains antecedent and subsequent events. Some of these antecedent events function as discriminative stimuli; others are neutral and exert no systematic reinforcing influence. These antecedent and subsequent events must be defined in terms that produce reliable observations. Such questions are raised as: What occurs in the environment after a designated behavior occurs and how frequently does this behavior produce this event? As discussed earlier, such observations form the basis for hypotheses about the controlling aspects of the environment.

Measurement of Behavior Strength. After behavior has been specified as it occurs in a described environment, some measure of the strength of the behavior is obtained prior to initiation of changes in the environment. The basic measure of behavior strength is that of frequency of occurrence within designated periods of time. Thirty-five units were completed during the first day, forty-two on the second, thirty-eight on the third, and so on. John became involved in four arguments during the first hour, three during the second hour, five during the third hour, etc. This rate of behavior under pretreatment environmental conditions serves as a baseline against which future measures of behavior strength can be evaluated. The frequency of behavior may be recorded continuously over a designated time period or at certain specified intervals within a time period. A teacher may keep a total count of the number of disruptive comments which a retarded adolescent makes in a social adjustment class which meets for 60 minutes daily. This may be done through a cumulative marking of each occurrence on a card which the teacher keeps on his desk. Some observers have found a wrist counter to be convenient for this purpose (Lindsley, 1968). Tate

(1968) described a system of automatic mechanical recording of work behaviors. Regardless of the procedure followed in recording frequency, the data produced by continuous recording can be translated into rate of performance. The recording of frequency of disruptive comments may produce such rate data as: "15 disruptive comments per 60 minute period or one comment every 4 minutes over the 15 days of baseline observation."

The value of continuous recording over specific time periods is illustrated in the following report of a retarded client attending a work training

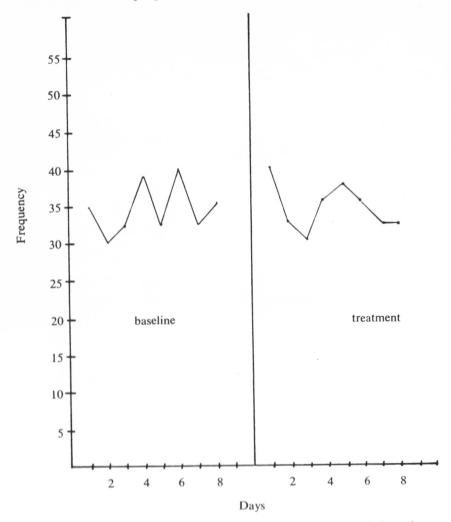

Figure 9.1. Average Rate of Performance for 15-Minute Periods under Baseline and Treatment Conditions

program. Recording was made of client's production under baseline conditions of monetary reinforcement provided at the end of the work day and based on the number of items completed. Each completed item was dropped down a chute and was automatically recorded on a counter. Accompanying recording devices printed the number of items completed every fifteen minutes and provided a permanent record of performance. In an effort to increase the rate of production, an added feature of intermittent social reinforcement during work periods was added. A female counselor,

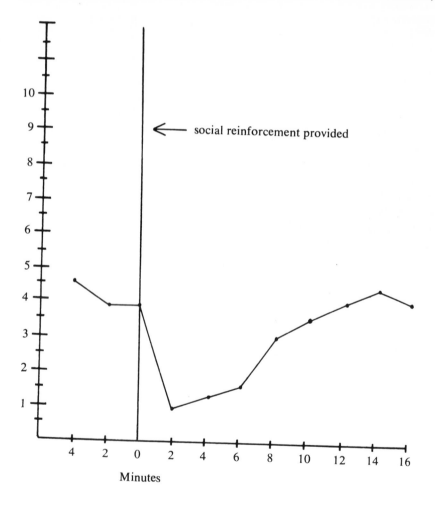

Figure 9.2. Average Rate of Performance under Conditions of Social Reinforcement

a rather attractive young lady, would pass by the clients' work table on the average of six times an hour and provide social attention in the form of praise (for example, "You are working hard today." "Keep up the good work." "I'm proud of your good performance."). The comments were made following appropriate work behavior. An examination of performance records presented in Figure 9.1 revealed no reliable change in the rate of production even though casual observation of the client suggested that his production rate was noticeably higher than prior to initiation of the social reinforcement procedure. The recording procedure was changed in order to obtain a continuous rate record. This record revealed that following social reinforcement, there was a definite decline in the rate of production for four or five minutes, after which there was a steady increase which reached a level considerably above that observed during the baseline period. Figure 9.2 presents a daily record which illustrates this effect. The social reinforcement provided by the attractive female supervisor created temporary but consistent disruption of the response rate. The social reinforcement procedure was effective, however, as higher performance was evident for a few minutes on the average out of every 15 minute period. The disruptive and the reinforcing effects of the social attention offset each other, with the result that the overall rate was comparable to the baseline rate. The reinforcing agent was changed from a female to a male counselor, with the result that a consistently higher rate of production was obtained. The temporary disruptive effect of social reinforcement disappeared.

In other instances it may not be desirable or feasible to record every occurrence of a behavior. The frequency may be extremely high and relatively stable over time. A sample of the frequency of occurrence would be representative of continuously recorded data. The supervisor or teacher may not be able to observe and record continuously due to other responsibilities. Under these circumstances, a time-sampling procedure may be followed. The initial five minutes of each 30 minute period during a 6 hour work day may be selected for continuous recording. In other instances, the observer may use a glance and record procedure. At designated times, the observer would note if the client was engaging in the specified behavior. No further recording would be made until the next designated time. In this manner a representative sample of the behavior would be obtained.

Again, quantitative frequency data are essential for evaluating the effectiveness of behavior modification programs. In other instances, measures of magnitude, duration, or latency may be the most appropriate measure, or these measures may be used in combination with frequency measures. As these data provide the basis for evaluating treatment effectiveness, it is necessary that measurement be taken over a sufficient time span to produce reliable or stable rate data. There will be variation in frequency from one

observation period to the next. The baseline data should be stable enough to enable the observer to discern later changes in the characteristics of the data which may coincide with treatment effects.

Initiation of Treatment. After a stable measure of behavior strength has been obtained, the treatment procedure is initiated. This will most frequently involve some change in the environment in which the baseline data were obtained. As the treatment procedures are initiated, the behavior is recorded in the manner followed in baseline recording. In some instances it will be desirable to record behavior strength from the moment of initiation of the treatment procedures. In other instances, a recording of behavior strength may be initiated after the treatment procedure has been in operation for a period of time. In any event, there must be a recording of the behavior during or following treatment in order to compare it with pre-treatment behavior strength.

Demonstration of a reliable change in the strength of the behavior after initiation of the treatment procedure provides some assurance that the treatment procedure was critical to the behavior change. As discussed in an earlier chapter, however, a replication procedure or some other means of demonstrating more precise control is desirable to eliminate the possibility that the behavior change is not due to uncontrolled and unidentified factors. Features of more precise evaluation designs are discussed by Sidman (1960) and by Gelfand and Hartmann (1968).

PROGRAM ANALYSIS

After a program has been designed on the basis of data obtained from the clinical behavior analysis, the program is implemented with an analytic orientation. Lindsley (1964) has described a general schema for evaluating the effectiveness of various components of a program designed to influence operant behavior. This schema, combined with other aspects of a functional analysis of behavior methodology described previously, provide a most helpful methodology for the behavior therapist who wishes to evaluate the effectiveness of various components of the program which has been designed.

A program designed to influence a specific target behavior or pattern of behavior consists of:

A. *Antecedent events.* (AE) These refer to the materials, instructions, physical surroundings, and the like, which are designed to influence the occurrence of the behavior.

B. *Behavior.* (B) This refers to the specific behavior in terms of form, strength, and the like, which the program is designed to develop and strengthen.

C. *Contingency*. (C) This refers to the arrangement between the occurrence of the behavior and the subsequent change in the environment. This subsequent change may be positive or aversive. It may be presented or removed.

D. *Subsequent events*. (SE) These refer to the consequences that follow, or are produced by the occurrence of the behavior. These events may serve a positively reinforcing, negatively reinforcing, neutral, or punishing function.

The target behavior program components are illustrated in Table 9.2. The example provided represents one phase of a behavior modification program designed to develop functional reading skills in a mildly retarded young adult.

If John is not successful in reaching the desired performance level (for example, the behavior may not occur, the behavior may occur in an irregular fashion, or the behavior may occur in an imprecise form), consideration must be given each component of the program. The antecedent events may be inadequate. The print may be too small, the room may contain various distracting stimuli, the attractive personal characteristics of the teacher, especially of the opposite sex, may be presenting stimuli which emit behaviors which interfere with attending to the cards. The task may be quite aversive as a result of previous punishing experiences with reading tasks, and the like. The contingency may be inappropriate for the behavior required. An FR 2 or even a continuous reinforcement schedule may be required to strengthen the behavior. The consequences may have very low

Table 9.2. Target Behavior Program Report

Name of Client: John K. Jackson	*Date of Analysis:* July 20, 1970
Behavior Therapist: Janelle K. Huitt	*Location of Program:* LABAM

AE Components: John is presented with a series of 25 simple phrases and sentences typed on 3 × 5 cards. These are presented one at a time with the request: "What are these words?" or "Tell me what this says." He receives the set of cards twice daily during an early morning session.

B Components: John is to read the words on the card loud enough to be heard by the teacher sitting next to him. The card is to be read without error within 10 seconds of presentation.

C Components: John is reinforced on a CR schedule. Response refers to correct reading of a single card within 10 seconds of presentation.

SE Components: Token, provided after every correct response, is redeemable for a variety of tangible items (cigarettes, matches, playing cards, comb set, movie ticket, candy, costume jewelry, and cosmetic items). Items may be purchased at any time after daily session. Social reinforcement in form of praise is provided upon receipt of token.

reinforcement value. It may be, for example, that the items available are all provided John on a noncontingency basis by his family. If so, a change in the type of back-up reinforcers available would hold better promise of influencing the strength of the desired behavior. Finally, the desired behavior may be inappropriate. It may be that even under maximum discriminative and reinforcing conditions the behavior would not occur. The behavior may be too difficult for the person. The prerequisites for this behavior may not be in his repertoire or there may be other stronger behavior patterns that preempt the desired behavior. It may be possible that the behavior in the form desired is in the repertoire but the reinforcing conditions are not sufficient for the effort or difficulty requirements of the behavior. A simple, or otherwise different, form of the behavior may be required. In considering each of these program components, the behavior therapist (for example, teacher, counselor, supervisor) decides on which component or components should be changed on the basis of knowledge which he has about the client. He may suspect from past experience with the client that more frequent reinforcement is likely to effect more active participation. Or he may discover that the reinforcers are inappropriate. If the therapist is interested in producing a maximum program as rapidly as possible and is not concerned with which specific variables are in fact the deficit ones in the program, he may change two or more components at a time. However, in most instances it would be most desirable and feasible to change only one component at a time. In this manner, if all components were held constant except this one, the precise effects of this change could be evaluated by means of the functional analysis procedure described in the preceding section.

Summary

This chapter has described the behavioral analysis approach to obtaining information on which to base a program of education and rehabilitation. Aspects of this approach also provide means of evaluating the effectiveness of the program designed. One of the outstanding features of this approach is the manner in which behavior modification strategies evolve from the evaluation data. Such evaluation data provide considerable assistance both in identifying the specific learning variables which should be utilized in the behavior modification program and in specifying the relative emphasis which should be provided each of these variables.

Methods of Producing
Behavior Change

CHAPTER TEN

Behavior Treatment: General Considerations

Introduction

Although the behavioral characteristics of the mentally retarded which create concern for the educational and rehabilitation personnel are those which in one way or another are inappropriate to specific or general environmental requirements, the primary focus of the behavior modification program is on the development of more functional behavior patterns. The major problem area for which a program may be devised may involve the absence of behaviors which are deemed necessary or desirable by aspects of the environment. The person, for example, may be unable to read instructions and consequently be unable to function in a job which requires such behavior. He may sit for lengthy periods of time without working in a situation that requires constant work behaviors. In other instances, the primary concern may be one of excessive or inappropriate behaviors. Too much talking, walking, smiling, crying, laughing, fighting, or complaining may occur too generally or inappropriately at specific places or times.

The program goal becomes that of modifying behavior as it occurs in a given environment in such a manner that it becomes most appropriate to that environment. The unwanted behavioral deficits or excesses are defined in behavioral terms and not in "symptomatic" terms. This focuses treatment in the present and toward a direct solution to the presenting problem. The treatment procedures are selected on the basis of their being the most direct means of producing beneficial behavior change.

In planning for behavior change no attempt is made to identify the presumptive historically based origins of the problem behaviors because the treatment program focuses on the present behavior as it occurs under certain environmental events. Behavioral goals are stated in specific terms, for example, the number of work units completed in a unit of time, the number of appropriate social contacts initiated, the number of words read correctly, frequency of getting to work on time, the amount of time spent in attending behavior, the frequency and magnitude of designated emotional behaviors and the like. A change plan is developed which provides direction to restructuring-through-design a range of environmental events which are presumed to have an influence on the behavioral areas under consideration. Undesirable behavior may be prevented on occasion through restructuring the environment so that available appropriate behavior may become dominant and replace the inappropriate means of responding. It is not essential that the client be desirous of change or "motivated" to change although active participation in change efforts may well facilitate change. Such involvement, however, is not a *sine qua non* of change. In fact the person may not even agree with the program environment that behavioral deficits or excesses are present.

The therapeutic or change agents can involve a variety of persons other than the counselor, teacher, and client and may include parents, peers, work supervisors and others who can provide some programmatic discriminative and reinforcing events. These change agents have at their disposal a wide variety of behavior change techniques which may range from initiation of specific changes in the physical environment to such approaches as procedural or rule changes concerning consequences or patterns of behaviors and to modification of the manner and frequency of direct social or personal contact with the client. Although versions of verbal-insight therapy procedures may be of value to some retarded clients, in most cases more effective and efficient direct procedures are selected.

It should be emphasized that a program designed to facilitate the development of functional behavior patterns does not view the problem behavior nor the related program goals in isolation. The behavior is viewed as one aspect of a complex flow of behavior occurring in a complex and changing environment. The program emphasis is on development of positive behavior patterns, that is, those that result in positive consequences. The concern is with both the short-term as well as the long-term effects of influencing behavior development by certain means. Procedures designed to suppress or eliminate inappropriate behavior patterns are never used in isolation. In illustration, a person's behavior may be disruptive in the classroom. The teacher may use a mild punishment procedure in an attempt to control the disruptive behavior. She would view this behavior control technique as only the initial step in development of positive func-

tional behavior. She also provides systematic encouragement of behavior patterns which "take the place of" the disruptive behavior and which produce more appropriate consequences.

The behavior modification approach has been viewed by some rehabilitation personnel as being too molecular in its manner of dealing with complex human behavior, of being concerned only with isolated or fragmented elements of a person's total behavior pattern. This is an unwarranted criticism as the behavior therapist is quite concerned with the entire complex of behaviors which a person typically utilizes in given settings as well as with other related behaviors which are in his repertoire. In developing a program for promoting behavior change, he identifies behavioral deficits and excesses and views these in the context of a broader range of functional behaviors which characterize the person.

Likewise, a treatment procedure is selected on the basis of its anticipated effect on the total functioning of the person in his environment. A punishment technique such as social isolation, for example, would not be selected for use with a person who becomes quite upset when left alone or when criticized by peers or adults. An alternative procedure which produced more positive and less negative side effects would be selected.

In a consideration of the concept of functional behaviors, it should be recognized that any behavior which is maintained over time could be viewed as being functional in that it produces reinforcement. Disruptive behavior may be functional in that it produces peer attention which in turn strengthens the disruptive behavior. Disruptive behavior may persist in a specific environment as this behavior pattern is more likely to produce positive reinforcers than any other behaviors which the retarded may demonstrate. However, the disruptive behavior may be viewed as nonfunctional in the sense that it interferes with the development of other behavior patterns which potentially could produce reinforcers of greater magnitude, of a greater range and consistency and which would hold less likelihood of negative components.

Environmental Deficits

As noted in the preceding chapters, problem behaviors frequently are evaluated in the environment in which the behavior occurs. Such an exploration concerning possible functional relationships between problem behaviors and environmental conditions often reveals inadequacies in the general program environment which may well account for, or at least be significantly involved in, the development and maintenance of the presenting problem behaviors. Inadequate programs for the retarded range from those of unstructured activities, few requirements and excessive

tolerance for disruptive behavior to those which are highly regimented and which permit little spontaneous behavior to occur. In the former without clearly stated behavioral goals nor appropriate reinforcing components, the retarded person may find disruptive behavior or even general unresponsiveness the most reinforcing of his daily activities. This may be true either because these patterns most consistently result in teacher and peer attention or because these remove him from program activities which he finds aversive. In the latter, the retarded student develops no initiative or self-direction as he is told what to do and when to do it. It is not unusual for such a program environment to influence behavior mostly through aversive means.

Observation of groups of retarded adolescents and adults in such programs suggests that many have the possibilities for integrated school and work behavior and related social skills. On occasion they become involved in assigned tasks and perform satisfactorily. They appear to have the basic motor, sensory, perceptual, and cognitive skills necessary for more satisfactory performance. The major difficulties appear to reside in an inappropriate program environment. The following sections will consider a number of these environmental or program deficits, and offer a set of principles and techniques as a basis for dealing with these.

INADEQUATE REINFORCEMENT SYSTEM

As has been suggested earlier, one of the most apparent deficits in the life of the problem retarded adolescent and adult is that related to the "motivational" aspect of his behavior. Such an adolescent in the school-work program, for example, just does not perform. He frequently is "uninterested" in the academic classes as well as in the social adjustment curriculum. He does not persist at his task nor does he show any enthusiasm about his work. This is well illustrated by the following exerpt from a teacher report concerning one of her mildly retarded adolescents: "Jim does not seem motivated by anything that I can provide. He seldom becomes involved in any individual work assignments or in group activities. He just seems bored by the whole affair. At times, he will talk about his brother's new car or about the professional football game which he watched on TV the day before, but even these topics will not keep him interested for very long." Observations of the teacher-client interaction in such programs frequently suggest that an excessive amount of the student's behavior is maintained by negative reinforcement, cajoling, and by other aversive control events. In some settings the teacher may well be using the most advanced curriculum materials. The lighting in the classrooms may be judged to be excellent, the rooms to be well heated and ventilated, with the walls painted in soft, warm colors. It is not unusual to find that the supervisory personnel

are frequently kind, warm, and intelligent adults. But neither is it unusual to observe that the major principles of behavior influence are sorely neglected. Even though the rehabilitation personnel recognize that reward, incentives, or positive consequences are most influential factors in their own lives and further that particular incentives may be highly idiosyncratic, they remain relatively myopic in any systematic application of this knowledge to their own program. The rewards are frequently incidental or noncontingent, are of limited reinforcing value (for example, grades, approval, being correct), too infrequent, and too far removed from the behavior which the teacher or counselor wishes to strengthen.

It is crucial to recognize that within a group of retarded adolescents and adults who present special learning and behavior adjustment difficulties there are considerable individual differences as to those consequences which are in fact reinforcing. Additionally, the learning and performance difficulties presented by this group require a most systematic structuring of the total education and rehabilitation experience if the program goals are to be met. In recent experiences of the writer and his colleagues, it has been found in groups of problem mentally retarded clients that even money, for example, may have little reinforcing properties for many in the initial stages of a rehabilitation program. Apparently the secondary reinforcing qualities of money had never developed as its presence had not been associated in a systematic and frequent manner with backup reinforcers. As a result money as an incentive was of limited value in a program designed to strengthen or maintain behavior. In such cases, money acquired secondary reinforcing properties only after systematic and in some instances, prolonged, association with other more reinforcing events or objects.

PROGRAM INADEQUACIES

The relatively poverty stricken nature of many education and rehabilitation programs in relation to reinforcement is shown by the following examples. These programs, which serve a range of special education and rehabilitation clients, provide evaluation, education, work training, and social adjustment services. All are supported by a combination of public and private, local, state and federal funds.

Program A. This is a special prevocational work training program serving clients who previously either had been denied entrance into a work training program because of poor prognosis for productive employment or had been admitted but had failed to make satisfactory progress. The clients are paid on an hourly basis for participating in sheltered workshop activities. The same rate is paid to all regardless of production. Social urging and some inconsistent praise and approval is provided by one of the

workshop supervisors. Some of the clients sit for extended periods of time without working unless the supervisor reminds them to begin. Work rate for all is erratic. Work involvement is more consistent when the supervisor is present than when he is out of the room. In fact, when he leaves the room, work behavior disintegrates rapidly. In this environment it is evident that reinforcing events are inadequate both in kind and amount and are not sufficiently contingent upon appropriate work performance to influence it to the extent desired. As a result a range of highly inappropriate behavioral characteristics is being facilitated.

Program B. In this training workshop which stresses production, clients are paid a minimum hourly wage plus a bonus for production above the minimum rate. Very few of the clients earn more than the minimum wage. Checks for money earned are provided on a weekly basis. Although the clients can verbalize the pay schedule, such information is not sufficient to exert control over work behavior to influence a higher performance rate. The reinforcing events appear to be too far removed from the work behavior.

Program C. This is a secondary level special education class for mentally retarded adolescents who present a range of behavior management problems. A male teacher provides instruction in shop, physical education, math and social studies. A female teacher has responsibility for home-making skills, social skills, language arts and music. The male teacher is a strict disciplinarian. He believes that these boys can be handled only if they have a strict program which quickly punishes deviations from regulations. A range of aversive means such as sitting in the principal's office, losing recess privileges, and threat of dismissal from school is used. The female teacher, on the other hand, believes that all problems can be solved by understanding and warmth. Also believing that the adolescents have learned just about all they will ever learn, she provides a most flexible school program for the students. In this environment, considerable social reinforcement is provided. However, it is not related in any contingent manner to any particular behavior patterns. The major purpose served is to "keep the students happy."

EXCESSIVE RELIANCE ON AVERSIVE CONTROL

In addition to an inappropriate reinforcement system, many educational and rehabilitation programs are characterized by excessive utilization of aversive control. Behavior is negatively reinforced and thereby strengthened through termination of aversive conditions following initiation of appropriate behavior or through cessation of the inappropriate behavior. Inappropriate behaviors may be controlled by threat or other forms of punishment. Desired performance may be reinforced by removal of this

punishment or the threat of such. The teacher, for example, may verbally reprimand the adolescent for excessive talking during study period. As this is a most embarrassing experience, control of talking is reinforced as this removes the threat of reprimand. Although the possible negative consequences of such an approach are numerous and pervasive, one of the major difficulties resides in the fact that when this aversive control is removed through, for example, transfer of the client to another environment, the behavior control soon deteriorates. Appropriate behavior declines as it is not under positive reinforcement control. That is, the behavior was being controlled or suppressed by negative factors and not strengthened through positive consequences. Inappropriate behaviors may reappear as the aversive cues which controlled their appearance are no longer present in the new physical environment. The aversive control soon dissipates. This emphasizes the fact that punishment does not usually result in the elimination of behavior nor the strengthening of new means of behaving which are incompatible with the punished behavior. The punished behavior is likely to reappear when the aversive components are not present.

INADEQUATE CLARITY AND SPECIFICATION OF PROGRAM GOALS

An additional environmental deficit which impedes appropriate behavior development is that of lack of specification of the goals of the education or rehabilitation program. The goals of "preparation of the client for an independent work and living status" are admirable. However, program personnel frequently have limited specific knowledge of the skills required for such a status and further do not translate the rehabilitation goals into specific target-behavior terms.

LOW RELATIONSHIP BETWEEN PROGRAM GOALS AND PROGRAM EXPERIENCES

Another deficit that frequently is characteristic of education and rehabilitation programs for the mentally retarded is that the day by day experiences provided are not related in any specific programmatic manner to the program goals nor to the specific behavioral deficits or excesses which the client presents. Frequently there appears to be an absence of both a logical and an empirical basis for the experiences which are provided. A general work experience frequently is of little value to the client. This results not only in ineffectual progress toward goals but also renders more likely the development of a variety of inappropriate behavior patterns. This is illustrated in the following experiences recently observed in a rehabilitation training workshop. The work rate of three clients was quite low. Upon investigation it was noted that these clients worked only

about 20 minutes in an hour. Whenever work supplies were brought to them all clients worked rapidly until the supplies were exhausted and sat around loafing until the supervisor noted that they were not working and brought more supplies. Loafing and other inappropriate behaviors were being reinforced by a poorly organized environment. In another case involving a young woman described as having a low frustration tolerance, it was noted that she engaged in frequent emotional outburst involving yelling, crying and refusing to work. Almost routinely following this behavior, she was sent to the counselor's office to "talk it out." Such a procedure appeared to be reinforcing the temper tantrum behavior as it not only removed her from an aversive situation but also provided her with individual attention from a male counselor—an event which held significant reinforcement value for her.

POOR DISCRIMINATIVE COMPONENTS

As mentioned in the previous section, the client frequently does not know what is expected of him either because the cues or instructions provided have not acquired discriminative properties or because the cues are too infrequent to insure a continuous flow of appropriate behavior. Instructions or signals presented by the program may be too complex in that the retarded does not "understand" what is being requested. The signals may not be of sufficient magnitude or latency to attract and hold attention. The person may soon "forget" what he is to do and his behavior comes under the control of cues for unacceptable behaviors. Finally, the behavior in the form required by the program may not be in the client's present repertoire. Thus appropriate behavior, as defined by the program environment, will not occur.

In summary, program environments may produce many of the behavioral limitations and inadequacies characteristic of the mentally retarded. Inadequate reinforcement procedures, excessive aversive components, inadequate clarity of program goals, and poor relationship between program experiences and program objectives all function to render many programs anything but educational or therapeutic.

General Principles of Positive Program Development

The principles of positive behavior development to be discussed in this section are equally applicable to a wide range of programs provided in a wide array of settings. Utilization of these principles is equally essential for maximum behavior development whether the major interest is one of teaching basic academic skills to a group of moderately retarded or one of facilitating social and interpersonal skills in the mildly retarded adolescent and

adult. Coercive techniques are rejected. The rehabilitation program is organized to prompt, support, and strengthen positive behaviors that function to enhance the person's adjustment to the requirements of his world.

Elimination of bothersome behavior patterns, while desirable, is not the primary program focus. In many instances, development of functional behaviors—those that meet the requirements of the environment and produce positive reinforcement—results in disappearance of inappropriate and undesirable modes of behavior. The person learns to engage in behaviors that produce more valuable and more consistent consequences than those resulting from the inappropriate behaviors. There are other beneficial consequences of a program which emphasize positive behavior development. As suggested earlier, as the person acquires a repertoire of functional behaviors, idiosyncratic behaviors may still exist but are more likely to be overlooked or tolerated. The person is able to behave in a manner that produces positive feedback. He is able to contribute something to his environment. As Ayllon and Azrin (1968) commented, "the corporation president that mumbles to himself may be characterized as an eccentric genius. The unemployed individual that mumbles to himself is more likely to find himself recommended for institutionalization" [p. 23]. Development of more functional behavior, therefore, may well reduce the visibility of other patterns of behavior which are typically viewed as inappropriate and result in greater acceptability of the person by his social environment.

MAXIMIZING REINFORCEMENT
COMPONENTS OF THE ENVIRONMENT

In considering the design of a program environment based on concepts of reinforcement, one is faced with practical as well as theoretical problems. In a group program, for example, the problem becomes not only one of discovering those reinforcers which can be used with the group but also that of insuring that the reinforcers which are available are valuable to each individual comprising the group. This becomes a significant consideration in working with the behaviorally disturbed retarded as individuals differ considerably in reinforcer preference. Related questions of "How should the reinforcers be delivered?" "How can available reinforcers be maximized in effectiveness?" "Is the reinforcer more effective if the person is aware of what is available?" must be evaluated. Basic concepts of operant learning and related principles and methods of imitation learning discussed in earlier chapters can provide considerable direction to attempts to design an environment which is most supportive of effective learning and performance. These are summarized as follows:

1. *Rehabilitation goals are best met when reinforcement is provided systematically following desirable behavior.*

(a) *Behavior to be reinforced must be defined precisely in order to insure reinforcement delivery by the program personnel.* This requirement of specifying the behavior to be reinforced is not an easy one for education and rehabilitation personnel to fulfill, especially when complex behavior patterns are involved. However, it cannot be emphasized too strongly that this requirement must be met for successful program implementation.

(b) *A well defined and manageable reinforcement delivery procedure must be devised and followed closely by program personnel.* Not only must the behavior to be reinforced be clearly specified, but also the environmental conditions under which reinforcement is to be delivered must be specified. In many instances these conditions are easily met. For example, Zimmerman, Stuckey, Garlick, and Miller (1969), in a prevocational training program for mentally retarded adults, provided token reinforcement at the end of each six-hour work day, with the number of tokens dependent upon the amount of work completed. The performance-number of work units completed—was easily identified, and the procedure of delivery—tokens or marks at the end of the work period—was easily followed. Once the system was explained and understood by the clients, the reinforcement procedure was easily administered.

In other instances a specification of the behavior to be reinforced as well as the procedure of reinforcement create more difficulty. This was illustrated in a recent experience with a young retarded adult who engaged in sudden disruptive outburst in situations which required her to shift from one activity to another. A program was designed to reinforce both control of such emotional episodes and movement from one task to another whenever the work situation required this behavior. In this situation the behaviors to be reinforced and the reinforcement delivery system were difficult to program. However, the desired behavior patterns were broken down into manageable segments and gradually integrated into a complex and functional behavior pattern.

(c) *Generally, behavior is most efficiently developed and maintained when the retarded is informed of the desired behavior and of the reinforcement system, that is, of the contingency between behavior and consequence.* To insure that the client is sufficiently informed about the relationship between appropriate behavior and the availability of a reinforcing consequence, it is sometimes desirable to demonstrate the relationship. This may be done through modeling the sequence from the initiation of behavior under appropriate environmental cues through the delivery of the rein-

forcing event. To further emphasize the sequence, it may be desirable to guide the retarded through from initial signal to completion of reinforcement. This procedure was illustrated by Culkin (1968) in her study of highly disruptive adult retarded clients in a work adjustment program. The reinforcement procedure was initially described. Following this, the teacher demonstrated the behavior as well as the delivery of reinforcement. Finally, the client was guided through the sequence and permitted to exchange the token earned for a backup reinforcer.

Further, whenever there is a delay between the behavior and consequence, it may be valuable to verbalize the contingency involved. This may prove quite useful whenever a long chain of behavior is being required prior to reinforcement.

2. *Stimulus events which do in fact influence the behavior of individual clients must be used if their behavior is to be modified.* No a priori decisions should be made about what reinforcers are effective with specific clients. What will influence the behavior of given individuals is an empirical question to be answered by actual experience with the client. Reinforcing events which are known to be effective with most adolescents and adults may be found to be relatively uninfluential with the difficult mentally retarded client. What is reinforcing to one may not be to another. What is reinforcing at one time, may not be reinforcing at another. The influential reinforcers may range from highly generalized token reinforcers, and various forms of social contact, social interaction, praise, approval, and recognition to activities, privileges and tangible objects. Strict adherence to a predetermined type or set of reinforcing events will only impede behavior development. Social reinforcement frequently is depended on excessively by educational and rehabilitation personnel in their work with the retarded. The major deficiency of this type of consequence resides in the temporary nature of such an event. Unlike a token reinforcer which is enduring over time, once the social reinforcer is provided it quickly disappears as a physical stimulus event. It is not infrequently heard from educational personnel that "he seems to respond to my attention and praise but he will not stick to his task when I'm not praising him constantly," or "sometimes he responds well to my approval but frequently it has no effect on his performance." Social reinforcement, while a potentially powerful reinforcer for some, must be used in a discerning manner and frequently interspersed with other reinforcers. Bijou, Birnbrauer, Kidder, and Tague (1966) in a program designed to strengthen a range of desirable classroom and academic behaviors followed such behaviors with teacher praise and approval. No improvement in target behaviors was noted under these conditions. Teacher approval was not sufficiently reinforcing to influence these

types of behaviors in the classroom setting. It was found, however, follow-ing initiation of a token reinforcement system in which marks and numeri-cal scores were provided for appropriate behaviors, that higher rates of effective study and greater cooperation were obtained.

(a) *A wide range of reinforcing events should be available for use in educational and rehabilitation programs.* This range of events should be available continuously in order to provide instant flexi-bility to the teacher or supervisor in selecting an appropriate rein-forcer to insure continuous behavior development and mainte-nance. If a given reinforcer or group of events are used too frequently, satiation may occur. A condition of disinterest or bore-dom may result which is obviously inconsistent with appropriate behavior functioning.

(b) *Variations of a given reinforcing event should be explored for new sources of reinforcers.* In a secondary school program, for ex-ample, it may be found that watching television or short subject movies are effective reinforcing events. The reinforcement value of this type of activity may be greatly enhanced, both in absolute magnitude and in value, in reducing satiation by providing a wide range of topics, length of programs, color vs. black-and-white, sound vs. silent, contemporary vs. Laurel and Hardy type, and the like.

(c) *In an environment in which an attempt is being made to maxi-mize its reinforcing components, the value of reinforcing events can be enhanced by making each available in such a manner that selection of one does not preclude selection of another.* In a recent observation of a social adjustment program, clients had a choice during break period to spend time in the bowling alley or to watch television. Some clients always selected television viewing even though previous experience with these clients indicated that bowling was also a reinforcing activity. One available source of reinforcement was lost to the program due to the forced choice which the reinforcement delivery system imposed. A rescheduling of events could have taken advantage of both.

3. *Due to the idiosyncratic nature of reinforcers for this group, use of a token reinforcement system with a wide range of objects and events avail-able as backup reinforcers is usually most effective.* Zimmerman et al. (1969) used the following activities and items for which points earned in a workshop could be exchanged by their retarded clients:

1) a weekly 2-hour tour of industrial facilities and points of interest around Indianapolis (300 points per tour), 2) a weekly 1½ hour "arcade," which took place in the employee's lounge and included the opportunity to participate in table games, purchase refreshments with points, and be entertained by a local celebrity (200 points per arcade), 3) the daily opportunity to work extra hours (10 points per hour for each extra hour elected), 4) the daily opportunity to hold a conversation with (be counseled by) a staff member of the clients' choice (10 points per minute), and finally 5) tangible goods such as games, jewelry, and candy, which could be purchased twice a week from a portable canteen located in the guest dining room . . . [p. 36].

As another example, Lent (1968) used British half-pennies as token reinforcers which were exchangeable for privileges such as the use of a record-player or for a range of items from a store. For older clients the:

tokens take the form of marks on a gridded point card. The points on one side of the card can be redeemed for money; those on the reverse are 'privilege points' that permit certain activities. Once a week, on Bank Day, the girls receive the amount of money shown on the financial side of their cards, money that they may keep themselves, or if they prefer, bank under lock and key. At the same time, their privilege points are recorded for use later on [p. 53].

Ayllon and Azrin (1965) in providing a token economy for hospitalized psychotic adults—some of whom were retarded—provided a range of available reinforcers grouped in categories of items or events which (1) increased or restricted contact with other patients (for example, choice of bedroom, choice of eating group, choice of room divider), (2) provided opportunity of leave from the ward, (3) provided social interaction with staff, (4) provided recreational opportunities, (5) provided opportunity for attending religious services, and (6) provided a wide range of commissary items.

(a) *A tangible stimulus such as a token or mark will serve to overcome the delay between behavioral event and the later delivery of the reinforcers as these are physically present to represent the later reinforcer.* Further, a token reinforcement system is relatively simple to administer. Tokens are easily presented, are easily handled by clients, and can be kept by the retarded to represent or to remind him of the ultimate reinforcer. Behavior can be reinforced as it occurs. Tokens frequently can be provided without disrupting ongoing behavior. Even the more severely retarded can learn the value of a tangible token reinforcer. Additionally, the tokens can acquire rather powerful secondary reinforcement value and can be used to maintain behavior for extended periods

of time in the absence of backup reinforcers. This type of reinforcer is crucial for many retarded clients, especially in the early
phase of their rehabilitation program. Other reinforcers, such as
social approval or praise, are too fleeting. Once provided there is
nothing tangible to represent the approval. Further, the promise
of a reinforcer at the end of the day or week is too abstract for
many clients in the initial stages of developing a work or achievement motivation system.

(b) *Even with a token reinforcement system it is necessary to insure
that the token delivered, whether it consists of a poker chip, a foreign coin, a gummed star, a mark, a numerical score or actual
American money, does in fact have reinforcement value for the
person who receives it.* Lent (1968), in a program designed to
develop skills of personal appearance, occupational skills, social
behavior and functional academic subjects in groups of moderately retarded girls stated:

Our first task with each group of girls is to teach them that the tokens have
value. At first we do not reinforce with tokens at all. Instead we offer nontoken
rewards such as candy for desired behavior. Gradually, we substitute tokens
for food. When the tokens are first used, we allow the girls to exchange them
for food immediately. Then we increase the time between token exchange.
Eventually we are able to introduce saving by requiring several tokens for
certain purchases [p. 53].

In other instances the initial influence of a token reinforcement
system may be enhanced by providing tokens free of charge in the
program setting and permitting the clients to exchange these for
backup reinforcers of their choice. Once this relationship between
tokens and desired reinforcing events has been demonstrated, the
tokens can then be delivered contingent upon desired behaviors.

4. *Reinforcement to be most effective must occur immediately following
the behavior to be strengthened.* The more immediate the reinforcer is delivered following behavior, the more rapid the learning. Use of a token system permits the education and rehabilitation programs to utilize this learning principle.

5. *Generally, the greater the magnitude of the reinforcing event, the
greater the effect of the reinforcer on the behavior.* Behavior acquired
under a low magnitude reinforcer is less resistent to extinction than a
similar behavior pattern acquired under a higher magnitude reinforcer.
Learning can be enhanced by increasing the magnitude of the reinforcer.

6. *Behavior development and maintenance is best influenced when reinforcement is provided in a systematic manner.* Frequent reinforcement

with high magnitude reinforcers facilitates initial behavior development. It is necessary to continue reinforcing frequently until the behavior has gained some reliable strength. If reinforcement is discontinued or provided in an infrequent manner too early in learning, the behavior, even though it appears to be of considerable strength when reinforced frequently, may show rapid extinction.

Resistance to extinction (disappearance under periods of limited or infrequent reinforcement) can best be developed by gradually reducing the frequency of reinforcement following development of a relatively stable rate of behaving and by providing reinforcement on a variable schedule.

It should be noted also that once many behaviors have been acquired these can typically be maintained with reinforcers of less magnitude than required for rapid initial development. This is due partially (a) to the control which the schedule of reinforcement acquires over the behavior: this could initially be exerted only by the magnitude of the reinforcing event which the behavior produced, (b) to the reduction in the amount of effort required to engage satisfactorily in many behaviors once these have been acquired, and (c) to the acquisition of secondary reinforcement properties of environmental events which have been associated frequently with the behavior—reinforcement sequence. Conditions associated with the delivery of the reinforcing consequences of the desired behavior acquire some of the reinforcing properties of these events and may begin to serve a reinforcing function.

7. *Behavior which is of low strength and can be superseded easily by other behavior patterns has been reinforced too infrequently and/or with reinforcers of low magnitude or value.* An application of this relationship is seen in the reinforcement procedures followed by many training and sheltered workshops for the retarded. In these settings, the major reinforcing event provided by the workshop for appropriate work behavior is the paycheck which is presented weekly or biweekly. For many retarded adults with rehabilitation difficulties, the reinforcer is too infrequent, that is, too far removed from the behavior patterns which the program attempts to strengthen. As a result of this practice, many clients do not acquire highly appropriate work skills.

8. *The effectiveness of a given reinforcer can be enhanced by depriving the person of that reinforcer for a period of time.* During a state of deprivation, reinforcing events which generally are unimportant may gain noticeably in reinforcement properties.

9. *The effectiveness of a given reinforcing event can be enhanced by reducing the availability of other preferred reinforcing events.* An adolescent

in a special education class may respond to the approval of the teacher but finds more reinforcing the attention of peers, which he obtains generally through disruptive behaviors. Removing the person from the physical proximity of his peers and thus increasing the availability of teacher approval for appropriate behavior will enhance the reinforcing properties of the teacher.

10. *The effectiveness of a reinforcing event which presently has little influence may be enhanced by the client's observation of others consuming or utilizing the reinforcer.* This is especially true if the person observed is highly preferred by the observer—a peer, teacher, or friend whom he attends to.

11. *Stimulus events may become effective reinforcers by permitting the client to sample or to be exposed to these events, especially if such initial participation produces other events which are reinforcing to him.* This procedure of developing reinforcer effectiveness is especially pertinent to the difficult mentally retarded client as there are few events which are reinforcing to him in the education or rehabilitation program. Typically, he has had infrequent experience with many potential reinforcing events and thus presents an impression of being disinterested in those aspects of the environment which to many persons are rather rewarding.

In view of this, it is valuable to expose the client to a variety of events and activities that are available and which could serve as reinforcing events for behavior patterns which are to be developed. Visiting the zoo, attending sports events, shopping, riding a train, taking a trip, and playing cards, for example, may all become reinforcing events after the retarded client participates in these.

In some instances it will be necessary to teach the person through systematic reinforcement to develop the skill required for participation in an activity. Once this is acquired, the activity can become a reinforcing event for other behavior patterns. This was illustrated by Lent (1968) in his education program for moderately retarded adolescents:

> It might be necessary at first, for example, to reward a girl for taking the smallest step toward painting a picture—for approaching the easel, say, or for touching the paint brush. Later, the girl receives tokens only when she has painted for some time. Still later, the activity itself may become desirable and therefore reinforcing, and we can *require* tokens for the privilege of participating [p. 53].

Finally, many retarded adolescents and adults have considerable hesitancy about entering into or trying out new events. Various types of activities (for example, eating new foods, playing new games, visiting new

places, meeting new people) may prove to be high preference activities after exposure. The rehabilitation program must insure that the retarded has a positive exposure to these events.

12. *The effectiveness of many reinforcers available in a rehabilitation or educational program is reduced as these same events are provided on a free basis.* In such a "welfare" state, reinforcers are available on a basis that is noncontingent—that is, provided whether the appropriate behavior occurs or not. Providing these reinforcing events following appropriate be-havior, and only following appropriate behavior, will add considerably to the effectiveness of the program. For many clients, behavior will be main-tained once it has been developed only to the extent that reinforcers are provided on a well delineated contingent basis. Ayllon and Azrin (1965) found this to be true in work with severely disturbed adults in a residential facility. During a baseline period, the adult workers readily performed their duties following which token reinforcers were provided. During a later period of 20 days, token reinforcement was provided in the morning prior to going to work with the comment: "You'll get your tokens each day whether or not you work. Of course, we are very pleased with your work and would like you to continue working . . ." [p. 368]. Time spent in work activities dropped to a minimal level under this contingency, but quickly returned to the original level of performance upon reinstatement of the reinforcement-following-work contingency.

13. *The kind and/or magnitude of the reinforcing event must be appro-priate to the effort or behavioral requirements of a given task.* There must be a reasonable match between the degree of difficulty of the task and the amount or magnitude of the contingent reinforcers. Social approval, in illustration, may be a valuable event to reinforce and thus maintain low rate work behavior, but not of sufficient magnitude to maintain high rate work behavior. In attempting to implement this relationship between diffi-culty level of task and magnitude of reinforcing event, it should be recog-nized that the difficulty level of a task will vary considerably from person to person. Additionally, the value of any reinforcing event will vary widely from person to person, and for the same person, from one occasion to another. Thus, to insure high strength, there should be a constant eval-uation of the match between behavioral requirements and reinforcing consequences.

14. *Behaviors which are highly probable in a designated environment may be used to increase the strength of other behavior patterns which are less likely to occur.* This is accomplished by arranging the program environ-ment so that the low preference activity will precede the availability of

high preference activities. The implications of this relationship are most significant to educational and rehabilitation programs as the relationship makes available a wide range of potential reinforcing events which are available naturally in the environment. High preference activities are identified through observation. As an example, Peter, an adolescent attending a prevocational work training program, would initiate a conversation with the teacher on every possible occasion. He, however, exhibited erratic work behavior. The teacher, in attempting to develop a "positive relationship" with the client, frequently spent significant periods of time talking with Peter. A program consultant, noting the high preference value of conversation with teacher, rearranged the contingency such that conversation was available after, and only after, a period of appropriate work behavior. Not only did Peter's work improve significantly, but further, the teacher had more time for activities other than conversing with Peter.

15. *Stimulus events which may serve as reinforcing events for retarded clients may be identified by asking the client what he prefers, by providing a wide range of potential reinforcers and permitting client to select those he would like, by interviewing parents and peers, and by observing the client in his general activity choices.* Events so identified may not be stable reinforcing events. Further, these procedures may not identify other events which may prove to be reinforcing after reinforcer sampling or exposure. This wide range of sources of information concerning possible reinforcing events, however, should emphasize that for every client there is an array of stimulus events which have or could acquire reinforcing properties.

16. *A specific stimulus event may lose some or all of its reinforcing properties either temporarily or on a more permanent basis.* Too much reinforcement or prolonged use of the same or a limited number of reinforcing events can result in this effect. If progress in learning or performance is not satisfactory, the role of the reinforcing components should be evaluated. An increase in magnitude may have a beneficial effect. Usually, however, under these conditions, it is best to use a different kind of reinforcer for a period of time. Disuse or unavailability of the previous reinforcer for a period of time may result in a return of its reinforcing properties.

17. *It cannot be assumed that the retarded client knows that a reinforcer is being provided for certain behaviors.* Reinforcement effects may be enhanced if a verbal account of the relationship is provided, especially in those instances in which a prolonged time delay exists between behavior and the delivery of the reinforcer.

18. *The schedule on which reinforcement is provided may be used to enhance the influence of reinforcing events.* Performance that has been

brought systematically under control of an intermittent reinforcement schedule in which reinforcement is provided infrequently may be maintained for long periods of times by a limited amount of reinforcement. That is, under such previous learning conditions given reinforcing events can become considerably more effective in maintaining behavior than would be possible in the absence of such schedule training.

19. *The retarded who display significant learning problems are not as generally influenced by various classes of social reinforcement as is 'true of other retarded peers with successful learning histories.* In addition, social events such as praise, attention or approval are momentary events and may not adequately represent over time the later delivery of tangible reinforcers. Therefore, the usefulness of such social events as close physical proximity, praise, approval, and attention must be evaluated empirically before assuming that this class of events has satisfactory reinforcement properties. In some instances, social events may even have aversive properties.

20. *Performance correlated stimulus events which represent progress toward the goal of reinforcer presentation may enhance the reinforcement properties of these final goal events.* These stimulus events may be auditory (for example, the supervisor providing verbal information such as "you now have only 15 problems to solve") or visual (for example, a marker rising in a thermometer—type chart and getting closer to the goal as a function of the rate of performance).

21. *Daily charting of performance on behavioral graphs and goal setting for subsequent performance sessions will serve as reinforcing procedures for some retarded clients.* The responses charted may include such behaviors as number of arithmetic problems solved, number of pages read, number of assembly items completed, or even the number of reading errors, number of assembly items rejected as below quality standards and the like. In work with moderately retarded adolescents, Jens and Shores (1969) demonstrated that behavioral graphs served to facilitate performance rate on assembly type tasks. Following daily work periods, each adolescent observed the work supervisor as he counted the number of assembly items completed and, after being informed of the total, then observed the supervisor as he charted the total number on a line graph. In this manner, each adolescent was able to obtain feedback concerning his performance rate on a day to day basis and also to obtain a visual account of his relative performance across days.

22. *Competition among group members or between groups may serve to promote satisfactory learning or performance.* Under conditions of compe-

tition, the reinforcing properties of available goal objects may be enhanced.

23. *The attainment of behavior goals set by means of a verbal contract between the counselor or teacher and the client may serve as a reinforcing event.* This type of arrangement will serve to increase the self-control and self-reinforcement characteristics of the client. In initiation of such a procedure, it is important that simple contracts (agreements) be set in order to insure success without undue delay. The amount and complexity of behavior required and the time required to complete the contract can be increased as success is attained.

MINIMIZING AVERSIVE COMPONENTS OF THE ENVIRONMENT

1. *A program that utilizes punishment or other aversive procedures as a major approach to influencing behavior will not promote appropriate behavior development or functioning.* Such a program approach creates negativism, excessive avoidance behavior patterns, negative emotional reactions and generally limited positive behavior development. Although it is sometimes easier to control inappropriate behavior through punishment or threat of punishment, positive behavior development requires control procedures based on positive reinforcement. It should be recalled that punishment merely serves to discourage that behavior which produced it. It does not strengthen appropriate behavior. An alternative approach to elimination of inappropriate behavior would consist of identifying the reinforcing events which support the behavior and rendering them contingent only upon appropriate behavior. If this is impossible or impractical, a strategy of development of competing behavior patterns by means of other reinforcing events having greater value can be pursued.

2. *Aversive stimulation should be used as infrequently as possible.* Such should be used only after careful consideration of positive behavior control procedures supports a punishment or negative reinforcement strategy.

3. *Whenever aversive events are used, these should be viewed as temporary measures and replaced as quickly as possible with positive reinforcement approaches.* The period during which behavior is suppressed by the aversive components of the environment should be used for the reinforcement of new behaviors that are incompatible with the punished behaviors. As the appropriate competing behaviors gain strength, there is a concomitant reduction in the need for procedures using aversive events.

4. *When aversive stimulation is used, it should be presented in a choice situation.* The client should have a clearly delineated choice between appropriate behavior and positive reinforcement on the one hand and inap-

propriate behavior and aversive consequences on the other. Such an alternative response situation results in maximum suppression by a given intensity of punishment. In representing such a choice situation to the client, the program personnel should insure that the client has the appropriate behavior in his repertoire, that the available reinforcer is of sufficient value to the client, and that he has had experience in receiving the positive reinforcer as a consequence of the desired behavior. It may be necessary to model the behavior and the positive consequences or to guide the client through the behavior reinforcement sequence. Also considerable prompting may be needed initially to insure positive behavior. These procedures will increase the possibility that the client will engage in the positive behavior when in the choice situation.

5. *If punishment procedures are used, the preferred approach would be one of delaying the delivery of positive reinforcers which are available only through appropriate behavior.* Other punishment procedures of presentation of aversive events carry connotations of incompetence, inadequacy, rejection, lack of respect, and the like.

6. *If it is necessary to use punishment, this procedure should represent only one small aspect of a program experience which provides considerable positive reinforcement for appropriate behavior.* Again, a program that utilizes procedures involving excessive aversive components is a poor program and is inconsistent with concepts of positive behavior development.

RELATING PROGRAM GOALS TO PROGRAM EXPERIENCES

1. *The rehabilitation program to be provided should be designed in terms of its contribution to the attainment of specific behavior goals.* The initial step in developing a program of experience is that of defining the behaviors which will serve as program goals. As emphasized in the preceding chapters, there is no adequate substitute for descriptive and readily defined behavioral terms in designing program goals. Many clients are referred for rehabilitation programming after having failed on a job placement. Reasons for failure are not infrequently stated in such vague terms as "unable to get along with authority figures," "cannot tolerate frustration or pressures of job," "negativistic." Such global terms provide little basis for program development. The behavior patterns forming the basis for the program should be described in terms that are meaningful to both rehabilitation personnel and client alike. Although complex behavior patterns are difficult to define in terms of behavior units which can be dealt with directly, successful program experiences require that this be accomplished. Otherwise there can be no reliable means of evaluating the usefulness of particular aspects of the program.

A detailed change plan should be developed for each client. This would include an identification of the materials presented, the discriminative cues provided, the behavior required, the reinforcement to be provided, as well as the contingency involved. Stimulus discrimination and response differentiation components must be specified. Every experience provided should meet the test of the question, "How is this experience related to the development of the specific target behaviors identified as program goals?" If program components cannot be justified in terms of their contribution, these should be discarded.

2. *The target or goal behaviors should be those involved in the work and social community in which the retarded client is likely to be residing.* Those behavioral skills which are most likely to be reinforced in that future environment should be selected for programming. Examples of such behaviors include those of following instructions provided by supervisory personnel, evaluating the adequacy of one's performance, control of disruptive behaviors, appropriate interaction with peers and authority personnel, persistence at a task in the face of difficulty, and the like. If a behavior pattern is unlikely to be required in the future environment of the client, why should the program attempt to teach it? If the behavior is infrequently used, it will soon be forgotten unless considerable overlearning is provided. As most is forgotten soon after learning, it is critical that only essential behavior goals be selected for programming.

In setting program goals in specific behavioral terms and components, it becomes necessary to identify both the behaviors to be taught or strengthened as well as to provide some indication of the environment in which the behavior patterns will be used. For example, assume that a rehabilitation program is being designed to train a laundry worker. The skills deemed desirable may be those of (a) preparing the ironing board, iron, and clothing for ironing, (b) ironing clothing satisfactorily, (c) folding and hanging clothing, and (d) cleaning work materials and area following completion of task. The behavioral goals for preparing a client to be a laundry worker in a residential facility for the retarded where quality of work is of less concern than quantity of work would be different from those goals associated with training the person for commercial laundry or household employment. Therefore, the skill level to be attained must be included in the description of the behavior goals. Failure to do so will result in unnecessary program failures as illustrated in the following case of Jane.

This nineteen-year-old mildly retarded female had been trained in the food service department of a private residential facility for the retarded. She was neat and pleasant, dependable, and showed some enthusiasm about completing her work assignments without delay. She was rated high on the twelve categories of behaviors which were deemed related to food

service work. On the basis of this report, she was placed in the food service department of a short-order restaurant in the community as a general helper and given such tasks as washing dishes, cleaning tables, placing certain foods on plates, preparing ice for water glasses and the like. In these tasks she was expected to work independently without supervision or reminders. Within one week she was returned to the residential facility as being unable to perform the simple food service tasks assigned to her. In evaluating her failure, it readily became apparent that the conditions under which she was trained were quite different from those present in the commercial restaurant. In the facility she was the best trainee as others were more severely involved. Thus, relative to the performance of the other institutional workers, she was outstanding. Additionally, the work tasks were highly structured and routine. She knew what to do and she followed a set schedule. She had sufficient time to complete her task before being asked to initiate another one. She had to make few independent decisions. There were no time pressures or requirements to move quickly from one task to another in a nonroutine manner.

One of Jane's peers also had been trained to be a salad chef in the low pressure, highly supportive environment of this program. She lasted only two days when placed in a drugstore. Work came in rush periods which required quick performance in short periods of time. These two cases illustrate the necessity in the development of the training program for a client of both a specification of the skills required in fulfilling a job and a description of the environment in which the person is to use the skills acquired.

Rehabilitation programs that provide recreational experiences in an effort to teach leisure time skills should emphasize those which are likely to be utilized (reinforced) in the future. Rug weaving, for example, may be a most enjoyable recreational activity. It may be used to provide the client with experiences of success and to reinforce a generalized behavior pattern of creativity or expression and of becoming involved in new activities. Whether such a program does in fact contribute to these traits, of course, is an empirical matter. It is not an activity, however, that is likely to be reinforced in the future independent living arrangements of the retarded as no weaving loom will be available for such activity. Thus, the rehabilitation program should carefully designate the function of various activities. It is even possible that some rehabilitation programs create maladaptive behaviors by reinforcing such activities as attending movies frequently, skating, golfing, bowling, and swimming. After being placed in an independent employment status where income is rather marginal, the retarded adult finds that he no longer can participate in these activities because he cannot afford to pay the expenses involved.

In summary, education and rehabilitation program personnel should be informed as to what behavior patterns will be possible and reinforceable

in the occupational and social environment of the retarded client. The program should be designed to teach those behavior patterns which are relevant to that environment. The following types of questions become pertinent: "In what type of environment will the person reside?" "What is the sociology of that environment?" "What behaviors are likely to be acceptable to, tolerated by, or actively maintained by this postrehabilitation training environment?"

3. *A program designed to strengthen and maintain the final behavior goals will consist of a series of well sequenced experiences which move the person closer to the final target behaviors.* This guideline is illustrated by aspects of a program provided by Lent (1968) and his colleagues. In this program to train moderately retarded adolescent girls to use a sewing machine, a series of 17 task components was developed. These included such behavior skills as machine preparation, discrimination of thread color, threading machine, winding bobbin, placing material under machine, using thread cutter and sewing a curved line. Each skill consisted of a series of specific performances. In illustration, the skill of threading machine consisted of the following performances which were to be completed in the following sequence:

(a) Places spool on spool pin
(b) Holds thread in left hand
(c) Places right hand on spool of thread on spool pin
(d) Pulls thread across the machine head and down into hook
(e) Pulls spring up until the thread is caught in the spring
(f) Pulls thread up and through the take-up lever eye
(g) Pulls thread through the hole directly under needle screw and catches it in hook
(h) Pulls thread from hole on right side of needle through to the left side, and places the thread between the foot [p. 61].

4. *The training program should require at a given time those behaviors that are presently in the client's repertoire.* Frequently these will be only approximations of the final target behavior. Reinforcement must be provided these approximations or initial performances of a chain and gradually behavior patterns which more closely resemble the final target behavior.

The training program must be designed to provide as much assistance as is necessary to insure successful progress. The program must match the requirements of the individual client. This program individualization and flexibility is illustrated in the previously mentioned program provided by Lent (1968) and his colleagues to train moderately retarded adolescents

to use a sewing machine: "the instructor always provided the model while describing what she was doing. This description was then given in the form of instructions to the *S*. If the *S* did not respond, the instructor placed the *S*'s hand or foot in the correct position and helped the *S*. The instructor faded the helping process until the *S* could perform the response above" [p. 60].

5. *The client should understand clearly what is expected of him at all times.* This can be accomplished through a verbal description accompanied by demonstration or modeling of the desired behavior. The client can be instructed to role play or try out the desired behavior, with appropriate correction being provided by program personnel. In other instances the desired behavior may be modeled by an adult or peer, preferably one with high prestige or status to the client. The systematic presentation of a reinforcer following appropriate behavior must be included. It is essential that the client engage in the modeled behavior so that it can be strengthened through reinforcement. It is insufficient to show or tell the retarded client what to do; he must do it to insure that he is able to do so. In this manner alterations of the behaviors being acquired can be prompted by verbal, observational, or physical guidance means.

The implementation of these guidelines is illustrated in the following description of the Lent (1968) program of training for moderately retarded adolescent girls:

> The training program used the principle of imitation, i.e., the instructor provided a model of the appropriate response to be performed by the *S*, asked the *S* to perform the same response, and then responded to correct imitations with praise. The generalized reinforcer, consisting of marks on a card was supplied intermittently, and usually at the end of a learning sequence. If a *S* failed to perform the required responses in a step, she was taken to the preceding step. The procedure was followed until the responses required in each step were considered to be adequate by the instructor [p. 60].

6. *The behaviors required for successful adjustment to the rehabilitation program may be different in critical aspects from those required for independent functioning in a nontherapeutic competitive environment.* As a result the program should replicate as closely as possible the various requirements of the future environment and prepare the client to meet these. An excessively therapeutic, highly structured, and benevolent environment may actually impede independent adjustment as such an environment does not train the retarded client to deal with certain negative, unpredictable, and unavoidable experiences which are an inevitable aspect of an independent living status.

It is highly essential that the reinforcement characteristics (for example,

type, amount, schedule) of the future environment be emulated in the training program. Sudden shift from a work environment in which frequent and high magnitude social and tangible reinforcers have been provided to an environment which provides reinforcing events of a different kind and on a different schedule (for example, bi-weekly paycheck instead of the training program schedule of twice weekly) can produce considerable difficulty to the client.

DEVELOPING APPROPRIATE DISCRIMINATIVE
CONTROL OVER BEHAVIOR

1. *It is not unusual to discover that desired behavior may be in the client's repertoire, but not under control of the stimulus elements of the rehabilitation program.* Discriminative control of desired behavior can be gained by insuring that a distinctive cue precedes and if possible accompanies the behavior as it is reinforced.

2. *As the behavior is in the early stages of gaining strength in a specific environment, it may be helpful to provide redundant and distinctive cues to serve as events which mark the time and place in which the behavior will produce the reinforcer.* As the behavior gains in strength, the redundant cues may be faded gradually. In illustration, in teaching highly distractible clients to persist at their work and to refrain from attending to irrelevant aspects of the immediate environment, redundant auditory cues may be provided by the instructor through means of an earphone worn by the client and connected to the instructor's desk. In such an arrangement, the instructor can provide frequent prompts of "Keep working now. Look at your task. Show me how fast you can work" and the like. As the work behavior becomes stronger, the prompts can be faded gradually and eventually terminated. The work task and surrounding stimuli will come to provide the discriminative control over continued high-rate work behavior.

3. *The controlling properties of certain stimulus events may be enhanced by carefully structuring the environmental and behavioral components of the program.* This may be accomplished by (a) simplifying behavioral alternatives, (b) reducing the number of stimulus events which are discriminative of competing behaviors, (c) scheduling reinforcers to compete with inappropriate behaviors, (d) setting specific and well delineated behavioral expectations and limits, and the like. Each of these will serve to emphasize the relationship between behavior patterns that result in reinforcement and specific stimulus events which precede these behavior-reinforcement sequences. The program must insure consistency in reinforcing behavior which occurs under certain stimulus events and in nondelivery of

reinforcers on those occasions in which the behavior occurs in the absence of these program events.

4. *Finally, the program should provide prompt discriminative feedback concerning correctness or appropriateness of a behavior pattern.* The relationship between appropriate discriminative cues and desired behavior should be represented to the client, either by means of model demonstration, role playing, or verbal descriptions.

CHAPTER ELEVEN

Behavior Treatment: Program Development and Strategies for Modification of Behavior

Development of Individual Treatment Programs

With the principles of positive behavior development discussed in the previous chapter as background, the steps involved in developing a behavior treatment program for an individual will be reviewed. Program development can be a relatively simple endeavor in some instances and a most complex one in others. Optimal success in behavior change endeavors can be realized only under the conditions of a highly individualized program which guides the experiences provided the individual. Education and rehabilitation programs may be provided on a group basis; nevertheless, since all persons in a group are not alike in terms of such factors as level of behavior development along program-related dimensions, types of reinforcing events which are most influential, availability of prerequisite behaviors, and the like, the experiences provided the group must be tailored to each person if maximum benefit is to accrue.

DESCRIPTION OF TREATMENT GOALS

The initial step in program development is a delineation of the types of environmental requirements for which the retarded client is being prepared. The mentally retarded becomes a rehabilitation client because the counselor has concluded that the retarded is unable to meet the behavioral re-

quirements of various aspects of work, social, interpersonal, etc. environments. That is, there is a significant discrepancy between the behaviors required in these settings and what the retarded does do. He works too slowly, he is unable to travel independently, he is unable to budget his earnings sufficiently for independent management, he is unable to tolerate the jesting provided by peers, he becomes too emotional and disruptive when under pressure to perform, he is overresponsive to criticism, he is too inattentive, he does not persist at his work task for a sufficient length of time, he makes too many disruptive comments or talks too much at inappropriate times, he objects too frequently to supervisory advice, he becomes angry when thwarted, and the like. He behaves in a manner in one, five or along dozens of different behavioral dimensions that is insufficient in meeting the requirements in certain life situations.

The first step, therefore, in development of an individualized treatment program consists of an enumeration of environmental requirements in terms of the behavior which the person must exhibit. "He must maintain a designated production rate throughout the daily work period." "He must anticipate material shortages and signal the supervisor for more." "He must be able to shift from one assembly task to another without loss of production rate." "He must be able to maintain production rate on repetitive tasks." "He must be able to work for a full week between pay checks." "He must be able to read at a fifth grade level." "He must be able to budget his earnings and be able to live on $75 per week." "He must follow the instructions provided by the work supervisor without argument." *These environmental requirements become the long-range program goals, objectives, or terminal behavior patterns.*

DESCRIPTION OF PRESENT BEHAVIORS

The second step in development of an individual treatment program becomes one of describing the client's present behavior in relation to each of the behavioral requirements enumerated in step one. "He presently is able to meet 50 percent of the minimum production rate." "He presently reads at a third grade level." "He spends whatever money he has without apparent regard for future needs." "A shift from one assembly task to another results in hyperactive behavior and a loss by 15-25 percent in production rate." *These behavioral characteristics become the starting point of a program of behavior change.* These are the present behaviors which must be changed in one way or another. As discussed in the preceding chapter on behavioral evaluation, other related data are obtained which provide direction to the program which is being developed. In discovering that a retarded adult has no functional reading skills, it would be helpful to know what his skill levels were in such related areas as vocabulary, visual and

auditory discrimination, visual and auditory memory, and the like. As another example, in discovering that a retarded client could not perform a certain work task, it may be valuable to know the level of functioning in such related behavioral areas as eye-hand coordination, sitting for lengthy periods of time, persistence under frequent auditory distractions, attending to various critical visual cues and distinguishing these from irrelevant ones, and the like. The behavior analysis as described in the previous chapter would provide data concerning the client's present level of functioning in the required and related behavioral areas.

SPECIFICATION OF TARGET BEHAVIORS

The discrepancy or difference between the environmental requirements and the client's present level of performance defines the task of the treatment program. *This difference defines the program content and target behavior goals.* "Increase rate of production by 25 percent." "Increase functional reading skills by two grade levels." "Reduce disruptive talking during work hours by 25 percent." "Eliminate arguments with supervisor." In relation to each target behavior area, it may be necessary to set a series of subgoals which are sequenced in such a manner that the final behavior goals are gradually attained. A reading program will be organized around a large number of specific steps including lessons in vocabulary building, increasing comprehension of materials heard and read, memory for materials read, and the like. In planning the program, the long-range or terminal behavior goals must be organized into a series of discrete steps which begin with the present behaviors exhibited by the client. Each subgoal or step is translated into specific behaviors required in meeting this subgoal. The program task then becomes one of influencing the development of these target behaviors under specific environmental conditions. The target behavior, again, refers to the immediate behavior which the program is designed to develop. It may be viewed as that behavior which the program will reinforce at any specific stage of the program. The target behavior will change frequently in the direction of the terminal behavior goal. The target behavior at any stage of the program may represent only the beginning segment of a complex chain of behaviors or perhaps a poor approximation of the desired terminal behavior. As an illustration, the succeeding target behaviors in a program designed to teach an excessively shy retarded adult to approach strangers and ask for various types of information (for example, directions, time, bus schedule, prices, availability of certain merchandise) may be as follows: (1) approach a friend and ask previously rehearsed questions, (2) accompany friends as they approach and ask strangers for information, (3) approach friends who are in the presence of strangers and ask the friends for information, with the information being

provided by the strangers, (4) approach and ask questions of a new acquaintance, (5) approach an acquaintance of a friend and ask questions when accompanied by the friend, (6) approach a stranger and ask questions while accompanied by a friend, (7) approach a stranger and ask simple questions, (8) approach a stranger and ask for more detailed information. As the client is able to accomplish each target behavior step, he is required to attempt the next. If he is unable to move from one step to the next, the program is redesigned, either to include a series of smaller target behavior steps or to include different discriminative or reinforcing components.

As discussed previously, the basic question confronting those who organize the treatment program becomes that of "How can the program be structured in order to promote continuous behavior change from the present level and mode of behaving to the terminal behavior objectives?" If at any time, program components cannot be defended either logically or empirically as representing a step in the direction of developing and strengthening the terminal behaviors, these parts of the program should be discarded. Every component of a program must be defended in terms of the manner in which it contributes to the development of a designated target behavior. In turn, the meaningfulness of the target behavior must be defended in terms of its relevance to the terminal behavior goal.

PROGRAM DESIGN

The final consideration becomes that of designing a behavior modification environment to promote the development of the terminal behavior goals. Such a program plan would include a description of the environmental setting in which the program will be implemented as well as a description of the specific treatment procedures to be followed. The specific program provided at any given time to influence specific target behaviors is described in terms of the four components of the Target Behavior Program Report as discussed in Chapter 9. The target behavior treatment program becomes the central feature of the Behavior Modification Program Report as depicted in Table 11.1. As noted in this table, the Program Report should include a specification of the procedures to be followed in evaluating the effectiveness of the treatment program as well as suggestions concerning alternative program procedures to be used in the event that sufficient progress is not realized.

The general strategies selected to influence the target behaviors as well as the specific aspects of these procedures will depend upon numerous factors. These factors would include such variables as the nature of the problem behavior, the factors which presently control the client's behavior, the specifics of the client's reinforcement hierarchy, the setting in which the

Table 11.1. Behavior Modification Program Report

Name of Behavior Therapist: _____

Name of Client: _____

Date of Program: _____

Terminal Behavior Goal:

Present Behavior:

Target Behavior Program: (Describe details of AE-B-C-SE components):

Procedure for Evaluating Treatment Effects:

Alternative Treatment Procedures:

---

behavior modification program is to be initiated, the characteristics of the people available to implement the program, and the like. For example, the procedures used in a program designed to strengthen behavior which is in the person's repertoire but which does not occur in the desired place would differ from the procedures used to eliminate undesirable patterns of behaving. The reinforcement procedure used with an individual who is relatively uninfluenced by social reinforcers would differ from that used with an individual who is highly responsive to praise and approval.

There are three general classes of behavior modification procedures,

each related to a type of behavior change. First, there are procedures available for *establishing* a new response. Next, there are procedures which are designed to *increase the strength* of behavior and to insure the continuation of the behavior in future settings. Finally, a group of techniques is available for *decreasing the strength* of behavior. Common to all of these are procedures for developing environmental control over designated behaviors.

Techniques for Establishing and Strengthening Behavior

The techniques used to influence the development of a new behavior or to influence the strength and consistency of a response pattern presently in the person's repertoire are based primarily on the principles of reinforcement.

REINFORCEMENT OF SUCCESSIVE
APPROXIMATIONS: BEHAVIOR SHAPING

It has been emphasized that behavior is strengthened by certain events which follow the behavior. Operant behavior which does not produce positively reinforcing events or which does not terminate some present aversive conditions will not develop in strength. In positive reinforcement, behavior is strengthened by those consequences which the behavior produces. In most programs it would be desirable to have the person select those reinforcers which he would prefer to have or experience. A listing of available reinforcers from which the person may choose would facilitate appropriate reinforcer selection. Addison and Homme (1966) and Clements and McKee (1968) have described the use of this "reinforcement menu" procedure.

In designing a program to influence the strength of a behavior, it is necessary to consider such additional procedures as reinforcer deprivation and reinforcer sampling, for example, to increase the strength of the reinforcing events selected for use. The basic factor to remember is that behavior must be followed consistently by events which are in fact reinforcing to the client and which are of sufficient magnitude in relation to the nature of the desired behavior. Programs frequently fail, not because the consequent events are not reinforcing to the individual, but rather because the person's state of deprivation is too low in relation to the reinforcer or because the reinforcer is not of sufficient magnitude in relation to the desired behavior. Social reinforcement, for example, may be quite sufficient to strengthen and maintain attending behavior during a class in current events but may be totally inadequate to strengthen attending and work behavior during a class in mathematics. As noted in the preceding chapter, a token economy system provides great flexibility in dealing with the mul-

tiple variables associated with optimal reinforcement procedures. Birn-brauer and Lawler (1964), Birnbrauer, Wolf, Kidder and Tague (1965), Burchard (1967), Lent (1968), Montgomery and McBurney (1970) and Zimmerman, Stucky, Garlick and Miller (1969) provide excellent descriptions of token reinforcement programs designed to influence various work, social, and academic behaviors of the mentally retarded. These, and recent reports and critiques of token economy programs by Krasner (1970a, 1970b) and Ayllon and Azrin (1968), should be consulted by those initiating a token economy program.

The use of a reinforcement procedure to strengthen behavior obviously depends upon the initial occurrence of the desired behavior. The behavior cannot produce a reinforcer until it occurs in the form required by the contingency in force. In some instances, the desired behavior may be in the person's repertoire, but not under control of appropriate environmental events. Thus, the behavior may never occur at the desired time or place or may occur only infrequently and therefore will not be reinforced in this setting. The task in these instances becomes one of arranging the prompting and reinforcing components of the environment in a manner which will insure that the behavior will occur and will be reinforced.

This is illustrated by a recent experience with a twenty year old mildly retarded client who demonstrated rather erratic work behavior in a work training program. Jack presented a most frustrating pattern of behavior. On occasion, he would attend the work training program and engage in excellent work behavior. He would be quite attentive to the task, work rapidly without distraction, and produce at a high rate. More characteristically, however, he would either refuse to enter the workshop or, if he did actually enter the workshop, he engaged in various disruptive and negativistic behaviors. It was evident that appropriate work behaviors were in his repertoire in the form required by the work environment. However, such behaviors did not occur with sufficient frequency to warrant adjustment to the workshop requirements. The task became one of strengthening the appropriate work behaviors and bringing these under the control of the work environment.

A behavioral analysis revealed that reinforcement procedures were inconsistent, were not provided in proximity to the desired work behaviors, and further that use was not being made of classes of reinforcing events which were readily available and quite powerful in magnitude. It was discovered that conversation with staff members, especially with young adults and even more especially if females were involved, was a highly desirable event. After providing this event (that is, conversation with young female staff members) contingent upon successful workshop performance, work behaviors increased in frequency of occurrence. As the work behaviors

became stronger, the frequency and time of the reinforcing conversation with adults were reduced and gradually withdrawn as the contingent consequence of work behavior. Again, behavior of the desired form which was in the repertoire, but of low strength in the work environment, was strengthened by rearranging the reinforcing components of the environment.

In other instances, the desired behavior is not present in the form desired. Even the most powerful reinforcer available under the most optimal prompting conditions would be of no value in these cases. Such a state calls for a procedure of behavior shaping by reinforcing successive approximations of the desired behavior. In this manner, through a series of occurrences in which closer and closer approximations of the desired behavior are reinforced, the retarded acquires the behavior. The initial approximations may be quite different from the final behavior goal. These must be reinforced, however, as these form the basis for similar behaviors which represent closer approximations of the final goal behavior.

In behavior shaping, various techniques are available to get the client to engage in the behavior which can be reinforced. These *prompting* techniques include verbal instruction, physical guidance, precise environmental arrangement, and modeling or demonstration. The client may be told what he should do in certain situations. "John, when the bell rings, you are to go to the supply room." "Sue, after you finish, put the dishes in the sink." In other instances, the instructor may provide physical guidance. In illustration, he may take the client's hands and move him through a difficult motor movement. Crosson (1969) describes the use of several of these prompting procedures in his work training program for severely retarded adults. In initiating the training procedure, "the trainer demonstrates each of the component behaviors in their proper sequence and prompts the trainee to immediately model the behavior. This can be accomplished by verbal or gestured command although it is occasionally necessary to 'mold' the response by physically guiding the trainee through an approximation of the appropriate topography" [p. 815].

The desired behavior may be demonstrated by a peer or the instructor as the client observes. This response exposure should also include a demonstration of the consequences of desired performance along with a verbal description of the contingency involved. Following observation, the client should rehearse what he has observed and be reinforced promptly for successful approximations. The imitated behavior could be shaped further by means of verbal or gestured instructions and physical guidance. The value of such demonstrations is illustrated in the following case of a severely withdrawn adolescent who spent most of her time sitting on the floor of her room with her head in her lap. One aspect of the treatment pro-

gram called for her to sit in a chair in an effort to increase her exposure to social stimulation. The behavior therapist had been unsuccessful in getting her to sit in the chair under the conditions of verbal prompts and physical guidance. The client promptly sat in the chair, however, after observing a peer demonstrate the behavior pattern of getting off the floor, sitting in the chair and of receiving and consuming the food reinforcer provided.

A study reported by Kliebhan (1967) provides further illustration of the value of modeling in influencing the acquisition of desired behavior. In this study, mildly retarded clients enrolled in a job training program were exposed to a model who performed the task engaged in by the clients. The model demonstrated the behaviors involved in both appropriate rate of performance as well as quality of performance. In comparison with a control group which had been exposed to a training procedure which relied heavily on verbal prompting, the performance of this "exposure to model" group was superior in production rate and in quality of work completed.

It would be possible also to facilitate the occurrence of behavior by restricting the response possibilities and thus rendering more likely the occurrence of the desired behavior. The development of skills of attending to and persisting at a work task, for example, may be facilitated by removing distracting visual or auditory stimulation. This strategy was followed in a project concerned with the development of basic sheltered workshop skills in a group of hyperactive and highly distractible severely retarded adults. The clients were trained one at a time in a small room with minimal irrelevant visual and auditory stimulation. This training environment greatly restricted the response possibilities and rendered more likely the occurrence of the desired behaviors. As the work skills increased in strength, the clients were moved through a series of environments which represented a closer approximation of the final workshop one.

These various prompting techniques are used to increase the likelihood that some behavior will occur which approximates the target or terminal behavior goals. The prompted behavior will not be strengthened, however, unless followed by reinforcement. As the behavior is brought under control of the reinforcing aspects of the environment, the behavioral requirements are gradually shifted in the direction of the more complex goal behavior.

As the behavior gains in strength and more closely approximates the goal behavior, it becomes desirable to remove gradually the prompting cues. The verbal instructions, gestural cuing, modeling, physical guidance, response restriction, or whatever combination is being used, should become less conclusive and less frequent. During the *fading* procedure, other components which are more natural to the behavior and to the environment in which it is expected to occur assume the discriminative stimulus function. The work table and materials begin to cue or control the work behavior.

The instructor's verbal prompt of "keep working now" is no longer needed as this prompt or control is assumed by natural components of the environment. This was illustrated by Culkin (1968) in her work with a group of highly disruptive retarded clients in a work training program. During training, both visual and auditory prompts were successfully used to obtain consistent work behavior which was of higher quality than that present prior to introducing the prompts. The prompts were used to emit behaviors of attending to the task, persisting at the task, and working rapidly. These prompts, presented through earphones worn by the trainee or by means of a signal box located on the work table, were gradually removed as the desired behaviors increased in strength. After complete removal of the prompts, the desired behaviors were maintained by the discriminative components of the natural work environment. Culkin observed considerable individual differences among these retarded clients in terms of the relative influence of various prompting procedures. Some were quite influenced by visual prompts; others were more influenced by auditory prompts. This observation emphasizes the necessity of individualizing prompts as well as other components of the behavior modification program.

Although the prompt should be removed as quickly as possible, care should be taken not to remove it too suddenly as the behavior may stop. At the same time, artificial prompts should not be maintained for an excessive length of time as these may become powerful discriminative stimuli without which the behavior will not occur.

Again, in a behavior shaping program, full appreciation must be given to individual differences. All will not acquire new approximations at the same rate, respond to the same prompts, or be influenced by the same reinforcing events or magnitudes.

CHAINING DEVELOPMENT OF COMPLEX BEHAVIORS

Behavior shaping through reinforcement of successive approximation of desired behaviors is useful in building relatively simple performances. After responses have been acquired, however, it is possible to link or chain these together into more lengthy and complex behavior patterns. These behavior patterns are linked together by stimulus events which serve both to reinforce the behavior which produced it and to set the occasion for additional performances. It will be recalled from an earlier discussion that discriminative stimulus events acquire secondary reinforcing properties through consistent association with the reinforcement which follows the performance. An increasing number of behavior links can be added to a chain as a consequence of these stimuli. These intervening stimuli come to reinforce the preceding behaviors and cue the occurrence of subsequent behaviors. These intervening stimuli maintain their discriminative and reinforcing

properties due to the reinforcing consequences of the entire chain or be-havior pattern. In illustration, a complex behavior chain consisting of walk-ing into the cafeteria, picking up a tray and utensils, selecting food, paying for the food, finding a table, sitting at the table, and finally consuming the food is maintained by the final reinforcement associated with consuming the food. None of the behavior chain would occur in the absence of the final consequence. None of the links in this chain would be maintained unless it was a necessary step in the chain. Each link in the chain is maintained by various conditioned reinforcers which serve the dual function as discrimina-tive stimuli for the next link in the chain. Conditioned reinforcing properties are attached to a wide range of stimuli which are consistently present during the development of various links in the chain. These stimuli could consist of various auditory, visual, tactual, and olfactory cues, cues from the person's own behavior, verbal cues such as "Now I've finished that. I must start the next item" and the like. Such implicit verbal responses actually represent critical links, with discriminative and reinforcing aspects, in behavioral chains. The development of such self-maintaining links represents one of the goals of behavior modification programs for those with a verbal repertoire.

In developing a complex chain of behavior, it is frequently desirable to begin backwards and provide reinforcement for the final performance of the chain. After this response occurs with some strength whenever distinct discriminative stimuli are present, an additional performance is required prior to the final performance which results in reinforcement. As new links are added to the chain, more and more behavior is required prior to rein-forcement. In building such response chains, it is important to insure that each new link has acquired suitable strength before adding an additional link. Otherwise, the chain will be eliminated completely. Careful sequenc-ing of response chains, with attention provided initially to insure that each link in the chain produces some distinctive stimuli, can result in the acqui-sition of complex behavior patterns.

An example of strengthening a chain of work behaviors in a group of severely/profoundly retarded nonverbal adults will illustrate this pro-cedure. The work task consisted of placing a leather washer on a four-inch long nail, putting eighteen completed units to a box, closing the box, and stacking it in a basket located on the edge of the work bench. Initially, the clients would not even sit in a chair at the work table. The first task became one of shaping the behavior of approaching the work table, sitting in the chair and facing the work area. This was accomplished by reinforcing approximations of this behavior using gestural and physical guidance prompts. Once this was brought under reinforcement control, the chair and work table became discriminative stimuli for the behavior of approaching the table, sitting in the chair and facing the work area. Next, response pat-

terns involved in the work task were shaped. It will be noted in the following description that the last performance in the response chain was strengthened initially and gradually linked to each preceding performance until the entire chain from approaching the work table to completion of task was developed. Tangible (food) and social reinforcers were provided after the last performance in the chain, that of stacking the box in the basket, was completed. The performances were strengthened in the following order: (1) Stacking closed boxes into basket. (2) Closing boxes of nails that had been filled and stacking them in basket. (3) Placing 18 nail/washer units in box, closing box, and stacking box in basket. (4) Placing 18 nails through 18 leather washers which had previously been placed on a specially constructed jig, removing completed nail/washer units and placing into box, closing the box, and stacking box in basket. (5) Placing 18 leather washers in 18 slots of jig, placing 18 nails through leather washers, removing completed nail/washer units and placing into box, closing box, and stacking box in basket.

At this stage, the performances of the chain were linked to the initial performance of sitting at the work table and facing the work area. With the chain completed the person would walk into the workshop, approach his work area, sit in the chair, face the work table, pick up the leather washer, place 18 washers in the 18 slots of the jig, pick up 18 nails and place them through the washers, remove the completed units and place in a box, close the box and stack the closed box in a basket. Each link in the chain was initiated by stimulus components of the task which also served as reinforcers for the preceding performance. For example, picking up a nail served as a cue for placing the nail through the leather washer. This also served a secondary reinforcing function for the preceding performance of placing the washer in the slot of the jig. As noted earlier, these stimulus components gain their discriminative and reinforcing functions through association with the final tangible and social reinforcement provided at the end of the response chain.

INFLUENCING RESPONDENT BEHAVIORS

It will be recalled that respondent behaviors are controlled by preceding stimulus events. A program designed to influence a range of respondent emotional behaviors becomes one of influencing the stimulus functions of various environmental events. It may be desirable to neutralize an event which controls either positive or negative emotional reactions. In other instances it may be desirable to substitute either a positive or an aversive stimulus function for a present neutral one. The techniques associated with eliminating the respondent control features of stimulus events will be discussed in the following section. The procedure of developing a new posi-

tive or aversive stimulus function for a neutral stimulus is a relatively simple one. The neutral events must be paired with the presentation of a stimulus event having established positive or aversive properties. After a series of pairings, the previously neutral event will acquire the stimulus properties of the paired event. The teacher or counselor who provides positive reinforcers to the retarded clients acquires some of the positive features of the reinforcers. In the same manner, the teacher or counselor who delivers aversive stimuli will acquire some of the aversive properties of these events. After conditioning, the presence of the counselor or teacher, in this latter situation, will elicit emotional reactions which may be labeled as unpleasantness, fearfulness, or dislike.

These respondents and associated stimulus properties exert an influence on a wide range of other respondent and operant behaviors. It will be recalled from Chapter 5 that certain stimulus-response interactions, which have been labeled as setting events, influence other behavior patterns which follow. These setting events render more likely the occurrence of certain subsequent behaviors. An environment which produces certain respondent behaviors with aversive or unpleasant stimulus components interferes with positive behavior development and functioning. Such emotional states disrupt and otherwise interfere with appropriate behavior functioning. In contrast, the environment which produces positive emotional states renders more likely the occurrence of such appropriate behaviors as cooperativeness, compliance, and friendliness.

These relationships can be used to good advantage by program personnel. Encouragement, statements of future consequences, support, friendliness, and the like may create emotional states which render more likely the occurrence of a wide range of appropriate behavior.

Just as some persons function best under conditions of positive setting events, it is true that some retarded clients will function appropriately only following punishment or the threat of some aversive consequences. In these cases, it is necessary to build the value of positive setting events by a rich experience of contingently provided positive reinforcement.

NEGATIVE REINFORCEMENT: THE DEVELOPMENT
OF ESCAPE AND AVOIDANCE BEHAVIORS

As noted, the strength of behavior can be influenced in those instances in which the behavior terminates an aversive event. Such a procedure of negative reinforcement, while not usually the preferred method of influencing behavior strength in a behavior modification program, can be of value in selected instances. It may not be possible, as an example, to maintain a highly disruptive client in a group program due to the management problem which is created. The development of more appropriate behavior

patterns through positive reinforcement may require more time than is available. Thus, it may be necessary to impose a highly aversive set of contingencies in order to create a learning situation in which competing avoidance behaviors may be developed through negative reinforcement. As the appropriate behavior occurs, the aversiveness is terminated and the preceding behavior is reinforced negatively. The person is able to avoid the aversive consequences as long as he behaves appropriately. Appropriate behavior terminates the threat of the aversive consequences. Behaving inappropriately reimposes the threat of the aversive consequences. The conditioned aversive events may well consist of a threat of removal of positive reinforcers by means of a response cost procedure. The client can avoid the response cost contingency by behaving in a nondisruptive manner.

Additionally, in a program designed to promote positive behavior development, negative reinforcement can be used to produce desired behaviors which can be strengthened further and eventually controlled by positive reinforcement. Much law abiding and self-control behavior has gained strength through a combination of negative and positive reinforcement. Such behaviors remove the threat of aversive stimuli, for example, fines, reprimands, disapproval, rejection, etc., and may produce the counterpart in positive reinforcement, for example, approval, acceptance, and the like.

The operation of negative reinforcement or the termination of aversive conditions has a strengthening feature in addition to that associated with development of escape and avoidance behaviors. Any stimuli which are associated consistently with the termination of an aversive event may acquire secondary positive reinforcer properties. The procedure of building a new stimulus function in this manner has been termed *aversion relief*. This technique to change the stimulus properties of events in the client's environment is described in a clinical study by Solyom and Miller (1967). In this study, stimuli which controlled phobic reactions were changed from aversive to positive by associating them with the termination of shock. As the stimulus functions were changed, the phobic reactions disappeared. Thorpe, Schmidt, Brown, and Castell (1964) report similar success with this stimulus substitution procedure in work with a range of nonadaptive behaviors.

Techniques of Developing and Maintaining Control of Behavior

Aspects of the environment come to exert powerful control over behavior. Upon the occurrence of these events, specified behaviors occur promptly and consistently. Further, behavior comes to persist for extended periods in the absence of apparent reinforcement. This section will review the procedures whereby behavior patterns come to be controlled by positive and

aversive components of the environment. Additionally, techniques to insure that behavior will be maintained after the termination of the treatment programs will be described.

DEVELOPMENT OF POSITIVE DISCRIMINATIVE CONTROL

The better the behavior of the mentally retarded is controlled by specific aspects of the environment, the more the likelihood that he will obtain the reinforcers available in that environment. As noted previously, one of the major deficits associated with the retarded is the lack of specific stimulus or environmental control of behavior. Behavior patterns needed for adaptation frequently are in the repertoire; these behaviors just do not occur on certain occasions with the reliability needed to produce consistent reinforcement. The behaviors are not functionally matched to the requirements of his environment.

This deficit can be overcome by systematic discrimination training in which a strategy of differential reinforcement is followed. As noted in earlier chapters, stimulus components of the environment which are present when a behavior is reinforced acquire some control over the future occurrence of that behavior. These events mark the occasion for the behavior. If a given behavior is reinforced a number of times in the presence of consistent and distinctive stimulus events, these events gain discriminative control over the behavior. Whenever these stimulus events are presented, the behavior follows. The development of this environmental or stimulus control depends upon consistent differential reinforcement. When the behavior occurs under a specific stimulus event, the behavior is reinforced. Whenever the behavior occurs under any other stimulus events, reinforcement is not provided. In this manner, certain aspects of the environment come to control the occurrence of certain behaviors.

Adaptive behavior difficulties of the retarded may result from insufficient differential reinforcement. Rehabilitation programs, either through poor design or as a result of a therapeutic attitude that inappropriate behaviors should be tolerated, may inadvertently teach the retarded to behave in an indiscriminate manner across various occasions. When the person is removed from the program or therapy, however, he obtains much less reinforcement due to the fact that the behavior is reinforced only on certain occasions and not on others. In illustration, a rehabilitation program may provide social reinforcement in the form of praise or approval following appropriate behavior. The program may also provide powerful social reinforcement in the form of "counseling" whenever the person engages in inappropriate behavior. As a result, the environment does not acquire precise differential control over the two patterns of behavior.

Every behavior modification program must include a strategy of precise

discrimination training. Distinctive cues consistently presented whenever behavior is reinforced will result in a repertoire which will match the reinforcement requirements imposed by various environments.

ROLE OF REINFORCEMENT PATTERNS IN BEHAVIOR CONTROL

In order to function independently, the retarded must be able to maintain a wide range of performances under conditions in which reinforcement is provided only on infrequent and irregular occasions. One important factor, which is related to whether or not the retarded person is able to behave in a stable manner under these conditions, is the manner in which he is able to progress from conditions of frequent reinforcement to conditions of infrequent reinforcement.

If the person's performance is developed under conditions of frequent reinforcement and he is required suddenly to perform under infrequent reinforcement conditions, even if the total magnitude or value of the reinforcement is the same, the behavior in all likelihood would reduce in quantity and perhaps would even extinguish.

The preferred technique to use in a program to insure maintenance of the behavior is to move through a number of small intermediate steps or schedules and gradually require an increasing amount of behavior prior to providing reinforcement. Typically, a history of even small values of intermittent schedules results in much more persistent behavior during periods of nonreinforcement than is characteristic of prolonged periods of continuous reinforcement.

These relationships between stability of behavior and schedules of reinforcement provide meaningful explanations for many cases of rehabilitation failure involving the mentally retarded. In an effort to provide an optimal rehabilitation environment, the retarded client is provided frequent reinforcement. Under such a schedule, highly appropriate and stable work and related behaviors may appear. However, when removed from this environment and placed in one in which reinforcement is less frequent and more irregular, the highly valued behavior patterns are frequently lost. The worker is not as attentive, his rate is reduced, work quality declines. The previously described relationships between the schedules by which preceding reinforcement has been provided and the maintenance of behavior patterns would suggest that even brief experiences during the rehabilitation program with an intermittent reinforcement schedule which approximated that of the job would have greatly increased the likelihood that the behaviors would have been maintained. Ideally, the client would have had prolonged experiences with reinforcement on an intermittent schedule similar to that which is followed in the work setting.

Likewise, as the client is moved from easy tasks to more difficult ones in

a training program, it is essential for a smooth transition that there be a gradual and systematic shift from continuous success on the easy task to partial success (reinforcement) on the more difficult ones. The difficult tasks must be organized into small easier segments and redesigned into more complex units as success is obtained. During these intermediate steps, the client learns to function on a small intermittent schedule. As the behavior is maintained on this schedule, the difficulty of the tasks can be increased slowly. In this manner, the client will be able to tolerate greater periods of difficulty without extinction of problem solving or persistent behavior. A rapid transition from easy to difficult, however, would have resulted in rapid reduction in the work behavior. It is essential that new requirements are not increased too quickly. A small and systematic change in the reinforcement schedule is a necessary requirement if highly stable behavior is to be achieved under conditions of infrequent reinforcement.

The speed with which a fixed-ratio schedule, for example, can be changed from one of frequent to one of infrequent reinforcement must be determined empirically. The performance must initially be reinforced frequently (that is, on small fixed ratios) and gradually moved to less and less frequent reinforcement. The pace by which the size of the ratio is increased is dependent upon the effects that changes have on the behavior. If the behavior is maintained upon change, an additional small change in ratio should follow after some experience. If the shift is too great or too rapid, the client may become discouraged and withdraw or develop other defensive (avoidance) behaviors that will remove him from the situation. In this manner, a once positive situation can become an aversive one.

These concepts concerning schedules of reinforcement suggest an explanation of many of the behavioral deficit characteristics that are usual with the retarded client. It is possible that a great deal of behavior that is in his repertoire does not appear because of the nature of the schedule on which reinforcement is available in the environment. Too much behavior is required prior to reinforcement delivery. The retarded is unable to maintain behavior in terms of this schedule. Laboratory studies suggest that the deficit may well be alleviated if the client is provided a systematic experience in making a transition from frequent to infrequent reinforcement.

In work with the more severely involved retarded, it is noted frequently that behavior does not come under the typical reinforcement schedule control. Behavior is frequently erratic, with persistence and rate of output minimal unless the person is under optimal reinforcement conditions of immediate and frequent delivery of a high preference reinforcer. Stamm (1970) reports a procedure which appears to have utility in some instances in assuming the smooth development of the usual schedule control. A response correlated continuous counter in the form of a distinct visual cue was used to denote progress toward reinforcer presentation. Groups of severely re-

tarded adults were trained to perform a simple operant response under a fixed schedule of 100. After a stable rate of performance under this schedule, the response correlated counter was introduced. This counter consisted of a series of small lights mounted above the response apparatus. After the completion of each response, one of the lights would turn on and remain lighted until the hundredth response at which time a reinforcer was delivered. All lights would turn off and the process started again. The correlated counter influenced a significantly higher response rate for all subjects not already responding at a high rate and in typical fixed-ratio schedule form. In addition, the correlated counter facilitated establishment of fixed-ratio controlled response patterning. Thus, the use of such a stimulus device may prove useful in overcoming the discriminative and schedule control deficits which characterize the more severely involved and behaviorally disruptive retarded.

DEVELOPMENT OF AVERSIVE STIMULUS CONTROL

Those aspects of the environment which are associated with the occurrence of aversive events come to exert control over those behaviors which escape from or avoid these aversive events. These events acquire conditioned aversive properties and serve as discriminative stimuli for behaviors which terminate the events. Thus, aversive stimuli can be used to build new stimulus functions. Stimuli which are nonaversive can acquire aversive features by systematic pairing with the onset of aversive events. These newly acquired conditioned aversions can be used in programs to control and to strengthen various behavior patterns.

In those instances in which various techniques of behavior control, strengthening, or elimination involving aversive stimuli are used, it is essential that distinctive cues are provided on a consistent basis. The effectiveness of conditioned aversive stimuli in controlling behavior depends to a great extent on how closely these correlate with the actual aversive event. A supervisor who threatens a client with aversive consequences will exert control only if the threat has been closely correlated with the actual aversive event. A threat that has not or which on occasion does not produce the aversive consequence will not influence the behavior of the person threatened. In some cases the verbal threat does not gain discriminative control until it is presented in a loud, harsh voice and accompanied by a frown and threatening gestures. As these in combination, and only these, have preceded the delivery of the threatened aversive consequences, these acquire control functions.

SHIFTING THE NATURE OF CONTROL FACTORS

One goal of a behavior modification program may be that of shifting the mode of control from aversive to positive events. As has been noted on

several previous occasions, it is not unusual for a large segment of the behavior of the retarded to be under the control of aversive events. Behavior
is maintained as it escapes from or avoids aversive conditions. Both appropriate and inappropriate behavior may be so controlled. A history of punishment and negative reinforcement associated with limited positive social
reinforcement and with being ridiculed, ostracized, rejected, and avoided
can produce generalized avoidance behavior. The person may appear to
be uninterested and aloof. In other instances, appropriate behavior of
attending school, following directions provided by the supervisor, interacting with peers without disruption, completion of task assignment and the
like may all represent aversive control. The retarded adolescent may
attend school in order to avoid detention, complete work assignments in
order to avoid remaining after work hours, follow supervisory instructions
as a means of avoiding the lengthy lecture which he will receive from the
counselor following an argument, and the like. If the aversive control components were suddenly removed from the environment (for example,
through dismissal of supervisor, removal of the possibility of delivering
punishment through administrative regulation, etc.), there may be a dras-
tic change in behavior. Incidence of disruption, limited task completion,
arguments with supervisor, absenteeism, and the like would tend to
increase.

It becomes desirable to bring these appropriate behaviors under positive
environmental control. This is accomplished gradually by providing positive reinforcement whenever the desired behavior occurs. As the behaviors
are controlled increasingly by positive factors, the aversive control components—the threat and punishment—can be removed. Except under the
most ideal conditions, most behaviors will still be influenced somewhat by
aversive aspects of the environment. The important factor, however, is that
the predominant mode of control become positive in nature. The person
may refrain from arguments with his supervisor because he is somewhat
fearful of the consequences of such activity. However, it is most desirable
to insure that he is positively reinforced consistently for following supervisory instructions. Again, the appropriate behavior is predominantly controlled by positive factors.

In some instances, the shift from aversive control to positive control becomes a most difficult task because so much of the behavior is under aversive control or because specific escape or avoidance behaviors may be of
high strength. The behavior modification program must be sensitive to the
nature of the control factors and utilize strategies which will insure a gradual shift to positive control. The initial aspects of the program may well include the continuation of punishment or other aversive control elements of
the environment for a period of time. As positive reinforcement for appro-

priate behaviors begins to exert control, the aversive procedures are concomitantly reduced in frequency and intensity and eventually terminated if possible.

Techniques for Eliminating Behavior

There are two basic techniques used in a program to weaken or eliminate operant behavior patterns. These techniques of extinction and punishment are frequently supplemented by a procedure of reinforcement of alternate or competing behaviors. Finally, respondent or emotional behaviors are eliminated through operations of extinction and counterconditioning.

EXTINCTION OF BEHAVIOR UNDER
POSITIVE REINFORCEMENT CONTROL

As discussed in an earlier chapter, an extinction technique may be used in a program designed to eliminate undesirable behavior. This involves the removal of those consequences which are reinforcing or maintaining the behavior. This is easier said than done in many instances as most behaviors are maintained by multiple consequences. However, in those instances in which there is some strong hypothesis about the nature of the controlling consequence, the extinction procedure may be initiated. In planning a behavior modification program it is necessary to specify the operations of the procedure. "How will the reinforcing consequences be removed?" becomes a critical operations question.

Whenever an extinction procedure is used in a behavior modification program, preparation should be made for the possible appearance of two undesirable side effects. First, there may be an initial, although temporary, increase in the frequency or magnitude of the problem behavior after reinforcement has been discontinued. This effect will disappear, however, if the program is persistent in its nonreinforcement strategy. Secondly, an extinction procedure may produce frustration reactions in the early phase of discontinuance of reinforcement. The intensity and duration of these effects is dependent upon the history of reinforcement of the behavior under extinction. As noted earlier, an intermittent reinforcement schedule will produce fewer frustration behaviors than a schedule which reinforced on every previous occurrence of the behavior. Knowledge of the possible reactions will do much to insure that, once begun, an extinction procedure will be used with facility.

When using an extinction operation, it is imperative that the reinforcement is *not* provided once the program has begun. If reinforcement is provided prior to complete extinction, the behavior may show a rapid increase in strength and a further resistance to extinction.

An extinction procedure is seldom used in isolation except perhaps in cases of simple behaviors. The program should be designed to promote some alternative means of behaving in the situation. Otherwise, the extinction procedure will only result in the removal of the control components of the behavior. Such a procedure does not teach the person what to do. For example, an adolescent may spend excessive time in class attempting to attract the attention of his peers. Peer attention may be maintaining the disruptive behavior. If the environment could be engineered such that peers would not attend to him at those times during which the disruptive behavior was occurring, such disruptive behavior should drop out. However, some alternative behavior is likely to replace this pattern. This replacement behavior may be just as undesirable as the disruptive behavior unless the program teaches some alternative appropriate behavior. Additionally, the diminution of social reinforcement (peer attention) may result in other undersirable reactions. He may feel rejected, isolated, unliked, with the result that various emotional behaviors will further compound his adaptation to the situation. These factors render it essential that an extinction procedure be used in combination with other behavior change strategies. In this instance, other appropriate means of obtaining peer attention should be provided. Under such conditions, the person can obtain peer attention by means of behaviors which will replace these previous disruptive behaviors eliminated through nonreinforcement. The simultaneous reinforcement of incompatible or alternative behaviors adds greatly to the usefulness of an extinction procedure.

ELIMINATION OF AVOIDANCE (DEFENSIVE) CONTROL

Escape and avoidance behavior gains strength initially as such behavior terminates or reduces the frequency or intensity of aversive events. Thus, that behavior is strengthened and maintained which successfully results in the termination or removal of those present stimulus conditions which are aversive or which postpone or decrease the possibility that present or available positively reinforcing events will be removed. As long as there is some indication that either class of events (that is, presentation of aversive conditions or removal of positive conditions) will be produced by given behaviors, these behaviors will remain in strength. Avoidance behavior is maintained by some distinct preaversive or conditioned aversive cues. Upon presentation of these cues, avoidance behavior occurs which terminates the possibility that the aversive conditions will occur.

The very nature of avoidance conditioning results in an increased possibility that avoidance behavior will occur the closer the person gets, physically or temporally, to the aversive event. Also, after avoidance conditioning, such behavior may be controlled cognitively. That is, the preaversive

stimulus controlling the avoidance behavior may consist of the person's thoughts about the aversive event. The person may merely think about an aversive situation and engage in behavior which avoids that situation.

Under these conditions, it is frequently difficult to get the person to refrain from engaging in the avoidance behavior. Until the person is actually exposed to the previously aversive situation, or to an approximation of it, the aversiveness of the situation will not be reduced nor can the nonoccurrence of the aversive events in the situation weaken the avoidance behavior. Unless the person approaches the previously aversive situation and discovers for himself that the situation is no longer aversive, avoidance behavior will not be weakened. His behavior will be controlled by historical conditions and not by present reality conditions. It is true, of course, that the conditioned or preaversive stimulus events, after repeated nonreinforced exposure, will gradually lose their acquired aversive properties. However, this typically is an extremely slow process, especially if the aversive conditions with which the conditioned events were associated were intense or frequent.

All too frequently the person not only learns to avoid the specific aversive components of an environment; he also comes to avoid the entire situation. The retarded adolescent who is punished severely by a workshop teacher may avoid the school situation entirely. He may drop out of school and refuse to return. Even if the workshop teacher is no longer employed by the school, the adolescent may refuse to return due to the conditioned aversive properties of school.

Also compounding the elimination by extinction is the fact that the avoidance behavior may be further strengthened by positive reinforcement. In illustration, the retarded adolescent who avoids engaging in a work training program by spending his time with a group of drop-outs may be reinforced positively for being with the group during school hours by the social attention, approval, and the like, which he obtains from the group. Thus, a class of avoidance behavior, reinforced both negatively and positively, becomes even more resistant to extinction.

As avoidance behavior is controlled by stimulus events which serve both discriminative and reinforcing functions, one major set of behavior modification procedures is designed to change the control features of these stimuli. In such a program designed to eliminate avoidance behavior, the person must be exposed repeatedly to the threatening situation under the condition that the feared consequences will not occur. If the conditioned aversive event, which serves to reinforce that behavior which terminates it, can lose its aversive properties, the avoidance behavior should extinguish through nonreinforcement. For example, the retarded adolescent must be exposed to the feared supervisor without the occurrence of rejec-

tion, reprimand, physical punishment or any other feared consequence. The techniques of *forced exposure* by preventing the avoidance behavior and that of *gradual exposure* to threatening situations which are increasingly similar to the aversive stimuli represent approaches to eliminating avoidance behavior through removing the aversive components of the controlling stimuli. A second approach involves the strengthening of approach behavior which competes successfully with the defensive reaction. Although such a procedure will change the stimulus functions of the aversive events, the major focus of the procedure is on the approach behavior.

Forced Exposure. In this procedure, the person would be placed in the presence of the conditioned aversive stimuli and prevented from engaging in avoidance behavior. The person is thus exposed to the stimulus components which control avoidance behavior without the occurrence of the feared consequences. Such forced exposure may eliminate the avoidance behavior under future presentation of the conditioned aversive cues. However, there is some evidence (for example, Miller, 1948; Page, 1955) that such a procedure does not neutralize the conditioned aversive components but rather results in the development of other avoidance behaviors. Thus, such a procedure as compared to routine extinction or to graded or gradual presentation does not appear to be the most valuable one to follow. The feared stimuli appear to retain some of their aversive properties. Additionally, clients not only appear to be more susceptible to further aversive conditioning but also, as Polin (1959) has suggested, the reestablished avoidance behavior appears to be more resistant to extinction.

Gradual Exposure. The extinction procedure which has considerable merit involves the repeated exposure of the person to stimulus events which are increasingly similar to the conditioned aversive events maintaining the avoidance behavior. Initially the conditioned aversive stimulus is presented at weak intensities. As the aversive properties of these stimuli are neutralized through nonreinforcement (that is, through nonoccurrence of the primary aversive event which provided initial strength to the conditioned stimulus), stimulus events which more closely approximate the conditioned aversive events are provided. In arranging these exposures, the presentations must be gradual enough to insure that a complete avoidance response does not occur.

The process of deconditioning of the feared stimulus events can be facilitated in some cases by providing information concerning the new contingencies. Informing the person that the feared consequence is no longer present or that it will occur only under conditions which differ from those previously in force may result in approach behavior. This exposure without the feared consequence will contribute to the extinction of the conditioned aversive properties of the situation.

Shaping Approach Behavior. A final procedure, and one which is used frequently in combination with the gradual exposure techniques, involves the positive reinforcement of behaviors which approach the feared situation and thus compete with the avoidance behaviors. The client who is fearful of a situation, person, or activity would be exposed to increasingly similar approximations of the feared event and at the same time reinforced positively for getting into closer and closer physical proximity of the feared event. The positive reinforcement not only strengthens the approach behavior but also serves as a conditioned stimulus for an antagonistic respondent reaction.

ELIMINATION OF LOW FRUSTRATION TOLERANCE

It is not unusual to observe that many problem clients exhibit a quick disposition to engage in various disruptive respondent (emotional) and operant behaviors in situations which require them to perform in a prescribed fashion. There is present a low frustration tolerance. The person quickly ceases to function appropriately in the absence of continuous and immediate reinforcement or whenever he is provided task requirements which involve some difficulty or effort. These behaviors represent a combination of factors which may involve:

1. A limited history of intermittent reinforcement which predisposes the person to frustration behaviors when placed in a situation which reinforces on a schedule different from a continuous one.
2. Positive reinforcement of the nonadaptive behaviors by an environment which "gives in" to the demands of the client in order to avoid more serious management difficulties.
3. Negative reinforcement of the nonadaptive behaviors by an environment which permits the person to escape or avoid situations whenever these behaviors occur.

A program which seeks to modify these behavior patterns must be designed to provide systematic training in intermittent reinforcement and to provide positive reinforcement for carefully identified appropriate behaviors.

REINFORCEMENT OF COMPETING BEHAVIORS

The elimination of behavior through procedures of extinction and punishment does not teach the person what to do. The elimination of disruptive behavior by an extinction procedure, for example, does not provide the person with any new way of behaving which will result in positive reinforcement. A procedure of reinforcement of appropriate behaviors represents a valuable alternative approach to extinction and punishment procedures. The behavior reinforced should preferably be incompatible to the unde-

sired behavior patterns. A client who spends excessive time away from his work table would be reinforced positively for time spent at the work table. This approach would strengthen the desired behavior instead of control it aversively as would occur if a punishment procedure would be used.

In instances which do not permit the strengthening of behaviors which are physically incompatible with the undesired behaviors, it would be desirable to change the reinforcement contingencies so that the reinforcement which supports the undesired behavior is shifted to become contingent upon the desired performance. In this manner, the reinforcement remains available, but can be produced only by the desired behavior.

Finally, if it becomes necessary to use a punishment procedure, reinforcement of alternative behaviors becomes a necessary adjunct to the punishment procedure. The program should include procedures for systematic reinforcement of behaviors which are desired and which will provide positive reinforcement in the natural environment of the client.

In using a procedure of reinforcing alternative behaviors as a means of elimination of undesired behaviors, it is essential that the prompting and reinforcing components be maximized in order to insure success. It will be desirable to inform the person of the behavior which will result in reinforcement through verbal description, behavior rehearsal, or through observation of others being reinforced for the desired behavior. As nonadaptive behavior frequently is under powerful discriminative and reinforcement control and as respondent reactions frequently accompany and perhaps even exert some control over such behavior, it is necessary to delineate carefully the operations which will be followed in the behavior shaping program. Procedures discussed in the preceding chapter which will maximize the reinforcing components of the program should be used.

PUNISHMENT: PRESENTATION OF AVERSIVE EVENTS

In some instances, it is difficult to control certain behavior patterns except through manipulating aversive conditions. It may not be possible to control the reinforcers which support the undesired behavior. The behavior may be highly disruptive or dangerous. The behavior may be so frequent that it prevents the occurrence of other desired behaviors. As will be described in Chapter 13, it is not unusual to find that a large segment of the behavior of the severely and profoundly retarded is of a disruptive and undesired form. Due to limitations in reinforcer effectiveness, among other things, it is difficult to influence the rate of occurrence of behavior patterns which have been present for a number of months or years. Among the less seriously involved, such behavior as promiscuous sexual activities, although carrying the dangers of unwanted pregnancies or venereal disease, are nonetheless highly reinforcing. It is difficult to control by competing be-

haviors due to a lack of effective reinforcers that are as powerful as those associated with sexual activities. If such behaviors cannot be controlled by other means such as providing the person with realistic information about the dangers involved, by providing alternative means of obtaining competing reinforcers, or by reinforcing abstinence, it may be necessary to utilize a punishment technique involving the presentation of aversive consequences. Such consequences should be immediate, obvious, and directly resulting from the specific behaviors which are to be eliminated. In this manner, behaviors which avoid the aversive consequences are most likely to result.

The punishment operation to be most effective should include the following considerations. The presentation of the aversive consequences must be immediate, must occur on every occasion of the undesired behavior, and must be of an intensity which will successfully offset the reinforcing effects of the maintaining stimuli. It is most desirable to deliver the punishing consequence as soon as possible after the initiation of the undesired behavior. A delay may result in the punishment of appropriate behavior.

It is important that the treatment program be structured so that advantage can be taken of the reduced likelihood of the undesired behavior following punishment. The treatment personnel must be ready to reinforce any other desired behavior which may occur during this suppression period.

The treatment program should be careful to avoid providing the punishing stimuli with secondary positive reinforcer properties. If the client is provided considerable positive reinforcement following punishment, and only following punishment, it is possible for the aversive events to become discriminative for later delivery of positive reinforcement. In this manner the undesired behavior will be reinforced by the later delivery of positive reinforcement.

As noted earlier, the use of aversive stimuli may produce undesirable side effects. The person delivering the punishing consequences may acquire secondary aversive properties. The use of intense aversive consequences may produce widespread disruptive emotional states which result in other patterns of undesirable behavior. As is discussed in Chapter 13, however, careful supplemental use of positive reinforcers for appropriate behavior offsets some of the possible negative side effects.

TIME-OUT AND RESPONSE COST

The reader will recall the discussion in Chapter 6 of two additional punishment procedures, those of time-out and response cost. In using a *time-out* procedure, the person is removed from a range of positive reinforcers contingent upon inappropriate behavior. Following the occurrence of the inappropriate behavior, the person is removed from the environment in which

he has previously received positive reinforcement or in which is available a range of reinforcers. To be effective, such removal must in fact be aversive. The degree of aversiveness associated with removal from one environment and placement in another which is assumed to be less reinforcing is dependent upon the magnitude of reinforcing elements in the initial environment. If the environment contains highly reinforcing elements which will not be available in the isolation area, contingent removal of the person from that environment can be aversive and exert a punishment or behavior deceleration effect. On the other hand, as noted previously in the description of the Striefel (1967) study, removal of the retarded from some environments and placing them in socially isolated ones may have a neutral or even a reinforcing effect which strengthens, rather than weakens, the contingent behavior pattern.

The *response cost* procedure represents an additional technique for the elimination of inappropriate behaviors. In this procedure, the retarded loses reinforcing events which he has in the environment. This loss is immediate and is contingent upon inadequate behavior. Such a response cost procedure is easy to administer in a program based on a token economy as the treatment personnel are able to remove tokens possessed by the retarded contingent upon inappropriate behavior. Burchard (1967), in a program designed to control a variety of inappropriate behaviors in a group of mildly retarded delinquent adolescents, used a response cost procedure. He charged the adolescents a certain number of tokens following the occurrence of specified behaviors. At the same time he reinforced the adolescents with tokens for engaging in appropriate behavior. The response cost procedure influenced the control of various disruptive behaviors.

ELIMINATION OF RESPONDENT BEHAVIOR

Although the topic of elimination of conditioned respondent behavior (emotionality) has been described in the previous section on avoidance behavior, a more systematic, albeit brief, presentation of the related behavior modification procedures will be presented.

Many neutral events in the environment acquire emotion-arousing properties through being paired with other aversive stimuli which control the emotional responses. These conditioned aversive events become excessive under conditions of intense or frequent aversive experiences and control emotional responses which interfere with the development or occurrence of a range of adaptive behaviors. As a result the person is too frequently in a state of heightened emotionality and develops a series of escape and avoidance behaviors which terminate the aversive conditions.

One procedure, although generally an ineffective and inefficient one, which may be used to eliminate the respondent patterns is that of extinc-

tion. The conditioned aversive stimulus which controls the emotionality is presented on numerous occasions, but without the occurrence (reinforcement in the respondent conditioning paradigm) of the primary aversive consequences. Repeated presentation will result in the gradual loss of the conditioned aversive properties. A workshop supervisor who reprimanded a client in a loud threatening manner will gradually lose his conditioned aversive properties after repeated exposure in the absence of further outburst. Again, while a procedure that is available, it is not the preferred one as the time required for extinction of the conditioned emotionality is excessive. Furthermore, in many instances, as noted in the earlier section on avoidance behavior, extinction may never occur as the person completely avoids exposure to the supervisor. He never discovers that the supervisor no longer will provide aversive consequences as he refuses to attend the work training program.

A procedure which may be used to speed up the extinction process and concomitantly to substitute a positive antagonistic respondent for the conditioned emotionality is that of *counter-conditioning.* In this procedure, responses which are antagonistic or incompatible to the undesired conditioned emotionality are presented along with stimuli which are similar to those which control the conditioned emotionality. Positive antagonistic responses involving, for example, varying degrees of relaxation and of sexual excitement have been used to counteract anxiety or other forms of conditioned emotionality. The treatment procedure is based on what Wolpe (1958) has called the reciprocal inhibition principle: "If a response antagonistic to anxiety can be made to occur in the presence of anxiety-evoking stimuli so that it is accompanied by a complete or partial suppression of the anxiety responses, the bond between these stimuli and the anxiety responses will be weakened" [p. 71].

Initially, then, it is necessary to utilize an anxiety-neutralizing stimulus that is sufficiently strong to counteract the respondents typically elicited by the conditioned aversive event. Secondly, the conditioned aversive events are presented initially in weak form so that the antagonistic stimulus conditions can extinguish the anxiety-arousing properties of the aversive stimuli. The conditioned aversive cues are gradually presented in stronger and stronger form until their aversive properties are extinguished and further have acquired properties of arousing the antagonistic respondents. Finally, the anxiety-reducing and the aversive stimuli are presented contiguously with sufficient frequency for extinction of the emotionality to occur. Bandura (1969), Kanfer and Phillips (1970), Lang (1970), and Wolpe and Lazarus (1966) should be consulted for a thorough description of the techniques as well as for a critical examination of the research and clinical literature concerning the utility of this counter-conditioning procedure.

Generality of Treatment Effects

One of the primary concerns of education and rehabilitation programs is with the generalization of behavior change to those environmental situations outside the therapeutic or rehabilitation situation. There is concern also for the question of maintaining the change over extended periods of time. It is expected for example, that a program which teaches a client to control disruptive verbal behavior in a work training environment, should also result in skills of behavior control in other settings. Additionally, it would be hoped that improvement in two classes of nonadaptive behavior, for example, would result in positive change in other classes of undesired behavior.

An evaluation of the behavior modification literature would suggest that behavior change does in fact generalize across stimulus situations as well as across response classes. Additionally, behavior changes have endured over extended periods of time. At the same time there are numerous reports which indicate that little stimulus or response generalization was noted.

In view of these conflicting results, it is important to provide as specifically as possible for generalization of behavior changes across situations by insuring similarity between both discriminative and reinforcing components of the therapeutic and natural environments. Behavior will not be maintained unless provisions are made for periodic reinforcement. Resistance to extinction can be facilitated by providing experience with intermittent reinforcement. However, even under the most favorable reinforcement history, behavior will not be maintained unless reinforcement is provided.

In a program of behavior change, no assumption should be made that spontaneous improvement will be made across behavior classes unless there is suitable evidence that the behaviors are functionally equivalent or otherwise related along pertinent learning variables. Generally, plans should be made to deal specifically with every problem area, with the orientation being one of "Wait and see." If spontaneous favorable changes occur in untreated areas, program emphasis should shift to unchanged problem areas.

Where Should Behavior Treatment Occur?

As noted previously, the traditional approach to treatment of difficult problems of adjustment removes the person from his natural surroundings and provides "therapy" in an artificial environment. The behavior modification approach treats the behavior in the environment in which it occurs. If it becomes necessary to deal with behavior difficulties in an unnatural setting,

the program must provide for a set of transitional experiences to insure generalization of the new behaviors to the natural environment. No assumption is made, as is true in many therapy systems, that "insight" or some other nebulous internal happening will prompt extensive behavior change.

If the retardate is disruptive in the classroom, this behavior is dealt with in that setting. If the client has a "poor work attitude," this is specified in terms of actual behavioral occurrences and each of these is treated in the setting in which it occurs. For example, if the client has excessive arguments with his work supervisor, has emotional outburst while working, and is unable to get along with his peers during break periods, these are handled if possible in their natural surroundings. If this is not feasible, for example, with the problem of peer interactions, it may be necessary to influence the development of certain related behaviors in a simulated peer relationship. Through behavior rehearsal, for example, the client would be taught new behavioral alternatives which he would use during the break period in relating to his peers in the work setting. Whenever it becomes necessary to treat the behavior in some setting other than the natural environment, the client should be expected to perform in the natural environment under the guidance of the treatment program prior to treatment termination. It is necessary in many cases to restructure the natural environment in any one of a variety of ways in order to insure the occurrence and reinforcement of the appropriate behavior.

Personnel Involved in the Treatment Program

As has been emphasized earlier, people in the client's natural environment should "administer" the change plan whenever possible. This would include such people as the teacher, supervisor, family members, counselor, and peers. The behavior modification specialist becomes directly involved in the treatment plan only in those instances where more familiar and readily available persons are unable to fulfill the requirements of the treatment plan. This strategy of utilizing natural environment personnel is based on the assumption that the most powerful reinforcers are in the hands of those who reside in the client's world. Secondly, the problem of generalization of treatment effects is eliminated. If the behavior is brought under the control of natural components of the environment, there is no concern for transferring the effects from the artificial conditions of the treatment environment to those present in the natural environment.

Applications to Development of Adaptive Behavior of the Moderately and Mildly Retarded

The previous chapters have provided the conceptual, principle, and techno-logical basis for the behavior modification approach to adaptive problems presented by the mentally retarded. This chapter, and the two to follow, present data relative to applications of this approach to the mildly, moder-ately, severely, and profoundly retarded. The present chapter provides a review of applications to the mildly and moderately retarded in school and occupational and social adjustment training settings, with a final section devoted to the behavior approach to counseling.

Applications to the School Setting

It is not infrequently heard, even within special education circles, that the mentally retarded cannot develop concepts, do not generalize, do not learn incidentally, cannot deal with abstract materials, have difficulty retaining what has been acquired and are generally slow learners in the acquisition of any new behaviors. None of these statements is in fact supported by re-liable experimental data. There is no suitable evidence that such a general and unitary deficiency exists. Retardates do develop concepts, they do gen-eralize from one learning setting to other settings, they do learn materials incidentally, they do deal in abstractions, and while it is true that they do learn less rapidly than the nonretarded in many areas, they are not slow

learners or poor retainers in *every* area of endeavor. In fact some research studies suggest that some mildly retarded under certain reinforcing conditions learn and retain at a rate comparable to that of their normal peers. Generally it is noted that associations once learned are fairly durable. It can be concluded that it has not been demonstrated that the retarded have a set of learning characteristics which is peculiarly descriptive of them or which separates or distinguishes them from contrast groups of nonretarded children and adolescents. The present section will focus on the pertinent question of "what can be done to facilitate most optimal learning by the school age mildly retarded" or "under what circumstances does the retardate perform best?" This type of question takes the teacher away from the theoretical and esoteric and into the realm of the practical. Translated into classroom procedures, the general question becomes more specifically:

1. What can the school environment, including the teacher, do to facilitate the efficient and effective development of new behavior by the mentally retarded student? The term behavior as used in this section, refers to the development and retention of any new response pattern, including traditional academic ones such as word recognition, speed of reading and concept formation as well as behaviors such as social graces, friendliness and self-confidence.
2. How are these behaviors strengthened to the point that these become a functional and natural part of the retardate's general behavior repertoire?
3. How can behaviors which are present but undesirable be weakened and eliminated?
4. Finally, how can the environment evoke or control appropriate behaviors in a reliable fashion?

Such an orientation avoids self-defeating concern with what the retardate cannot do and focuses on what can be done in a program designed to optimize learning. The focus then is on *how* the retarded can learn. The major concern is on the technology of facilitating learning and on designing an appropriate environmental setting in which learning will progress in an orderly manner.

This focus on designing an appropriate learning environment is critical as special education in secondary level programs for the mentally retarded is confronted with some of the most difficult problems of the entire school system. The curriculum is generally ill-defined and poorly related to ultimate goals, students in the program have a long history of failure and unsuccessful experiences in the school environment, social relationships with non-retarded peers are frequently poor or nonexistent, the students have only minimal achievement motivation (that is, school activities have not

acquired positive reinforcing properties), the reinforcing aspects of the environment are typically too limited in kind or magnitude, and the educational methods are seldom highly appropriate to the characteristics of the retarded adolescent.

As a result, an unusually large number of students present severe learning and personal-social adjustment difficulties. These are the adolescents that later present the difficult problems for the vocational rehabilitation agency. In a sense, the educational program inadvertently teaches these adolescents to avoid learning situations, especially those involving any obvious cognitive skills, and to avoid competitive situations if there is much likelihood of failure. Additionally, such experiences significantly decrease the possibility that the adolescent will acquire general work skills involving both persistence of effort over extended periods of time and concern about quality performance.

Observation of a large number of retarded adolescents presenting a range of learning and behavior problems suggested the following:

1. Many of the school activities have low reinforcement value to the retarded. In fact, large segments of the program have active aversive characteristics. This is related to numerous factors. Reinforcers available such as grades, teacher approval, and status for successful performance are of low magnitude and too restricted in range. Bijou, Birnbrauer, Kidder, and Tague (1966), for example, found that teacher approval following desirable classroom behavior and correct answers to academic materials produced little sustained studying behavior in a group of mildly retarded children and adolescents. These educators concluded that teacher approval and praise did not have reinforcing functions for this group. Additionally, many of the available reinforcers are too abstract, too far removed in time, and too inconsistently and infrequently provided contingent upon desired performance of approximations of this performance. It must be recognized that many of the school activities required of the retarded are in essence quite difficult and require considerable effort for successful performance. This places heavy demands upon reinforcing events which are comparable in magnitude to the effort required. Additionally, many activities required by the school program are highly unlikely to be reinforced outside the school setting. Thus, such behaviors have no functional relationship to reinforcers which are available in the person's life. Such performances are said to lack relevance.

2. Many special education students are characterized by an excessive amount of disruptive behavior. Bijou et al. (1966) described the retardates in their study as being characterized by refusal to study or comply with teacher instructions, temper tantrums, fighting, and pouting. Burchard (1967) reported such behaviors as fighting, lying, cheating, physical and

verbal assault and temper tantrums. The disruptive behavior may develop as it removes the adolescent from being involved in aversive tasks. In other instances, as the retarded is unable to engage in the behaviors required, he may engage in other behaviors which are disruptive relative to the initial task requirement. It is also possible that disruptive behavior is reinforced by the attention that it receives from peers and teacher.

3. There is a relative dearth of positive reinforcement available to the retarded in the school setting. An undesirable amount of the behavior that is present is under aversive (mostly threat of punishment) control. The aversive control serves to decrease the likelihood that appropriate behavior will occur in areas other than the specific areas being punished. This serves to decrease the spontaneity or curiosity of the adolescent.

4. Under these circumstances, immediate reinforcement becomes more influential than delayed reinforcement. Thus, reinforcers under the control of agents other than the teacher exert an unfavorable amount of influence over the retarded. The cigarette behind the building, freedom from the social studies class, conversation with the girls at the soda fountain—all these exert more control over the behavior because they bring more immediate reinforcement than the prospect of a good grade or the approval of the teacher or parent.

From this brief account, it is evident that the emphasis in a successful education program for the educable mentally retarded must be a positive one. The major behavior control procedures must be based on positive reinforcement and not on such aversive techniques as threat, coercion, and punishment. To insure a positive orientation, a workable motivational system must be viewed as an essential aspect of the program which seeks to strengthen academic and appropriate social behaviors. Additionally the development of prerequisite academic behaviors (study skills) must be viewed as a basic and essential program goal. This involves the strengthening of such desirable behaviors as sitting quietly, paying attention to instruction, beginning to work without undue delay, working productively for sustained periods and initiating a new task upon completion of a previous one. As these behavior patterns are being developed, the program must also be designed to weaken and eliminate such disruptive behaviors as talking loudly, negativism, fighting, teasing, excessive motor activity, and daydreaming because these compete with appropriate study skills. These behaviors typically decrease in strength as the child experiences success in the school program.

If the retarded is not succeeding in the school program, one must look at the environment for the reasons underlying this lack of success and should under no circumstances assume it is the retardate's fault he is not learning. Placing the responsibility for inadequate behavior development on the re-

tarded adolescent assumes he does what he *wants* to or is in the *mood* for and controls his behavior at will. A positive environmental approach to education of the mentally retarded rejects this unacceptable position. If the person is not succeeding, then the program is at fault: the materials are too difficult, the behavior required is too complex for his present level of development, the environment is structured in a manner which does not facilitate performance or else the consequences of behavior are ineffectual for this child. This positive approach, while not an easy one to assume, is one that will result in the best satisfactory development of the retarded.

EVALUATION

Evaluation is the first step in structuring the learning environment for the adolescent retarded. The emphasis in evaluation is on what the person can do and not on his deficits or limitations. Focusing on a person's deficiencies or limitations does not benefit anyone. It merely reveals what the person cannot do. A program cannot be built on what a person cannot do, but rather must start from what he can do. Terms such as deficiency and disability emphasize the negative components of a developmental level and in a real sense are derogatory as the danger is present that these will be used to explain the limited behavioral development instead of searching for environmental deficits which may be impeding learning. A positive teaching approach requires that we know about what the retarded can do in a variety of behavior areas. The student's behavioral limitations should be translated into present behavioral characteristics. As an example of the deficiency orientation, it might be said that an adolescent has a short attention span, shows little persistence or does not respond to visual stimulation for extended periods of time. The positive approach, instead of emphasizing what the child cannot do, would merely describe the adolescent in terms of his present behavioral characteristics. In illustration, this adolescent, under certain circumstances will engage in certain behavior; this adolescent will attend to and interact with the instructional environment for up to ten minutes at a time; this adolescent responds better to auditory stimulation than to visual stimulation in the typical teacher-student relationship. Knowing these and having knowledge or hypotheses about how learning is best promoted, the teacher is then in an optimal position to devise a program which will result in systematic growth and development.

Although not conclusive, the following types of data are valuable in providing direction to specific program planning and in selecting the particular teaching techniques deemed the most likely to succeed with the retarded student.

Intelligence Test Data. Such data as mental age, intelligence quotient, and the like provide some general global information which suggests guide-

lines as to the present level of general learning skills and to the general rate of academic development which could be expected. It should be emphasized, however, that this is a relatively gross measure as specific skills vary widely within groups of moderately and mildly retarded adolescents with comparable MAs or IQs. Expected grade level cannot be predicted perfectly on the basis of the mental age of the retarded because the relationship between level of academic skill development and mental age is not great enough for individual prediction. Although it is generally assumed for example, that an individual with a mental age of six to six and one-half should be able to develop beginning reading skills, many retardates in this mental age range have not acquired some of the basic preacademic skills involving such areas as visual and auditory discriminations, visual-motor coordination and vocabulary knowledge. More specific information evidently is required for individualized program development.

Achievement and Diagnostic Tests. These tests provide more specific types of data concerning skill development or level of functioning within specific academic areas. General achievement tests provide knowledge of a level of functioning which can form the basis for selecting curriculum materials to which the child should respond in a successful manner. Other tests which provide information about more specific functional skills (for example, Illinois Test of Psycholinguistic Abilities, Frostig's Developmental Test of Visual Perception) can provide information to guide specific developmental and remedial activities. There is some suggestive evidence that specific language and perceptual skill areas are "educable" and remediable.

Observational Data. A great deal of valuable information is obtainable only through observation of the person in various structured and unstructured and in work and play settings. Examples of pertinent questions include "How long does he attend, study or engage in difficult problem solving activities?" "How well does he attend to verbal or other auditory stimulation in contrast with visually presented instruction?" "How much individual attention is required for productive work or persistence in the face of difficulty?" "How frequently does he make disruptive comments?" "What are the consequences of his undesirable behavior?" These observations should be as objective as possible. By noting that an adolescent is able to work productively only for 5-10 minutes at a time, engages in disruptive behaviors an average of 10 times daily and does not reduce this frequency when such behavior is followed by verbal reprimand, the teacher has (1) obtained a baseline in terms of which future progress can be compared and (2) identified a behavior change procedure (that is, reprimand) that is ineffectual. Again the objective of this evaluation procedure is to obtain data concerning the work and study skills so that a

program can be provided that will be complementary to these skills. The behavioral analysis outlined in Chapter 9 gives direction to the evaluation procedure.

Reinforcing Consequences. One of the most basic principles of learning is that behavior which is followed by a desirable consequence will increase in strength. Recognition of the crucial role which this law of reinforcement assumes in the learning of the retarded suggests a consideration of those environmental events which are reinforcing. As noted in the behavioral analysis outline, the evaluation should identify a range of stimulus events which will influence the learning of the retarded. This frequently is a difficult undertaking because the range of individual differences among the retarded is great. However, the teacher is in a most favorable position to identify the effective reinforcers and to utilize these in her daily activities to influence the retarded student.

PROGRAM OBJECTIVES

The evaluation data form the basis for the specification of reasonable program goals for the retarded student. Such goal setting in the school setting should be developed in every area of behavior development and should be stated in small units of time and related specifically to the program that is presented day by day to the student. Such goal setting is an end result of an integrated process based on a variety of factors, including objective test data, history of rate of behavior change in similar areas, type of materials, nature of instructional program, level of skill development at initiation of program, and the nature and manner of reinforcement procedures.

INSTRUCTIONAL PROGRAM: CONTENT AND METHODOLOGY

The set of experiences provided the retarded student throughout the day, week and semester must be designed to meet the persisting life behavioral goals which have been set. This requires that the daily instructional program, whether in the area of teaching the adolescent word recognition or of facilitating appropriate peer interaction, be so organized and presented that each experience adds to the development of the person. If every experience in the program does not contribute to the growth and development of the student then the legitimacy of these as meaningful elements of the program must be questioned. This requirement places a strenuous responsibility on the teacher as she must continually evaluate the effectiveness of her content and teaching methodology in promoting the program goals. The program experiences must not only be intimately related to the program goals and persisting life objectives but also must not be too easy or too difficult to impede continuous growth. In either case, appropriate progression toward the program goals is not evident. Just as much damage

can be done to the student when the program is too easy as when the program is too difficult.

To summarize the program development process, the teacher initially identifies the behaviors (for example, reading 25 basic words, counting by two's up to 20, attending to instructions which are presented verbally, decreasing by 15 percent the number of disagreements which John has with his peers during recess period) to be strengthened, eliminated, or otherwise altered and states these educational goals in behavioral terms: What environmental events are to be utilized (for example, specific materials, individual study booth, verbal and visual instructions, use of the classroom aide, prompting by passing the child's desk every five minutes) in order to develop new behavior, to strengthen present behavior and to insure the continuation of present behaviors under new environmental conditions? The adolescents may be provided tokens for appropriate behaviors. A specified number of tokens may be exchanged for a five-day privilege card which entitles him to leave early at dismissal time, leave his desk without permission, get a drink of water at any time, and the like. What program will be followed in decreasing or eliminating the occurrence of undesirable behaviors under certain situations (for example, horseplay while working) or under all conditions (for example, apathy)? Sulzbacher and Houser (1968), in illustration, used a response cost procedure on a group contingency basis to control disruptive behavior displayed by various class members. Each occurrence of a specified disruptive behavior from any member of the group of mildly retarded students in a classroom setting, resulted in loss of recess time for the entire group, There was an immediate deceleration of the behavior. Such a procedure took advantage of the natural social consequences of peers to control the very behavior which they had previously maintained through social attention. If satisfactory improvement is not realized, the teacher is in a position to indentify the source of difficulty (for example, content, method of instruction, behavior requirements, or reinforcement events and procedures used) and to initiate immediate and specific changes in the program.

CIRCUMSTANCES THAT FACILITATE LEARNING

The role of the special education teacher is to provide a total program which will maximize the learning and performance of her students. Although the program must be highly individualized for optimal results, a number of guides are available to assist her in her general program development endeavors. The following represent some of these.

1. The instructional materials should be selected to complement the learning characteristics of the retarded students. The content and pace of reading materials developed for instructional use with the nonretarded

child, for example, changes too rapidly for effective use with the retarded child. There is not sufficient repetition of a word in such materials for the retarded adolescent to effectively acquire and retain the word.

2. Many retarded adolescents present uneven skill development across behavioral areas and require highly individualized instruction in these specific areas of limited development. This characteristic places further demands (1) on the instructional materials selected as most materials assume even development across a number of cognitive, perceptual and motivational areas and (2) on the teaching procedures used as the retarded student usually experiences pronounced difficulty of learning in these areas.

3. Effective learning is facilitated when new concepts and skills are developed through a gradual and systematic progression from what is known. Concrete materials and related experiences involving doing should be used whenever possible in fostering the development of concepts. Additionally, the program is designed to insure the elicitation of the to-be-learned response. Immediate knowledge concerning the correctness of a response or immediate correction in the event of a wrong response facilitates effective learning.

4. Use of materials and methods of presentation which utilize multiple sense modalities facilitates learning and performance. Such materials and methods increase the attention responses of the learner and increases the likelihood of effective discrimination of the relevant cues from the irrelevant ones.

5. Generalization or transfer is facilitated by a set of systematic transitional experiences. The teacher should not assume that generalization or transfer from one situation to another will occur—she must program for it. Concepts presented in recurring spiral-like fashion in varied meaningful contexts are more readily generalized than those presented in isolation.

6. Although repetition in itself does not insure learning and effective retention, repetition that results in reinforcement does strengthen behavior. This repetition to the point of overlearning should not be restricted to the initial learning experience. Once a behavior is in the student's repertoire, use should be made of this new behavior in a variety of experiences and settings. This improves both retention and transfer.

7. Learning and retention are facilitated when the materials involved are familiar and meaningful, for example, when the associations to be formed are between familiar events. Familiar events should be used especially in teaching new concepts. Learning is facilitated whenever the retardate is able to apply distinctive verbal mediators to distinguish materials to be learned. When new materials are presented, the students should be prompted to apply verbal mediators to these materials.

8. Although the retarded do learn incidentally, best learning occurs in

a systematic program. Learning should not be left to chance or to fortune. Learning is insured through a well-sequenced interesting program of experience which is designed around the specific characteristics of each student.

9. The program should be so designed that continuous success is attained. Most retardates have experienced an excessive amount of failure and have received little systematic reinforcement for attentive and persistent work behavior. The retarded *can* learn. If they are not successful, the program is ill designed, that is, requiring too much of the student at the time of failure.

10. A history of failure (that is, nonreinforcement for problem solving attempts; aversive consequences for failure to reach the behavior goal set by an unperceptive environment) has resulted in development of numerous behavioral characteristics which interfere with effective academic, social and affective learning. Low frustration tolerance, excessive emotional outbursts, limited self-confidence and self-control, hesitancy to become involved in new or competitive experiences, refusal to continue problem-solving effort in the face of difficulty, and the like all have evolved out of a poor learning environment which either has failed to match behavior requirements to present behavioral characteristics or to present reinforcing consequences for appropriate behavior. These inappropriate behavioral characteristics are not inherent components of "mental retardation," but rather consequences of a retarded, insensitive and blindly-demanding environment. An environment which minimizes failure and systematically reinforces self-adequacy and self-control will greatly enhance active learning.

11. Distributed practice facilitates learning and retention. If instructional sessions are too long and require too much attention and effort, learning is inefficient.

12. Frequent review facilitates long-term retention.

13. Better learning occurs in a given period of time if a smaller number of tasks is learned to a high level of acquisition than if too many different tasks are presented, especially if the tasks are highly similar. Too many new things should not be presented at one time.

14. Memory can be facilitated if each lesson contains material which is highly dissimilar to that which precedes or follows it in the daily class schedule. Rest periods should be provided between lessons. If materials are similar, overlearning would facilitate retention. The most important materials should be presented at the beginning or at the end, as these are materials most likely to be remembered.

15. Discrimination learning is facilitated by increasing the distinctiveness of the stimuli involved. This can be done by presenting multidimen-

sional cues, by increasing the disparity between the stimuli and by teaching labels for the stimuli in pretraining sessions.

16. The program in every area of learning should proceed in small steps from the known to the unknown. Progress in academic subjects is best achieved by systematically presenting materials which gradually require more complex behaviors.

17. In various types of learning it is best to move from easy materials to difficult materials. Developing a set to succeed or a warm-up effect provides increased impetus to task involvement and persistence when the problems become difficult.

18. Speed of performance (reading, writing, etc.) should not be stressed until accuracy has been attained.

19. Speech and the environmental events, objects, or situations which the verbal symbols represent should be correlated in experience. For example, a verbal description of an experience should be followed by actual involvement in which the student uses the verbal behavior to describe the experience.

20. If a given task is not learned, the program should break this task into smaller, specific components and then teach these smaller segments in sequence. After acquiring skill in one, the next is then learned. All are interrelated with one serving as a building block for the next.

21. Learning is facilitated by arranging the instructional environment so that the retardate responds to and interacts with the materials presented. Attention and persistent productive work can be enhanced by presenting redundant or excessive cues for appropriate behavior, by presenting novel cues, by reducing response alternatives and by providing highly desirable reinforcing events following the behavior to be learned.

22. Behavior which is followed by an appropriate consequence will increase in strength (frequency of occurrence). This behavior principle requires that the program (1) does have reinforcing events available which will in fact influence a given student and (2) is organized in such a manner that the reinforcement is available following desired behavior. It should be noted that what is reinforcing to one pupil may not be reinforcing to another. For this reason, a token reinforcement system is recommended. Although social reinforcement in the form of praise, approval or attention is effective with some retarded children, these events show quick satiation effects or are rather unreliable reinforcing events for others, especially with those who display highly disruptive and antisocial behavior patterns. Additionally, the reinforcing effectiveness of a given event (for example, smile, grade, attention, trinket, token, privilege, peer interaction) may vary considerably from time to time. Further, the reinforcing effectiveness of certain events can be influenced by conditions of deprivation and satiation.

Learning will be facilitated best in that environment which has a wide range of reinforcing consequences. Those programs which depend solely on teacher approval and grades will have considerable difficulty in influencing the entire class in a positive manner. It is frequently noted that the retarded have "low motivation," "limited interest" or a "poor attitude" toward learning. These behavioral characteristics are best dealt with by providing a varied program based on positive reinforcement. Bijou et al. (1966) and Burchard (1967) used tokens for a range of prerequisite academic, academic, and appropriate social behaviors. Bijou et al. found that check marks by teachers in a token booklet which each student carried with him represented a useful procedure to provide and keep records of token reinforcement. A completely filled booklet could be exchanged for a variety of tangible and social events.

23. Most effective learning occurs when reinforcement is provided contingent upon and immediately following the performance. If there is a delay between behavior and reinforcement, other irrelevant behaviors are likely to occur and be reinforced. Programmed instructional materials and the use of teacher aides to provide immediate reinforcement are particularly relevant within this context. Burchard (1967) demonstrated the necessity of providing reinforcement on a contingent basis. He provided reinforcement contingent upon a desired behavior in a classroom setting and later provided the reinforcers on a noncontingent basis but still requesting the same behavior. The desired behavior dropped drastically when reinforcement was provided noncontingently, even though the same amount of reinforcement was provided.

24. The program must carefully avoid the reinforcement of inappropriate behaviors. In a recently observed mildly retarded adolescent, high strength disruptive behaviors (for example, talking out of turn, laughing at inappropriate times, poking peers, getting out of chair) were reinforced by the person being sent out of the classroom and being required to sit in the hall. The class, concerned with teaching quantitative concepts, was rather aversive to the boy. His being dismissed from class removed him from the unpleasant task of working arithmetic problems, being reprimanded by the teacher for poor performance and the like. Further, social reinforcement, such as attention, is a powerful reinforcer for some retardates. A teacher who attends to a range of inappropriate and disruptive behaviors may inadvertently strengthen these behaviors. The teacher can structure her attention in such a manner that it only follows appropriate behavior. Under such conditions, desired responses are strengthened which compete with inadequate ones.

25. Behavior which is being learned can be strengthened best if reinforced on every occasion of its appearance. As learning progresses, rein-

forcement should be provided less and less frequently and on a varied schedule. This intermittent reinforcement procedure increases the likelihood that the behavior will be maintained for longer periods of time when the environment does not provide reinforcement. However, it must not be assumed that behavior will continue without reinforcement. Birnbrauer, Wolf, Kidder, and Tague (1965) found that upon removal of token reinforcement for appropriate academic behaviors, some students showed rapid and pronounced change in their behavior. Not only did quality and quantity of academic behaviors decline, there was also an increase in disruptive social behaviors.

26. In teaching new behaviors (for example, academic, social, or motor), the program should be highly distinctive and consistent during the early stages of learning. The student should know what behaviors are required, and should be provided distinctive prompting and discriminative cues for these behaviors. These cues will come to control the desired behaviors if reinforcement systematically follows the behavior.

27. Development of discriminative responses should precede presentation of more complex constructed responses. Prior to requiring the child to write or to recognize a written word, for example, the child initially is provided experience in visually discriminating that word from other similar ones.

28. Approximations of the final behavior to be learned should be reinforced initially. As these occur with some frequency, behaviors which closer resemble the final target behaviors are next required prior to reinforcement. Such a procedure of rewarding successive approximations of the desired behavior requires considerable skill and patience on the part of the teacher. It also requires that a well delineated program be available. The teacher must know what social, perceptual, verbal, reading, etc. behavior to reinforce and how this behavior relates to larger or more skillful response segments.

29. The teacher should recognize that some behaviors are developed as these remove the student from a source of aversive or unpleasant stimulation. The retardate, for example, may learn to engage in disruptive behaviors or to complain of physical ailments as these remove him from program requirements. If these behaviors are present, it must be assumed that the program is unpleasant and is not providing sufficient success experiences (that is, reinforcement).

30. As stated, the program should provide opportunities for the retardate to use newly acquired behaviors in new situations and in increasingly difficult situations. Unless behaviors are used and reinforced these will be lost.

31. Behavior which has a low likelihood of occurrence (for example,

finishing an arithmetic assignment, working without disruption, seeking permission prior to leaving work area) can be strengthened by following the occurrence of these behaviors with an activity that the child enjoys or prefers. Any teacher can make use of this principle as every child has some activities that he prefers over others.

CONCLUSION

Continuous positive behavior development of the mentally retarded in a school setting can be insured by a well organized program which systematically adds to current behavior characteristics. A positive educational approach provides meaningful and consistent reinforcement for learning and performance. The teacher is challenged to believe not only in the inherent worth and integrity of the mentally retarded, but also to instill an enthusiasm for learning and living by providing a systematic positive environment which constantly encourages involvement and expression.

Application to Occupational Training Setting

Lent (1968) describes the application of a range of behavior modification procedures in the training of moderately retarded adolescent and young adult females who lived in a state residential facility. The program is designed to train the girls in the four general areas of personal, social, occupational, and functional academic skills. The program areas are broken down into a series of well defined behavioral components. These small segments become the target behaviors which are shaped into increasingly complex units of behavior until the terminal behavior goals are attained.

The program is based on a token economy system. Clients are informed concerning the behaviors which result in token reinforcement. In illustration, at various stages of the program, the following "ways to earn tokens" were available: putting clean laundry away, doing laundry, sitting properly, speaking properly on telephone, polishing shoes, following directions willingly, and shaving legs and underarms. In addition to receiving tokens for appropriate behavior, the client may lose tokens by engaging in inappropriate behaviors. Following such behaviors tokens are simply removed in an unemotional fashion. Examples of these behaviors include: refusal to do cottage work, teasing peers, fighting and arguing, not wearing bathrobe, unmade beds, sitting on floor or with legs sprawled, and inappropriate address to adults.

Tokens are exchangeable for a wide range of backup reinforcers. Examples of the events used include: special parties, playing record player, swimming, canteen, movie, riding bicycle, walks on campus, watching TV,

shopping downtown, rodeo, parties in another cottage, and local phone calls. The cost of events varied. The clients are encouraged to save in order to be able to purchase some of the more expensive events.

In addition to positive reinforcement and response cost procedures, the program has used a time-out strategy with some success. Following inappropriate behavior, the adolescent may initially be placed in a designated area of the room which signifies to the client and her peers that her behavior is unsatisfactory. If this is not sufficient to terminate the inappropriate behavior, the client is next placed into a time-out room.

The Lent project is most impressive for a number of reasons. The program is well organized and detailed. A wide range of different behavior modification procedures has been demonstrated to be effective in promoting change in a wide range of behavioral areas. Clients have been "normalized" to the extent that satisfactory community adjustment has been realized.

Burchard (1967) has described a training program designed to develop a repertoire of socially acceptable behaviors in mildly retarded adolescent boys with histories of delinquent behavior. Positive reinforcement for appropriate school and work behaviors and punishment procedures involving time-out and response cost have all produced reliable behavior change.

Zimmerman, Overpeck, Eisenberg, and Garlick (1969) report on techniques used in a sheltered workshop with multihandicapped retarded clients. An isolation-avoidance procedure was effective in increasing production rate in some clients. In this procedure, after baseline production rate is obtained, client is informed that he is expected to produce at a certain rate. Failure to do so would result in his being isolated from the group of fellow-workers and placed at a work table some 50 feet from the group. Visual access to the group is blocked by plywood partitions. Reliable increment in production rate has been obtained from a number of clients. When the avoidance contingency was removed, a permanent gain in production rate followed. The writers report this to differ from results obtained when tokens are removed. In their experience, at least half of their clients whose production had increased with token reinforcement showed a decline to initial baseline after tokens were removed.

The brief account of these three studies provides illustration of the application of a behavior modification approach to the development of vocational and related behaviors of the moderately and mildly retarded. These studies provide support for the concepts of positive program development emphasized in the preceding chapters. In addition, as noted by Zimmerman et al., such studies demonstrate that rehabilitation personnel can "do their own thing" in a systematic way: "He should (a) specify his behavioral target in observable, objective terms, (b) systematically monitor the defined

behavior, (c) define his treatment in such a manner that others can employ it, and (d) assess its effects on the behavior under conditions in which his treatment is applied systematically" [p. 334].

Counseling the Mentally Retarded

Mentally retarded adults experience a variety of problems in adapting to the natural and social demands of their environment. The more complex the environmental demands, the greater the adaptive behavior problems of the retarded and, concomitantly, the problems faced by those concerned with their vocational guidance and counseling. Neff (1968) succinctly describes the repertoire of behaviors required for a minimally successful work adjustment:

> He is able to distinguish the workplace both from home and the playing field and adjust his behavior accordingly. He is able to leave his home to go to work without falling apart in the process. He is capable, within limits, of looking and behaving like the other members of his work group. He can live a public life as well as a private one and can reduce his needs for intimacy without undue deprivation. He can regulate his life by the clock, to the degree that the job requires. He can permit himself to be supervised by strangers, without being rendered so angry by supervision that he cannot function, or so servile that he loses all initiative. He can relate to his fellow-workers in ways that they deem acceptable [p. 131].

In general, it is not unreasonable to conclude that the mentally retarded experience a variety of work-related problems which must be dealt with by those involved in his rehabilitation.

A number of observational and experimental studies provide a more specific picture of the problems which must be dealt with in a rehabilitation program. Baller (1936), Charles (1953), and Baller, Charles, and Miller (1967), studied the vocational and social adjustment of a group of retarded subjects and noted that they could adequately perform most unskilled, many semiskilled, service, and a few skilled jobs. However, it was reported that extensive vocational training and counseling services were necessary in order to maintain social and vocational adaptation. Peckham (1951) noted that retarded workers frequently failed on jobs because they lacked personal-social amenities to adjust satisfactorily to job-related social situations. Edgerton (1967) indicated that formerly institutionalized adults, who had been deemed sufficiently independent to be placed in the community, experience significant adjustment problems and were particularly concerned about: (1) obtaining more information relative to skills necessary to earn a living; (2) adequate management of sex, marriage,

and reproduction; and, (3) utilization of leisure time. Johnson (1950), Johnson and Kirk (1950), and Baldwin (1958) noted that retarded students attending regular public school classes were psychologically and socially rejected by their nonrelated peers. Bothersome or inappropriate behavior characteristics, rather than low intelligence, were generally reported as the crucial factors resulting in low acceptance or in active rejection. Lapp (1957) made the additional observation that many retarded just had no special characteristics to contribute to a group and thus were not accepted as a group member. DiMichael and Terwilliger (1953) characterized personal and interpersonal problems of the retarded as centering around undesirable personal attitudes, exaggerated opinions of their skills and wages, sex problems, lack of interest in and motivation for work, difficulties in obtaining suitable jobs, and slowness in acquiring job skills. Excessive day dreaming, nervousness, hyperactivity, withdrawal, general lack of social skills, poor self-concept, and low motivation (Ayers and Duguay, 1969; Hannen, 1968) have also been noted. Thus, it may be concluded that the retarded manifest a wide variety of vocational, emotional, and social problems which limit their adaptability to an environment requiring independent functioning. Also, it is not unreasonable to assume that the adaptive behavior problems experienced by the retarded are not unlike those of the nonretarded and that counseling and psychotherapy would be included as part of a total rehabilitation program designed to ameliorate these problems.

In light of these multiple problems the basic objectives of vocational rehabilitation programs for the retarded are: 1) to establish them as productive workers in the community; 2) the development of motivational systems emphasizing the importance of performing to the best of their ability and establishment of the reinforcing properties of work; and 3) the development of skills of personal-social responsibilities including adjustment to social, personal, and family stress. In general, the objective is to develop adaptive behavior repertoires.

Individual counseling and psychotherapy have traditionally been viewed as treatment procedures in the total rehabilitation program for the retarded. Yepsen (1958), an authority in mental retardation, has suggested that counseling is characterized by an "interpersonal relationship which takes place when one seeks to influence the behavior and attitudes of another person or persons" and is essentially applicable in the same manner to both retarded and nonretarded individuals or groups. Counseling and psychotherapy routinely entails a one-to-one (face-to-face) verbal instruction between more knowing (counselor) and less knowing (client) persons. According to Bialer (1967), neither medical treatment (for example, drug therapy), physical treatment (for example, speech therapy), nor

teaching should be included within this framework. Such an approach is undertaken to resolve such personal difficulties as intrapsychic conflicts, emotional disturbances, weak ego-strength, inadequate self-concept, poor attitudes, poor emotional or behavioral control, depression, lack of motivation, and neurotic disorders, and to provide information sufficient to assist the client in resolving problems of personal, social, and vocational adaptation.

TRADITIONAL COUNSELING APPROACH

Counseling and psychotherapy procedures, while varying greatly in specific character (Bialer, 1967; Carkhuff and Berenson, 1967), are based predominately on various psychodynamic theories of behavior (personality) development and change. That is, it is generally assumed that any observable behavior characteristic which is inappropriate is viewed as a symptom or manifestation of some more basic, underlying defect in one's personality structure and/or dynamics. The therapy focuses on modification of these underlying difficulties, with the related assumption that the observable problems (symptoms) will concomitantly abate. This has been characterized as a "medical" or "disease" orientation or model (Kanfer and Saslow, 1965; Maher, 1966; Ullman and Krasner, 1965), the basic tenets of which may be characterized as follows:

1. It is assumed that there is an underlying origin or cause of behavior and consequently maladaptive behaviors cannot be directly treated since these are merely symptoms of deeper causes; the symptom can be removed only by eliminating the cause.
2. Changed behavior is not really of importance unless the basic cause is dealt with. Symptom (behavior) treatment only results in temporary reduction of problem behavior.
3. Change in verbal behavior, thoughts, or ideas is invariably accompanied by changes in other classes of behavior outside the counseling setting.
4. Insight is essential for effective treatment.
5. Verbal therapy sessions represent equivalent actual life situations and experiences.

The applicability (effectiveness and efficiency) of this model, both in theory and practice, to the amelioration of the adaptive behavior problems of the nonretarded (Eysenck, 1952, 1960, 1961; Krumboltz, 1964, 1966; Levitt, 1967) and the retarded (Gardner, 1967b; Leslie, 1968) has been questioned. With respect to the retarded, Gardner (1967b) suggested that counseling and therapy practices based on the disease model orientation are a luxury that psychologists and counselors working with the retarded

can ill afford and questioned both its usefulness and efficiency in addition to the counselor's role in the diagnosis and treatment of maladaptive behavior within this context. Gardner indicated:

> Psychotherapy, as commonly practiced, requires considerable investment of time and energy and, in light of available personnel and financial resources, can be provided to only a select few. I would take the position that we could not seriously view such expensive undertakings as solutions to anything and that our resources should be invested in a search for new ways of effectively and efficiently modifying the behavior of the mentally retarded . . . [p. 30].

As an alternative, the writer offered a social learning model based on the principles and techniques of learning theory for conceptualizing both behavior development and methods of behavior change. Others, however, have directly criticized this position and defended the traditional medical model (for example, Halpern, 1968) or indirectly supported its continued use with the retarded (for example, Ayers and Duguay, 1969; Sternlicht, 1966b).

Halpern (1968) suggested: (1) that research which indicates that traditional one-to-one verbally oriented counseling and therapy procedures are inadequate (for example, Eysenck, 1952, 1961) cannot be generalized to the retarded population because retardates were not subjects in the cited research; (2) psychotherapy is appropriate when retardation is psychogenic in nature and thus not a luxury; and, (3) refuting a theoretical position does not *ipso facto* refute treatment techniques derived from it, and vice versa. In view of these obvious differences of opinion, a closer examination of both theory and fact relative to the usefulness and efficiency of psychotherapeutic procedures with the retarded thus appears to be needed.

Critical reviews by Eysenck (1952, 1961) and others (for example, Levitt, 1967) suggesting that traditional psychotherapy and no treatment are about equally effective may be methodologically equivocal (for example, Bergin, 1963) and the results not generally applicable to the retarded population since treatment samples from this population were not used. However, there remains a paucity of evidence which supports the use of traditional psychotherapy with the retarded, and, alternatively, would suggest that such procedures are neither appropriate, useful nor efficient.

Traditional counseling and therapy, as noted previously, relies heavily upon one-to-one verbally oriented techniques. Thus, one's general intellectual level, and particularly general verbal skills and skills relating to verbal control over other classes of behavior appear to be critical for treatment to be effective. Krasner (1965) suggested that psycotherapy is a verbal modification process between two people, in which one (the more knowing therapist or counselor) seeks to change the verbal behavior of another (the

less knowing client). Moreover, Krasner suggested that "if changes in verbal behavior have consequences for change in other kinds of behavior, the systematic modification of verbalization is itself a treatment" [p. 230]. That is, it is assumed that changes in verbal behaviors will result in changes in behaviors which the verbal content represents. In illustration, if psychotherapy results in changes in verbal behavior from "I do not like to work and will not cooperate with my supervisor," to "I like to work and will cooperate with my supervisor because I can get along better if I do so," it is assumed that there will in fact be a change in work and work related behaviors. The verbal behavior will gain control over and give direction to other overt (non-verbal) behaviors in other settings. However, with respect to the adult retarded who is experiencing significant behavior adjustment problems, this assumption appears tenuous.

One of the significant psychological (functional) deficits which characterize the mentally retarded adolescent and young adult who present personal and social behavior difficulties is the lack of adequate verbal control of overt (nonverbal) behaviors. Stimulus events other than verbal ones provide the major discriminative or control influence over classes of behavior. In many instances, the control or functional relationship has not developed between verbal behaviors and other classes of behaviors which the verbal content represents. The retardate can be encouraged to say "I will do that" or "I should not do that" but frequently he does not reflect these verbally expressed intentions in overt behavior. In other instances such relationships between verbal cues and other classes of behavior are distorted or even may have lost their control function. The retardate frequently does not behave in a rational fashion or does not have "self-control" over his behaviors, that is, he is unable to direct appropriate behaviors or to make a rational decision in a choice or conflict situation as he does not have the appropriate verbal mediational responses which have strong or sufficient stimulus control over other classes of his behaviors. Moreover, the retarded exhibits a deficiency of appropriate intraverbal or mediational responses necessary for organization, storage, and retrieval of information and the establishment of situationally appropriate overt behavior. Thus, they fail to act "rationally," "logically," or "intelligently" on the basis of environmental contingencies. A treatment approach that aims merely at development of insight or an expanded system of verbal behaviors does not insure systematic change in other behavior areas. What the retarded adolescent or adult says or may be taught to say may or *may not* be related to other classes of behavior. The treatment strategy must go further and promote the development of verbal behaviors as powerful discriminative cues for other classes of behavior as these other behaviors occur in natural settings. This can best be done by reinforcing the occurrence of verbal be-

haviors that immediately precede or occur concomitantly with other behaviors. This seldom is accomplished in traditional counseling. A study of Doubros (1966) represents a step in the right direction even though it falls short of the aforementioned strategy.

Doubros (1966) studied the effects of deliberate and systematic manipulation of retardates' verbal behavior as a therapeutic technique. Therapy sessions often became exercises in memorization of critical, appropriate verbal patterns, upon which selective reinforcement was contingent in order to provide verbal cues which may gain discriminative control of overt behavior outside the therapy environment. However, no attempt was made to insure that the newly learned verbal responses were actually made and reinforced in critical social and interpersonal situations. This study, labeled by the writer as behavior therapy, merely attempted to shape new verbal responses in an isolated artificial office setting. Two case illustrations of this technique were provided. One male had received weekly 45 minute therapy sessions for six months, and the other eleven months of office and playroom sessions. Although no statistical analysis of the data was presented, behavioral graphs suggested a treatment effect in that there was a reduction in inappropriate behaviors outside the therapy environment. However, it was apparent that for both subjects a significant reduction in deviant behavior occurred during the baseline period, prior to the initiation of the verbal conditioning therapy. Thus, factors other than the reinforcement of classes of appropriate verbal behaviors could well have accounted for the reported effects.

Brodsky (1967) described a study designed to assess the changes, both in verbal behavior as a function of changes in nonverbal behavior as well as changes in nonverbal behavior as a function of changes in verbal behavior, in two institutionalized retarded males (ages 17 and 25) with low rates of social behaviors. Both had high rates of verbal behavior, but rarely initiated nor engaged in sustained social contacts. Treatment consisted of providing one with token reinforcement for social behavior (interacting with another person described as a gregarious mongoloid) in a laboratory setting and the other with reinforcement for social statements (such as "I like to play with Jane") during standardized clinic sessions. Results indicated that the person reinforced for social behavior in the laboratory behaved more socially in a playground situation whereas the subject receiving reinforcement for social statements showed no increase in overt social behavior on the playground. It was noted that reinforcement of social behavior led to increased prosocial verbal behavior. Thus, the results, although limited by the small sample, failed to support the assumed relationship between verbal and nonverbal behavior change. Also, it suggests that it may be more efficacious to bypass verbally oriented therapy and *repro-*

gram directly in the appropriate social environment. Again, it would appear that verbal behaviors, if these are to function as discriminative cues for other classes of behaviors, should accompany these other behaviors as they occur in the natural environment. Reinforcement of the verbal behavior-other behavior sequence can strengthen the control relationship between the two.

The results of the Doubros (1966) study, combined with conclusions which may be drawn from verbal learning research with the retarded (for example, Borokowski and Johnson, 1968; Penny, Seim and Peters, 1968) further qualify the use of verbally oriented therapy with the retarded. This research indicates that the retarded, when confronted with paired-associate verbal learning tasks do not spontaneously generate effective verbal mediators, nor use them appropriately when provided, in associating stimulus and response items. This suggests that their intraverbal behaviors (thinking or verbal associations) are relatively ineffective. That is, appropriate associations are absent or distorted. To the degree that this is true, the acquisition of "insight," (for example, verbal understanding or description of corelationships between behavior histories and contemporaneous events) which is deemed crucial in psychotherapy, is limited and the possible control of verbal behavior over classes of nonverbal behavior is greatly reduced. More studies are needed which systematically investigate the degree to which verbal response classes of the retarded may be differentially conditioned and the degree to which these response classes, acquired independently of any discriminative association with other nonverbal behaviors, may in turn exercise control over nonverbal behavior. Until more data are available, the assumption that the retarded have good verbal control over nonverbal behaviors remains only a hypothesis needing empirical verification.

Little systematic data assessing the relative usefulness and effectiveness of psychotherapeutic procedures with the retarded are presently available. The available information is, at best, ambiguous. Sternlicht (1966) concluded a lengthy review of individual and group psychotherapy procedures with the retarded by noting that "therapeutic work in this field, however, still lacks sufficient theoretical and empirical basis. A major shortcoming in this area is efficient research dealing with *outcomes* of psychotherapeutic treatment" [p. 349].

On the basis of Sternlicht's conclusion and the failure to find suitable research to support the efficacy of personal counseling and psychotherapy with the retarded, it may be concluded that neither salient psychotherapeutic *process* nor *outcome* variables have been delineated nor independently manipulated in order to determine their relative usefulness with the mentally retarded. As Baumeister (1967) noted, "to put it bluntly, maybe

the typical psychologist has developed no unique and effective skills relevant to the *modification* and *control* of retarded behavior" [p. 5]. Carkhuff and Berenson (1967) suggested a possible cause for this:

> Counselors and clinicians have, for too long, settled for apparent insight as the criterion for success, with little or no concern for the behavior of the patient outside of, or following therapy. Perhaps most significant, the complexity of our abstractions, and their vague implications for therapeutic treatment are so far removed from behavior and life that assessing efficacy takes the form of crude judgments based upon modifications of hypothetical dynamics. The dynamic, living, breathing person is lost in labels [p. 87].

Prior to a description of characteristics of a behavioristic approach to modifying the behavior of the mentally retarded, an example taken from the pages of a recent issue of *Mental Retardation* illustrates so well some of the major deficiencies of the traditional psychotherapy or counseling approach. In this paper Jones (1969) sought to "establish the utility and efficiency with which counseling can be done with the mentally retarded" [p. 19]. However, Jones provided not even a hint of objective data concerning the effects of his counseling efforts on the behavior of the retarded client. Although initially identifying excessive fantasy behavior as an area of concern, he concluded that:

> exposure to a concerned therapist on an intensive schedule enhanced the establishment of trust and a feeling of acceptance on the part of the client, two vital factors in establishment of rapport . . .

and

> If . . . goals include treatment of apathy, establishment of drive objects and motivation and building of ego strength, it is felt that intensive counseling programs can make meaningful contributions to these ends [p. 21].

Jones does not present any conceptual or empirical relationships between excessive fantasy behavior and any of these other "personality" constructs. Apparently, he assumed some degree of functional relationship among these but the nature of this was not identified. He makes no mention of the specific therapy techniques used, the specific behavioral effects of therapy, nor of the evaluation procedures used to assess therapeutic effects. Although he speaks of extensive diagnostic testing, there is no conceptual or procedural framework provided for translating the testing data into treatment strategies. As a result of these and related deficiencies, it is not at all surprising that counseling and psychotherapy with the retarded remains a vague, ill-defined, and suspect form of behavior intervention.

BEHAVIOR APPROACH TO COUNSELING

It appears that a functionally integrated analytic approach to the conceptualization of behavior development and behavior control (treatment) is
needed rather than reformulations of theories, principles, and practices
which are ineffective. What is required is a minimal number of theoretical
statements, operationally defined and subject to empirical verification, accounting for acquisition of both deviant and nondeviant behaviors with
unambiguously derivable treatment procedures. A natural science approach (Bijou, 1966b) to the acquisition and control of human behavior
offers an effective, efficient, and parsimonious basis for behavior theory and
clinical practice. This is particularly true with respect to the counseling
and guidance of the retarded.

As noted in previous chapters, the broad area of learning theory, particularly operant and respondent learning, provides the basis for the applied
analysis of behavior (Baer, Wolf, and Risley, 1968), and related clinical
treatment techniques. The applied or functional analysis of behavior is
based upon analytic behavioral application of "sometimes tentative principles of behavior to the improvement of specific behaviors, and simultaneously evaluating whether or not any changes noted are indeed attribut-
able to the process of application—and if so, to what parts of the process.
In short, analytic behavioral application is self-examining, self-evaluating,
discovery oriented . . ." [p. 91].

A number of different labels have been attached to this position, for
example: social learning (Gardner, 1967b), behavior facilitation, behavior
modification (Krumboltz, 1966; Carkhuff and Berenson, 1967), behavior
therapy (Wolpe, 1966), and the psychological model (Ullman and
Krasner, 1965). Regardless of the label, the approach is behavioral, with
emphasis upon getting an individual to do something efficiently as a function of the manipulation of the events controlling his behavior. Thus, the
clinician or therapist:

> . . . studies what subjects can be brought to do rather than what they can be
> brought to say; unless, of course, a verbal response is the behavior of interest.
> Accordingly, a subject's verbal description of his own nonverbal behavior
> usually would not be accepted as a measure of his actual behavior unless it
> were independely substantiated [Baer, Wolf, and Risley, 1968, p. 93].

Unlike the traditional or disease model approach to psychological treatment, the learning theory approach is technological, analytic, and provides
for conceptual clarity and relevance of treatment to conceptual principles.
It is technological in that the techniques and procedures for effecting specific behavior change are completely delineated. Thus, neither "play ther-

apy," "psychotherapy," "self-awareness," "insight," nor "social reinforcement" are technological descriptions. However, "the S was given token reinforcers, redeemable for back-up reinforcer every hour, on a variable ratio schedule for making eye contact with the counselor during therapy" is technological. Technological sufficiency permits unambiguous understanding and precise replicability.

A technological approach to behavior change, moreover, requires reliable quantification of the behavior under consideration in order to provide succinct, objective, and unambiguous definition of these behavior(s) and the relative change in their rate, intensity, and/or topography as a function of the treatment procedures. Reliable observation of specific behavior is possible outside of the laboratory or clinic and in the natural environment. Reliable, objective observation provides the basis for direct measurement and change of specific nonadaptive behavior.

The learning theory approach is analytic in that the clinician has achieved an analysis of, or an "explanation of," behavior in the degree to which he exercises control over it. This is contrary to Bijou's statement (1966b) that "many of the conventional approaches to counseling aim to get into and as near as possible to the *presumed* internal processes and conditions of the individual so that *hypothetical* causes may be modified. The behavioral science approach aims to get into and as near as possible to the *actual* situation in which the problem may be modified" [p. 34].

All behavior, both those labeled adaptive and maladaptive, are assumed to be learned and are conceptually a function of the same variables which are, or potentially may be, manipulatable. There is no concept of the unconscious nor of a pathology underlying the "symptomatic" behavior. Behavior is a sympton of nothing. It may be controlled by, or serve to control other behaviors, but these functions must be demonstrated. The behaviors dealt with are observable, and more importantly, quantifiable. Also, their manipulation is possible through the analysis of their reinforcement history and present environmental contingencies.

The learning model requires that specific problem behaviors be dealt with. As Bijou (1966b) observed, "it is *not* advantageous to try to reorganize, in one fell swoop, the 'whole personality' or even attempt to modify some hypothetical part of the personality such as the 'sense of ego-identity.' If such global objectives do in fact refer to changes in behavior, then the units selected to be changed are much too large to manage well" [p. 34]. Moreover, as Carkhuff and Berenson (1967) have suggested, there is less chance of explaining away failures in terms of client resistance, or lack of readiness for therapy when treatment focuses on specific problem behaviors.

The learning theory approach provides conceptual clarity to counseling theory and behavior change. Unlike the psychodynamic orientation, theoretical statements are subject to operational definition and empirical verification. The techniques of behavior control are related to the principles and concepts of learning theory. The clarity and parsimony thus permitted facilitate the systematic development of clinical techniques rather than a grab-bag of counseling and therapeutic tricks.

The behavior modification or learning approach, however, may create problems for counselors trained in the psychodynamic tradition in that it requires him to assume a new role: "instead of conceiving of the counselor as a reflector of feelings, or an explorer of resources, or a habit changer, or a remediator of self-concepts and values, or a releaser of repressions, we might come to think of him as a behavioral engineer—one whose job it is to arrange and rearrange the environment in order to bring about desired change in behavior" [Bijou, 1966b, p. 44].

This would include, as Gardner (1967b) suggested, functioning as a consultant-educator to rehabilitation and day care facilities for the retarded and as specialists in arranging optimal learning experiences in the real world. Moreover, it may be more efficient, and of less expense in terms of professional time and money, to function mainly as a trainer of those who have natural contact with the retarded, that is, teacher, attendant, nurse, parent, and others. Tharp and Wetzel (1969) provide well documented evidence that such "mediators" can exert a profound positive effect when trained to function in a contingency management environment. Zeilberger, Sampen, and Sloane (1968), as another example, successfully demonstrated that the frequency of "disobedience" behaviors can be decreased and "obedience" increased in the home by arrangement of differential reinforcement contingencies by parents. Adequately trained paraprofessional personnel who interact with the individual continuously in his "real" world may be more efficient and effective in changing behavior than a "qualified" psychologist or counselor who interacts with him only occasionally in an artificial world of office or playroom.

The psychodynamic orientation has not provided the integral relationship between theory and clinical practices in vocational counseling with the retarded. Particularly the goals of counseling and therapy have been poorly defined. Additionally, specific techniques are ill-defined and only vaguely related to theory. That is, even though diagnosis may be stated in terms of a theory, the therapist is still confronted with the question: "Just what do I do in order to change the behavior of the client?" In contrast, a learning orientation stresses the statement of goals in behavioral terms: "Stating goals of counseling in terms of observable behavior will prove

more useful than stating goals in terms of inferred mental states as 'self-understanding' and 'self-acceptance' " (Krumboltz, 1966 p. 153).

These goals should be differentially and specifically determined for each client. For example, if a therapy goal were one of developing a "healthier" or more "positive" identification as a worker the counselor would need to: (1) specify the behaviors taken as evidence of a poor identification as a worker; (2) specify the conditions under which these behaviors occur; (3) establish the functional consequences controlling these behaviors; and (4) determine their rate of occurrence. Moreover, the responsible clinician will need to state behaviorally the therapy objective, delineating (1) who will act, (2) when and under what conditions they will act, (3) the specific behaviors to be dealt with and how they will be influenced, and (4) a criterion for assessing the relative success or failure of the treatment. The details of this approach have been delineated in previous chapters.

Although requiring the counselor to acquire a new or different professional role and thus creating a certain amount of cognitive dissonance, the learning theory approach contributes much to him. Some of the contributions, as noted by Carkhuff and Berenson (1967) are: (1) he is provided with a system of well defined procedures; (2) there is a high level relationship between treatment goals and techniques of behavior change; (3) there is more effective involvement in behavior change beyond the therapy hour; (4) he quite naturally looks for ways of making transitions from therapy to real life; (5) it dispels the concern for transference/counter-transference neurosis; (6) it requires that more attention be paid to nonverbal cues affecting behavior change; and (7) it provides an opportunity for not only eliminating maladaptive behavior but also for establishing adaptive ones.

More systematic applied behavior research obviously is needed to determine the parameters of behavior control techniques most effective in facilitating behavior change with the mentally retarded. Questions raised by Halpern (1968) are relevant in this respect: "Which technique works best, under what circumstances, and with whom?" [p. 50]. While the questions are appropriate, the conceptual and procedural orientations assumed by traditional counseling and psychotherapy models have been and remain inappropriate. More specifically, it appears pertinent to ask such questions as: What are the antecedent stimulus conditions which are most effective in controlling behavior; what is the nature of the behavior to be changed in frequency, intensity, or amount; what are the reinforcement or consequent events currently maintaining the behavior; and, what are the effective reinforcement contingencies of schedules for shaping and maintaining more adaptive behaviors? The learning theory orientation provides both conceptual and operational guidelines for answering these questions.

Applications to Development of Adaptive Behavior of the Severely and Profoundly Retarded

Education and rehabilitation endeavors with the severely and profoundly retarded differ in several quantitative and qualitative dimensions from similar endeavors with the moderately and mildly retarded. The major concern is not one of "How can the client be best prepared for an independent or semi-independent social and vocational status?" but rather one of "How independent can this person become in the sheltered environment of home or residential facility in which he is to reside?", with the related question of "What type of environment must be developed in order to maximize the behavior potential of this person?" Education and rehabilitation efforts take on a more basic character. The goals become those of developing toileting, feeding, grooming, and other self-care skills, and of developing basic works and work-related skills. Those persons involved in the rehabilitation of these adolescents and adults become educators in the fullest sense of the word. Such an educator is concerned not only with adjustment, however simple it may be, to the world of work and its related implications but also with the total life adjustment of the retarded in a sheltered environment. In this perspective, however, occupational skills become nonetheless important as such skills can spell the difference between a life filled with inactivity or undirected activity and a life that includes meaningful involvement in the world of work. Work skills, and the opportunity to use

these in a simple remunerative environment, add dignity and personal worth to the life of the more severely retarded adolescent and adult.

The position that the retarded, regardless of his severity of disability, has a right to an opportunity to develop self-care skills and to learn to work productively is consistent with the behavior modification viewpoint that behavioral limitations cannot be assumed on an a priori basis to be due to internal factors. The more severely retarded has a right to an environment which is designed to promote positive behavior development. As his limited behavioral repertoire is not due to illness, he should not be pampered or pitied, but rather should be provided an opportunity to learn and to perform. Residing in an environment that provides continuous total care regardless of the person's degree of involvement or potential contribution, creates dependency and contributes significantly to the person's total behavioral inadequacies. An environment that respects the integrity and dignity of the more severely retarded, on the other hand, will be arranged in that manner which will maximize the possibility for learning and performance of a range of skills of independence.

Although learning and performance in the more severely retarded are influenced and controlled by the same set of factors which influence learning and performance in all other retarded persons, some specific problems are present which influence the manner in which a program of behavior change is designed and implemented. The more important of these factors include:

1. The more severely retarded has a relatively limited behavior repertoire. In teaching new patterns of behavior it may be necessary initially to teach a number of the basic components rather than, as is done with the more able person, to integrate available behavior into a new chain or pattern. He also has less behavior to use to compete with nonadaptive behavior. As a result, a program concerned with eliminating behaviors frequently must use direct means of dealing with nonadaptive responses.

2. There is a limitation in the events which have reinforcing properties. This limitation is seen most drastically in the area of secondary reinforcing events. It is sometimes difficult to identify any events that have secondary reinforcing properties. Further, as associative learning occurs so slowly in the more severely retarded, it is difficult to empower events with secondary reinforcing properties. This restriction in secondary reinforcing events renders difficult the development of positive environmental control over behavior. There is little work or achievement motivation present. That is, engaging in work or completion of a task may have little or no reinforcement value. A long life of inactivity, noninvolvement, lack of persistence, and a limited history of contingent reinforcement all add to the difficulties faced by a program devoted to positive behavior development.

3. It is frequently difficult with the more severely retarded to develop conditioned aversive events. Such discriminative events as "Stop" or "No" and other more direct warnings or threats may acquire no control function. This, in combination with the limitations in positive environmental control due to a relative paucity of secondary reinforcing events, creates additional problems of management and rehabilitation of the adolescent and adult.

4. There is a limitation in the use of language, both receptive and expressive. This restricts the use of verbal events as discriminative stimuli (for example, "Stop that and come here." "Start to work now.") and as secondary reinforcing events (such as, "good job," "keep up the good work"). Additionally, this limitation restricts the development of self-cuing and self-reinforcement procedures. As a result, the possibility of self-control and self-regulation is greatly reduced.

5. Skills in imitating the behavior of others are frequently poorly developed or absent. Such a deficit greatly hampers the development of many self-care, social, and verbal behaviors. Bry (1969), for example, found in work with the profoundly retarded that observation learning as defined by Bandura (1969) does not occur unless such imitated behaviors are associated precisely with positive reinforcers. As will be described later, a program which initially encourages the person to imitate the behavior of the teacher may produce generalized imitative behavior patterns.

6. Skills in attending to relevant cues in the learning environment are frequently poorly developed. This renders discrimination difficult, with the result that precise environmental control over behavior is poor.

7. The severely retarded frequently present high rate disruptive behaviors which are highly resistant to change. For example, many severely and profoundly retarded engage in repetitive self-stimulatory or stereotyped behaviors. These may involve simple repetitive behaviors such as body rocking or arm flapping or may involve more disruptive behaviors—repetitive screaming or chattering or various forms of emotional outburst involving physical aggression toward peers or other persons in the immediate environment.

8. A low frustration tolerance along with hyperactivity and limited persistence all add difficulties to a behavior development program. Behavioral requirements that differ from the routine or even interference with ongoing behavior may result in disruptive emotional outburst. Attention is difficult to attract and to hold. Thus the development of new responses and the process of bringing these under precise environmental control become major tasks.

9. The generalization of learning from the environment in which the behavior was acquired to other similar environments is sometimes difficult.

An example of this is seen in the report of Giles and Wolf (1966) in their attempt to toilet train the severely retarded. Although stimulus generalization did occur, a retraining period was frequently needed as the retarded person was returned from the training environment to the living unit. Behavior maintenance thus becomes a critical problem of technology and must not be left to chance.

In spite of these and related difficulties, recent reviews (for example, Gardner and Watson, 1969; Nawas and Braun, 1970; Watson, 1967) have demonstrated that the severely and profoundly retarded can acquire a wide range of skills and, under appropriate environmental conditions, can maintain these skills over extended periods of time. Residential facilities are gradually shifting from that of care and life maintenance to that of training and rehabilitation. The shift is quite slow in numerous instances as the severely and profoundly retarded have been viewed as helpless and quite incapable of any independence. An environment has been provided to take care of all life-sustaining needs of the person. He has been fed, clothed, toileted, and kept warm and dry in the better facilities. He has been viewed as being unable to take care of even his more basic needs.

Within the last decade a revolutionary change has occurred in programs for the severely and profoundly retarded. In fact, some activities of this revolution represent some of the most exciting work available in application of behavior principles to the treatment of developmental, behavioral, educational, and rehabilitation problems. It has been demonstrated that at least a significant degree of the behavioral limitations of the more severely retarded reside in a poorly constructed environment which impedes rather than facilitates the development and maintenance of adaptive behavior. As noted in an earlier chapter, treatment programs utilizing this systematic application of behavior modification procedures have demonstrated that the more severely retarded can develop language, motor, perceptual, cognitive, affective, social, self-help, and work skills that render them more independent and more able to experience a meaningful personal and social existence.

The initial section of this chapter is devoted to a review of the behavior modification procedures used and the results obtained in a number of studies involving the severely and profoundly retarded. Although many of the studies are concerned with the modification of the behavior of the adolescent or adult, studies will be described that report data on the younger retarded person. These studies of younger persons are included as behavior modification techniques are utilized which have applicability to the older person. The final section of the chapter will summarize the procedures followed in developing and implementing a program of behavior modification for the severely and profoundly retarded.

As noted earlier, certain characteristics of the more severely retarded render difficult any efforts at behavior development and modification. This emphasizes, however, the need for utilizing every useful behavior modification approach that is available. Limited language and general cognitive skills, a rather primitive social motivation system, and a restricted range of stimulus events which are controlling or reinforcing all render behavior shaping attempts with this group quite difficult. In addition, for a large number of severely and profoundly retarded a disproportionate amount of their total behavior is of a sort that creates considerable management problems. It is not unusual to find in this group such behaviors as dangerous self-mutilation, violent and unpredictable temper outbursts, physical attacks on peers and attendants, chronic and high rate repetitive movements, disruptive screaming and crying, and destruction of windows, clothing, furnishings, and the like.

As there are no essential differences in the behavior modification procedures used with various clinical, developmental, educational, and vocational problem areas, the discussion will revolve around the various techniques available for increasing and for decreasing the strength of designated behavior patterns.

Procedures for Elimination of Behavior Patterns

A significant emphasis in many of the clinical studies and reports which describe behavior modification techniques with the retarded has been that of eliminating or reducing in frequency or severity specific inappropriate behavior patterns. Three general techniques have been used in programs to eliminate undesirable behavior. First is that of extinction which involves the removal of those contingent stimulus events which are maintaining the behavior. The report of Wolf et al. (1965), described in an earlier chapter, illustrates the successful use of this procedure in eliminating excessive vomiting behavior and related tantrumlike behaviors. The second major strategy involves the use of various techniques having aversive components. Finally, behavior modification programs have used a strategy of developing behavior patterns which are incompatible to or which compete with and replace the inappropriate behavior patterns. Peterson and Peterson (1968), in illustration, reinforced a range of behaviors which competed with self-destructive behaviors of a retarded boy. In fact, most studies which use an extinction or punishment procedure to eliminate excessively occurring inappropriate behavior patterns report the concurrent reinforcement of appropriate ways of behaving. Studies frequently report that these new ways of behaving add considerably to the effort to reduce and eliminate the punished behavior. In other instances, the aversive com-

ponents associated with certain environmental events can be extinguished
by a combination of repeated graded presentations of the conditioned
aversive stimuli and the concurrent reinforcement of more appropriate behaviors in the presence of the feared event. Blackwood (1962) illustrates
this approach in his work with a retarded person who exhibited a fear of
walking down steps.

EXTINCTION PROCEDURES

Although useful in dealing with relatively simple behavior patterns or behavior patterns which are maintained by reinforcers which the treatment
personnel may control, an extinction procedure used in isolation has not
produced too much success in work with the severely and profoundly retarded. As noted in the discussion of extinction of operant behavior in
cies, especially of complex behavior and behavior of long standing, is usu-
Chapter 6, the analysis and control of the pertinent reinforcing contingen-
ally a difficult undertaking. In addition, the reader will recall the reports
of Bucher and Lovaas (1968) that in cases involving self-destructive or
aggressive behaviors, an extinction procedure could be a dangerous strategy as the person may seriously injure himself or others.

PUNISHMENT PROCEDURE

Some treatment procedures which have gained recent consideration in
work with the severely retarded are those having aversive components.
Many of the reports describing experience with punishment have been
products of relatively new clinical research programs aimed at creating a
more effective total rehabilitation environment for the retarded. Few have
been products of systematic experience in clinical treatment programs.
This is not surprising as most clinical treatment personnel categorically
reject the use of punishment procedures as legitimate behavior change approaches. Punishment procedures are typically viewed as inhumane, deplorable, unethical, and nonprofessional. This attitude is perhaps understandable in relation to the mentally retarded in residential settings as
various punishment techniques all too frequently have been used as punitive measures instead of as treatment techniques used in a deliberate
systematic fashion. In addition, it is assumed by many that the decelerating
effects of punishment are temporary and that punishment produces undesirable side effects, including disruptive emotional states and disruption of
social relationships. It even appears that these attitudes and extrapolations
from animal research have greatly restricted the clinical use of punishment
with the retarded. For example, a review chapter on the moderately and
severely retarded as recent as 1966 reported no studies in this area (Sprad-

lin and Girardeau, 1966). In general it appears that punishment is frequently rejected as a treatment procedure, not on the basis of an objective evaluation of scientific data, but rather on the basis of ethical, philosophic, and sociopolitical considerations.

In view of this restrictive attitude and in consideration of the recent experience which numerous people are reporting, it should be valuable to examine the question, "What does punishment do to the behavior of the severely and profoundly retarded?" To accomplish this, studies that evaluate the use of punishment with persons exhibiting severely retarded behavior are reviewed, including a few studies with children who have been labeled autistic or schizophrenic. More specifically, information relevant to the following and related questions will be sought: How effective are punishment procedures in treatment of inappropriate behaviors of the severely retarded? If effective, are such behavior changes temporary? What "side effects" are produced by punishment? With what types of behavior is punishment most effective? Such an evaluation of available data will provide an empirical basis for decisions by treatment personnel concerning the use or rejection of punishment procedures. In addition, a critical evaluation of the studies will provide direction to future investigations, both in terms of identifying design and methodology deficiencies which must be considered if more reliable data are to be obtained and in terms of identifying a range of parameters in need of study.

Punishment procedures that have been used with the retarded can be grouped into two classes on the basis of the operations followed. The first class includes those procedures that result in the *presentation* of certain stimulus conditions following a response to be eliminated. These would include: (a) primary aversive stimuli, for example, electric shock (Tate and Baroff, 1966), (b) physical restraint, for example, strapping to chair or bed (Hamilton, Stevens and Allen, 1967), placing in restraining jackets (Giles and Wolf, 1966), and (c) conditioned aversive stimuli, for example, "No" paired previously with removal of food and physical restraint (Henriksen and Doughty, 1967). The second class includes those procedures which result in the *removal* of certain stimulus conditions following the to-be-eliminated behavior. Various procedures of time-out from positive reinforcement, for example, placement in an isolation room following inappropriate behavior (Wiesen and Watson, 1967), illustrate this class of pro-procedures. On occasion the time-out is used in combination with a response cost (Weiner 1962) procedure, for example, subject is isolated and in addition loses certain tangible positive reinforcers which are available to him (Hamilton and Allen, 1967).

In most of the studies to be described, regardless of the specific punish-

ment procedures used, subjects not only had alternative response possibilities available in the punishment situation but in addition were provided positive reinforcement for more suitable alternative behaviors. Azrin and Holz (1966) emphasize that such an alternative response situation results in maximum suppression by a given intensity of punishment. Although desirable as a treatment strategy, such a procedure does, however, confound the contributions of punishment and positive reinforcement in subsequent behavior change except in those studies which utilize a precise functional analysis design. Further, the reader should note that the applied research reports reviewed vary greatly in terms of the nature of the data presented. As much of the work represents recent pioneer efforts at studying the effects of punishment on human problem behavior in a clinical setting, it is mostly of a preliminary or case study nature. Only a few of the studies used analytic designs (for example, a reversal technique) which would render possible the demonstration of reliable control over the observed behavior changes. In most of the work reviewed, a therapy procedure (that is, baseline-treatment) was followed which precluded the demonstration of a reliable (replicated) functional relationship between punishment and subsequent behavior changes. Finally, except in a few instances, no objective data were obtained concerning "side effects." The limitations which these design characteristics place on both the reliability and generality of the reported results will be discussed following a review of the studies.

Primary Aversive Stimulation. The presentation of primary aversive stimulus conditions contingent upon inappropriate behavior has been used in a number of behavior modification programs in an attempt to eliminate self-destructive, aggressive, and disruptive behaviors. In a recent report, Bucher and Lovaas (1968) describe the application of electric shock in suppressing the high rate of self-destructive responses of three retarded subjects with psychotic-like behavior. All had long histories of self-injurious behavior, all were hospitalized, and all were kept in constant restraints. In all cases the self-destructive behaviors were suppressed immediately and virtually eliminated after a series of response contingent electric shocks usually delivered by a hand-held inductorium and distributed over a small number of sessions.

Risley (1968) used shock to control dangerous climbing behavior in a hyperactive brain-damaged girl described as asocial, with no speech or imitative behaviors. Repetitive head twisting was eliminated by a procedure of shouting at and shaking the child. Previous withdrawal of attention, isolation for ten-minute time-out periods contingent upon the climbing behavior and reinforcement of incompatible behaviors all proved noninfluential. As the behavior was dangerous to the child and destructive to the

home, and as the child's aggressive behavior toward her younger brother was causing parental concern, it was felt that an effective control procedure having immediate effects was needed.

Shock was applied by a hand-held inductorium to the child's leg contingent upon climbing behavior. Climbing behavior, which was occurring at the rate of one climb every ten minutes, was eliminated in a laboratory room after six contingent applications of the shock over eight sessions. No climbing occurred in the therapist's presence during the subsequent twelve sessions but did reappear in the following session. No shock was administered during the subsequent eleven sessions, with climbing occurring an average of 4.9 times per hour. As the author emphasized, "Clearly, the effects of the shock punishment were reversible (not permanent)" [p. 29]. A single response contingent shock again eliminated the response, with no further climbing occurring during the next 59 sessions.

The procedure was applied in the home where the inappropriate climbing was at an average rate of 29 times daily. The rate was reduced to two per day within four days of response contingent shock, with a zero rate obtained within a few additional days. Aggressive behavior against the younger brother resulted in shock. Within three weeks this behavior rate was reduced to zero and was not reported to occur during the subsequent 70 days of follow-up. The repetitive head rolling behaviors were virtually eliminated within ten sessions of response contingent shouting ("stop that") and vigorous shaking.

In evaluating the question of possible negative side effects associated with the use of a punishment procedure, Risley concluded that "the most significant side effect was the fact that eliminating climbing and autistic rocking with punishment facilitated the acquisition of new desirable behaviors" [p. 33]. Both frequency of eye contact with the therapist and rate of imitation behavior were increased. Risley suggested the possibility that stereotyped behaviors of deviant children are "functionally incompatible" with the development of new socially desirable behaviors. In the case reported, socially appropriate behaviors were established as stereotyped behaviors were eliminated.

Tate and Baroff (1966) described the successful use of response contingent electric shock in work with a nine year old blind boy residing in a state institution for the mentally retarded. The boy engaged in various self-injurious behavior (SIB) including head-banging, face slapping, punching his face and head with his fist, hitting his shoulder with his chin and kicking himself. He was reported to enjoy bodily contact with others. The child spent most of his time restrained in bed. Electric shock was used in this case on the assumption that such aversive consequences would result in rapid deceleration of the SIB. This was deemed essential as the risk was

present that further SIB would completely destroy the retina of his right eye in which some light-dark vision was present. An earlier treatment procedure consisting of brief termination of physical contact with an adult produced dramatic results but was replaced by the primary aversive stimulation procedure. This time-out procedure will be described in the following section.

Shock was delivered to the lower leg contingent upon SIB. Previous baseline rate of SIB was approximately two per minute. Following response contingent shock a rapid deceleration effect was noted, with only 20 SIBs of light intensity observed during a five and one-half hour period (average of .06 responses per minute) on the first day following shock. On the second day there were only 15 SIBs during the entire day (rate of .03 per minute). During subsequent days, subject spent nine hours daily out of bed. Subject was observed for 167 days after the beginning of shock, with no SIBs observed during the last 20 days of treatment.

After initiating use of electric shock, these writers observed that no deleterious emotional or social interaction effects were evident. On the contrary, punishment frequently resulted in a more alert, cooperative, smiling, and relaxed child. Bucher and Lovaas (1968) and Luckey, Watson, and Musick (1968) reported highly similar reactions of decrease in whining, fussing and crying and an increase in alertness, affection, and general social responsiveness in their similar treatment of retarded and autistic children. In all cases, these new behaviors were provided ample reinforcement by the therapists and other caretaker personnel having contact with the child.

Hamilton and Standahl (1969) reported success with the shock-punishment procedure in obtaining rapid deceleration of a variety of behavior deviations in the severely and profoundly retarded, including such problem areas as window-breaking, rectal digging, rumination, and physically abusing other residents. In each instance a brief electric shock was administered following the occurrence of the target behaviors. These writers noted, however, that in some cases responses which occurred at a high rate were not rapidly suppressed. Furthermore, the decelerated behavior did not readily generalize to no-shock conditions in all cases. A procedure for dealing with these problems was evaluated in work with a twenty-four-year-old female institutionalized for over fourteen years who exhibited limited self-care skills and no intelligible vocalizations. Her most characteristic behavior consisted of low-pitched high intensity screams which occurred during most of her waking hours. Two other types of vocalizations described as "mooing" and "chattering" were also present.

During base rate sessions consisting of eight daily one-half hour periods, a shock apparatus was strapped about subject's waist to acclimate her to this equipment. During treatment (days 9–26) shock was administered

following each growl which occurred during the last 15 minutes of each daily 30 minute session. The shock intensity was increased after day 18 following an apparent adaptation effect. During base rate sessions growling was emitted at an average half hour rate of 330. No effect on growling was evident during the first two days of the treatment sessions. During the next three treatment sessions there was a sharp reduction in growling during the shock periods and to a lesser extent during the no-shock periods. During the next five days of treatment there was a change from a generalized marked suppression of growling to a return to pretreatment level during both shock and no-shock periods. After the shock intensity was increased, an immediate suppression effect was evident. Growling was effectively eliminated during the shock condition. Examination of the frequencies of chattering and mooing, however, indicated that the training was singularly specific to the growling—no effect was noted on these other classes of vocalization. In the second phase of the treatment program, shock was administered whenever growling occurred during two one-half hour periods five days a week. At this time subject was allowed to wander freely on the ward or in the outdoor play yard. By the eighteenth treatment day, growling was practically eliminated during these two one-half hour sessions. The average growling frequencies dropped from 25.5 in the morning and 19.2 in the afternoon during the first 17 treatments sessions to an average rate of 2.2 and .8 respectively during sessions 18–32.

During phase three the program was expanded to a 24 hour basis. Shock was delivered on a loosely defined intermittent punishment schedule by a shock stick carried by ward personnel. Growling responses gradually diminished over the next three months of the treatment program. Subject was followed for one year with the observation that the behavior rarely occurred at all. Thus it appears that a distributing behavior that initially had occurred many thousands of times daily had been, for all practical purposes, eliminated following the contingent use of mild shock.

White and Taylor (1967) administered electric shock as a consequence of ruminating gestures of two profoundly retarded adults. Although not presenting adequate quantitative data, the writers reported an impression that the response contingent shock did significantly interrupt the ruminating behavior in these two subjects. In a related study, Luckey, Watson, and Musick (1968) reported the use of mild electric shock to reduce the frequency of vomiting and chronic rumination by a severely retarded boy. Rumination had been present for over a year in the hyperactive, destructive boy. Vomiting episodes started about 12 months prior to initiation of the response contingent shock. Medical and psychiatric treatment had failed to control these behaviors. With the use of a portable radio-controlled shock apparatus, the therapist delivered shock immediately following vomiting or rumination behaviors. These behaviors dropped from a

daily average of 13 occurrences during the first 4 days of treatment to a near zero level during the following 94 days of treatment and follow-up.

Birnbrauer (1968), in work with a profoundly retarded adolescent, found response contingent electric shock to be effective in suppressing several bothersome behaviors but noted that the effects were highly response-specific. The application of shock to one response had no reliable effect on other behaviors.

In addition to these studies using obvious primary aversive stimuli as the major treatment strategy, a few studies are available that report the use of a combination of primary and secondary aversive stimulus consequences or stimulus conditions that differed noticeably in physical intensity. Wiesen and Watson (1967), in an attempt to eliminate soiling in a six year old institutionalized severely retarded boy, required him to remain in the soiled clothes for five minutes prior to bathing. In addition bathing was completed in water that was maintained at below room temperature. The writers reported that soiling—which had occurred as often as nine times per day before treatment—was extinguished with very rare reoccurrences. Evaluation of the specific effect of these punishment procedures was not possible as these contingencies were one aspect of a program which also used a time-out procedure in an effort to extinguish other undesirable behaviors. This study will be discussed in more detail in the following section concerned with procedures using removal of stimuli conditions. Marshall (1966) reported success in toilet training an autistic child through use of· mild punishment consisting of slaps on the buttocks for soiling behavior and food reinforcement for correct responses.

Physical Restraint. Henriksen and Doughty (1967), Giles and Wolf (1966), and Hamilton, Stephens, and Allen (1967) all report the use of physical restraint as a deceleration procedure. Henriksen and Doughty, in a program to eliminate undesirable mealtime behaviors of rapid eating, eating with hands, stealing food, hitting others at table, and throwing trays on floor, interrupted the misbehavior and held the subject's arm down in his lap. Secondary aversive cues of verbal disapproval were developed by pairing these cues with movement restraint.

Giles and Wolf placed subjects in restraining jackets, attached them to the end of a rope, and/or retained them in a crawl pen as a negative consequence of soiling behavior. These events were not used to physically restrict behavior but rather as aversive consequences to suppress its occurrence. The authors conclude: "This study suggests that aversive stimuli, such as restraining jackets, can be used briefly, yet effectively, to modify inappropriate behavior when distributed for short intervals contingent upon that behavior" [p. 780].

Hamilton, Stephens, and Allen (1967) used a combination of time-out

from positive reinforcement and physical restraint in a program to eliminate a variety of aggressive and destructive behaviors in five severely and profoundly retarded adolescents and adults. Following occurrence of the target behavior, the subject was placed in a time-out area from 30 to 120 minutes, during which time she was either restrained to a padded chair bolted to the floor or, with one subject, restrained to her bed. High frequency head and back banging was quickly eliminated in the first subject. The second subject's behavior of frequent undressing throughout the day (for example, 12 times on the day preceding initiation of program) was reduced to an occasional occurrence after one week.

Subject 3 illustrates the value of application of response contingent punishment over the use of the same negative conditions in an unsystematic manner. Due to a number of bothersome behaviors, including the habit of breaking windows with her head, subject 3 was restrained to her bed for extended periods of time prior to initiation of treatment. She averaged one broken window daily during the short periods when she was released for eating, bathing, toileting, and exercising. Following initiation of the program, whenever a window was broken the subject was immediately restrained to her bed for two-hour periods, with no attention provided beyond that essential for medical treatment of cuts from the broken glass. Within a week this behavior had dropped to a minimal frequency. During the next seven weeks only eleven windows were broken, after which the behavior did not reoccur during an eleven month follow-up period.

Following the elimination of prolonged restraint and window breaking, two other classes of behavior, body-slamming and clothes tearing, were selected for deceleration programming. The occurrence of either behavior resulted in immediate bed restraint. After a few weeks, the behavior virtually dropped out and remained so over an extended follow-up period.

Abusive behavior occurring at an average rate of five incidents a week was reduced within a month to an average of one incident a week in subject 4 following systematic response contingent restraint in the time-out chair. Subject 5 exhibited a wide range of disruptive behavior, mostly involving fighting, making intolerable demands on staff, and defying authority. Much of this behavior was eliminated and that which remained was reduced in severity following response contingent time-out in the restraint chair.

Hamilton and Stephens (1968) used time-out as a strategy to reduce disruptive behaviors prior to initiating a program of reinstating speech behavior in an emotionally disturbed nineteen year old retarded female. The program of behavior deceleration was highly effective and rendered it possible to utilize positive reinforcement procedures in the program of speech development.

Conditioned Aversive Stimulus Presentation. As suggested earlier, Henriksen and Doughty (1967) paired facial and verbal disapproval with the onset of movement restraint and later used the aversive stimuli alone to suppress inappropriate eating behavior. Although unable, due to the confounding effects of other variables, to account for the ensuing behavior changes solely in terms of the presentation of conditioned aversive stimuli, the writers did speculate that the obtained results could be attributed to these aversive cues. Whitney and Barnard (1966) used a similar procedure with positive results in elimination of inappropriate eating behavior in a profoundly retarded fifteen-year-old-girl.

Giles and Wolf (1966), after exploring the effects of a variety of stimuli in an effort to eliminate inappropriate toilet behavior in a severely retarded boy, found that placing a blindfold on him created an aversive condition. The use of this consequence in combination with physical restraint was followed by the elimination of inappropriate behaviors.

Watson and Sanders (1966) and Watson (1966) used a chain of aversive stimuli as a means of eliminating undesirable behavior of severely retarded boys after experiencing little success in extinguishing the behavior following attempts with an extinction procedure and a schedule of differential reinforcement of low rate of responding (see Watson, 1967). A response in the absence of the discriminative stimulus (S^D) produced a time-out signal that the S^D would not reappear for 15 seconds. Continued responses produced a firm and moderately loud vocal "No," with an electric shock following subsequent responses. In this higher-order conditioning paradigm, the vocal "No" and the time-out stimulus gained aversive properties. The writers reported this to be a very effective procedure and found it necessary to use the shock very infrequently after an initial introduction to this technique.

In the Tate and Baroff (1966) article discussed earlier, the writers reported that the buzzing sound produced by the shock stick which occurred upon delivering electric shock became an effective conditioned aversive stimulus following a few pairings. Refusal to eat and drink, inappropriate hand posturing, saliva-saving and excessive clinging to people were all brought under control by use of the buzz without actually delivering the electric shock. Similar conditioning effects were reported by Risley (1968).

Removal of Stimulus Conditions. In addition to the typical extinction procedure of removal of the reinforcing consequences associated with the given behavior, a *time-out* from positive reinforcement and a *response cost* procedure have been used successfully as behavior deceleration techniques with the retarded. Although Verhave (1966) defines a time-out procedure rather simply as a period of time during which positive reinforcement is not available, Leitenberg (1965) indicates that there is no single set of operations which adequately defines time-out from positive reinforcement.

It becomes apparent in reviewing various time-out procedures used in studies with the retarded that considerable variation exists among the specific operations followed. The reader may wish to review the discussion in Chapter 6 of the basic operations which define response cost and time-out procedures.

In a study mentioned in Chapter 4, Wiesen and Watson (1967) describe the behavior treatment of an institutionalized severely retarded boy who exhibited excessive attention getting behavior. This behavior, directed toward adults, was described as "almost unbearable" and consisted of constant grabbing, pulling, hitting, untying shoelaces, and the like. It was further noted that this boy totally ignored other children. It was hypothesized that the excessive high rate of responding (over six responses per minute during the base rate observations) was being maintained by the social attention which such behaviors brought.

Elimination of this highly disruptive behavior and development of peer social interaction were identified as the treatment goals. One element of the treatment procedure, that of removing the child from the presence of the reinforcing adults immediately following inappropriate attention seeking behavior, is based on the suggestion from experimental and treatment studies that time-out from positive reinforcement functions as an aversive event and thus decreases the strength of the preceding behavior (for example, Ferster and Appel, 1961; Wolf, Risley, and Mees, 1964). A time-out procedure consisting of removal of the boy from all possible social reinforcement and placing him outdoors for five minute periods were made contingent upon excessive attention seeking behavior. Concurrent tangible reinforcement was made contingent upon appropriate interaction with peers. An interesting aspect of this procedure consisted of the manner in which reinforcement was provided this behavior. Over the 21-day treatment program, peers presented the tangible reinforcement to Paul whenever he interacted with them. These peers were in turn reinforced by the attendant counselors. Removal of clothing and soiling behaviors which were observed to occur during the isolation or time-out period resulted in an extension of the aversive consequence condition. Additionally, following soiling, "no bathing was permitted until five minutes had elapsed and water temperature was maintained at below room temperature" [p. 51].

This treatment program produced a rapid decrease in the rate of attention seeking behavior. Although the child was removed a large number of times during the first few days of the program (over 40 times during the first day), this decreased rapidly. "Soiling, which had occurred as often as nine times per day before conditioning, had been extinguished with only nine episodes of spontaneous recovery" [p. 51]. Rate of social interaction behaviors were reported to become a "major response."

Blackwood (1962), Giles and Wolf (1966), and Whitney and Barnard

(1966) all used brief interruptions of meals as an aversive event to eliminate behaviors of profoundly retarded subjects which interfered with development of simple self care skills. Peterson and Peterson (1968), in a
program designed to eliminate the self-injurious behaviors of a severely retarded boy, successfully used time-out from primary (removal of food)
and secondary (brief termination of social interaction) reinforcement. An
additional punishment procedure of requiring the child to walk across the
room and sit in a chair was included. These procedures functioned as mild
forms of punishment and facilitated the reduction of the inappropriate behaviors.

Edwards and Lilly (1966) and Hamilton and Allen (1967) used time
out plus response-cost to control inappropriate mealtime behavior of severely and profoundly retarded females. Both report virtual elimination of
a wide range of bothersome behaviors including line-breaking, food-throw-
ing, food stealing, food-smearing, and tray-throwing. The basic treatment
procedure was one of removing the subject from the dining area without
the rest of her meal. Hamilton and Allen obtained a rapid and permanent
reduction in inappropriate dining room behavior from the daily average
of 60 during baseline. A 12 month follow-up revealed a daily average of
less than one inappropriate response.

As reported earlier, Hamilton, Stephens, and Allen (1967) were quite
successful in the use of time-out plus physical restraint in eliminating a
variety of inappropriate behaviors in severely retarded subjects. Hamilton
and Stephens (1968), in work with a retarded nineteen-year-old girl, and
using the same procedure of time-out plus physical restraint, were successful in rapid elimination of inappropriate behaviors including floor-rolling
and screaming. Success with a social isolation consequence was evident in
this case even though the subject was described as being consistently socially isolated, withdrawn, and interacted with no one on the ward. Follow-up for six months and longer revealed only infrequent recurrences of
these behaviors.

Tate and Baroff (1966) used a brief time-out from physical contact in
an effort to eliminate undesirable self-injurious behavior in a blind boy.
Previous observations of this subject strongly indicated that physical contact with people was reinforcing to him and that being alone, especially
when he was standing or walking, was aversive. A three-second time-out
from physical contact period immediately followed each occurrence of a
self-injurious response. In addition, during a time-out period the therapist
ceased conversation with the subject. A median average rate of 6.6 responses per minute was obtained for five control days prior to the initiation
of time-out procedure. This average declined sharply with the initiation of

the time-out procedure to an average of .1 responses per minute. The results of this study indicated that the relatively simple procedure of immediate brief withdrawal of physical contact produced a dramatic reduction in the frequency of chronic self-injurious behavior. The usual extinction procedure of ignoring the behavior was not effective in reducing its frequency of occurrence.

A brief time-out period of two minutes used in combination with a procedure of providing positive reinforcement for acceptable behaviors was reported by Bostow and Bailey (1969) to result in elimination of extreme disruptive and aggressive behavior in institutionalized retarded residents.

As suggested earlier, in all studies using a time-out procedure, alternative behaviors were not only present but routinely were reinforced positively in a systematic manner. These studies support the statement of Azrin and Holz (1966) which reflected the animal and laboratory human research that "time-out can be a very effective punishment stimulus if the organism has available an alternative response that is unpunished and that will produce the reinforcement" [p. 392].

Discussion. As documented in recent reviews (Azrin and Holz, 1966; Church, 1963; Marshall, 1965; Solomon, 1964), the effects of punishment depend upon the parameters of the aversive stimuli in combination with characteristics of the subject being punished. In the studies reviewed in this chapter, types of punishment and subject characteristics as well as behavioral effects varied greatly. These effects are summarized in this section and similarities to results of general laboratory research noted.

The reader should note that most of the treatment studies reviewed were conducted in the natural setting in which the subjects resided. The primary focus of most studies was that of applied or treatment research and not of basic research, although some would qualify as acceptable behavior modification research endeavors. Furthermore, as suggested earlier, few of the treatment studies utilized a punishment procedure in isolation. Most frequently, alternative responses concomitantly resulted in reinforcement. Finally, subjects continued to live in a rather complex social environment which was not under control of the treatment personnel. In this environment it was not unusual, once the punished behavior reduced in intensity and frequency, for the social environment to attend to and reinforce appropriate behaviors of subjects who were previously ignored or actively avoided due to the obnoxious and inappropriate responses which they exhibited (for example, Hamilton and Stephens, 1968; Tate and Baroff, 1966; Whitney and Barnard, 1966). Even though punishment was the only independent variable which was manipulated in a systematic manner, other reinforcement variables were possible contributing factors to resulting be-

havior changes. Therefore, behavior changes should be viewed in such cases as a combination of punishment effects and positively reinforced competing responses.

In evaluating the question of the reliability of the data reported in the studies, certain deficiencies in experimental design are evident. None followed a treatment versus control group procedure. Only a few (for example, Lovaas et al., 1965; Risley, 1968; Tate and Baroff, 1966) met the rigorous requirements of a "single organism, within-subject design" (Dinsmoor, 1966; Honig, 1966; Sidman, 1960, 1962), that is, provided demonstration of a causal relationship between punishment and behavior change through a replication design. Most are case studies which described the treatment procedures used in work with single subjects or with small groups of subjects. In most instances the results must be viewed as therapy data, that is, data showing only a nonreplicated correlation between behavior change and punishment. These deficiencies however, are generally characteristic of most behavior modification/behavior therapy studies as documented in recent *Psychological Bulletin* reviews by Gelfand and Hartmann (1968) and Leff (1968). In fact as Baer, Wolf, and Risley (1968) have suggested, the very nature of applied behavior analysis frequently renders a reversal or replicated procedure impossible. These authors commented that "application typically means producing valuable behavior; valuable behavior usually means extra-experimental reinforcement in a social setting; thus, valuable behavior, once set up, may no longer be dependent upon the experimental technique which created it" [p. 94].

For those studies which produced therapy data, additional criteria must be used in evaluating the adequacy of the results obtained. In most of the studies reviewed (a) the target behaviors were specified and well delineated, enabling reliable observations of the occurrence-nonoccurrence of the behavior being treated; (b) reliable (over time) base rate information was provided; (c) description of the specifics of the treatment procedures was provided; (d) quantitative measures of treatment effects were obtained; and (e) follow-up data extending beyond the treatment period were provided. Leff (1968), recognizing the general deficits in experimental design in behavior modification studies dealing with a wide range of techniques and behavior problems, additionally suggested that the studies should be evaluated with respect to the extent to which dramatic changes in behavior followed treatment and which were maintained over a period of time following termination of treatment. He implied that procedures which evoked behavior changes meeting these criteria and which contribute substantially to the general social development of the individual should be viewed as having clinical treatment significance. Many of the studies concerning the mentally retarded did report dramatic, long term changes which evidently contributed significantly to the general adapta-

tion of the individual to his social and physical environment. In conclusion, although the results should be interpreted with caution as most studies reported could be criticized from a rigorous experimental design viewpoint, the consistency of positive results along with a consideration of the nature of the behavior change do provide a basis for the following generalizations.

Is punishment effective with the severely retarded? As noted earlier, punishment as a behavior modification procedure has been rejected by most treatment personnel as an appropriate or effective strategy. The question of the effectiveness of punishment as a treatment procedure in use with the severely and profoundly retarded, nonetheless, is an empirical one and cannot be answered on an a priori theoretical or philosophic basis.

The studies reviewed provide support for the general conclusion that punishment procedures do contribute to behavior change in the severely and profoundly retarded. Studies that utilized response contingent electric shock, physical restraint, conditioned aversive stimuli, and time-out from primary and/or secondary reinforcement all reported success in the deceleration of a wide range of inappropriate behaviors in both children and adults.

In the majority of the studies reviewed, especially those involving intense stimulation, punishment procedures were used only with chronic high frequency behavior which occurred in individuals who potentially were only minimally responsive to the more typical procedures of behavior change. In many cases punishment was used as a "last resort" strategy, only after other procedures of behavior change produced minimal results. For example, Watson (1966) reported little success in eliminating undesirable responses in severely retarded boys when using extinction or a differential reinforcement of low rates of responding procedure. The writer reported that the behaviors were quickly eliminated following the use of a chain of aversive consequences, consisting of time-out, a vocal "No," and electric shock. Likewise, Bucher and Lovaas (1968), Giles and Wolf (1966), and Risley (1968) reported that aversive consequences were used only after positive reinforcement had been found to be ineffective in modifying the behavior.

In summary, studies have reported the deceleration of behavior of severely and profoundly retarded individuals following response contingent punishment. Further, punishing one response does appear to greatly aid the acquisition of other available ones (for example, Blackwood, 1962; Henriksen and Doughty, 1967; Risley, 1968; Whitney and Barnard, 1966).

Are the effects of punishment temporary? Is there a relationship between the intensity of punishment and the degree of response deceleration? In contrast to Skinner's position (1938, 1953, 1961) that punishment does not weaken operant behavior but merely produces temporary suppression,

recent studies provide support for the position that punishing stimuli may produce long term deceleration effects (for example, Appel, 1963; Azrin and Holz, 1961; Karsh, 1963; Walters and Rogers, 1963). This is especially true, as Solomon (1964) has noted, when "the response-suppression period is tactically used as an aid to the reinforcement of new responses that are topographically *incompatible* with the punished ones" [p. 241]. Azrin and Holz (1966) in evaluating the "temporary effect" question conclude from their comprehensive review of basic laboratory studies that "punishment really does 'weaken' a response in the same sense that other procedures for reducing behavior 'weaken' behavior. Indeed, punishment appears to be potentially more effective than other procedures for weakening a response" [p. 436].

With few exceptions, the studies involving retarded subjects described in the present review reported deceleration results which extended considerably beyond the treatment period. As noted earlier, in most instances positive reinforcement was used for the instatement and acceleration of alternative, although not in every case incompatible, responses, for example, attention and praise was provided following desirable behavior, food which was withdrawn after inappropriate behavior was returned following appropriate social responses. Although few of the studies provided data relative to the theoretical issue of whether the deceleration of performance of the punished response was due to a weakening of the habit or whether the reinforced competing responses merely displaced the punished behavior, such an issue is of minor importance in a program designed to evaluate treatment procedure as long as the punished behavior does not reappear. In summary, there is some support for the position that the deceleration effects of punishment are not temporary when used in a broader program of behavior instatement and acceleration of social responses.

Bucher and Lovaas (1968), in commenting on the durability of behavior suppression following electric shock, suggested that the "post-treatment" environment would be rather critical as subjects in their studies demonstrated rather extensive discriminations among adults, physical settings, and the like. That is, if behavior is suppressed in one environment, it is not necessarily suppressed in another. This was supported by Hamilton and Standahl (1969) and Risley (1968). If the environment that previously reinforced the shock-suppressed behavior remains unchanged, it is highly likely that the behavior would reappear. These studies demonstrated, however, that response contingent punishment provided in new situations did result in systematic elimination of the behavior.

Although no study was concerned with a parametric analysis of punishment (that is, none evaluated the possible effects, for example, of varying the length of time-out or the length or frequency of electric shock), the studies using electric shock do provide some suggestions concerning the

relationship between the intensity of the punishing stimulus and the behavioral effect. White and Taylor (1967) reported that their subjects adapted fairly quickly to a mild shock of approximately 400 volts at 1 milliamp. The writers felt that shock at this intensity might have functioned even as positive reinforcement. The voltage was increased to approximately 500–700 volts before it appeared to exert a punishment effect. Hamilton and Standahl (1969), after obtaining behavior suppression effects initially, found an adaptation effect to electric shock delivered through two electrodes attached to a belt worn around the subject's waist. The punished behavior returned to pretreatment level and was decelerated only after the shock intensity was increased. Although no definitive position evolves from the data, there does appear to be some suggestion that for the severely/profoundly retarded a relationship does exist between intensity of punishment and behavior suppression effect. Obviously studies that vary intensity of punishment in a systematic manner are needed.

Does punishment produce disruptive and chronic undesirable emotional states or general chronic behavioral disruption? Punishment frequently is not used in a behavioral modification program due to the belief that aversive stimuli produce undesirable emotional states. Behavioral rigidity, general disruption of cognitive processes, production of neurotic syndromes, suppression effects not specific to the response punished, and chronic emotional maladjustment are but a few of the negative side effects attributed to punishment (Azrin and Holz, 1966; Church, 1963; Solomon, 1964).

This question was not evaluated satisfactorily by the studies reviewed. However, many expressed a concern for this question and presented relevant anecdotal reports. Contrary to expectations, widespread behavioral improvement rather than disruption was generally reported. Risley (1968), after careful evaluation of behaviors which occurred in the punishment (shock) sessions, concluded that "no suppression of other behaviors was noted, either through generalization of the punishment effect or through conditioned 'emotional' suppression, correlated with the punishment of the target behaviors. . . . The brevity of the general suppression directly produced by the shock, if any, is indicated by the subject obtaining and consuming food within 70 sec. after the first shock" [p. 33].

Tate and Baroff (1966) reported that on control days when no re sponse-contingent punishment was in effect. The subject "typically whined, cried, hesitated often in his walk, and seemed unresponsive to the environment in general" [p. 283]. On experimental days, during which withdrawal of physical contact followed a self-injurious response, subject "appeared to attend more to the environment stimuli, including the experimenters; there was no crying or whining, and he often smiled" [p. 283]. This provides a dramatic example of the possible beneficial effects which response contin-

gent punishment can exert on individuals who exhibit chronic high frequency maladaptive responses. After initiating use of electric shock, these
writers reported the observation that shock produced no observable deleterious effects in emotional state or in social interaction. On the contrary,
punishment frequently resulted in a more alert, cooperative, smiling, and
relaxed child. Bucher and Lovaas (1968), Lovaas et al. (1965), and
Luckey, Watson, and Musick (1968) reported highly similar reactions of
decrease in whining, fussing, and crying and an increase in alertness, affection and general social responsiveness in their work with severely retarded
and autistic children. These changes in behavior were reported to result in
a positive change in the behavior of attendants and nurses toward the subjects. As valuable behavior appeared, the social environment was more
likely to attend to and reinforce a wide range of other appropriate behaviors.

In summary, although caution must be exercised in generalizing from
these reports, it appears that emotional or behavior disruption is not a necessary result of punishment when used with the severely and profoundly
retarded. Conversely, it should not be assumed that the side-effects of
punishment should always be neutral or desirable. As suggested by Bucher
and Lovaas (1968) the reinforcement history of subjects should influence
the specific side-effects which result. Obviously, this complex question requires further investigation.

*Is social disruption a consequence of the use of punishment with the
severely retarded? Do symptom substitution and/or other negative side
effects occur?* The purpose of punishment is to eliminate specific inappropriate behaviors and to leave intact other behavior patterns. One of the
dangers of using a punishment procedure is that the treatment personnel
will acquire some properties of an aversive stimulus and evoke escape and
avoidance behavior. Thus, potentially social disruption may occur in subjects who least need such behavior strengthened. The present writer agrees
with Colwell's (1966) argument that punishment as frequently used in
institutions for the mentally retarded is likely to produce negative reactions to authority figures. In such settings, punishment often is inappropriate both in frequency and intensity and in its proximity to the punished
behavior.

Punishment applied appropriately, however, holds promise of being
effective without precipitating harmful side effects of social disruption.
This is supported by data and anecdotal reports from studies of Risley
(1968), Hamilton et al. (1967), and Whitney and Barnard (1966). Risley
(1968) evaluated the effects of electric shock on frequency of eye contact
with the adult delivering the punishment. Hutt and Ounsted (1966) have
predicted that increasing the level of arousal and anxiety of a child would

result in a decrease in eye contacts. Contrary to this theoretical position, frequency of eye contact actually increased. This was the only observed change in the subject's behavior toward the therapist. No punishment related aggressive behavior was noted toward any person or object in the laboratory or in the home, even following punishment of the subject's aggressive behavior toward his brother. One side effect which could be labeled as "symptom substitution" was observed. When climbing on a bookcase was punished, the subject began to engage in a topographically similar behavior of chair climbing. This behavior was quickly eliminated when also punished and no other undesirable behaviors appeared.

Risley concluded that "the most significant side effect was the fact that eliminating climbing and autistic rocking with punishment facilitated the acquisition of new desirable behaviors" [p. 33]. Both frequency of eye contact and rate of imitation behavior were increased. Risley suggested the possibility that stereotyped behaviors of deviant children are "functionally incompatible" with the development of new socially desirable behaviors. In this case reported, socially appropriate behaviors were established as stereotyped behaviors were eliminated through punishment.

Hamilton, Stephens, and Allen (1967) reported no cases of negative sympton substitution or any other undesirable side effect. They concluded that "on the contrary, residents whose unacceptable behaviors were suppressed as a result of the punishment procedure were judged by the ward personnel to be more socially outgoing, happier, and better adjusted in the ward setting" [p. 856]. Whitney and Barnard (1966), after controlling inappropriate eating behavior by means of physical restraint, verbal punishment, and time-out, noted that subject no longer removed her clothing, did not play with her feces, nor take food from other residents.

White and Taylor (1967) presented some interesting ideas concerning the positive side effects of electric shock punishment in their comments that the procedure "appears to afford a means of developing an interpersonal relationship as it presents a stimulus to the subject which is powerful enough to serve as an identifiable reinforcer. Both subjects, apparently as a consequence of the treatment, appeared to be more aware of and interact more with the examiners than other staff members" [p. 32]. And later: "the noxious conditioning procedure seems to work well in eliminating responses in patients where it is important to communicate on a physiological level" [p. 33].

In summary, although the data are limited, the studies reviewed would support the cautious position that it is possible to use punishment with the severely and profoundly retarded without producing social disruption or other negative side effects.

Is punishment effective in eliminating self-destructive behavior? It is not

unusual for the retarded in a residential setting to be placed in restraints throughout the day due to high rate self-destructive behavior (for example, Bucher and Lovaas, 1968; Hamilton, Stephens, and Allen, 1967; Tate and Baroff, 1966). When physically possible, subjects engage in head banging, window breaking, slapping, scratching, biting, eye gouging, and the like. Basic laboratory research (for example, Holz and Azrin, 1961; Muenzinger, 1934) provides a possible explanation for the development of this rather paradoxical masochistic behavior. The aversive stimulation of self-injurious responses becomes discriminative for subsequent presentation of positive reinforcement and, theoretically, acquires secondary reinforcement properties. It is difficult in analyzing such behavior in the retarded, however, to identify any subsequent reinforcement conditions and to control the contingencies so as to reduce the discriminative and reinforcing properties of such self-destructive behaviors.

Response contingent application of aversive stimuli differing from those which are directly related to the self-destructive behavior has been used successfully to disrupt and eliminate such habits. Bucher and Lovaas (1968) and Tate and Baroff (1966) using electric shock, and Hamilton, Stephens, and Allen (1967), using a physical restraint-time-out procedure, reported dramatic treatment results. Apparently the punishing stimuli can be effective in these cases due to their pure aversive properties, that is, these stimuli have not acquired positive reinforcing function.

Is punishment effective with the unsocialized profoundly retarded? For many severely and profoundly retarded with minimal social language or social conscience, such behaviors as chronic masturbation, rectal digging, feces smearing and eating, chronic self-stimulation, and reingestion of vomitus are correct-incorrect or acceptable-unacceptable only in terms of the immediate stimulus consequences. No social amenities, superego, internal controls, or the like can be counted on to provide controlling cues of conditioned aversive consequences for such unacceptable behavior. In addition, in many instances it is difficult to identify reinforcers which are powerful enough to compete successfully with those that apparently maintain these behaviors.

In such instances, response contingent aversive stimuli in combination with systematic positive reinforcement would appear to facilitate the development of alternative behaviors which would replace these highly unacceptable responses. Punishment would be used to "define" the incorrect response and to render more likely the occurrence of correct ones (for example, Blackwood, 1962; Edwards and Lilly, 1966; Hamilton and Standahl, 1969).

With what types of behavior is punishment most effective? As noted in the review of studies, punishment operations have been effectively used

with a wide class of behaviors, ranging from specific habit disorders to chronic high rate stereotyped responses. While no research program has reported systematic investigation of this question, Hamilton et al. (1967) have provided some observations concerning the types of behavior which responded most favorably to punishment procedures. These observations provide a suggestive basis for further research. In work with a number of retarded subjects presenting a variety of problem behaviors, these writers reported punishment to be very effective in rapid and total elimination of single specific behavior which occurred with little variation in frequency or type and which seldom involved direct interaction with others (for example, clothes tearing, head-banging). Single specific behaviors which occurred with variable frequency and/or intensity and which typically involved interaction with others (such as physical abuse of others) required longer treatment periods and seldom were completely eliminated. General misbehavior consisting of a wide variety of inappropriate behaviors was reported to show least dramatic improvement, although marked improvement was obtained even in complicated cases of this kind. These observations were generally supported by the punishment studies reviewed.

What punishment operations produce the most rapid and long-lasting results? Data from laboratory and clinical studies suggest that punishment will be most effective as a treatment procedure if the following conditions are met:

1. Behavior should be punished initially on every occurrence.

2. Punishment should be delivered immediately following the behavior and in close space proximity to its occurrence. Timing is an important variable with the more severely retarded. The timing of punishment to coincide with response onset represents the most effective procedure.

3. In order to gain the greatest suppression effect, punishing stimuli should be presented at maximum intensity initially and not increased gradually. Additionally, once an influential aversive stimulus has been identified, the punishment procedure should not be terminated until complete and prolonged suppression is attained.

4. Punishment of any one behavior should not be carried out over an extended period of time in order to avoid recovery or adaptation effects. New intense aversive stimuli are more effective than previously used intense stimuli.

5. Delivery of punishment should be separate from delivery of reinforcement in order to avoid punishment becoming a discriminative cue for positive reinforcement.

6. Alternative response possibilities should be available that would provide the same or greater reinforcement than produced by the punished response. The response-suppression period should be used to reinforce in-

compatible new responses which will provide suitable reinforcement. As Baer (1970) has noted, "punishment is most effective as a behavior removing technique. . . . Punishment is not an efficient technique of behavior building" [p. 248]. Therefore, punishment should be combined with extensive positive reinforcement of other behaviors.

7. If punishment operations involving presentation of physical stimuli are not possible or feasible, a procedure of time-out from positive reinforcement or removal of reinforcers available to the subject may be effective.

8. For maximum effectiveness of time-out, those stimulus conditions (that is, events, objects, persons) that are most meaningful to the subject should be selected for withdrawal.

9. In a program of elimination of several problem areas, work should be done only with one at a time. In addition, punishment appears to be most effective with single specific behaviors that occur with little variation in frequency or type and that seldom involve direct interaction with other persons. Behaviors that occur with variable frequency and that typically involve interaction with other persons usually require longer treatment periods. More complex behavior patterns show the least dramatic improvement but may show sufficient change in frequency or intensity to render these more responsive to other techniques of behavior modification.

How can punishment be justified in view of ethical and humanitarian issues? As implied, the unsystematic use of aversive stimuli as a punitive measure is deplorable. Such use should not be tolerated as it violates basic concepts of human dignity as well as principles of behavior change. Furthermore, such use is likely to produce only negative consequences. Studies that have been reviewed, however, provide support for a position that aversive consequences used in a *systematic* manner can be effective in treatment of a variety of undesirable behavior patterns of the severely and profoundly retarded. Although it is a technique of sharply limited applicability, it is suggested that, when other techniques of behavior change or control are either not effective or hold promise of being highly inefficient in terms of time or personnel costs, it would be most humane to use those procedures that produce desirable results. The alternative of categorically rejecting procedures involving aversive consequences regardless of their potential value would be, it would appear, both unethical and inhumane.

Watson (1967) provided some most pointed comments concerning this issue:

> If such aversive consequences would contribute to delivering the severely or profoundly retarded child from his present subhuman state and help to make his behavior more "normal," this is a direct contribution toward his becoming a "more complete and happier person." Using the same kind of rationale,

doctors give children painful shots with hypodermic needles, make painful physical examinations, cut people open and remove part of their internal organs, and give them painful electric shock "treatments" [p. 15].

Finally, it appears from an ethical viewpoint that every behavior treatment procedure which holds promise of facilitating the personal development of the severely and profoundly retarded must be objectively evaluated and utilized when deemed appropriate. Biased value judgments should be replaced, or at minimum, tempered by professional responsibility. Conversely, it is recognized, of course, that no treatment procedure, including those involving punishment operations, should be categorically applied to any problem or subject population. Decision to follow any treatment regimen should be a deliberate, well-formulated, clinical one arrived at only after careful considerations of questions of effectiveness, efficiency and possible side effects.

Conclusions. As Solomon suggested in 1964, studies of the effects of punishment have been hampered unnecessarily by certain unscientific legends concerning this stimulus condition. Although most of the studies reviewed could be criticized from a rigorous functional analysis position, the deficiencies in methodological sophistication are somewhat offset by the consistency and nature of results provided which call into question some of the more stultifying of the legends. As a general conclusion, the studies reviewed lend some support to the feasibility of application of a variety of punishment procedures in work with the severely and profoundly functioning person and, as Risley (1968) has suggested, "do serve to limit the generality of extrapolations from past research which contraindicates the use of punishment" [p. 34]. The results call for an empirical approach to the question of the efficacy of punishment and rejection of a categorical position that would not facilitate continued investigation of the behavior effects of these procedures.

It is quite apparent that considerable research must be completed prior to the general acceptance of punishment as a treatment approach. Examples of specific research questions which evolve out of the studies reviewed include: (a) Are the behavior suppression effects of punishment specific to the behavior punished as well as to the situational cues present during punishment? Birnbrauer (1968), Bucher and Lovaas (1968), Hamilton and Standahl (1969), and Risley (1968) all commented on the highly specific suppressive effects of punishment. Risley reported that suppressive effects did not even generalize to behavior that was topographically quite similar to the punished behavior. How reliable are these observations? (b) What are the specific side effects of punishment? Writers

who commented on this question expressed surprise that there were significant positive side effects. How general are these effects? (c) Is the "functional incompatibility" hypothesis of Risley (1968) tenable? If so, with what classes of stereotyped behaviors? Could such a concept lend some assistance in decision making concerning the appropriateness of punishment in specific cases?

These are merely representative of the extensive work with a wide range of problems, types, and intensities of punishment stimuli, and subject characteristics which must be completed prior to presenting a definitive statement of the effects of punishment. Until further data are available, use of punishment techniques in clinical practice should be preceded by a careful consideration of alternative procedures. In those instances in which punishment is the treatment of choice, highly controlled procedures of delivery of punishment, and measurement of effects as dictated by a functional analysis of behavior approach, should add considerably to its clinical value.

Development of Competing Behaviors

In view of the difficulty involved in the effective use of an extinction procedure and considering the inapplicability of various punishment procedures for some problems of behavior development and performance, it is frequently desirable to follow a strategy of strengthening behavior patterns which compete with the inappropriate behaviors. Hollis (1967), in illustration, ignored temper tantrum behavior and delivered food reinforcers only following appropriate behavior. Similarly, Gorton and Hollis (1965), in teaching a range of self-care and socialization skills, ignored inappropriate behavior and reinforced only those that were consistent with the behavior goals set for each client. After the appropriate behaviors, gained sufficient strength through resulting in positive reinforcers, these behaviors successfully competed with the undesired performances.

The strategy of strengthening response patterns that compete successfully with undesired behaviors is especially appropriate in dealing with chronic stereotyped and self-manipulatory behavior. The program used in work with one severely retarded adult will be described to illustrate this procedure. As noted earlier, a significant number of institutionalized, severely and profoundly retarded adults engage in chronic excessive stereotyped and self-manipulatory behavior. In addition, many respond little in a meaningful manner to their social and physical environment. In more severe cases, the stereotyped activities fill most of the person's time and are incompatible with behaviors which would lead to more meaningful and effective interactions with the environment. The stereotyped be-

haviors include such categories as body rocking, head rolling, head banging, hand-before-eyes, slapping, poking, rubbing, scratching or biting self, sucking and mouthing objects, nonsocial vocalizations, arm flapping, leg swinging, restless pacing, whirling, twirling, smelling objects, and placing the hands over ears. These stereotyped and self-manipulatory behaviors not only decrease the opportunities for learning new appropriate behaviors, but also render control of behavior by appropriate environmental sources (for example, ward staff) more difficult. Even when the person does respond to the social or physical environment, attention frequently is maintained only for momentary periods of time. The result of this isolated, self-directed behavior is that the person receives little positive feedback from his environment. The possibility is greatly reduced that the retarded would do something that would result in a positive response from the environment. This paucity of positive feedback due to the person's limited behavioral repertoire further supports the repetitive, nonsocial behavior. In summary, the person engages in little meaningful interaction with the environment, is under little specific environmental control, maintains an appropriate attention set only for limited periods of time, and does little that produces desirable environmental consequences.

Observation of a group of adolescents and young adults who are "chronic stereotypers" suggests that some of them engage in rather complex motor behaviors and exhibit a level of motor dexterity and sensory acuity which would render them likely candidates for participation in simple but meaningful work activities. The task for the therapeutic environment becomes one of shaping response patterns which could compete with the stereotyped behaviors and further one of developing some consistent environmental control, both discriminative and reinforcing, over this more desirable competing behavior.

Research seems to support the theory that stereotyped behaviors are self-stimulatory in nature and may reflect inadequate response repertoires which do not offer more adaptive alternatives of obtaining reinforcement. It should be noted that the institutionalized severely and profoundly mentally retarded often spend a great deal of time in situations where opportunities for more meaningful interaction with their environment are quite limited or even absent. The person spends many hours in day rooms with other similarly retarded individuals. Toys and other objects are often limited or nonexistent and few severely retarded individuals reach a level where spontaneous, cooperative social interaction is possible. The ward personnel are kept busy with the physical care of these individuals (for example, dressing, toileting, and the like) and have little time to provide active social stimulation. There is certainly almost nothing for the individuals to do during many of their waking hours and there is little general

environmental enrichment available to them. It is not surprising, under these circumstances and considering the limited behavioral repertoires present, that many engage in chronic self-stimulatory activities.

There is evidence pointing to the fact that stereotyped behavior can be at least somewhat influenced by environmental conditions and specifically by those conditions that offer alternative behaviors; and there is evidence supporting the inverse relationship between environmental manipulation and self-stimulatory behavior. This evidence leads to the conclusion that it may be possible to significantly lower the frequency of stereotyped behaviors in severely and profoundly retarded individuals by getting such persons involved in meaningful competing tasks or activities. It is possible that if the retarded could be stimulated to engage in behaviors that provide him with reinforcing conditions available in the external environment, his self-stimulation behavior would decrease in frequency or magnitude.

The purpose of the program to be described was to gain some impressions concerning the possibility of developing rehabilitation techniques for promoting the development of simple work behaviors in the "chronic stereotyper" which would serve to compete successfully with this stereotyped behavior. Behavior shaping procedures based on principles of operant learning were used in teaching the work behaviors. More specifically, attempts were made to bring some simple work behaviors under specific and reliable environmental control, to teach the person to continue task behaviors over extended periods of time, to teach a simple work motivation system, that is, to render task participation a reinforcing activity and to teach a relationship between appropriate behavior and a desirable consequence, and to reduce the frequency of stereotyped behaviors in both the work as well as the nonwork situation.

In devising a program to meet these objectives, it was evident that tasks appropriate to the abilities of the severely and profoundly retarded must be provided and secondly some effective procedure must be found to involve the unresponsive, detached person in these tasks. As suggested, severely and profoundly retarded individuals with chronic stereotyped behaviors are relatively unresponsive to their environment and difficulty is often encountered in getting them involved in any purposeful activity. A procedure of behavior shaping using considerable prompts and a rich reinforcement schedule was selected to teach a simple motor task which would compete with certain classes of stereotyped behavior exhibited by the client.

The retarded client was a thirty year old ambulatory institutionalized retarded male who demonstrated no expressive and extremely limited receptive language at the beginning of the program. He has been labeled as mentally retarded due to uncertain causes. He was institutionalized at the age of seventeen because he was unmanageable at home. A recent psy-

chological evaluation describes him as being slightly retarded in motor development, severely retarded in social-personal development, and profoundly retarded in language and in intellectual functioning. During previous psychometric evaluation, he earned a mental age of 25 months on the Leiter International Performance Scale, but it was noted that some 60–70 demonstrations of the tasks were necessary before the client would respond to the urging of the examiner. The client had been reported to exhibit a very high level of complex stereotyped compulsive and ritualistic behaviors. Stereotyped behaviors were noted some thirteen years earlier at admission to the institution and have been present throughout this time.

Prior to the initiation of the behavior shaping program, levels of stereotyped behaviors which the client exhibited were obtained. He usually engaged in stereotyped behavior constantly except when moving from one spot to another. The behavior usually consisted of violent body rocking while simultaneously flapping his arms, manipulating his hands in front of his eyes or grimacing. The most frequently occurring stereotype behaviors were those of body rocking, hand-before-eye, rubbing self, and arm flapping. He also engaged in considerable facial grimacing. Most of the behaviors involved active use of the arms and hands in rather gross types of movements. Work tasks were used initially which utilized the arms and hands in gross movement.

A simple visual-motor task was used in the initial phase of the program. In this phase an attempt was made to gain some specific external stimulus control over some specific operant behavior which would compete directly with some of the classes of stereotype behaviors present in the client. The client, while standing and facing the task, was first taught to pick up a rubber ball and drop it through a hole located at eye level. (See Fig. 13.1) A variety of candies, cereals, cookies, and nuts were used as reinforcers. These were provided initially on a continuous reinforcement schedule. After this behavior was occurring with high regularity whenever the ball was presented, the client was taught a simple discrimination. A light-on over the drop chute was a signal for the response to occur, and a light-off a signal for no response of ball dropping.

After obtaining stimulus control over this response, an additional discriminative stimulus was presented. The light to the left of the ball cup when turned on was a discriminative stimulus for the client to place his hand on top of the ball while the ball remained in the cup—a "get ready" response. Following a short time delay, the cue for placing the ball through the chute was presented. An appropriate operant was reinforced. After these operants were brought under reliable stimulus control, the task was changed to a two-hole and then to a three-hole discrimination problem.

The next step in the program consisted of changing the reinforcement

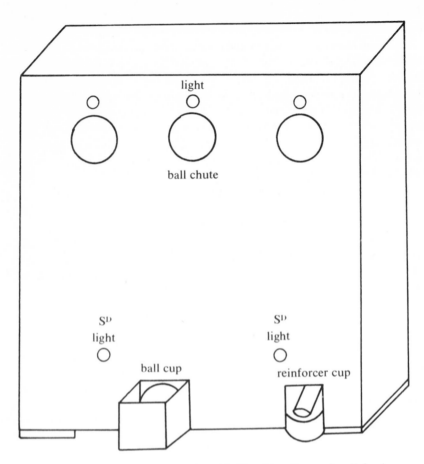

Figure 13.1. Task Apparatus Used in Teaching Competing Behavior

schedule and of increasing the length of the work sessions. The schedule was gradually shifted through an increasingly large fixed ratio and later into a VR20 schedule. Time spent in sessions was increased from an initial period of 5 to 10 minutes to 45 to 55 minutes. As the reinforcement schedule was changed from a continuous reinforcement through a fixed ratio and to a variable ratio one, it was necessary to teach an additional discrimination so that the client would not spend excessive time looking at the reward cup in anticipation of reinforcer presentation. A red light-on over the food cup and an accompanying buzz immediately preceded and overlapped reward presentation and soon came to control the food cup-looking response.

This phase of the program lasted for 21 daily sessions extending over a 31 day period. The following results were obtained and gave direction to the next phase of the program:

1. Client was responding reliably and with high rate to the simple work task. Some specific behaviors were reliably emitted upon presentation of specific environmental cues. Whenever these cues were presented, stereotyped behavior ceased and did not reappear until the S^Ds were absent. It is interesting to note that the "time-on" or "get-ready" light interrupted the stereotype behavior and emitted highly reliable attending responses. The program had been successful in bringing some simple behaviors under specific stimulus control. These behaviors successfully competed with the stereotype behavior.

2. Client was able to persist at this task with high rate performance over periods up to 55 minutes. This was quite contrary to the momentary attention noted in client prior to conditioning.

3. Client acquired a primitive achievement or response motivation system. The task activity apparently acquired positive reinforcing properties. The supposition that the task activity became a reinforcing one was supported by the observation that as the client approached the work area, he frequently would run to the work table and would stand waiting for the "time-on" light to be presented. During this time stereotype behavior was at a minimum. Upon "time-on" presentation, he would immediately begin the task at a rapid pace. In addition, upon presentation of the S^D for reward delivery, there was no delay in retrieving and consuming the reinforcer nor was there a time delay between reward presentation and continuation of the task. A final observation supported the supposition of the development of a relationship between appropriate task behavior and reinforcement. After change of the reinforcement schedule from a continuous to an intermittent one, the client would look toward the reward cup and display obvious agitation at the absence of the reward. Stereotype behavior increased greatly at these instances. He did, however, readily adapt to the changed schedule and after a few days of experience with the new schedule, his "cup-looking" behavior soon came under the control of the S^D for reward presentation.

Following this initial success in teaching behaviors that interrupted the chronic stereotype movements during the work sessions, the client was taught, by means of similar behavior shaping techniques, a series of other tasks that required an increasing amount of attention, persistence, and more complex manipulative eye-hand coordination behavior. Some tasks required up to four different steps for completion. These included sorting and bagging golf tees and marbles. This training phase culminated in teaching the client a task he now engages in while attending a sheltered

workshop with a group of other severely and profoundly retarded adults. During this phase, the client was taught a token reinforcement system and is presently able to work for three or four days for 60 to 80 minute sessions before exchanging tokens for back-up reinforcers.

Level of stereotype behavior in the living unit reduced noticeably over the five months of the program. Observation of the client in the work environment revealed no stereotype behavior during task participation. Other significant changes observed in the work setting and in the living unit include increased attention to the presence and behavior of his peers and increased social interaction with staff.

It is evident that during the experience reported there have been some dramatic changes in the behavior of the client described. He became under sufficient environmental control to maintain appropriate work behavior in a group setting. During daily work activity, stereotyped behavior seldom is observed. He is noticeably more sociable and responsive to meaningful variations in the environment. It is felt that with further intensive individual training, even more appropriate work, social and other cognitive behaviors will develop.

Development and Strengthening of Behavior

As documented earlier, numerous studies have demonstrated that the systematic use of reinforcement procedures can facilitate the development of a variety of skills of eating, dressing, toileting, grooming, socialization, locomotion, language, and work. Examples of procedures used in some of these areas will be presented to illustrate the application of the behavior shaping and chaining concepts presented in previous chapters.

Eating. Bensberg, Colwell, and Cassell (1965), Gorton and Hollis (1965), Spradlin (1964), Whitney and Barnard (1966), and Zeiler and Jervey (1968) provide excellent examples of programs designed to teach the severely and profoundly retarded self-feeding skills. Self-feeding is relatively simple to teach because such behaviors are reinforced immediately by the food. Also, once established, these skills are maintained through continuous reinforcement in the natural environment. In teaching self-feeding, the trainer provides necessary prompts of physical guidance initially. The spoon is placed in the retarded person's hand, and assistance is provided in holding and filling it. The trainer then assists in moving the spoon toward the mouth. The trainer removes his prompt before reaching the mouth and requires the retardate to complete the movement. Reinforcement for this last segment of the response chain is provided by the food. The trainer gradually reduces the assistance that is provided until the person is able to complete the entire performance himself. The same

procedure of reinforcement of successive approximations of the final performance is used in teaching cup-holding, drinking, and other skills related to self-care in the feeding area.

Dressing. Bensberg (1965), Bensberg et al. (1965) and Minge and Ball (1967) describe step-by-step programs for teaching dressing and related self-care skills to the profoundly retarded. The program devised by Minge and Ball was designed to teach skills of attention, coming to the technician, sitting down, remaining seated, standing up, removing shirt or dress, removing pants, removing socks, pulling on shirt or dress, pulling on pants, and putting on socks. In teaching each skill, the retarded person was provided a simple verbal direction and a gesture or physical guidance to insure the correct response. Food reinforcement and praise promptly followed. Prompts were removed as self-independence was gained. More complex responses were required prior to reinforcement until the skill was acquired. The following is an example of the steps and sequence followed in teaching the person to remove her pants:

1. Use elastic-banded cotton pants. Child should be seated, with pants nearly off; over one foot only. She removes them, with technician:
   a. placing patient's hands on pants and helping pull them off, plus spoken direction.
   b. pointing to pants, plus spoken direction.
   c. giving spoken direction only.
2. Patient is seated with pants at both knees. She removes them, with technician:
   a. pointing at pants, plus spoken direction.
   b. giving spoken direction only.
3. Patient either seated or standing, pants all the way up. She takes them off when the technician:
   a. points at the pants, plus spoken direction.
   b. gives spoken direction only. [p. 865].

In order to increase the reinforcement value of the food used, breakfast and lunch were provided in training sessions. Each correct response was reinforced by a spoonful of the meal. For some clients who were relatively nonattentive to the training program, a period of food deprivation was initiated in order to increase the discriminative and reinforcing properties of the food reinforcer. Such a procedure resulted in better progress for these clients. This and similar programs illustrate the position that has been presented throughout this book that the behavioral limitations of the retarded frequently reside, not in the individual, but within an inadequate learning environment. As this environment is modified to accommodate the

requirements of the severely and profoundly retarded, behavior development does occur.

Toileting. One of the more difficult self-care skills to teach the severely and profoundly retarded is toileting. Some most creative and sophisticated applications of learning concepts, however, have been illustrated by programs designed to teach toilet training skills. Beginning with the critical article of Ellis (1963), reports by Baumeister and Klosowski (1965), Dayan (1964), Giles and Wolf (1966), Hundziak, Maurer, and Watson (1965), and Watson (1968) have provided rich information to guide the technician in a toilet-training program. The Baumeister and Klosowski report of their experience with the profoundly retarded emphasized the need for intensive, systematic, and prolonged programming. The general procedure followed in all reports was that of immediate positive reinforcement of elimination on the toilet. Reinforcers usually consisted of food items, but also included a range of other events that were found in individual analysis to be effective. Giles and Wolf and Hundziak, Maurer and Watson reported successful transfer of the newly acquired skills from a training ward to the home ward. The Watson (1968) report describes an automated behavior shaping device for use in toilet training. Recognizing that a response to be acquired must be reinforced with minimal delay, and further recognizing that elimination responses may easily go undetected and thus unreinforced by the trainer, Watson developed a "toilet trainer" which automatically detects the initiation of an elimination response and provides instant reinforcement:

> It consists of an aluminum framework which covers the conventional toilet bowl. It is equipped with a seat, a foot rest, arm rests, and a photoelectric cell trigger. The interior of the toilet bowl is bathed with light beams focused on photoelectric cells. Whenever a beam is broken a pulse is transmitted to a reinforcement dispenser, and a reinforcement is delivered. Either defecation or urination will trigger the reinforcement switch. In order to prevent the child from activating the device with a hand or foot, three safety switches must be closed before it will operate [p. 22].

Work Skills. Although the last chapter describes a program designed to develop work behaviors in the retarded adult, including the severely and profoundly involved, the experience of Crosson (1969) is given brief attention as it provides illustration of task analysis as a basis for shaping work behaviors. Crosson challenged the philosophy that is held by many sheltered workshops that work should be found that the severely retarded can do. He provides an alternative argument that the severely retarded can be taught to perform work that is available and thus can be viewed as a productive worker. The initial step in programming a task environment re-

quires a specification of the behavior units which make up the task response sequence. Generally, the more severely retarded the trainee, the more discrete the behavior specifications should be. After analyzing the task into behavior components, the cues which can be associated with each operant must be identified. As discussed in an earlier chapter on response chaining, these cues become both discriminative for subsequent behaviors and reinforcing for preceding operants. At times, the stimuli that are integral parts of the task are not prominent enough and must be intensified so as to develop control over the response.

In teaching a task, it frequently is found that some parts of the response sequence are more difficult than others. As these require more intensive training, these should be taught in pretraining sessions. In beginning the training, the trainer demonstrates the desired behavior and guides the trainee through the operant or sequence pattern. These segments should be reinforced and repeated several times prior to adding new components. Crosson recommends a reinforcement procedure of dropping the reinforcer in a clear plastic cup visible to the trainee. This procedure is similar to that described by Stamm (1970) as a correlated counter. Such a procedure provides frequent reinforcement for ongoing behavior and the tangible nature of the event is sufficient to bridge the time delay between behavior and eventual primary reinforcement of food consumption. Continuous reinforcement is provided until the terminal behaviors are controlled by appropriate discriminative cues. Prompts are gradually faded until the task behaviors come under the control of task stimuli. As the specific operants are acquired, the tangible reinforcement is removed and the operant becomes a natural part of a longer chain of responses. And finally, "when the trainee's performance stabilizes, as evidenced by increasing consistency in rate of emission of the correct sequence of responses, reinforcement is gradually phased to higher order schedules, eventually matching the 'natural' incentive program of the work environment" [p. 816].

Crosson reports the use of this training procedure in work with a group of severely retarded males in the age range of sixteen to thirty-four years. He analyzed a drilling machine operation into approximately 100 operants. Within this sample, he found that little more than 50 percent of the operants were present in the repertoires of the subjects, and further that some 10 percent of the operants required intensive shaping and/or discrimination training. He was able to teach the required task performance in a relatively short period of time. This study emphasizes that the behavioral deficiencies are not of an all-or-none fashion. Upon initial evaluation, the severely retarded clients could not perform the task satisfactorily. However, they did have more than half the required behaviors and were able to meet the necessary performance criterion with appropriate train-

ing. The task limitations resided in a poorly designed learning history and not within the "severe mental retardation."

Imitation Behavior. As a final example of behavior development through positive reinforcement in the severely and profoundly retarded, the reports of Baer, Peterson, and Sherman (1967) and Bry (1969) on development of imitation behavior will be described. As noted in a previous chapter, various behavior acquisition, extinction, inhibition, and facilitation effects may result from observation of the behavior of others. The observer tends to imitate that which he observes, especially if the model has high reinforcement value to the observer. This imitation tendency apparently contributes considerably to the acquisition and performance of behavior for most individuals. However, as suggested in the initial section of this chapter, it is not too unusual to observe that the severely and profoundly retarded show little or no skills in imitating the behavior of a model. In the absence of such imitation skills, it becomes even more difficult to strengthen new behaviors. A whole range of speech, motor, and social skills become almost impossible unless the person can be taught a general skill of imitation.

Baer et al. (1967) and Bry (1969) demonstrated that a generalized skill of imitation can be developed as a result of specific training procedures. Baer et al. used a basic procedure of teaching a series of discriminated operants. A discriminative stimulus ("Do this" presented by the trainer and followed by his demonstration of some behavior), a correct response (imitation of demonstrated behavior), and reinforcement after the correct response (presentation of food) define the elements of the procedure. The initial training was accomplished by shaping, prompting, and fading. After demonstation of the behavior, the retarded person was assisted physically in making the response. The physical guidance prompt was faded as the person began to imitate the behavior following demonstration. Following the development of a number of imitated responses, the training procedure included some demonstrated behaviors which were never reinforced. Later, a procedure of chaining together old and new imitations was begun. After extensive motor performances were acquired, verbal imitation behaviors were programmed. Finally, new trainers were introduced to insure that the person's imitative repertoire would generalize to persons other than the original trainer. These procedures produced highly developed imitation skills in these severely retarded subjects. They not only imitated demonstrations which were reinforced but additionally imitated other behaviors of the model which were never reinforced directly. Bry (1969), on the other hand, reported in her work with a small group of profoundly retarded persons that imitation did not take place unless the imitated behavior was associated with a positive reinforcer. It was reported, however,

that once the retardates acquired skills in imitating simple behaviors such as putting a spoon in a basket or tapping the table, they were able to imitate more complex self-grooming skills.

These studies would suggest that more attention should be provided to teaching basic skills of imitation when these skills are not present. Such generalized imitation skills greatly increase the performance possibilities of the more severely retarded.

Effective Program Development

It is evident from the preceding review that the severely and profoundly retarded can acquire a wide range of skills, some of which are quite complex. Behavior development is frequently slow and difficult with the older and more severely retarded. In view of both the limitations presented in the initial section, and of more general cognitive deficits, it is essential that programs of behavior development and modification be precisely developed. Programs devised to influence the behavior of the severely and profoundly retarded, whether concerned with teaching a basic self-care skill, a perceptual-motor skill or a more complex work skill, must take advantage of every available behavior principle if success is to be realized. The following guidelines represent some of the more important factors which should be considered.

1. A program should include a precise specification of the terminal behavior goals and a detailed delineation of the basic operant subunits which comprise this behavior. Rather simple behavior chains may be exceedingly complex for the profoundly retarded. The identification of simple operant units which can be taught separately and later integrated into a more complex sequential chain is desired.

2. The behavioral analysis preceding program development should include a precise description of the skills which are presently in the person's repertoire. The Crosson (1969) study illustrates the value of this procedure. Although the severely retarded adults could not perform the criterion work task they required intensive training in only 10 percent of the basic operant units. The intensive pretraining of these added greatly to the efficiency of the training program.

3. The program procedures should insure that the to-be-learned response, or some acceptable approximation of it does occur. The liberal use of "crutch cues" to insure the desired response should be programmed. If the desired response does not occur with high frequency from the beginning of the program, the behavior unit expected is too complex. The concern should be one of keeping inappropriate responses to a minimum. It is easier to remove "crutch cues" than it is to remove wrong responses. If an

inappropriate response is made, there should be an immediate correction if possible and a subsequent confirmation (reinforcement) of the corrected response.

4. Identification of effective reinforcers prior to initiation of the training program is essential. Although tokens may become powerful generalized reinforcers for the more severely retarded, the program must have available the most effective tangible reinforcers. The learning possibilites are highly limited for the severely and profoundly retarded. Behavior development and related appropriate environmental control can be maximized by maximizing the training program. As emphasized throughout the book, the reinforcing components of a program are of major importance.

Procedures of deprivation, reinforcer sampling, reinforcer exposure, use of a correlated counter, the availability of a range of reinforcing events, and the like should be utilized. Food is an effective reinforcer for most severely and profoundly retarded. Additionally, as noted by Spradlin and Girardeau (1966) and Nawas and Braun (1970), participation in various activities, visual (for example, movies), auditory (for example, music), and tactual (for example, vibration) stimuli, as well as socially related stimuli may serve as effective consequences.

5. It should be remembered that behavior is lost if it is not reinforced. The severely and profoundly retarded require more frequent reinforcement for behavior maintenance than the less severely involved require.

6. The reinforcement delivery system must be arranged to insure immediate reinforcement. This is of great importance to the severely and profoundly retarded due to minimal cognitive skills and restricted secondary reinforcement components of the learning environment. There must be little time delay between behavior to-be-strengthened and the reinforcer, especially in the early stages of response development.

7. Zeaman and House (1963) have provided sufficient data that the more severely retarded have unusual difficulty in attending to the relevant cues in a learning task. It becomes necessary, therefore, that measures be taken to insure that the person does focus on relevant discriminative cues. This may be done by creating more distinctive cues or by using systematic prompts to assist the learner to attend to the relevant aspects of the environment.

8. Behavior that is acquired in a special training environment typically will not generalize to a different environmental setting. If the discriminative and reinforcing aspects are modified too abruptly or drastically, newly acquired behaviors will show rapid deterioration. Considerable overlearning and gradual change in the control components of the environment would add to the stability of newly-acquired behavior and add to its transfer from one setting to another.

Applied Behavioral Technology in a Vocational Rehabilitation Setting

Introduction

The projects described in this chapter represent components of an ongoing research program of the Jewish Vocational Service of Milwaukee (J.V.S.) in which concepts of learning and motivation are being applied in the design and testing of sheltered workshop systems for retarded and emotionally disturbed adults. The primary objective of the methods being developed is to establish work environments which maximize the performance of clients in producing consignment goods which meet the production requirements of sheltered work.

THEORETICAL RATIONALE

Some rehabilitation personnel believe that the more severely retarded and emotionally handicapped adults have potential for useful, productive activity. The development of such potential, however, depends upon the availability of effective educational, rehabilitative, and training methods

C. G. Screven, University of Wisconsin—Milwaukee; Joseph A. Straka and Richard LaFond, Jewish Vocational Service of Milwaukee. This project has been supported by the Jewish Vocational Service of Milwaukee, the Rehabilitation Services Administration of the Department of Health, Education, and Welfare, and the Wisconsin Division of Mental Hygiene.

appropriate to the perceptual, conceptual, and behavioral deficits of such a population. Recent developments in the experimental analysis of behavior and in educational technology (for example, Glaser and Reynolds, 1965; Skinner, 1969) provide a conceptual and methodological basis for the realization of the educational and productive work potentials of such persons.

This chapter describes specific examples of the application of behavioral technology. Our approach may be characterized as descriptive, with little commitment to preexisting formal theories other than the framework provided by various learning and related concepts. Procedures derive from the operant methodology associated with Skinner and his associates. Operant methodology emphasizes the *pliability* of behavior, that is, the idea that most definable behaviors can be modified by the manipulation of specific environmental consequences of behavior such as "reinforcers" and "punishers" and by the schedules which correlate these consequences with behavior (Skinner, 1969). Work and other learning behaviors are made up of many "bits" of behavior which are modifiable by altering their immediate consequences.

The rate or frequency of any definable behavior, including the behavior of the more severely retarded in workshop and concept learning stiuations, reflects the circumstances of previous learning as well as existing contingencies in the immediate environment which maintain behavior by continuing to reinforce it. The frequencies of any definable behavior may be brought under control, or changed in favor of more desirable behaviors, by imposing *new* contingencies between successive approximations of the desired behaviors and their immediate consequences.

In actual practice, a particular positive or aversive event is selected and tested, and is eventually accepted or rejected for use with a particular workshop client on the basis of whether or not the desired control over the client's behavior is obtained through its use. Reinforcers are chosen from those objects and activities in the immediate environment which the client himself is observed to select or seek, such as talking with a supervisor, listening to loud music, or taking walks, and the like (see Premack, 1959, 1965). Once an effective reinforcer is determined for a particular client, access to the reinforcer is made contingent on performance of the work (or training) task—or approximations of them.

In recent years, the feasibility of such an approach for the modification and control of problem behaviors in various institutional and applied settings has been demonstrated. Studies reported in previous chapters have indicated clearly that retarded persons are subject to the same laws as others and are indeed influenced by the reinforcing consequences of their actions.

GENERAL METHODOLOGY

A more complete technology of rehabilitation requires the development of additional procedures and devices which can work in practice in the management and rehabilitation of the mentally and emotionally handicapped. Specific answers to the following types of specific questions are required for the development of this technology:

a. What kinds of positive reinforcers, in addition to, or other than money, can be used with most retardates in work settings and administered on precise schedules without losing their effectiveness?

b. If a token economy is to be established, what options work best, given the realities of rehabilitation workshops, and how are they to be established and maintained?

c. What are the most efficient means of controlling or suppressing undesirable behaviors (for example time-outs, loss of tokens, avoidance schedules, payment for privilege of engaging in the undesirable behavior) in sheltered work?

d. Many mentally handicapped persons may have good potential for carrying out productive work, but only within a carefully defined prosthetic environment (see Lindsley, 1964) where greater stimulus support, more frequent reinforcement, and more careful control of contingencies are provided. If so, what are the features of such a prosthetic work environment, and can such an environment be provided within practical cost limitations?

e. Are there devices and supportive discriminative stimuli that can automate some of the features necessary to maintain attention span and the ability for continuous work? Such automation would reduce unpredictable and unprecise management of supervisors, and probably reduce costs.

f. How can the facts concerning the different performance properties of different schedules of reinforcement (Ferster and Skinner, 1957) be adapted to better achieve the objectives of sheltered and rehabilitative work settings?

g. What are some practical ways for training supervisory personnel to administer the controls and contingencies required in a sheltered work environment?

Efforts of the Milwaukee research program have been directed at providing tentative answers to these and related questions.

Until recently, most of these efforts have been concentrated in an adult day-care facility for severely retarded adults at the Jewish Vocational Service of Milwaukee known as the Adult Basic Learning Center (ABLC). Within this facility, the staff is exploring the kinds of work-environments

in which moderately to severely retarded and emotionally disturbed persons can carry out productive work reliably and effectively, ways of utilizing multimedia programmed learning procedures and teaching machines for teaching the retarded basic vocabulary and conceptual skills, and procedures for modifying specific behavioral characteristics of individual clients. In other projects, operant procedures are being applied to gain the attention and cooperation of several custodial clients in developing some simple conceptual and social abilities.

The client population consists of males and females between the ages of 16 and 40, with tested IQs ranging from not measurable to approximately 70. They are characterized by extremely short attention span, emotional instability, social inadequacy, and an assortment of visual, auditory, speech, and motor handicaps. Most of these clients have a long history of complete work inadequacy and originally were assigned to the ABLC with little expectation that productive work activity was possible.

The ABLC facility consists of three experimental workshops, individual workshop "shaping" rooms, rooms for automated teaching machines, an individual behavior modification area, an operant laboratory room, and various rooms used for providing positive reinforcers (including a store, a music room, a game and social room, and a physical recreation area). One of the workshops is completely automated. Its ten work stations are operated from a control room equipped with one-way mirrors and programming equipment, so that the client does not interact with supervisory personnel. The other two workshops are normally not automated and are used to develop and test alternative procedures for arranging the workshop environment. A supervisor is normally present in these shops to provide work assignments and reinforcers.

Recent funding from the Rehabilitation Services Administration has allowed the extension of experimental workshop projects to a wider range of handicapped clients and sheltered work settings within the Jewish Vocational Service Agency. The task of this extended project is to develop, test, and establish practical workshop systems in actual sheltered workshop settings which include the various practical limitations and characteristics, human and nonhuman, usually associated with rehabilitation agencies. To accomplish this, three levels of operation are involved: *a systems laboratory, pilot workshops,* and *sheltered workshop field tests.* The broad functions of each of these levels may be described as follows:

Systems Laboratory. This small experimental facility accomodates six clients and investigates types of reinforcers, intermittent schedules, stimulus controls and devices and other work arrangements in relation to work efficiency. Concern here is with the controls, reinforcers, devices, and work systems which can be demonstrated to work effectively with particular

types of clients prior to attempts to apply them in particular work settings. The laboratory is expected to provide the framework from which specific work systems for pilot shops can be generated. Each of the six stations has a display panel for various visual and auditory stimuli, coin-token-candy dispenser, scoring and timing devices, a small screen for displaying slides, speaker and headphones, and an S-Box (described later). An adjoining control room contains programming equipment, recorders, counters, running time meters, etc.

Pilot Workshops. Three pilot workshops serve as "miniature" workshops (accomodating six persons), where particular work control systems can be tested and modified under simulated workshop conditions. Pilot workshops may be designed for a specific client population or for certain work tasks, etc. Present pilot workshop projects involve a middle level assembly task with moderately retarded clients, a higher level workshop task, and a system for training and controlling maintenance tasks carried out by clients with community potential.

Sheltered Workshop Field Tests. Pilot work systems which produce superior work performance and generalized work behaviors in a pilot workshop are then introduced into one or more of the 15 sheltered work areas of the Jewish Vocational Service involving clients and work tasks of the same type and functional level as used in earlier testing except that regularly assigned work supervisors and clients are involved. Individual and group records of hourly and daily production, tardiness, social disruptions, self-control, meeting work standards and rules, and the like, are obtained for at least three weeks prior to the test period, as well as during the tests; and modifications are made in the system as necessary. Poor systems are returned to the pilot shop level for further testing.

Through successive testing, modification and retesting at both pilot and sheltered workshop levels, we expect to develop effective and practical work systems which meet the needs and practical conditions of actual sheltered workshop tasks and client abilites.

Motivational Systems

The effective use of a reinforcer to strengthen behavior requires that the reinforcer *immediately follows* the desired behavior. Reinforcement strengthens the behavior occurring *at the time* of reinforcement, not the behavior occurring earlier in the day or week. Even minutes or seconds delay of reinforcement can strengthen the wrong behavior and cancel its desired effect.

But, in actual workshop practice, the dispensing of specific potential reinforcers such as candy, soda pop, access to activities, etc. during actual

320 Methods of Producing Behavior Change

work is disruptive of the work and, in general, unfeasible. Not only are the mechanics of on-the-spot delivery to the client difficult, but dispensing such reinforcers can disrupt the ongoing work activity itself since the client stops work to partake in them.

One solution to this problem has been the use of signals (lights, sounds) which are presented during work and which identify steps toward later reinforcement (for example, lights may accumulate on a matrix as work is completed, with a fully lighted matrix associated with a reinforcement break, tokens, etc.).

Another approach is to utilize intrinsic audio reinforcers such as taped music or voices individually administered during work for brief periods (5-10 seconds.). Such audio reinforcement need not interfere with on-going work.

In our own program, we have found that such transient reinforcers, while effective, must eventually be followed up with other reinforcers of greater importance to the clients, such as take-home items, edibles, social activities, money, and the like. Access to such reinforcers, of course, must be postponed to after-work periods. Since the objects and activities which are most reinforcing to retardates may vary from day to day and even moment to moment, a large variety of reinforcers should be available from which the client may choose.

In the usual day care center for the mentally handicapped, most of the activities of great interest to the clients are readily available to them. Great efforts are made to provide as positive and stimulating an environment as possible through toys, games, dances, singing, walks, stories and sensory motor exercises. In addition, attention from staff is easily available and readily "manipulated" by the clients. While such activities are probably worthwhile and valuable, they are also the main resources for positive reinforcement. These resources are available "free," they are not contingent on his productive activity except on the client's own terms. In such circumstances, it is difficult, if not impossible, to secure or sustain the attention or cooperation of the client in other less attractive activities, such as learning to count, speak, read, dress, eat, listen, groom themselves, or engage in productive work. In order to secure the cooperation of the client in such matters, it is necessary to take advantage of as many of the potential reinforcing activities as possible which are available within the immediate environment. These must be isolated and the client then given access (in limited exposures) to them only for those behaviors related to desired learning or behavioral goals.

In the Milwaukee project, many of these sources of positive reinforcement for the clients have been isolated from the daily work and learning activities of the clients and made available at certain times and places for

tokens earned in relation to performance. Outside of these areas, conversations with the clients, attention by staff or by visitors to irrelevant client solicitations in the hallways, etc., are kept at a minimum. Quarter-size aluminum tokens serve as generalized reinforcers for a wide range of productive activities. These tokens have little value in themselves, but are the only means of gaining acess to the reinforcing areas and to the reinforcing events therein. The tokens, therefore, acquire reinforcing value which can substitute as immediate reinforcers until they can be traded in. Such a token economy is currently a popular procedure in various applied institutional settings.

Clients actually obtain more positive reinforcers than are normally available in such day care or social welfare facilities, except that these are available only on a *contingent* basis; they are not "free" but only for appropriate, productive behaviors. Emphasis is on the positive control of behavior rather than on coersive, aversive control. This means that so far as possible, control of undesirable behavior is obtained through the selective reinforcement of more desirable alternative behaviors and the minimizing of sources of positive reinforcement for the undesirable behaviors.

All except custodial clients within the ABLC facility earn tokens from work and learning activities or from individual experiments being conducted by staff. Available items and activities of potential reinforcing value are isolated in four areas: a *"store,"* a *music-dance* room, a *"social"* room, and a *motor* area. Clients pay one-token to enter any of the areas and one additional token for each subsequent time period (usually 5 or 10-minutes), within the area. At the end of each time period, all room lights turn off (controlled from outside) and clients must pay another token to turn them back on. This light-off system is helpful in establishing a sharp cutoff of the reinforcement intervals which is independent of the teacher who is conducting the room's activities and is readily discriminable by the retarded individuals. If a client is out of tokens, he must leave the room and wait in a "holding room" which is a comparatively neutral environment with a minimum of stimulation, social opportunities, etc. The holding room is not used for punishment, but simply as a "boring" waiting area less desirable than the other areas.

Clients may move from area to area provided they have the tokens required. The reinforcement areas may be briefly described as follows:

The Store. A colorful, gayly decorated room with a glass counter filled with candy and take-home items (rings, play watches, hair ribbons, combs, bracelets, plastic cars, etc.) shelves of rentable mechanical toys, a pinball machine (one token per ball), a pop machine, and a "bank" where tokens can be converted to cash (one penny per token). Costs of items vary; most candy is one token; a picture book is three tokens, a ring or bracelet may

cost five tokens. Clients are not given formal training in prices, but learn token uses and procedures with experience. Most new clients spend all of their tokens for take-home trinkets and games. However, many higher level clients gradually settle down to spending a few tokens for store items and saving most for cash to take home where it apparently serves as an explicit symbol of success, status, etc.

The Music Room. Contains a record player, piano, and sufficient space for dancing if desired. Favorite records are played, group singing around the piano, dancing, clapping, noise making, etc. make up typical activities in an open, indulgent, expressive situation. At the end of each time segment, during the lights-off situation, the phonograph power also turns off, the teacher stops all actions, and the clients generally quiet down. Each client must place a token in a special wall box before the lights will go on again. Any client unable to do so because of lack of tokens is quietly let out of the room by the teacher. (Another staff member in the hall directs clients without tokens to the holding area.)

The Social Room. This room is designed primarily for social activities not available in other areas, for example, the opportunity for the full attention of a favorite staff member, conversation with another client, guessing games, imitation games, drawing, coloring, etc. Other items which do not fit in other areas may be placed here. Sometimes one particular item may turn out to be a powerful reinforcer for a client. For example, one male client cared only for picture books of scientific or mechanical materials and would spend almost all of his time (and tokens) paging through such material. Though not social, such books were made available to him in this room.

Motor Area. A large, physical recreation area containing a trampoline, floor mats, a basketball, etc. Such activities, of course, combine with opportunities for social interaction and expression. Because this area is located some distance from the ABLC facility, access to it is available only following lunch periods. Also, a "holding" area for those who run out of tokens is located at the other end of the same room with chairs facing toward a wall.

Reinforcement areas are made available to clients with tokens at specific periods during the day. The most common schedule is shown in Table 14.1 along with the schedule for work periods. The lunch hour, although it is a potential source for token based positively reinforcing activities, is not included in the token system because of staffing and other difficulties.

All tokens earned during the day must be used during that day. As shown in Table 14.1, just prior to leaving the agency, clients trade in remaining tokens, if any, for pennies.

Table 14.1. Outline of Schedule of Activities and Contingencies for the Token Economy of the Milwaukee Program Facility

	Activities	Contingencies
8:30 A.M. to 11:00 A.M.	workshop tasks	10-second audio reinforcement contingent on work (presented on ratio or interval schedules) tokens contingent on completion of 1½ hour work period .
	teaching and programmed learning sessions individual behavior modification individual experiments	tokens contingent on completion of teaching-learning-unit (on teaching machine, etc.) tokens, M&Ms, fruit-loops, etc., contingencies dependent on particular requirements
11:00 A.M. to 11:30 A.M.	exchanging tokens in store, music room, social area	1 token for entry, each area 1 token for each 5 (or 10) minutes in an area tokens for individual store items tokens for cash (1 token = 1 cent)
11:30 A.M. to 12:30 P.M.	lunch	
12:30 P.M. to 1:25 P.M.	token exchanges: store, motor area, walks (occasionally)	As above
1:20 P.M. to 2:50 P.M.	workshop and other tasks described above (same as 8:30–11:00)	Same as 8:30–11:00 period
2:50 P.M. to 3:05 P.M.	token exchange for pennies	1 penny per token
3:05 P.M.	leave agency	

Workshop Procedures

The primary objective of the workshop procedures is the development of an efficient system for motivating and maintaining effective work and work-related behaviors for the moderately to severely retarded adult.

Several approaches to the control of work behavior with the severely retarded will be described here along with some illustrative procedures, feedback and reinforcement devices, and results of the more promising systems. One such system, designed for the severely retarded, utilizes in-

dividual responsive-signaling devices and audio reinforcement in an auto-mated workshop system. Another system is designed for less severely re-tarded clients for larger scale operation and utilizes a simple timing device at each station which determines the time interval within each work unit which must be completed and reinforces client accordingly. The results of several applications to sheltered workshops are described as follows:

AN AUTOMATED WORKSHOP SYSTEM

This workshop system was developed through various stages for use with the severely retarded. It utilizes a responsive "stimulus box" at each of 10 individual work stations programmed from a remote control center. Se-verely retarded clients work without direct human supervision at consign-ment tasks for 2½ hour sessions of continuous work twice a day.

Each work station consists of a small work space (about 2 × 3 feet), an adjustable overhead focused light, earphones, and a "stimulus-control box" to be described below. There are two unpartitioned work stations to a work bench, arranged in U-shape along three walls in an enclosed room. Clients enter the workshop on arrival in the morning (at 8:30 A.M.), go to their assigned stations, put on their earphones (when in use) and work until 11 A.M., when they collect tokens from an automated token dispenser, and go to one of the reinforcement areas (the store, music room, etc.). On arrival in the morning, in hallways, etc., clients are given an absolute minimum of attention or conversation from staff since these are available only in reinforcement areas for tokens.

The Stimulus-Control Box. The function of such a device at a work sta-tion is to provide for the client precise and consistent information during work concerning important aspects of his work (speed, errors, inadequate attention, undesirable social behavior, and the like). It also provides a form of nondisruptive positive reinforcement for acceptable performance that will sustain attention over the work period until other reinforcers are available. There are, of course, many possibilities; for example, electric counters that provide a cumulative record of work (not usable with the severely retarded), charts that pictorially chart progress toward a work goal, lights that display number of subgoals achieved, sounds that signal a work objective or signal errors or other undesirable behavior, and so forth. The development and testing of various possibilities is one of the ob-jectives of the Milwaukee program. The Stimulus-Control Box, or S-Box, is one such device.

Figure 14.1 shows front and back views of the S-Box. It is designed to provide wide latitude in the manner of providing feedback and online rein-forcement to the client while working. Its principle features, shown in Figure 14.1 may be described as follows:

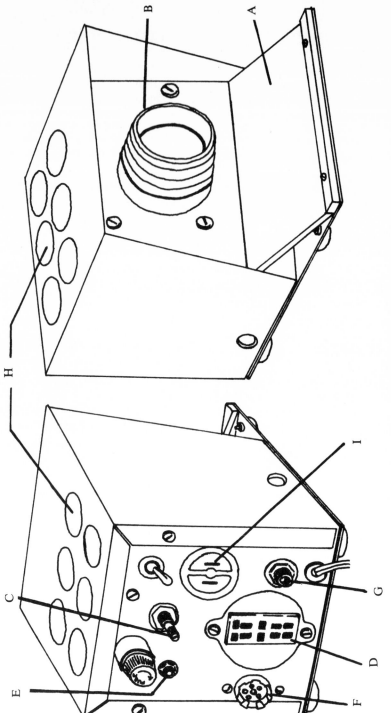

Figure 14.1. Front and Rear Views of S-Box Used Individually with Clients in Automated Workshop

Response key. (A in Figure 14.1). The angled key pressed by the client upon completion of each work unit. It momentarily flashes and clicks when pressed once. After one press, the key is "dead" for up to 9 successive seconds of no presses (preset by internal timer) thus discouraging multiple presses. The client learns to regard this flash-click as approval of his work and a step toward a reinforcing event.

Reinforcement interval (RI). Reinforcing events can be programmed to occur during a brief (up to 10 seconds) interval as a function of time or ratio of key presses administered manually by a remote control hand buttons or automatically by programming apparatus connected to input plug (D in Figure 14.1). On those trials on which an RI is programmed to occur, pressing the key produces onset of the larger center (red) light (B in Figure 14.1), a bell chime, and lighting up of the response-key itself. In addition to these events, other events may be programmed to occur during the RI period. For example, any automatic dispenser may be plugged into reinforcer plug (E in Figure 14.1) and an M&M or a token may be presented at each RI. Or a slide or movie projector may be operated from this same plug during RIs. An audio circuit has been provided so that recorded music or other audio may be fed into audio input plug (F in Figure 14.1) and heard by the client during RI periods through earphones plugged into the S-Box (G in Figure 14.1). The length of each RI is adjustable up to 10 seconds from an interval timer. At the end of RI, the lights and other RI conditions automatically go off signalling a return to the normal work condition. The Milwaukee Project has experimented with the use of a wide range of RI events from using the light-chime alone to tokens, M&Ms, projected color slides of familiar persons and scenes, and such audio as rock music, varying unfamiliar noises, recorded praise from a staff member, recorded segments of favorite TV programs, and live personalized comments from a teacher via a microphone.

Time-out (TO). In normal use, the S-Box has its own internal "on" light visible through round windows on top (H in Figure 14.1); an individual overhead focused work light, plugged into 110 v. a.c. outlet of S-Box (I in Figure 14.1), is also controlled through S-Box circuitry. The "time-out" circuitry allows the teacher to turn off, from a remote switch, lights, sounds and other operating features of the S-Box including the overhead work light. In this TO condition, the S-Box becomes "dead" from the client's point of view, and continuation of the work chain and associated reinforcing event is impossible. The TO switch is operated manually and is used, for example, when work errors are observed or when undesirable behavior is occurring. TO intervals depend upon circumstances but, in practice, are seldom longer than 15 seconds.

Recording system. Each key press, RIs, and time-outs are recorded by

counters and other recording equipment located in a control room attached to the workshop.

Workshop Operation. During pre-workshop training (called "shaping sessions"), the client learns to press the white key of the S-Box upon completion of each work unit (as defined during training). The key then briefly flashes and clicks, signalling the client to deposit his completed unit in a "finish box" (or bag attached to the work bench) and to begin the next unit. Each key-press is registered in the control room on counters which advance the client's program toward the RI events. Only one key-press is registered since a "dead" period follows each key-press so that extra or repeated presses by client will have no effect (see above).

While various ratio and interval schedules have been employed in the workshop, the most common reinforcement schedule has been the fixed-ratio schedule for presenting of the RIs; that is, after the client presses the key a fixed number of times (representing completion of a fixed number of work units), the next key press produces a 10-second RI (chime plus light and other accompanying events). At various times, these accompanying events have included M&Ms, tokens, slides, and audio. However, the use of audio, such as music, the voices of familiar staff members, or recorded favorite TV programs have proved to be least disruptive of ongoing work and effective enough to maintain attentive work activity over the 2½ hour work period. For the audio RI condition, clients must wear earphones, plugged into the S-Box. The audio material is most effective for most clients when varied from RI to RI and day to day. These variations may involve variations in the kinds of music, different voices, different content, and so on. One of the more effective types of audio consists of the recorded voice of a favorite teacher simulating a conversation with the (unnamed) client (clients in this case usually talk back to the S-Box during these "conversations"). The teacher may also use a microphone to directly talk to a client during an RI, using the clients name.

Since the audio input to the client is independently controlled by circuits within each S-Box, each client hears only what is going on "on line" during the 10-second RI for his particular S-Box.

Time-Out Punishment. The TO procedure is used to provide feedback and suppression of careless work habits or undesirable or disruptive behavior at the time of their occurrence. TO has the advantages of being easily discriminable, mildly aversive to most clients, of short duration, minimally disruptive of ongoing work activity, and being mediated by a "machine" rather than another person. Many severely retarded persons have been highly sensitized to failure and human aversive control. If methods for controlling work and other behaviors are to emphasize *positive* reinforcement for acceptable behavior rather than punishment for

unacceptable behavior, the methods for letting the client know he is doing poorly or behaving badly must not negate the positive aspects of the work activity itself. We feel that the nonhuman S-Box mediated time-out procedure serves this purpose. When unacceptable behavior occurs, the S-Box operation simply stops (along with the opportunities it affords). Correcting the behavior that brought about the onset of TO immediately returns the client to the opportunity for work activity with its associated achievement, frequent positive reinforcing events during work, and eventual social reinforcers and acceptance. TO usually is manually controlled by a staff observer from the control room by operating a lever for the work-station involved. If it is known that a client is making errors on his work task, the observer (who can watch the client through a one-way mirror) waits until the error is apparently being made and then operates the TO lever. The TO may be applied for errors, disruptive talking or actions, for responding to another client's disruptive actions, for daydreaming, work stoppage, and the like. In all cases, it is administered only at the time such behavior is actually occurring. Errors or other undesirable behavior are never corrected or referred to by staff at times other than when they have just occurred. If work errors continue to be made, a staff member may attempt to correct it with the client during a time-out period; if correction requires more than this, the client is removed from the workshop and worked with individually in a shaping room. TO periods of from 5 to 10 seconds usually are effective in suppressing most undesirable behaviors if the positive reinforcing conditions related to the work task are intact. If 10 second TO periods prove to be ineffective for a client, we have usually found that there are more fundamental problems that need correction—for example, retraining, a change in reinforcing conditions. The same may be said when there is a frequent need for administering TOs. Those clients for whom direct social attention is a strong reinforcer will learn to bring about a TO and its associated attention if the RI reinforcers become satiated or are of little value to them. The TO condition usually consists of simply the temporary absence of a functioning S-Box and the opportunity for work. On some cases, it may be desirable to add an aversive stimulus to the TO condition. This may be done via an audio circuit of the S-Box which can provide white noise or other aversive audio stimulation during TO periods.

Pre-Time-Out Signal. A difficulty with the TO is that it forces temporary work stoppage when all that may be required is a signal to the client that his behavior needs correction. Our experience has indicated that even with severely retarded persons, if they know when they are making an error, most can and will correct the error by themselves. To provide such a signal and minimize work stoppage, we have used a "pre-time-out" warning signal, consisting of a rapid and repeated onset and offset of the TO condition

for about an 8-second period prior to onset of the actual TO condition. This appears as a flashing of the S-Box and overhead work lights. During training, the client learns that this means he is doing something wrong at the moment which, if corrected, will terminate the flashing signal and avoid the TO. Proper timing of this pretimeout signal by the operator is, of course, important because the client focuses on what he is doing at the moment of onset of the flashing. When used by a skilled operator, the method has proved most effective in controlling (suppressing) a wide variety of unwanted workshop behaviors and minimizing the need for actual TOs and work stoppages. Even under optimal conditions, however, some clients periodically "test" the TO system and apparently deliberately force a TO.

Training (Shaping) Procedures. Prior to actual participation in the automated workshop, each client is individually "shaped" to the desired level of work performance required by the particular task and by the workshop rules. A small room with a single work station simulating a workshop situation is used for shaping. The same S-Box is used, but with the manual hand-control attached by a long cord which allows the trainer-teacher to control the RI, TO and pre-TO conditions of the S-Box from inside or outside the room. Pressing one button sets up the S-Box so that the next key press by the client will produce the RI condition (the duration of RI can be preset or can be extended by holding the RI button down). Pressing another button on the hand control activated the TO condition and repeated pressing produces the pre-TO signal.

In training the new client to a new work task, the task is first broken down into a chain of small steps arranged in order. Using backward chaining, the work task is arranged and cued so that approximations of the required responses at any point are highly likely. Key discriminations may be cued with colors or by other means. In this backward chaining procedure, the client completes only the *final* part of the chain at first, then the final *two* parts, and so on backward until he must carry out each step in the chain from the beginning. For example, a coin-tube task involves (1) picking up an uncapped tube, (2) picking up a cap, (3) finding the L-shaped slot on the rim of the tube, (4) alligning the cap's nodule with this slot, (5) pressing the cap onto the tube's rim and into the slot, and (6) turning the cap clockwise in L-shaped slot without forcing. In initial training, the caps are already placed in the slots and the client needs only to perform the final step (Step 6). Later, he must take a cap from a supply box and so on until he finally must complete all 6 steps under the normal work situation, without errors. Such an arrangement minimizes the chances of error and when errors do occur they can be corrected by the teacher and the step mastered before proceding to the next step.

During the backward chaining phase of training and until the client is completing the full work chain smoothly, correctly, and without help, the teacher remains with the client. Since it is important that the client is able to perform the task without the control of a teacher, it is important that learning and practice of the skills involved develop as much as possible from the arrangement and cuing of the work chain itself and not from directions from the teacher. Therefore, direct teacher guidance during training is kept at a minimum. The teacher monitors the client's performance and difficulties and modifies the chain or adds cuing in order that the client's skills develop from the task itself rather than from the teacher.

In addition to the task itself, the client must also press the key on his S-Box as the final part of each work chain. Therefore, if this is a new client who is unfamiliar with the S-Box, pressing the key is the first task practiced by the client (usually only one trail is needed). The client is then shown the almost completed work unit and what to do with it. When he does this, the teacher points to the key which usually is immediately pressed without further prodding. At this stage, each key press produces an RI. No mechanical reinforcers are used during the RIs during training but only the direct expressive social actions of the teacher while the RI light is on. With onset of each RI, the teacher immediately expresses praise and excitement and places one token in the client's palm. Intense social interaction is maintained until offset of the RI light which is immediately accompanied by teacher silence. Even in early stages, the client will usually pick up another work unit and complete it and press the key without further prodding. Again an RI occurs, another token, and the situation is repeated. *Only* positive reinforcement is used in this early stage; errors are corrected as described earlier. As the chain becomes longer, more steps must be completed before the RI, which occurs only when the key is pressed at the end of the chain.

Tokens, of course, are being accumulated rapidly. After 8 or 10 tokens have been obtained and during an RI, the client is taken from the room to the store where he uses one token to enter and the others for items inside. After about five minutes, he is returned to the shaping room. Training in the significance of the TO condition begins upon return from his first or second store visit. Upon reentering the room, the S-Box is set in the TO condition (S-Box lights and work-light are off). As the client begins to sit down, the teacher exclaims "What! Look! The light is off!" The client stops. Both the client and teacher step back a few feet, wait, and watch the S-Box together for four or five seconds. The teacher then turns the lights back on and announces "The lights are on! You can work now!" The client sits down and is expected to continue work without further comment.

The results of this TO training are tested after the next trip to the store.

The S-Box light is again off upon their return and the teacher simply waits to see whether or not the client begins to sit down. Most clients do not but watch quietly until the lights go on. If a client does begin to sit down, the teacher repeats the above procedure as needed.

To establish the pre-TO situation, the teacher himself touches the S-Box in some obvious manner and then "punishes" himself with a short series of flashes followed by a TO. The teacher then turns to the client, apologizes for his "mistake," and says that he did something wrong and the light is off and they must get up and wait until the light goes on again. This procedure is repeated a second time and then tested with the client by presenting the flashing signal for some irrelevant response. If the client does not immediately terminate the response accompanying the flashing signal, further trials are given. Most clients in the present population have not required more than three pre-TO training trials to reach this point.

Using the above procedure, most clients in the ABLC population (excluding the custodial clients) are able to complete a work unit chain from the beginning smoothly and accurately without guidance in from one to two 30–40 minute sessions. At this point, training begins on intermittent reinforcement. This begins with the RI omitted upon completion of one of the work units. Client presses the key on the S-Box as usual, but receives no RI. Clients usually press several more times and then turn to the teacher who responds with the comment, "The bell does not always ring." The client returns to work. Upon completion of the next work unit, he again receives the usual RI. The RI ratio is kept at 2 to 1 for several trials, then moved to 5 to 1.

The terminal work behavior requires that the client work alone without the support or physical presence of a staff member. At the beginning of training, the teacher sits next to client at the work station. As soon as possible, the teacher monitors the client from a standing position over his shoulder. With subsequent trials, as the RI ratio is increased, the teacher moves farther and farther away. He approaches and interacts with the client only during the 10-second RIs.

As performance becomes smoother, the RI ratio is gradually increased to FR-10 and the teacher now moves out of the room altogether, closing the door to only a small crack. From outside, he is able to count the clicks of the key presses; after 9 clicks he presses his hand control RI button so that RI occurs with next press. With onset of RI, the teacher quickly opens door and approaches the client with a token, praise, etc., until its offset again.

This is continued until the client is able to exhibit smooth, accurate performance on an FR-10 RI schedule for a one-hour session in the shaping room. The client is then assigned to an individual work station in the experimental workshop where he is now expected to work for 2½ hours.

The teacher-trainer monitors the client during the first day in the experimental workshop, keeping the client on the same FR-10 RI schedule. However, direct social reinforcement during RI periods is no longer available and is replaced by the audio reinforcement system via earphones. The client is shown how to put on the earphones and is left to work at the same task used in training. Most clients readily adapt to this new procedure and are gradually moved from FR-10 up to FR-25 or more over the first week. In the event that performance deteriorates under the workshop conditions, the client is returned to the individual shaping sessions for further work on the difficulties encountered in the workshop.

Of course, sheltered work tasks often change from week to week and, with severely retarded clients, these changes usually require special training. When a new task is to be introduced, clients are given a brief individual training session (15–30 minutes) with the new work-task assignment. The new task is again chained backwards and the teacher provides help as necessary, making sure that the client has mastered each step before moving back to earlier steps. However, for experienced clients, such training usually moves ahead rapidly. An FR-10 schedule is used from the start and RIs are usually reduced to 5 seconds of social reinforcement.

Many variations are possible within this workshop situation. While fixed ratio schedules have been used most frequently, RI schedules on a variable basis have been tried as well as variable interval schedules (see Chapter 6). No important differences have been found in the performance of clients under variable vs. fixed schedules or, to date, even under variable interval schedules. Because it has been technically simpler with present equipment, we have used fixed ratio schedules as the primary schedule for the automated workshop.

Some of the results and some tentative conclusions regarding the automated workshop system described here may be summarized as follows:

a. Severely retarded clients, formerly believed to be unsuited for even the lowest level of sheltered work activity, work for a normal workshop day (about 4 hours of productive time and 2½ hours of uninterrupted stretches), producing consignment goods of acceptable quality and rates comparable to less handicapped clients. Day to day stability is greater than with regular workshop clients.

b. With simple assembly tasks, such as capping coin tubes, requiring less than 30 seconds to complete, stable results are most often obtained using RI reinforcement schedules below FR-30. Within this range, either variable or fixed ratios appear to produce relatively smooth, steady work output for several hours with little disruptive behavior from the more emotionally unstable clients. Figure 14.2 shows a typical 80 minute cumulative record of an emotionally disturbed and re-

tarded client who was working under ratio schedules of varying levels and types. Each record was obtained on a different day. Hatched marks represent RIs. Each record is obtained by a pen which moves sideways with each key press on a paper moving at a constant speed. Thus, the steeper the slope the faster the rate of responding (no responses at all result in a flat line). Note the smoother performance under lower ratios.

c. There are wide differences between clients in the size of the ratio that will maintain the smooth performance shown in Figure 14.2. A few clients on this same task would work well under ratios as high as 80–1; most do not. The more behaviorally erratic and disturbed individuals seem to require very low ratios (between 10 and 15–1 for the task represented in Figure 14.2). Many of the clients in this population, when subjected to conditions requiring sustained attention and effort, exhibit restlessness, attention getting, resistance, hostility, disruptiveness, and the like. While such characteristics usually disappear when placed in the automated workshop with effective RI reinforcement on low RI ratio schedules, these characteristics reappear when high RI ratios are introduced. For subjects who have not been in workshops for long, the tolerance for sustained attention under very high ratios breaks down rapidly, usually within 30 minutes. The tolerance for sustained workshop activity under very high ratios for clients who have worked under lower ratios effectively for long periods of time breaks down rather slowly. In fact, some individuals who have been accustomed to the routines of the automated workshop have continued to work effectively for a week without any RI reinforcement, although unstable work performance and disruptive behavior eventually return. The more precise roles of RI scheduling and ratio levels and other variables in the experimental workshop environment in determining the stability and efficiency of sustained workshop performance have yet to be determined.

d. Once a particular rate of performance has been established (under an optimal schedule), the client will maintain very similar rates minute to minute and hour to hour during those times when the client is actually working. However, under some conditions, clients may stop work for brief periods periodically producing a more unstable overall record. Stability and smoothness of work activity appears to be very sensitive to changes in the reinforcing conditions—both RI conditions and reinforcers available for tokens outside of the work area. Reinforcement can be decreased by the use of identical audio tapes for long periods, elimination of all audio during RIs depletion of store supplies, reduction in the number of tokens which can be earned, re-

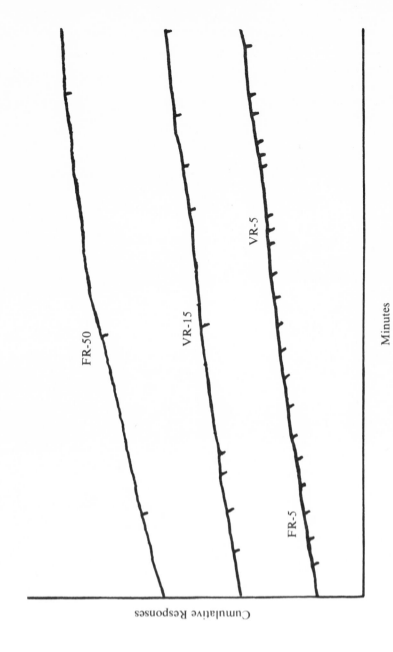

Figure 14.2. Sample Cumulative Record under Various RI Schedules from Three Separate Workshop Sessions of 40 Minutes Each

moval of the S-Box, and so on. Such changes gradually produce increased rates of inattention, carelessness, work-stoppages, time-outs, etc., all of which decrease stability of work output.

e. Among the RI audio reinforcers tried have been music, recorded voices simulating praise and positive comments about work, use of comments which are live personalized with name, etc. (via mike), use of unfamiliar sounds and noises, and a recorded TV program selected by clients (Divorce Court). No single audio mode results in more work stability than any other; if used repeatedly, all modes eventually result in gradual deterioration of work stability. Frequent and unpredictable changes in audio modes seem most effective. Music and voice modes appear to be less easily satiable. In one study, the role of sound during RIs was investigated in which sound (music and recorded voice) was provided *during* work and was silent during RIs. Stability and other behaviors were compared against pre and post-baseline performance obtained when sound accompanied RIs only. After 5 days without RI sound and with sound during work, stability began to decrease noticeably along with the need for increased use of pre-TOs and TOs for unacceptable behaviors. After three weeks, the contingency was reversed and sound was again present only during RIs. Work stability returned within two days for most clients. Of course, other sounds, rhythms, etc. played during work and perhaps directly related to the work task might facilitate performance rather than hinder it.

f. In addition to work activity itself, there is also indication of effects of workshop conditions on the behavior of the client in his home. Such effects are reflected by comments and actions by parents and guardians, particularly during efforts to establish baselines when some reinforcing conditions are being omitted during work. During the period described above when all audio reinforcement was removed during RIs, parents began complaining to the Agency or commenting that their son or daughter no longer liked to come in the morning. Some parents reported more than usual difficulties in control at home, and so forth. When all RI reinforcement was removed in another study, such problems became so bad that the test period was cut short. For clients who are well adapted to the workshop routine, there is some indication that home problems and loss of interest in the Agency due to a change in reinforcement conditions precede measureable changes in workshop performance by several weeks.

WORKSHOP II SYSTEM

The use of an automated workshop system such as the one just described with the need for remote control rooms, online audio reinforcement, etc.

is probably unfeasible for larger scale application in most sheltered workshops. Yet, the level, quality and stability of work output in most sheltered
workshops operated under normal conditions with less handicapped clients
leave much to be desired. Some type of stimulus-control and feedback system along with work-contingent positive reinforcement would probably
greatly improve the stability and productivity of many sheltered workshop
clients. The problem is to develop a system which the average work supervisor may operate without much training or professional background and
can be used without elaborate mechanical or electrical installations.

To investigate some of the alternatives available, Screven and Wrabetz
(1969) obtained baseline production data under normal workshop conditions on four retarded and emotionally disturbed clients (IQs between 40
and 80) outside the ABLC facility in a Developmental Sheltered Workshop at the Jewish Vocational Service. The work task which the clients had
been previously performing consisted of filling a tray with 12 red and 12
black checkers and loading these into a cardboard box. Baseline involves
no change in workshop conditions except that the four clients involved
were placed at the same work table in a large room in which about 23
clients were working at the same task. As was usual practice, clients received their pay at the end of each week based on a minimum rate *per
hour* (established by Agency through client rating) plus a piece rate bonus
of one cent per box produced over a pre-established minimum. As is usual
in such sheltered work settings, the clients were not aware of these bases
for their weekly paycheck. The check was just something that was given
them at the end of each week. Clients worked for 6 hours per day with two
15-minute break periods in the morning and afternoon and one-half hour
for lunch.

The left portion of Figure 14.3 shows the mean baseline performance of
the four clients in terms of mean units per hour for the particular task for
each of the six days of the baseline period. The left portion of Figure 14.4
shows the same data for each of the four individual clients. Daily output
was both variable and relatively low for all clients in terms of community
standard.

Following baseline, a simple contingency was then established between
cash payments and work output. Each client was given a fixed number of
checkers and boxes to complete in 20 minutes. This number was based on
the client's former baseline output, namely, two *units less* than formerly
completed in 20 minutes.

The stimulus-control unit was a simple mechanical kitchen timer placed
at each work station and set for exactly 20 minutes. The client was told to
complete his work before this clock rang. Upon completion of his allotted
work units, the client brought his finished work *and* his clock-timer to the

supervisor's table. If the client "beat" the clock, the supervisor complimented him and gave him two cents. He then took one box at a time from the client and paid him one cent each time, verbally emphasizing the relationship between each cent paid and each box. The client was then given supplies for another set of units to complete in 20 minutes, the clock was reset, and he returned to his station. The number of work units was increased by two additional units for each two successive trials on which the client beat his clock-timer. When he did not beat the clock and the clock's bell rang, he lost the two-cent bonus, but still received one cent for each completed unit.

With repeated daily sessions, the work period (and time between payments) was increased from 20 minutes to 30, 40, and finally 60 minutes, with the number of allotted work units adjusted for the same rate of work. This was done by increasing the clock setting and adding work units accordingly, until the 60-minute work period was reached.

After 9 successive days under the above conditions, the base payment of one cent per box was eliminated and for the following 5 work days a ticket was substituted with the amount earned written on it. Clients still received a cash bonus for beating the clock, which was now doubled to four cents. Payment for work, other than bonuses, was again received by weekly check, but the total check was based on output rather than hours worked.

The results on client work production for each of the 14 work days is shown in Figure 14.3 (group means) and Figure 14.4 (individual client output). As is readily apparent, the work output in terms of units per hour increased markedly almost immediately with increases of from 50 to over 100 percent. Day to day variability of production decreased. Removal of the immediate cash payments for work units completed with substitution of a ticket did not have a noticeable effect on any client.

Following the 14 experimental sessions, all contingencies were removed, along with the clock-timers, and the clients returned to the former baseline situation of weekly paychecks based on hourly rate plus bonus for production over minimum amount. Mean performance dropped sharply over the 6 day period. However, two of the four clients maintained their former rate and stability over the 6 days (they did come down later).

After the first few experimental sessions when the relationship between the money received and work output was clearly established, two of the clients (the two fastest producers) verbalized this relationship with some excitement and later did not seem to care about direct payment or the tickets so long as it was clear they were to be paid for their work output.

This study was later replicated by Screven, Derlin, and Huber (1969) using nine clients from the same workshop. The task was filling a counter

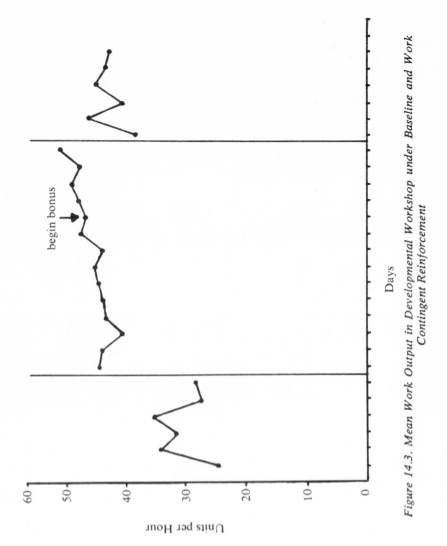

Figure 14.3. Mean Work Output in Developmental Workshop under Baseline and Work Contingent Reinforcement

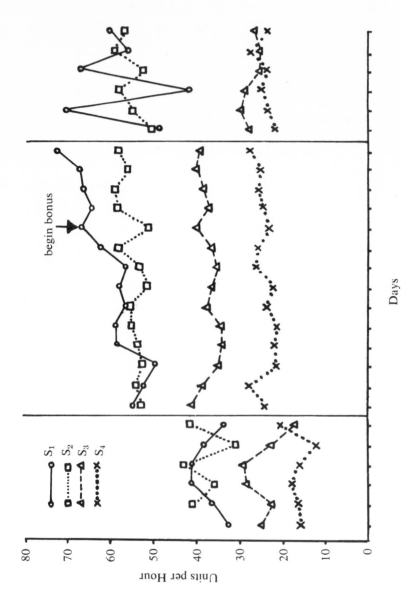

Figure 14.4. Work Output of Individual Clients in Developmental Workshop under Baseline and Work Contingent Reinforcement

board with 50 golf tees, putting these into plastic bags, and placing the bag in a finish tray.

The same procedures and equipment were used except that (a) clients remained at tables and supervisor came to client when client signalled he was finished with his allotted material and (b) different payments were used, namely:

First 5 days: ½ cent cash per unit plus a 4-cent beat-the-clock bonus.

Second 5 days: 1-cent cash per unit plus a 4-cent beat-the-clock bonus.

Third 3 days: No direct cash payment for work; no tickets; check was received at end of week; 4-cent beat-the-clock bonus remained.

Figure 14.5 shows the group mean performance (units per hour) for the nine clients for the 4 day baseline period, the 13 experimental work days, and a final 2 work days under original baseline conditions. Results were similar to the Screven-Wrabetz study. Instituting the pay and beat-the-clock contingencies were again effective in increasing production rates and stable day to day performance. These effects held under all three payment conditions. As in the earlier study, once the cash for work contingency was established, there was no effect on performance of removal of direct payments.

In both studies, inappropriate behaviors were greatly reduced or eliminated. Some clients formerly had regularly engaged in taking unapproved breaks from the workshop, constant complaining to and bothering of supervisor, and frequent tardiness. After instituting the contingencies, such behaviors virtually disappeared in all clients. These behaviors gradually began returning after return to the original workshop conditions.

Such results indicate the feasibility of applying behavioral techniques to sheltered work settings. Once the direct cash payment for completed work units can be eliminated, administration by the supervisor of the clock-timer procedure and bonus payments is a simple matter which should be adaptable to workshops of larger sizes with many different job situations. The delay in work payments apparently is not a serious problem, once the relation between work and pay is established. In the meantime, the clock-bonus payments serve both as a feedback device for keeping the client informed on how he is doing and, at the same time, as a source of more immediate and frequent positive reinforcement.

The most recent application of another approach to controlling work rate and stability in regular sheltered work settings is in the early testing phase. This involves the adaptation of a so-called "Sidman Avoidance" procedure to maintain stable work output at an optimal level. In Sidman Avoidance, the individual is placed in a potentially punishing situation in which punishment can be avoided (postponed) by performing some discrete task within a fixed time period. For example, a laboratory animal

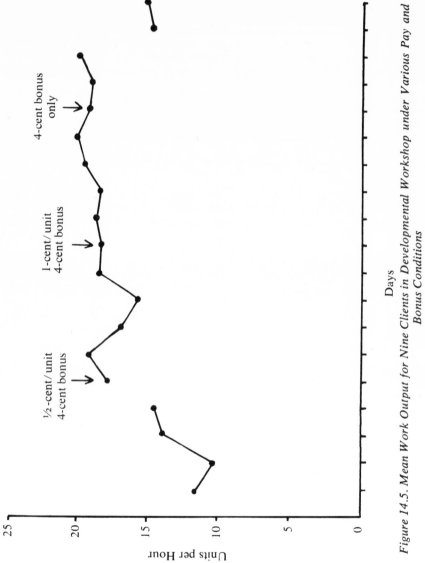

Figure 14.5. *Mean Work Output for Nine Clients in Developmental Workshop under Various Pay and Bonus Conditions*

may be on an electric grid and shocked without warning, say, every 20 seconds. But if the animal presses a lever within this 20 seconds, this resets the interval to 20 more seconds before the next shock. Provided the lever is pressed within 20 seconds after the previous lever press, all shock is completely avoided.

In our adaptation to the sheltered work situation, the shock has been replaced by the aversive event of having a number of finished work units taken away, or losing a part of a bonus already earned. The "lever" has been replaced by a spring platform mounted on a small black box. The prototype of the avoidance box is a small square box (4 × 4 × 3 in.) with two lights (yellow, red), an adjustable 0- to 90-second timer, a low volume buzzer, and a spring platform top. Upon completing each work unit, the client briefly places the item on the platform (pressing downward if necessary to produce a click) on his way to placing the item in the finish tray, or barrel. The timer resets to zero *with each press* and may be set by supervisor for the desired *maximum* time for task completion consistent with the client's abilities and previous performance. Completing each work unit within this interval keeps resetting the timer to zero and the avoidance box remains inert. If the work is *not* completed, the yellow light and a buzzing sound come on at the end of the preset interval. These cannot be turned off except by the supervisor. The yellow light alerts the supervisor who comes to the work station and silently removes x-number of completed items from the client's finish tray (or may perform some other aversive action such as taking back bonus tokens or money earned). He then turns off the light-buzzer with a special key (resetting timer to zero), and leaves. The supervisor must be careful not to engage in conversation with the client since conversation could have reinforcing value for some clients.

The second light (red) may be used by client himself when an interruption in work is necessary, such as replenishing supplies, or turning in completed trays. The client simply operates a switch for the red light which stops the timer operation. The red light signals the supervisor who can then judge if the break is legitimate. If the red light is misused, the supervisor treats it as a yellow light.

In current pilot tests, clients are given supplies for completing a fixed number of items and turn these in, first for direct cash payments and later, for end-of-the day or end-of-week payments. For positive reinforcement during work, various possibilities are being tested; for example, payment of cash or token for each completed finish tray, payment of fixed bonus of one token or one cent during work periods on variable-interval schedule, etc.

Pilot tests to date with individual problem clients in workshop settings have resulted in doubling and tripling of baseline production rates and

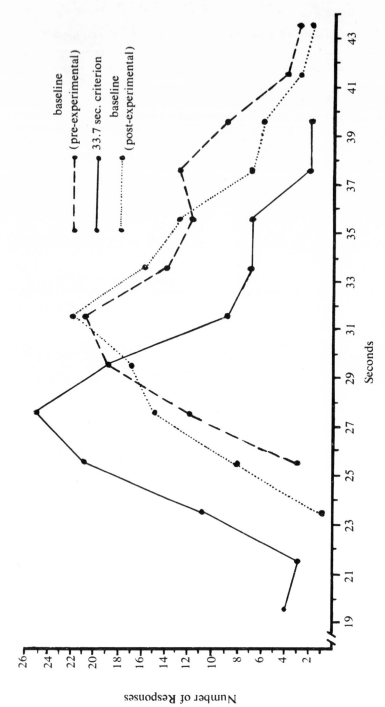

Figure 14.6. *Response Time Distribution of an Individual Client With and Without Avoidance Box Control*

good day-to-day stability of performance. Performance is being recorded in terms of frequency of work units completed plotted against times of completion as illustrated in Figure 14.6 with one of the present pilot clients—typical of results obtained with other clients to date. The work task was assembling four window shade brackets in a plastic bag for one token per 25 bags. As may be seen in Figure 14.6, use of the avoidance box lowered the distribution of response time well below those distributions of response time obtained both before and after the avoidance box procedure. The light-buzzer on the avoidance box and its associated mildly aversive action (the removal of only one completed package from the finish-tray) appeared to exercise a powerful effect on the client's behavior. Fidgeting and nonproductive attention stopped after the first 3 or 4 light-buzzer events and the client became highly attentive to the task with dramatic increases in rate. Quality of work also increased with errors dropping from 17 percent to 12 percent.

The pilot applications of the Sidman Avoidance procedure to date are encouraging. Not only are the results encouraging, but the system is relatively simple to administer and could be easily applied by a work supervisor or teacher. Timer-intervals can easily be readjusted to suit the particular capabilities and needs of the individual client and clients quickly adapt to the procedure. In the case of new work, of course, it is still important that provision is made for pretraining the clients in the components of the work chain as described earlier.

Teaching Procedures

Since the work potentials of a client may be limited by the lack of basic skills such as vocabulary, counting, color naming, and listening skills, the Milwaukee program has devoted considerable effort to procedures for teaching simple language and concept skills to the retarded client population within ABLC. The methods employed fall generally within what may be called *educational technology*. The technologies of programmed learning and responsive teaching devices, if wisely employed, can do much to meet the pressing needs of educating the retarded individual. Harnessing of these technologies could make far more productive use of both the teacher's and the client's time and more effective use of what is known about the processes of human learning.

Educational technology is a systematic effort to arrange the instructional process to facilitate specific learning outcomes. Desired learning outcomes are first formulated and performance tests are established which reflect these desired outcomes. An analysis is then made of the specific learning tasks likely to be involved. An instructional sequence is then designed in-

tended to produce the learning outcomes, utilizing whatever available modes and media (human and nonhuman) seem most efficient for this purpose. The system is then tried out in a representative teaching situation with the kind of student for which it is being developed and the results are evaluated. Based on these results, the instructional tasks and sequencing may be reanalyzed and modified and again retested until its performance with representative students justified its further application to a training program.

The teaching staff in the Milwaukee program have been trained in this process of defining learning objectives, developing an instructional sequence, testing it with ABLC clients, modifying the program, restesting, and so on.

The program has to date emphasized the techniques of programmed instruction and some of the staff have become skilled at developing programmed materials on simple concepts for the retarded. Programmed instruction started in the latter part of the 1950s when Harvard's B. F. Skinner (1954, 1958) advocated the application of established principles of learning to the instructional process. In its early stage, programmed learning became identified with teaching by machine and many crude devices came onto the market long before the know-how for the development of the programs to go with them.

Programmed instruction as a concept for the organization and sequencing of instructional events is basically a good one when separated from crude mechanical gadgets and bad programs. The method is particularly suited to the retarded individual if ways to elicit and maintain his attention are found.

The use of an automated teaching machine is most useful for this purpose but the machine must utilize both audio and visual materials and be flexible enough to not restrict the programmer or the client. Fortunately, contemporary teaching machines are no longer mechanical page turners. They can provide information in a variety of modes, including sound effects and the human voice to impart a "personal" quality, emphasize a point, "reward" correct answers (with "Great!" "Wow!" etc.) and "punish" careless answers. An important advantage of a machine is that if it can do a job well, it can then easily be replicated. If *one* machine is programmed to teach a basic vocabulary to groups of severely retarded reliably and effectively, then an unlimited number of these machines can be produced to provide this basic vocabulary to any desired number of other severely retarded persons! This contrasts with a teacher of the retarded, trained to do an equally good job, but who cannot be so readily duplicated in unlimited numbers! A good "teaching machine" containing an equally good program *simulates* a good tutor but, unlike the tutor, we can produce

as many more as we need and deliver them for use anywhere and anytime!

The limited facilities of the ABLC program have not allowed the use of such sophisticated devices as computers, "talking typewriters," and so on. The devices to be used required visual materials which could be printed or pasted on paper, edited and changed readily, and easily prepared for automated machine presentation. Recorded audio material had to be easily produced by teaching staff and correlated by them with the visual material on the machine.

The equipment selected was an MTA-400[1] with a matching-to-sample press-panel top diagrammed in Figure 14.7. Printed words, pictures, etc. appear in the large upper window (A); corresponding symbols, words, etc. to be matched to this upper word or picture appear in the four plexiglas windows below (B). The subject responds by touching one of these windows with the picture or word in it which he believes corresponds to the "sample" word or picture above.

Sound may be added to the visual portion of the program by a simple cassette tape recorder (Norelco "Carrycorder") to stop automatically on a beep tone placed by the teacher-programmer at any point on the tape she desires. When plugged into the existing audio circuitry of the MTA-400 device, the tape will automatically start when the client presses a correct window. The taped material may say "Good!" and go on to present supportive audio material for the new frame now showing on the machine. Incorrect responses do *not* start the tape. A "lock-out" feature prevents the machine from advancing while the tape is playing. Thus, the teacher may integrate and synchronize any audio material she wishes with the visual program.

Other devices, such as slide or movie projectors, may also be plugged into the MTA circuitry for additional visual presentations correlated with the teaching program material, or, if desired, contingent upon the client's performance.

The machine usually is used in a correction mode in which the machine advances only on correct. To further identify an incorrect response, a "time-out" system is employed in which a "house light" which lights the face of the machine (see C in Figure 14.7) turns off for a brief period whenever an incorrect panel is pressed. A TO interval of no more than 3 seconds works best, after which the house-light returns and the client must make another choice. This is repeated until he presses the correct window and advances the machine.

Clients who are unfamiliar with the machine first take a program on working the machine and the matching-to-sample method. The client is

1. Manufactured by Behavior Control Incorporated, 1506 West Pierce Street, Milwaukee, Wisconsin 53204.

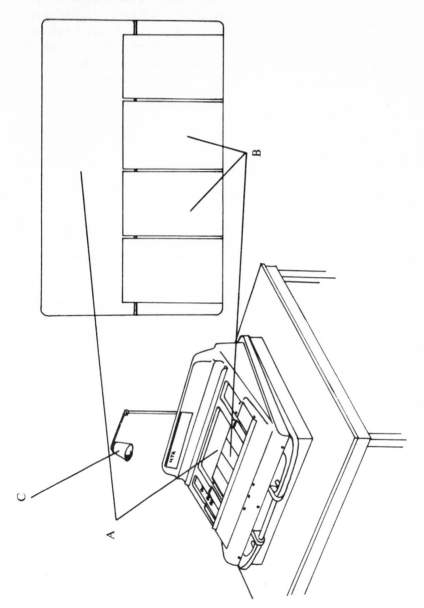

Figure 14.7. Teaching Machine with Press Panel Format Used for Automated Instruction

first brought to the individual room by a teacher and, after sitting down, is encouraged to press the window with a familiar picture in it. When he does, the machine advances and another picture appears in a different window. This process is repeated until a picture appears with a pretaped audio which says "Touch the picture in the window." The client is now under the full control of the machine and tape and the teacher leaves the room. Clients continue to work on the machine unattended to the end of the program (normally from 25 to 45 minutes). The teacher monitors the client from an adjoining observation room. Errors are recorded. At the end of the program, the tape tells the client he has finished and will receive some tokens, which are then given directly to the client by the teacher who returns to the room. The client is later returned to the same program for at least two more sessions or until he completes the program with no more than 5 percent errors for three successive sessions. He is then ready for other programs.

Motivational Considerations. For most clients, the operation and sounds of the machine itself and the accompanying audio seem to be sufficient reinforcement to sustain attention for programs up to one hour in length. When M&Ms or tokens have been automatically dispensed following a fixed number of successive correct responses (FR-10), error rates and time to mastery have usually increased. An M&M or token arbitrarily introduced in this way, draws the client away from the stimulus materials and without regard to where he may be in the program sequence. Nevertheless, it may sometimes be necessary to add to the reinforcing conditions accompanying the program, to sustain attention of less responsive clients or to carry the client through a series of more difficult discrimination frames. In this case, rather than using extrinsic reinforcers like tokens or M&Ms during learning, it has been more effective to use transient reinforcing events woven into the program itself; examples would be the teacher's voice praising the client following some of the correct responses, or occasional insertion of familiar cartoon characters or photos which simply pass by the viewing windows between appropriate frames.

However, because of the apparently intrinsic reinforcing properties of the machine-teaching situation itself for most of the clients, we have found such additional motivational props to be seldom needed. However, the teaching programs are taking place within a token economy, therefore, each client, at the *end* of each machine-teaching session, is given tokens to match those which would have otherwise been obtained in the same period in the workshop programs.

The machine format appears to be superior to nonmachine presentation in terms of number of errors made during learning, frequency of irrelevant behavior and loss of attention, initial posttest performance and successive

sessions required for mastery (three successive runs with less than 5 percent error). When machine programs have been placed on cards and presented by a skilled teacher in one-to-one sessions with the same sequencing and script, much difficulty has been encountered in maintaining attention.

Clients working at the machine do not attempt to leave the room and will work at the machine for as much as one hour, unattended. When away from the situation, participating clients often ask to go to "the game in that room." Access to the teaching machine room has become a reinforcing activity which can even be "sold."

Staff have reported a general increase in verbalization among normally nonverbal clients participating in the machine-teaching programs. Although unconfirmed, parents of these clients have reported that at home words and objects being taught by machine are being spontaneously vocalized.

Various programs in development include color naming, color discrimination, making small change, one vs two of something, listening skills, the i.t.a. alphabet, and a basic reading program. Frame sequences are first prepared on 5 × 8 cards and tested with clients with the teacher-programmer simulating the machine and tape as much as possible. Pre-post tests are given and on the basis of posttest results, frames are revised and retested with cards until the desired learning outcomes on posttests are obtained. The material is then transferred to the machine format. During this process, the staff learn to evaluate frame sequencing, methods for cuing successive approximations, and so on.

The teaching-machine program of particular interest is the basic reading program, concerned with the automated teaching of reading skills to the severely retarded. Its objectives include the teaching of visual vocabularies (word-picture matching), oral reading (word-naming) and listening vocabularies (sound-word matching) using a machine format which could be packaged for use with other retardates by unskilled persons.

The basic format and design of such a program for use in the automated teaching of both oral and visual matching of nouns is being developed and tested by Screven and Pace (1970). Working within a model suggested by Sidman (1969), Pace (1970) investigated some of the prerequisite skills necessary for the "emergence," without training, of oral and visual language skills and found, among other things, that after teaching the severely retarded to master only the visual relationships between familiar pictures and their nouns on an MTA-400 matching-to-sample program, the ability of the clients to orally name the words *emerged* spontaneously *without* direct training.

In order to better understand the formats and general problems, we shall describe a model suggested by Sidman (1969) and shown in modified form

in Figure 14.8. Figure 14.8 depicts the various relationships between spoken and written symbols and their corresponding nonverbal pictures (or object)-referents. The upper parts of Figure 14.8 (relation I and V) involve no written language, but only the relations of spoken sounds to their picture-referents. These are *prereading* relationships usually well established in children during nursery and preschool years and which provide the listening and speaking vocabularies of children. Most retarded persons, including the severely retarded, have adequate vocabularies of this type relating to familiar parts of their experience.

The lower parts of Figure 14.8 (relations II and VI) involve the relation of oral vocabularies to *written or printed* symbols or words. Relation II involves the ability to choose the written name for its spoken equivalent, and relation VI the ability to name this written word aloud.

The middle portion of Figure 14.8 (relations III and IV) involves the purely nonauditory ability to choose the correct picture (or object) when

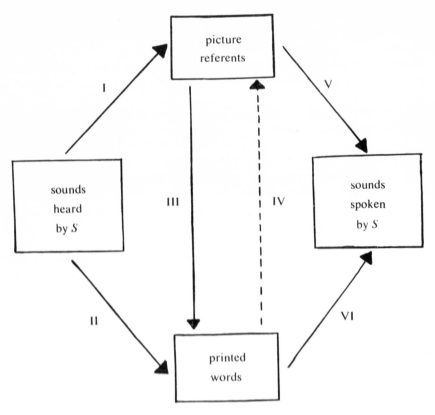

Figure 14.8. Schematic Diagram of Sidman Model for Language Relationships

seeing its written word equivalent (relation III) or vice versa (relation IV).

It is the relations in the lower and middle portions of this figure (II, III, and VI) that are most often absent or very deficient among retarded individuals. Of these equivalences, the only relationship which requires a live teacher to be present to confirm and correct the reading responses is relation VI. The other two equivalences can be programmed to be taught by machine and tape recorder. If methods can be developed which would allow equivalence VI to emerge, then the packaging of machine programs for reading is feasible.

Sidman's study showed, with one severely retarded adolescent, that relation VI did in fact emerge after the S mastered the auditory equivalence of sound-word matching (II). In the Milwaukee project, using four 3-letter words and the MTA-400, Pace (1970) replicated the Sidman study with four severely retarded Ss from ABLC and obtained the same result. He also found that this oral reading ability was still fully intact on a posttest given three weeks later.

Not only did oral reading emerge, but also word-picture matching ability (III) also emerged and remained fully intact after three weeks for all Ss. Thus, by teaching only *one* equivalence, sound-word matching, *two* other equivalences were also mastered at the same time without direct teaching efforts.

Emergence of oral reading (along with relation III) in this case followed mastery of the sound-word equivalence (II) on the machine. Pace also investigated whether such emergence would occur when only the non-auditory ability to match picture to word (III) was taught by machine, rather than equivalence II. Using a similar set of four 3-letter words and the same Ss, Pace found that the emergence of oral reading (VI) again occurred.

These results were based, however, on the use of familiar words and picture-referents such as *bed, cup, car, bug,* etc. Before training, pretests demonstrated that the Ss already had the sound-picture and picture-naming abilities represented by relations I and V. Another question is whether the oral reading (VI) would emerge by automating the machine teaching of II or III if unfamiliar picture-referents were used. Nonsense picture-referents were therefore substituted and a new set of four unfamiliar 3-letter words assigned (for example, *yen, boa, yaw,* etc.). Ss were first taught (by machine) the sound-picture equivalence of relation I using a meaningless design as the picture of the nonsense word; and then the sound-word equivalence II by machine. Both oral reading (VI) and word-picture (III) abilities emerged.

These results suggest that new vocabularies involving unfamiliar pic-

ture-referents can also be established via machine. However, emergence of equivalence VI was not complete for all words or *Ss* and, on the three weeks retention tests, relation VI had deteriorated still further. The non-auditory equivalence of III remained fully intact for all *Ss*. Screven and Pace are now investigating the use of more active vocal involvement by *Ss* at the machine during the learning of relations I and II for unfamiliar nonsense referents (for example, having S overtly imitate and repeat taped words) as a means of improving the emergence of oral reading of unfamiliar words by machine.

A word about the machine programs themselves, using a group of pilot clients in the ABLC, the specific details of the program, sequencing, etc., gradually emerged. Errors made by pilot *Ss* led to corrective changes until the sequencing, prompting and other characteristics yielded less than 5 percent errors and produced mastery on subsequent posttests (passing 67 discrimination frames with less than 5 percent errors three times in succession). What eventually evolved was a nonsymmetrical 270 frame program capable of producing mastery of any two nouns in from 3 to 4 individual sessions of about 15 minutes each.

All frames were matching-to-sample. However, in the program for teaching relation II, the "sample" consisted of hearing the word spoken through a speaker and the pressing the word in the window which matched it. (See Fig. 14.8). The program for relation III showed a picture in the upper window to be matched with a word appearing in the lower windows. Figure 14.9 shows examples of some of the "teaching" frames and some "discrimination" frames from the program designed for teaching relation III. *Bug* and *Cup* are the referent words being taught. In frames 19–21, a "filler word" (a word not being actively learned in the program) is being faded in in various positions; in frames 49–51, two filler words are involved and in frames 67–86, *bug* must be differentiated from three filler words. Frames 256–264 are examples of discrimination frames in which along with filler words, the referent word *bug* must also be differentiated from another familiar referent word, cow and vice versa.

These results support the possibility that oral and visual vocabulary could be "packaged" for automated administration to the severely retarded. However, when teaching word-pictures equivalence (III) for unfamiliar words and picture-referents, without additional auditory training, equivalence VI will not emerge. Apparently, when retardates do not have the entering abilities to relate word-sounds to their picture-referents or orally name these pictures, then the machine teaching procedure must incorporate some kind of audio-visual (sound-word and sound-picture) training and overt involvement if oral reading (VI) is to emerge. The question is whether this can be done entirely by a machine without the need of a teacher.

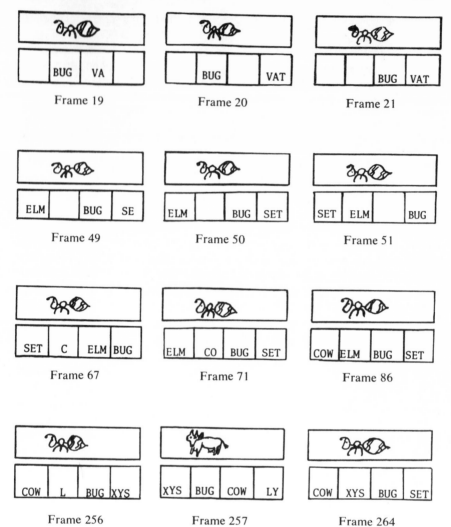

Figure 14.9. Sample Teaching and Discrimination Frames for Teaching
Word-Picture Equivalences

Single-Subject Behavior Modification

A number of clients within the ABLC facility have been unresponsive to
the procedures described. These have been custodial clients, profoundly
retarded, nonverbal, and autistic.

Use of the S-Box, at least in initial phases, has proved ineffective, even
when reinforcers of known value are used for RIs on a continuous reinforcement schedule. The *Ss* pay little or no attention to its signals or oper-

ation and continue to engage in stereotyping and other characteristic behaviors.

Therefore, a different apparatus was designed to provide the necessary discriminative stimuli and to structure the behavioral situation for the custodial clients as much as possible. This apparatus includes the essential functions of the S-Box, but these are provided on a much larger scale. The apparatus consists of three main parts: (1) a table surface on which objects, pictures, or work tasks can be placed for use by the subject, (2) a large, red divider-screen with two 100 watt lights which face the client and separate the client's side of the table from the experimenter's side, and (3) a 1 × 1 foot reinforcement box, open at one end, located to the left of the client. The large reinforcement box contains a bright internal light and a loud chime which operate only during reinforcement intervals; the open side allows *S* to reach in for the reinforcer. The "work" condition, when *S* is expected to *do* something, is always signalled by onset of the 100 watt lights on divider-screen and can hardly be overlooked.

In the established procedure which has been successfully used with custodial clients, the client sits on one side of a table and divider-screen, the teacher-experimenter on the other, where she records responses, operates the lights, presents objects or pictures, gives instructions, and provides reinforcers. The normal sequence of events is as follows:

   a. Between trials, the client, *S,* and the teacher-experimenter, *E,* sit in relative darkness for 30-seconds with a 5-watt "Between-trials" light providing the only illumination;

   b. The divider-screen is then lighted by the 100-watt "work" lights and *E* places a task under the screen for *S* to respond to, giving instructions if necessary;

   c. If *S* responds correctly, the work-lights go off simultaneously with the onset of the light-bell in the reinforcement box which now contains a reinforcer (usually an M&M or fruit-loop);

   d. *S* takes the reinforcer from the box while *E* comes around the table to *S* and provides direct attention and praise;

   e. After 20-seconds, the reinforcement light goes off, *E* returns to the other side of the screen, and the apparatus is back to the 30-second between-trials condition, which is then followed by a repeat of the above.

In Step *c,* if the client makes an *incorrect* response, displays inappropriate behavior, or does nothing for 20 seconds, the screen lights go off for 3 seconds, a "time-out," followed by a repeat of Step *b* above.

One example of a specific application of this system to a profoundly retarded girl will be described here.

Favreau (1969), used the above apparatus and system with a profoundly retarded 28 year old girl (M.A. about 2 years) to improve her

responsiveness to commands, increase cooperation and attention, and develop certain sound-symbol discriminations using letters of the i.t.a. alphabet. At the beginning of treatment, *S* was characterized by various stereotyped behavior, hyperactivity, almost complete lack of responsiveness to directions or requests from others, and frequent tantrum behaviors (kicking, clawing, screaming) when approached by other staff with any command. If placed at a work task of even the simplest nature, she would sit mutely, pounding her side, ignoring all efforts to get her to work, including tokens, candy, etc. The *S* was nonverbal, except for occasional repeating of the words "baby" and "mama."

Favreau first tested the use of the apparatus for securing imitative responses. Imitative tendencies were already present in some strength for this client and it was hoped that this would increase the chances for successful responding. Reinforcement during the 20-second RI combined direct attention and praise from *E* with a constantly changing set of reinforcers such as M&Ms and fruit-loops and an occasional take-home piece of jewelry. The imitation procedure for each trial on Step *b* (above), consisted of *E* standing up in view of *S* and performing some simple movement (for example, touching nose, touching ear) with the statement, "Do this." *S* was then expected to imitate this action.

The results were very encouraging. *S* moved from an average frequency of imitative responses prior to treatment of about 12 percent to an average frequency of between 70 percent and 100 percent.

These results led to trying to develop *S's* responses to commands. At Step *b*, *S* was shown three pictures (of a *ball*, a *shoe*, and a *cup*) and told "Show me the shoe in the picture," or "Show me the ball," etc. *S* was given 30 minutes of training on each session always followed by a 30-item criterion test requiring 30 responses to commands. The percent of correct responses to the 30 commands was recorded for each session. Prior to training, responses to the 30 commands was obtained *without* the use of the stimulus-control apparatus (reinforcers were given by hand).

The percent responses to commands for the 9 pretreatment sessions and the 12 experimental sessions are shown in the left-hand portion of Figure 14.10. As may be seen in Figure 14.10, pretreatment responses to commands were very erratic. After use of the apparatus and procedures described, the percent of responses to commands increased dramatically and remained so.

S was now given a matching task in which she was given an object (*cup*, *shoe*, *ball*) and three pictures and asked to place the object on the corresponding picture. The results, in terms of percent of 30 criterion test items, are shown in the right-hand portion of Figure 14.10. Again, *S* performed nearly all matching responses on most of the sessions.

The next step was to give *S* training in a matching-to-sample task similar

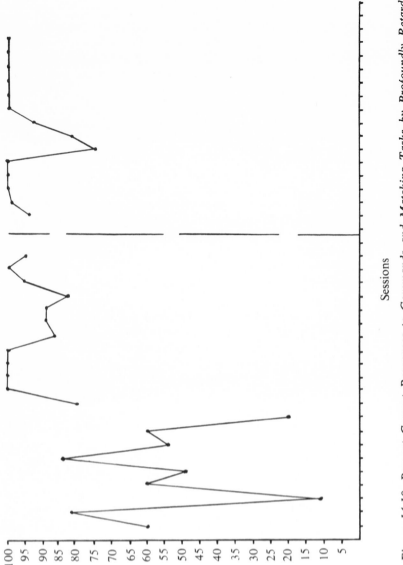

Sessions

Figure 14.10. Percent Correct Responses to Commands and Matching Tasks by Profoundly Retarded Client with Use of Stimulus Control Apparatus

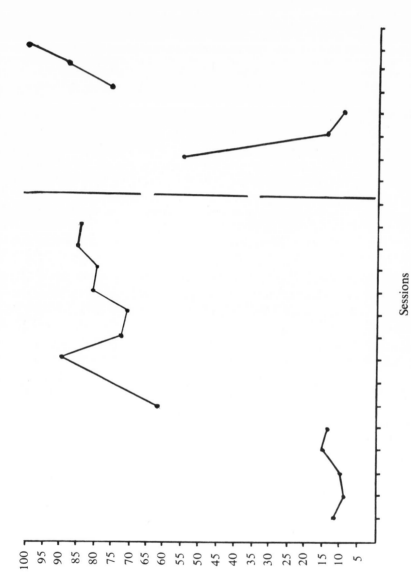

Figure 14.11. Percent of Correct Responses Made by a Profoundly Retarded Client for Matching-to-Sample (left) and Oral Naming of Pictures (right), under Baseline and Stimulus Control Conditions

:o formats used in programmed learning systems. In this situation, the S was given an object (ball, cup, or shoe) which she then had to place on its corresponding picture selected from among three pictures. The objects and the order of the pictures were changed on each trial. All other conditions were the same. S was first given a matching-to-sample pretest on each of five baseline sessions, followed by eight sessions using the control apparatus and procedure. Results are shown in the lefthand portion of Figure 14.i1. Again S's performance was very poor during pretest baseline sessions and rose sharply during experimental sessions.

The righthand portion of Figure 14.11 shows the results when the S's task required *orally* giving the name of whichever object was shown (equivalence V in Sidman's model shown in Figure 14.8). Pretreatment baseline date for three sessions are also shown. Again, the stimulus-control procedures appear critical in securing the S's cooperation and sustained attention needed for performance of the task.

In summary, this profoundly retarded girl, normally incapable of any prolonged attention or cooperation in responding to her environment, when placed in the highly structured situation provided by the stimulus-control apparatus and its contingencies, was able to perform various tasks requiring considerable attention at relatively high levels over many sessions. The characteristic behaviors of hitting her body, screaming, etc., were almost entirely absent during the sessions in which these procedures were used.

Taking advantage of the control obtained by this procedure, Favreau designed a program to teach this S the sound-symbol relationships of the i.t.a. alphabet in preparation for the possible development of reading skills. The first phase of this program has been completed and was successful.

The objective of this phase was to teach S the sound-symbol equivalence of three symbols of the i.t.a., *ee, æ, ie*. S was first required to imitate the sounds of each of the i.t.a. symbols, presented individually (at Step *b*). After reaching 100 percent performance on criterion trials, S was then required to *independently* give the sound of each symbol presented one at a time. This training was continued for successive ½-hour sessions until mastery. In the final stage, S was then shown *several* i.t.a. symbols and was required to touch the symbol corresponding to its sound (spoken by E). This is equivalence II of Sidman's model shown in Figure 14.8. Initially, only two symbols were presented together over a number of sessions until S reached 100 percent mastery, then *all three* symbols were presented together until 100 percent mastery, It took S four sessions to reach mastery of the two symbol discrimination and two sessions to master the three symbols.

It seems clear that this subject would not be able to work in a workshop situation in which the task and immediate work environment are not highly structured and controlled. However, the procedure and controlling apparatus which has been effective with this *S* would be cumbersome and impractical in any actual work setting. Given the control that the present apparatus and procedure afford, however, the question is whether it might be possible to transfer this control to an appropriate control system, such as the S-Box used with other clients, and obtain a degree of productive work from this subject. A plan is now in progress which is attempting to answer this question.

This plan involves the following steps: (a) training *S* for the performance of a simple work task (uncapping coin tubes) using backward chaining with the apparatus controls already familiar to her; (b) transferring environmental control from the present apparatus to the S-Box, teaching *S* to press the S-Box as a part of the work-chain; (c) reducing and eventually eliminating the between-trial interval; (d) introducing intermittent reinforcement with the S-Box; and (e) reducing the need for the direct intervention of *E* during reinforcement intervals.

The essentials of the approach being used to accomplish these steps involve, first, using *both* the present familiar control apparatus along with the S-Box during the shaping of the work task (uncapping coin tubes) and use of the S-Box key in the work-chain. After this initial training, using both units, the old control apparatus is gradually "faded out" until only the S-Box is in use. For example, one of the two 100-watt lights on the divider-screen is removed, then *both* are removed leaving only the work-light attached to the S-Box to serve this function, then the divider-screen itself is removed, then an FR-2 schedule is introduced, and so forth.

As a concluding statement, it has been emphasized throughout the book that even the more severely retarded can learn if the environmental conditions are appropriately arranged. A technology of environmental arrangement is slowly evolving. The methodology of an experimental analysis of behavior, wisely applied, holds promise of facilitating this development.

References

Addison, R. M. and Homme, L. E. "The Reinforcing Event (RE) Menu." *National Society for Programmed Instruction Journal,* 1966, 5, 8–9.

Appel, J. B. "Punishment and Shock Intensity." *Science,* 1963, 144, 528–529.

Ayers, G. E. and Duguay, A. R. "Critical Variables in Counseling the Mentally Retarded." *Rehabilitation Literature,* 1969, 30, 42–44, 50.

Ayllon, T. and Azrin, N. H. "The Measurement and Reinforcement of Behavior of Psychotics." *Journal of Experimental Analysis of Behavior,* 1965, 8, 357–380.

Ayllon, T. and Azrin, N. H. *The Token Economy: A Motivational System for Therapy and Rehabilitation.* New York: Appleton-Century-Crofts, 1968.

Ayllon, T. and Michael J. "The Psychiatric Nurse as a Behavioral Engineer." *Journal of Experimental Analysis of Behavior,* 1959, 2, 323–334.

Azrin, N. H. and Holz, W. C. "Punishment During Fixed-Interval Reinforcement." *Journal of Experimental Analysis of Behavior,* 1961, 4, 343–347.

Azrin, N. H. and Holz, W. C. "Punishment." In *Operant Behavior: Areas of Research and Application,* ed. W. K. Honig. New York: Appleton-Century-Crofts, 1966. Pp. 380–447.

Baer, D. M. "A Case for the Selective Reinforcement of Punishment." In *Behavior Modification in Clinical Psychology,* eds. C. Neuringer and J. L. Michael, New York: Appleton-Century-Crofts, 1970. Pp. 243–249.

Baer, D. M., Peterson, R. F., and Sherman, J. A. "The Development of Imitation by Reinforcing Behavioral Similarity to a Model." *Journal of Experimental Analysis of Behavior,* 1967, 10, 405–416.

Baer, D. M., Wolf, M. M., and Risley, T. R. "Some Current Dimensions of Applied Behavior Analysis." *Journal of Applied Behavior Analysis,* 1968, 1, 91–97.

Baldwin, W. K. "The Social Position of Educable Mentally Retarded Child in the Regular Grades in the Public Schools." *Exceptional Children*, 1958, 25, 106–108, 112.

Baller, W. R. "A Study of the Present Social Status of a Group of Adults Who, when They Were in Elementary Schools, Were Classified as Mentally Deficient." *Genetic Psychological Monographs*, 1936, 18, 165–244.

Baller, W. R., Charles, D. C., and Miller, E. L. "Mid-life Attainment of the Mentally Retarded: A Longitudinal Study." *Genetic Psychological Monographs*, 1967, 75, 235–329.

Bandura, A. "Vicarious Processes: A Case of No Trial Learning." In *Advances in Experimental Social Psychology*, Vol. II, ed. L. Berkowitz. New York: Academic Press, 1965. Pp. 1–55.

Bandura, A. *Principles of Behavior Modification*. New York: Holt, Rinehart and Winston, 1969.

Bandura, A., Grusec, J. E., and Menlore, F. L. "Vicarious Extinction of Avoidance Behavior." *Journal of Personality and Social Psychology*, 1967, 5, 16–23.

Bandura, A. and Menlore, F. L. "Factors Determining Vicarious Extinction of Avoidance Behavior Through Symbolic Modeling." *Journal of Personality and Social Psychology*, 1968, 8, 99–108.

Bandura, A. and Walters, R. H. *Social Learning and Personality Development*. New York: Holt, Rinehart and Winston, 1963.

Baumeister, A. A. "A Survey of the Role of Psychologists in Public Institutions for the Mentally Retarded." *Mental Retardation*, 1967, 1, 2–5.

Baumeister, A. A. and Klosowski, R. "An attempt to Group Toilet Train Severely Retarded Patients." *Mental Retardation*, 1965, 3, 24–26.

Bensberg, G. J. *Teaching the Mentally Retarded*. Atlanta, Ga.: Southern Regional Education Board, 1965.

Bensberg, G. J., Colwell, C. N., and Cassel, R. H. "Teaching the Profoundly Retarded Self-Help Activities by Behavior Shaping Techniques." *American Journal of Mental Deficiency*, 1965, 69, 674–679.

Berger, S. M. "Conditioning Through Vicarious Instigation." *Psychological Review*, 1962, 69, 450–466.

Bergin, A. E. "The Effects of Psychotherapy: Negative Results Revisited." *Journal of Counseling Psychology*, 1963, 10, 244–255.

Bialer, I. "Psychotherapy and Other Adjustment Techniques with the Mentally Retarded." In *Mental Retardation*, ed. A. A. Baumeister. Chicago: Aldine Publishing Company, 1967. Pp. 138–180.

Bijou, S. W. "A Functional Analysis of Retarded Development." In *International Review of Research in Mental Retardation*. Vol. I. ed. N. R. Ellis. New York: Academic Press, 1966. Pp. 1–20. (a)

Bijou, S. W. "Implications of Behavioral Science for Counseling and Guidance." In *Revolution in Counseling*, ed. J. D. Krumboltz. Boston: Houghton Mifflin, 1966. Pp. 27–48. (b)

Bijou, S. W. and Baer, D. M. *Child Development I. A Systematic and Empirical Theory*. New York: Appleton-Century-Crofts, 1961.

Bijou, S. W., Birnbrauer, J. S., Kidder, J. D., and Tague, C. "Programmed Instruction as an Approach to Teaching of Reading, Writing, and Arithmetic to Retarded Children." *Psychological Record*, 1966, 16, 505–522.

Bijou, S. W. and Sloane, H. N. "Therapeutic Techniques with Children."

In *An Introduction to Clinical Psychology,* eds. I. A. Berg and L. A. Pennington. New York: Ronald Press, 1966. Pp. 652–684.

Birnbrauer, J. S. "Generalization of Punishment Effects—A Case Study." *Journal of Applied Behavior Analysis,* 1968, 1, 201–211.

Birnbrauer, J. S., Bijou, S. W., Wolf, M. M., and Kidder, J. D. "Programmed Instruction in the Classroom." In *Case Studies in Behavior Modification,* eds. L. P. Ullman and L. Krasner. New York: Holt, Rinehart and Winston, 1965. Pp. 358–363.

Birnbrauer, J. S., Burchard, J. D., and Burchard, S. N. "Wanted: Behavior Analysts." In *Behavior Modification: The Human Effort,* ed. R. H. Bradfield. San Rafael, Calif.: Dimensions Publishing Co., 1970. Pp. 19–76.

Birnbrauer, J. S. and Lawler, J. "Token Reinforcement for Learning." *Mental Retardation,* 1964, 2, 219–289.

Birnbrauer, J. S., Wolf, M. M., Kidder, J. D., and Tague, C. E. "Classroom Behavior of Retarded Pupils with Token Reinforcement." *Journal of Experimental Child Psychology,* 1965, 2, 219–235.

Blachely, R., Stephenson, W. L., and Levy, L. A. "A Demonstration of Work as Therapy." *Summaries of Scientific Papers,* Paper No. 191, American Psychiatric Association Annual Meeting, St. Louis, 1963.

Blackwood, R. O. "Operant Conditioning as a Method of Training the Mentally Retarded." Unpublished doctoral dissertation, Ohio State University, 1962.

Borokowski, J. G. and Johnson, L. O. "Meditation and the Paired-Associate Learning of Normals and Retardates." *American Journal of Mental Deficiency,* 1968, 72, 610–613.

Bostow, D. E. and Bailey, J. B. "Modification of Severe Disruptive and Aggressive Behavior Using Brief Timeout and Reinforcement Procedures." *Journal of Applied Behavior Analysis,* 1969, 2, 31–37.

Brodsky, G. "The Relation Between Verbal and Non-Verbal Behavior Change." *Behavior Research and Therapy,* 1967, 5, 183–191.

Bry, P. M. "The Role of Reinforcement in Imitation by Retardates." Unpublished doctoral dissertation, University of Missouri, 1969.

Bryan, J. H. and Test, M. A. "Models and Helping: Naturalistic Studies in Aiding Behavior." *Journal of Personality and Social Psychology,* 1967, 6, 400–407.

Bucher, B. and Lovaas, O. I. "Use of Aversive Stimulation in Behavior Modification." In *Miami Symposium on the Prediction of Behavior, 1967: Aversive Stimulation,* ed. M. R. Jones. Coral Gables, Fla.: University of Miami Press, 1968. Pp. 77–145.

Burchard, J. D. "Systematic Socialization: A Programmed Environment for the Rehabilitation of Antisocial Retardates." *Psychological Reports,* 1967, 11, 461–476.

Burg, B. W. and Barrett, A. M. "Interest Testing with the Mentally Retarded: a Bi-Sensory Approach." *American Journal of Mental Deficiency,* 1965, 69, 548–552.

Carkhuff, R. R. and Berenson, B. G. *Beyond Counseling and Therapy.* New York: Holt, Rinehart and Winston, 1967.

Charles, D. C. "Ability and Accomplishment of Persons Earlier Judged Mentally Deficient." *Genetic Psychological Monographs,* 1953, 47, 3–71.

Church, R. M. "The Varied Effects of Punishment on Behavior." *Psychological Review,* 1963, 70, 369–402.

Clements, C. B. and McKee, J. M. "Programmed Instruction for Institutionalized Offenders: Contingency Management and Performance Contracts." *Psychological Report*, 1968, 22, 957–964.

Colwell, C. N. "The Role of Operant Techniques in Cottage and Ward Life Programs." Paper presented at meeting of the American Association on Mental Deficiency, Chicago, 1966.

Cromwell, R. L. "A Social Learning Approach to Mental Retardation." In *Handbook of Mental Deficiency*, ed. N. R. Ellis. New York: McGraw-Hill, 1963. Pp. 41–91.

Crosson, J. E. "A Technique for Programming Sheltered Workshop Environments for Training Severely Retarded Workers." *American Journal of Mental Deficiency*, 1969, 73, 814–818.

Culkin, W. "Use of Behavior Shaping Procedures to Increase Basic Work Skills of Retarded Young Adults with Difficult Behavior Problems." Unpublished doctoral dissertation, University of Wisconsin, 1968.

Dayan, M. "Toilet Training Retarded Children in a State Residential Institution." *Mental Retardation*, 1964, 2, 116–117.

DiMichael, S. G. and Terwilliger, W. B. "Counselor's Activities in the Vocational and Rehabilitation of the Mentally Retarded." *Journal of Clinical Psychology*, 1953, 9, 99–106.

Dinsmoor, J. A. "Comments on Wetzel's Treatment of a Case of Compulsive Stealing." *Journal of Consulting Psychology*, 1966, 30, 378–380.

Diven, K. "Certain Determinants in the Conditioning of Anxiety Reactions." *Journal of Psychology*, 1937, 3, 291–308.

Doubros, S. G. "Behavior Therapy with High Level Institutionalized Retarded Adolescents." *Exceptional Children*, 1966, 33, 229–233.

Edgerton, R. E. *The Cloak of Competence: Stigma in the Lives of the Mentally Retarded*. Berkeley: University of California Press, 1967.

Edwards, M. and Lilly, R. T. "Operant Conditioning: An Application to Behavioral Problems in Groups." *Mental Retardation*, 1966, 4, 18–20.

Ellis, N. R. "Toilet Training the Severely Defective Patient: An S-R Reinforcement Analysis." *American Journal of Mental Deficiency*, 1963, 68, 98–103.

Eysenck, H. J. "The Effects of Psychotherapy: An Evaluation." *Journal of Consulting Psychology*, 1952, 16, 319–324.

Eysenck, H. J. ed. *Behavior Therapy and the Neuroses*. New York: Pergamon Press, 1960.

Eysenck, H. J. "The Effects of Psychotherapy." In *Handbook of Abnormal Psychology*, ed. H. J. Eysenck. New York: Basic Books, 1961.

Eysenck, H. J. "The Effects of Psychotherapy." *International Journal of Psychiatry*, 1965, 1, 99–142.

Favreau, J. "Development of Response to Commands and Sound Symbol Discrimination." Unpublished manuscript, 1969.

Ferster, C. B. "Reinforcement and Punishment in the Control of Human Behavior by Social Agencies." *Psychiatric Research Reports*, 1958, Dec. 101–118.

Ferster, C. B. "Classification of Behavior Pathology." In *Research in Behavior Modification-New Developments and Implications*, eds. L. Krasner and L. P. Ullman. New York: Holt, Rinehart and Winston, 1965. Pp. 6–26.

Ferster, C. B. and Appel, J. B. "Punishment of S^Δ Responding in Match-to-Sample by Time Out from Positive Reinforcement." *Journal of Experimental Analysis of Behavior*, 1961, 4, 45–56.

Ferster, C. B. and Perrott, Mary. *Behavior Principles.* New York: Appleton-Century-Crofts, 1968.

Ferster, C. B. and Skinner, B. F. *Schedules of Reinforcement.* New York: Appleton-Century-Crofts, 1957.

Flanders, J. P. "A Review of Research on Imitative Behavior." *Psychological Bulletin,* 1968, 69, 316–337.

Gallagher, J. J. "Measurement of Personality Development in Preadolescent Mentally Retarded Children." *American Journal of Mental Deficiency,* 1959, 64, 296–301.

Gardner, J. M. and Watson, L. S. "Behavior Modification of the Mentally Retarded: An Annotated Bibliography." *Mental Retardation Abstracts,* 1969, 6, 181–193.

Gardner, W. I. "Effects of Failure on Intellectually Retarded and Normal Boys." *American Journal of Mental Deficiency,* 1966, 70, 899–902. (a)

Gardner, W. I. "Effects of Success and Failure with Institutionalized Mentally Retarded Adults." *Psychological Reports,* 1966, 18, 779–782. (b)

Gardner, W. I. "Use of the California Test of Personality with the Mentally Retarded." *Mental Retardation,* 1967, 5, 12–16. (a)

Gardner, W. I. "What Should Be the Psychologist's Role?" *Mental Retardation,* 1967, 5, 29–31. (b)

Gardner, W. I. "Use of Punishment Procedures with the Severely Retarded: A Review." *American Journal of Mental Deficiency,* 1969, 74, 86–103.

Gardner, W. I. "Use of Behavior Therapy with the Mentally Retarded." In *Psychiatric Approaches of Mental Retardation,* ed. F. J. Menolascino. New York: Basic Books, 1970. Pp. 250–275.

Gelfand, D. M. and Hartmann, D. P. "Behavior Therapy with Children: A Review and Evaluation of Research Methodology." *Psychological Bulletin.* 1968, 69, 204–215.

Giles, D. K. and Wolf, M. M. "Toilet Training Institutionalized Severe Retardates: "An Application of Operant Behavior Modification Techniques." *American Journal of Mental Deficiency,* 1966, 70, 766–780.

Girardeau, F. L. and Spradlin, J. E. "Token Rewards in a Cottage Program." *Mental Retardation,* 1964, 2, 345–352.

Glaser, R. and Reynolds, J. H., eds. *Teaching Machines and Programmed Instruction II. Data and Directions.* National Education Association, 1965.

Gorton, C. E. and Hollis, J. H. "Redesigning a Cottage Unit for Better Programming and Research for the Severely Retarded." *Mental Retardation,* 1965, 3, 16–21.

Guthrie, G. M., Butler, A., Gorlow, L., and White, G. M. "Nonverbal Expression of Self-Attitudes of Retardates." *American Journal of Mental Deficiency,* 1964, 69, 42–49.

Halpern, A. A. "Why Not Psychotherapy?" *Mental Retardation,* 1968, 6, 48–50.

Hamilton, J. and Allen, P. "Ward Programming for Severely Retarded Institutionalized Residents." *Mental Retardation,* 1967, 5, 22–24.

Hamilton, J. and Standahl, J. "Suppression of Stereotyped Screaming Behavior in a Profoundly Retarded Institutionalized Female." *Journal of Experimental Child Psychology,* 1969, 7, 114–121.

Hamilton, J. and Stephens, L. "Reinstating Speech in an Emotionally Disturbed Mentally Retarded Young Woman." *Journal of Speech and Hearing Disorders,* 1968, 33, 383–389.

Hamilton, J., Stephens, L., and Allen, P. "Controlling Aggressive and Destructive Behavior in Severely Retarded Institutionalized Residents." *American Journal of Mental Deficiency,* 1967, 71, 852–856.

Hannen, R. W. "A Program for Developing Self-Concept in Retarded Children." *Mental Retardation,* 1968, 6, 33–37.

Henricksen, K. and Doughty, R. "Decelerating Undesirable Mealtime Behavior in a Group of Profoundly Retarded Boys." *American Journal of Mental Deficiency,* 1967, 72, 40–44.

Hill, W. F. "Sources of Evaluative Reinforcement." *Psychological Bulletin,* 1968, 69, 132–146.

Hollis, J. H. "Development of Perceptual Motor Skills in a Profoundly Retarded Child: Part I, Prosthesis." *American Journal of Mental Deficiency,* 1967, 71, 941–952.

Holz, W. C. and Azrin, N. H. "Discriminative Properties of Punishment." *Journal of Experimental Analysis of Behavior,* 1961, 4, 225–232.

Honig, W. K., ed. *Operant Behavior: Areas of Research and Application.* New York: Appleton-Century-Crofts, 1966.

Hundziak, M., Maurer, R. A. and Watson, L. S. "Operant Conditioning and Toilet Training of Severely Mentally Retarded Boys." *American Journal of Mental Deficiency,* 1965, 70, 120–128.

Hunt, J. G. and Zimmerman, J. "Stimulating Productivity in a Simulated Sheltered Workshop Setting." *American Journal of Mental Deficiency,* 1969, 74, 43–49.

Hutt, C. and Ounsted, C. "The Biological Significance of Gaze Aversion with Particular Reference to the Syndrome of Infantile Autism." *Behavioral Science,* 1966, 11, 346–356.

Jens, K. and Shores, R. E. "Behavioral Graphs as Reinforcers for Work Behavior of Mentally Retarded Adolescents." *Education and Training of the Mentally Retarded,* 1969, 4, 21–28.

Johns, J. H. and Quay, H. C. "The Effect of Social Rewards on Verbal Conditioning on Psychopathic and Neurotic Military Offenders." *Journal of Consulting Psychology,* 1962, 26, 217–220.

Johnson, G. O. "A Study of the Social Position of Mentally Handicapped Children in the Regular Grades." *American Journal of Mental Deficiency,* 1950. 55, 60–89.

Johnson, G. O. and Kirk, S. A. "Are Mentally Handicapped Children Segregated in the Regular Grades?" *Journal of Exceptional Children,* 1950, 17, 65–68, 87–88.

Jones, J. G. "The Case of Mary." *Mental Retardation,* 1969, 7, 19–21.

Kalish, H. I. "Behavior Therapy." In *Handbook of Clinical Psychology,* ed. B. B. Wolman. New York: McGraw-Hill, 1965. Pp. 1230–1253.

Kamin, L. J., Brimer, C. J. and Black, A. H. "Conditioned Suppression as a Monitor of Fear of the CS in the Course of Avoidance Training." *Journal of Comparative and Physiological Psychology,* 1963, 56, 497–501.

Kanfer, F. H. and Phillips, J. S. *Learning Foundations of Behavior Therapy.* New York: Wiley, 1970.

Kanfer, F. H. and Saslow, G. "Behavioral Analysis an Alternative to Diagnostic Classification." *Archives General Psychiatry,* 1965, 12 529–538.

Kanfer, F. H. and Saslow, G. "Behavioral Diagnosis." In *Behavior Therapy, Appraisal and Status,* ed. C. Franks. New York: McGraw-Hill, 1969. Pp. 417–444.

Kantor, J. R. *Interbehavioral Psychology.* Bloomington, Ind.: Principia Press, 1958.

Karsh, E. B. "Changes in Intensity of Punishment: Effect on Runway Behavior of Rats." *Science,* 1963, 140, 1084–1085.

Keller, F. S. and Schoenfeld, W. N. *Principles of Psychology.* New York: Appleton-Century-Crofts, 1950.

Kerr, Nancy, Meyerson, L., and Michael, J. "A Procedure for Shaping Vocalizations in a Mute Child." In *Case Studies in Behavior Modification,* eds. L. P. Ullmann and L. Krasner. New York: Holt, Rinehart and Winston, 1965. Pp. 366–370.

Kliebhan, J. M. "Effects of Goal-Setting and Modeling on Job Performance of Retarded Adolescents." *American Journal of Mental Deficiency,* 1967, 72, 220–226.

Krasner, L. "Behavior Modification, Token Economies, and Training in Clinical Psychology." In *Behavior Modification in Clinical Psychology,* eds. C. Neuringer and J. L. Michael. New York: Appleton-Century-Crofts, 1970. Pp. 86–104. (a)

Krasner, L. "Token Economy as an Illustration of Operant Conditioning Procedures with the Aged, with Youth, and with Society." In *Learning Approaches to Therapeutic Behavior Change,* ed. D. J. Levis. Chicago: Aldine · Atherton, Inc., 1970. Pp. 74–101. (b)

Krasner, L. "Verbal Conditioning and Psychotherapy." In *Research in Behavior Modification,* eds. L. Krasner and L. P. Ullman. New York: Holt, Rinehart and Winston, Inc., 1965.

Krumboltz, J. D. "Behavioral Goals in Counseling." *Journal of Counseling Psychology,* 1966, 2, 153–159.

Krumboltz, J. D. "Parable of the Good Counselor." *Personnel and Guidance Journal,* 1964, 43, 118–123.

Krumboltz, J. D. and Thoresen, C. E. "The Effect of Behavioral Counseling in Group and Individual Settings on Information-Seeking Behavior." *Journal of Counseling Psychology,* 1964, 11, 324–333.

Lang, P. J. "Stimulus Control, Response Control, and the Desensitization of Fear." In *Learning Approaches to Therapeutic Behavior Change,* ed. D. J. Levis. Chicago: Aldine · Atherton, Inc., 1970. Pp. 148–173.

Lapp, Ester R. "A Study of the Social Adjustment of Slow-Learning Children who were Assigned Part-time to Regular Classes." *American Journal of Mental Deficiency,* 1957, 62, 254–262.

Leff, R. "Behavior Modification and the Psychoses of Childhood: a Review." *Psychological Bulletin,* 1968, 69, 396–409.

Leitenberg, H. "Is Time out from Positive Reinforcement an Aversive Event? A Review." *Psychological Bulletin,* 1965, 64, 428–441.

Lent, J. R. "A Demonstration Program for Intensive Training of Institutionalized Mentally Retarded Girls." Detailed Progress Report: January, 1967-January 1968. Public Health Service, U.S. Department of Health, Education, and Welfare, 1968.

Leslie, G. R., ed. *Behavior Modification in Rehabilitation Facilities.* Arkansas Rehabilitation and Research Center, Hot Springs, Arkansas, 1968.

Levitt, E. E. "The Results of Psychotherapy with Children: An Evaluation." *Journal of Consulting Psychology,* 1967, 21, 189–196.

Lindsley, O. R. "Direct Measurement and Prosthesis of Retarded Behavior." *Journal of Education,* 1964, 147, 62–81.

Lindsley, O. R. "A Reliable Wrist Counter for Recording Behavior Rates." *Journal of Applied Behavior Analysis,* 1968, 1, 77.

Lipman, R. S. "Some Test Correlates of Behavioral Agression in Institution-alized Retardates with Particular Reference to the Rosenzweig Picture Frustration Study." *American Journal of Mental Deficiency,* 1959, 63, 1038–1045.

Lovaas, O. I. "A Behavior Therapy Approach to Treatment of Childhood Schizophrenia." In *Symposia on Child Development,* Vol. 1. ed. J. Hill. Minneapolis: University of Minnesota Press, 1967. Pp. 108–159.

Lovaas, O. I., Schaeffer, B. and Simmons, J. Q. "Building Social Behavior in Autistic Children by Use of Electric Shock." *Journal of Experimental Research in Personality,* 1965, 1, 99–109.

Luckey, R. E., Watson, C. M. and Musick, J. K. "Aversive Conditioning as Means of Inhibiting Vomiting and Rumination." *American Journal Of Mental Deficiency,* 1968, 73, 139–142.

Lundin, R. W. *Personality: An Experimental Approach.* New York: Macmillan, 1961.

Lundin, R. W. *Personality: A Behavioral Analysis.* New York: Macmillan, 1969.

MacAulay, B. D. "A Program for Teaching Speech and Beginning Reading to Nonverbal Retardates." In *Operant Procedures and Remedial Speech and Language Training.* eds. H. N. Sloane, Jr., and B. D. MacAulay. Boston: Houghton Mifflin, 1968. Pp. 102–124.

Maher, B. *Principles of Psychopathology.* New York: McGraw-Hill, 1966.

Marshall, G. R. "Toilet Training of an Autistic Eight-Year-Old Through Conditioning Therapy: A Case Report." *Behavior Research and Therapy,* 1966, 4, 242–245.

Marshall, H. H. "The Effects of Punishment on Children: A Review of the Literature and a Suggested Hypothesis." *Journal of Genetic Psychology,* 1965, 106, 23–33.

Meyerson, L., Kerr, N. and Michael, J. L. "Behavior Modification in Rehabilitation." In *Child Development: Readings in Experimental Analysis,* eds. S. W. Bijou and D. M. Baer. New York: Appleton-Century-Crofts, 1967. Pp. 214–239.

Miller, N. E. "Theory and Experiment Relating Psychoanalytic Displacement to Stimulus-Response Generalization." *Journal of Abnormal and Social Psychology,* 1948, 43, 155–178.

Miller, N. E. and Dollard, J. *Social Learning and Imitation.* New Haven: Yale University Press, 1941.

Minge, M. R. and Ball, T. S. "Teaching of Self Help Skills to Profoundly Retarded Patients." *American Journal of Mental Deficiency,* 1967, 71, 864–868.

Montgomery, J. and McBurney, R. D. "Problems and Pitfalls of Establishing an Operant Conditioning Token Economy Program." *Mental Hygiene,* 1970, 54, 382–387.

Muenzinger, K. F. "Motivation in Learning: I. Electric Shock for Correct Responses in the Visual Discrimination Habit." *Journal of Comparative Psychology,* 1934, 17, 439–448.

Neff, W. S. *Work and Human Behavior.* New York: Aldine · Atherton, Inc., 1968.

Nawas, M. M. and Braun, S. H. "The Use of Operant Techniques for Modifying the Behavior of the Severely and Profoundly Retarded: Part II: The Techniques." *Mental Retardation,* 1970, 8, 18–24.

Pace, R. "The Role of Auditory-Visual Equivalences and the Applicability of Automated Programmed Learning Procedure in Teaching Severely Retarded Adults to Read." Unpublished doctoral dissertation, University of Wisconsin–Milwaukee, 1970.

Page, H. A. "The Facilitation of Experimental Extinction by Response Presentation as a Function of the Acquisition of a New Response." *Journal of Comparative and Physiological Psychology*, 1955, 48, 14–16.

Patterson, G. R., Jones, R., Wittier, J., and Wright, M. "A Behavior Modification Technique for the Hyperactive Child." *Behavior Research and Therapy*, 1965, 2, 217–226.

Peckham, R. A. "Problems in Job Adjustment of the Mentally Retarded." *American Journal of Mental Deficiency*, 1951, 56, 448–453.

Penny, K. R., Seim, R. and Peters, R. "The Mediational Deficiency of Mentally Retarded Children: I. The Establishment of Retardate's Mediational Deficiency." *American Journal of Mental Deficiency*, 1968, 77, 626–630.

Peterson, D. R. *The Clinical Study of Social Behavior*. New York: Appleton-Century-Crofts, 1968.

Peterson, R. F. and Peterson, L. R. "The Use of Positive Reinforcement in the Control of Self Destructive Behavior in a Retarded Boy." *Journal of Experimental Child Psychology*, 1968, 6, 351–360.

Poindexter, W. R. "Mental Patients become Employees." *Summaries of Scientific Papers*, Paper No. 84, American Psychiatric Association, Toronto, Canada, 1962.

Polin, A. T. "The Effects of Flooding and Physical Suppression as Extinction Techniques on an Anxiety Motivated Avoidance Locomotor Response." *Journal of Psychology*, 1959, 47, 235–245.

Premack, D. "Toward Empirical Behavior Laws: I. Positive Reinforcement." *Psychological Review*, 1959, 66, 219–233.

Premack, D. "Reinforcement Theory." In *Nebraska Symposium on Motivation*, ed. M. R. Jones. Lincoln: University of Nebraska, 1965.

Quay, H. C. and Hunt, W. A. "Psychopathy, Neuroticism, and Verbal Conditioning: A Replication of an Extension." *Journal of Consulting Psychology*, 1965, 29, 283.

Rachman, S. "Behavior Therapy." In *Sources of Gain in Counseling and Psychotherapy*, eds. B. G. Berenson and R. R. Carkhuff. New York: Holt, Rinehart and Winston, 1967.

Reynolds, G. S. *A Primer of Operant Conditioning*. Glenview, Illinois: Scott, Foresman and Company, 1968.

Risley, T. "The Effects and Side Effects of Punishing the Autistic Behaviors of a Deviant Child." *Journal of Applied Behavior Analysis*, 1968, 1, 21–34.

Roos, P. "Development of an Intensive Habit-Training Unit at Austin State School." *Mental Retardation*, 1965, 3, 12–15.

Rosenbaum, M. E. "The Effect of Stimulus and Background Factors on the Volunteering Response." *Journal of Abnormal and Social Psychology*, 1956, 53, 118–121.

Saslow, G. "A Case History of Attempted Behavior Manipulation in a Psychiatric Ward." In *Research in Behavior Modification: New Developments and Implications*, eds. L. Krasner and L. P. Ullman. New York: Holt, Rinehart and Winston, 1965. Pp. 285–304.

Screven, C. G. and Wrabetz, H. "A Programmed Work Environment for the Behaviorally Disturbed and Retarded Adult: I." Unpublished paper, 1969.

Screven, C. G., Derlin, R. and Huber, J. "A Programmed Work Environment for the Behaviorally Disturbed and Retarded Adult: II." Unpublished paper, 1969.

Screven, C. G. and Pace, R. A. "The Automation of Verbal Learning Skills for the Severely Retarded." Unpublished paper, 1970.

Sidman, M. *Tactics of Scientific Research.* New York: Basic Books, 1960.

Sidman, M. "Operant techniques." In *Experimental Foundations of Clinical Psychology,* ed. A. L. Bachrach. New York: Basic Books, 1962. Pp. 170–210.

Sidman, M. "Programmed Perception and Learning for Retarded Children." Paper read at 90th annual meeting of the American Association of Mental Deficiency. Chicago: May, 1966.

Sidman, M. "Reading and Auditory-Visual Equivalences." Unpublished paper, 1969.

Skinner, B. F. *The Behavior of Organisms.* New York: Appleton Century, 1938.

Skinner, B. F. *Science and Human Behavior.* New York: Macmillan, 1953.

Skinner, B. F. "The Science of Learning and the Art of Teaching." *Harvard Educational Review,* 1954, 29, 86–97.

Skinner, B. F. "Teaching machines." *Science,* 1958, 128, 969–977.

Skinner, B. F. *Cumulative Record.* New York: Macmillan, 1961.

Skinner, B. F. *Contingencies of Reinforcement: A Theoretical Analysis.* New York: Appleton-Century-Crofts, 1969.

Sloane, H. N., Jr., Johnston, N. J. and Harris, F. R. "Remedial Procedures for Teaching Verbal Behavior to Speech Defective Young Children." In *Operant Procedures and Remedial Speech and Language Training,* eds. H. N. Sloane, Jr. and B. D. MacAulay. Houghton Mifflin, 1968. Pp. 77–101.

Solomon, R. L. "Punishment." *American Psychologist,* 1964, 19, 239–253.

Solyom, L. and Miller, S. B. "Reciprocal Inhibition by Aversion Relief in the Treatment of Phobias." *Behavior Research and Therapy.* 1967, 5, 313–324.

Spradlin, J. E. and Girardeau, F. L. "The Behavior of Moderately and Severely Retarded Persons." In *International Review of Research in Mental Retardation,* Vol. I, ed. N. Ellis. New York: Academic Press, 1966. Pp. 257–298.

Spradlin, J. "The Premack Hypothesis and Self-Feeding by Profoundly Retarded Children: A Case Report." Parsons Research Center, Parsons, Kansas, Working Paper No. 79, 1964.

Stamm, J. M. "An Analysis of the Effects of a Continuous Counter on Response Rate under Fixed-Ratio Reinforcement of Retarded Adolescents and Young Adults." Unpublished doctoral dissertation, University of Wisconsin, 1970.

Sternlicht, M. "Fantasy Aggression in Delinquent and Nondelinquent Retarded." *American Journal of Mental Deficiency,* 1966, 70, 819–821. (a)

Sternlicht, M. "Psychotherapeutic Procedures with the Retarded." In *International Review of Research in Mental Retardation,* Vol. 2, ed. Ellis, N. R. New York: Academic Press, 1966. Pp. 279–354. (b)

Sternlicht, M. and Silverg, E. F. "The Relationship Between Fantasy Aggression and Overt Hostility in Mental Retardates." *American Journal of Mental Deficiency,* 1965, 70, 486–488.

Striefel, S. "Isolation as a Behavioral Management Procedure with Retarded Children." Working Paper, No. 156, Parsons Research Project, University of Kansas, 1967.

Sulzbacher, S. I. and Houser, J. E. "A Tactic to Eliminate Disruptive Be-

haviors in the Classroom: Group Contingent Consequences." *American Journal of Mental Deficiency*, 1968, 73, 88–90.

Tate, B. G. "An Automated System of Reinforcing and Recording Retardate Work Behavior." *Journal of Applied Behavior Analysis*, 1968, 1, 347.

Tate, B. G. and Baroff, G. S. "Aversive Control of Self-Injurious Behavior in a Psychotic Boy." *Behavior Research and Therapy*, 1966, 4, 281–287.

Tharp, R. G. and Wetzel, R. J. *Behavior Modification in the Natural Environment.* New York: Academic Press, 1969.

Thorpe, J. G., Schmidt, E., Brown, P. T., and Castell, D. "Aversion-Relief Therapy: A New Method for General Application." *Behavior Research and Therapy*, 1964, 2, 71–82.

Ullman, L. P. "Making Use of Modeling in the Therapeutic Interview," In *Advances in Behavior Therapy, 1968*, eds. R. D. Rubin, and C. M. Franks. New York: Academic Press, 1969. Pp. 175–181.

Ullman, L. P. and Krasner, L., eds. *Case Studies in Behavior Modification.* New York: Holt, Rinehart, and Winston, 1965.

Verhave, T. *The Experimental Analysis of Behavior.* New York: Appleton-Century-Crofts, 1966.

Walters, G. S. and Rogers, J. V. "Aversive Stimulation of the Rat: Long Term Effects Subsequent Behavior." *Science*, 1963, 142, 70–71.

Watson, L. S. "Application of Behavior Shaping Devices to Training Severely and Profoundly Mentally Retarded Children in an Institutional Setting." Paper presented at the meeting of the Midwestern Psychological Association, Chicago, 1966.

Watson, L. S. "Application of Operant Conditioning Techniques to Institutionalized Severely and Profoundly Retarded Children." *Mental Retardation Abstracts*, 1967, 4, 1–18.

Watson, L. S. "Applications of Behavior-Shaping Devices to Training Severely and Profoundly Mentally Retarded Children in an Institutional Setting." *Mental Retardation*, 1968, 6, 21–23.

Watson, L. S. and Sanders, C. C. "Stimulus Control with Severely and Profoundly Retarded Children under Varying Stimulus Conditions in a Free-Operant Situation." Paper presented at the meeting of the American Association on Mental Deficiency, Chicago, 1966.

Weiner, H. "Some Effects of Response Cost upon Human Behavior." *Journal of Experimental Analysis of Behavior*, 1962, 5, 201–208.

Whalen, C. K. and Henker, B. A. "Creating Therapeutic Pyramids using Mentally Retarded Patients." *American Journal of Mental Deficiency*, 1969, 74, 331–337.

White, J. C., Jr., and Taylor, D. "Noxious Conditioning as a Treatment for Rumination. *Mental Retardation*, 1967, 6, 30–33.

Whitney, L. R. and Barnard, K. E. "Implications of Operant Learning Theory for Nursing Care of the Retarded Child." *Mental Retardation*, 1966, 4, 26–29.

Wiesen, A. E. and Watson, E. "Elimination of Attention Seeking Behavior in a Retarded Child." *American Journal of Mental Deficiency*, 1967, 72, 50–52.

Wolf, M. M., Birnbrauer, J. S., Williams, T. and Lawler, Julia. "A Note on Apparent Extinction of the Vomiting Behavior of a Retarded Child." In *Case Studies in Behavior Modification*, eds. L. P. Ullman and L. Krasner. New York: Holt, Rinehart and Winston, 1965. Pp. 364–366.

Wolf, M. Risley, T. and Mees, H. "Application of Operant Conditioning Procedures to the Behavior Problems of an Autistic Child." *Behavior Research and Therapy*, 1964, 1, 305–312.

Wolpe, J. *Psychotherapy by Reciprocal Inhibition.* Stanford: Stanford University Press, 1958.

Wolpe, J. and Lazarus, A. A. *Behavior Therapy Techniques.* Oxford: Pergamon Press, 1966.

Yates, A. J. *Behavior Therapy.* New York: Wiley, 1970.

Yepsen, L. N. "Counseling the Mentally Retarded." In *Vocational Rehabilitation of the Mentall Retarded,* ed. S. G. DiMichael. U.S. Department of Health, Education and Welfare, Office of Vocational Rehabilitation, 1958.

Zeaman, D. and House, B. J. "The Role of Attention in Retardate Discrimination Learning." In *Handbook of Mental Deficiency,* ed. N. R. Ellis. New York: McGraw-Hill, 1963. Pp. 159–223.

Zeilberger, J., Sampen, S. E. and Sloane, H. N., Jr. "Modification of a Child's Problem Behaviors in the Home with the Mother as a Therapist." *Journal of Applied Behavior Analysis,* 1968, 1, 47–53.

Zeiler, M. D. and Jeruly; S. S. "Development of Behavior: Self-Feeding." *Journal of Consulting and Clinical Psychology,* 1968, 32, 164–168.

Zigler, E. "Research on Personality Structure in the Retardate." In *International Review of Research in Mental Retardation.* Vol. 1, ed. N. R. Ellis. New York: Academic Press, 1966. Pp. 77–108.

Zimmerman, J., Overpeck, C., Eisenberg, H. and Garlick, B. "Operant Conditioning in a Sheltered Workshop." *Rehabilitation Literature,* 1969, 30, 326–334.

Zimmerman, J., Stuckey, T. E., Garlick, B. J. and Miller, M. "Effects of Token Reinforcement on Productivity in Multiple Handicapped Clients in a Sheltered Workshop." *Rehabilitation Literature,* 1969, 30, 34–41.

Name Index

Subject Index